REVELATION

God's Word *for the* **Biblically-Inept**™ SERIES

Daymond R. Duck

STARBURST PUBLISHERS

P. O. Box 4123, Lancaster, Pennsylvania 17604

CARTOONS BY

Reverend Fun
(Dennis "Max" Hengeveld)
Dennis is a graphic designer for Gospel Films and the author of *Has Anybody Seen My Locust?* His cartoons can be seen worldwide at www.gospelcom.net/rev-fun/ and monthly in *Charisma* magazine.

Daymond R. Duck is the best-selling author of *On the Brink—Easy-to-Understand End-Time Bible Prophecy*. He is also a contributing author to *Forewarning—The Approaching Battle Between Good and Evil*. He has been interviewed on numerous Christian radio programs aired by some of the foremost prophetic ministries in the world. He speaks at prophecy conferences and preaches at revivals. He lives in Dyer, Tennessee with his wife Rachel, a registered nurse.

I wish to acknowledge the many long hours of hard work and invaluable help from my loving wife, Rachel. She worked behind the scenes, but her encouragement and commitment kept me going, and her research, definitions, suggestions, and editing made this difficult task much easier. Thanks honey.

To schedule Author appearances write: Author Appearances, Starburst Promotions, P.O. Box 4123 Lancaster, Pennsylvania 17604 or call (717) 293-0939

Website: www.starburstpublishers.com

CREDITS:
Cover design by David Marty Design
Text design and composition by John Reinhardt Book Design
Illustrations by Melissa A. Burkhart
Cartoons by Dennis "Max" Hengeveld

Unless otherwise noted, or paraphrased by the author, all Scripture quotations are from the New International Version of The Holy Bible.

To the best of its ability, Starburst Publishers has strived to find the source of all material. If there has been an oversight, please contact us and we will make any correction deemed necessary in future printings. We also declare that to the best of our knowledge all material (quoted or not) contained herein is accurate, and we shall not be held liable for the same.

INTRODUCTION

Welcome to *Revelation—God's Word for the Biblically-Inept*. It is the first book in a new series that will take the Bible and make it fun and educational. This is not the traditional hum-drum, boring Bible studies and commentaries you are used to seeing. It is a REVOLUTIONARY COMMENTARY™ that will change your outlook on the Bible forever. You *will* Learn The Word!™

To Gain Your Confidence

Revelation—God's Word for the Biblically-Inept is for those who are not interested in all that complicated stuff. You can be sure that I have tried to take an educational approach, but much effort has gone into keeping things simple. I always end up making things so complicated when I try to explain them, so my wife Rachel laughingly told me to use the "KISS" method.

Keep It Simple Stupid

She always seems to know what I am qualified to do. And, believe it or not, I have tried to do just what she said.

Jesus promised a blessing to all those who *read, hear* and *keep* those things written in Revelation. He also promised a curse on all those who add to, or take away from it. I take that seriously, so I have undertaken this project with great care. To help explain things in Revelation I will use the age-old *Golden Rule of Interpretation* which states: *When the plain sense of Scripture makes common sense, seek no other sense. . . .* The Bible explains itself. You do not need to go anywhere else. That is why I have included other verses of Scripture from the Bible to explain difficult areas of Revelation.

Why Study Revelation?

We are living in perilous times. The constant barrage of bad news has many people frightened and disturbed about their future. And now the year 2000 is just around the corner—a new millennium. Today, one out of every four Christian adults believe Jesus could return in their lifetime. Revelation is God's message to all of us who are concerned about the future. It reveals, unlike what many would like to believe, that the world is not going to get better, but worse.

Let's Get Started

(Let's Get Started)

> **Revelation 1:1**
> The revelation of Jesus Christ, which God . . .

(Verse of Scripture)

☞ **GO TO:**

Exodus 34:22, 23
(Pentecost)

(Go To:)

Revelation reveals that God is the one who is really in control. It encourages faith and perseverance, warns against making certain mistakes, and tells how to gain eternal life.

Anyone who picks up this book might ask, "Why study Revelation?" Here are seven good reasons:

1) Revelation is the Word of God (the Bible).
2) Jesus told us to watch for signs of things to come.
3) If we do not study Revelation our understanding of the entire Bible will remain *Biblically-Inept*.
4) Revelation reveals God's plan for the future.
5) A special blessing is promised to all those who read Revelation.
6) Revelation will change our lives.
7) Revelation will give us a concern for those who reject God and his Son, Jesus.

How To Study Revelation

As you study Revelation keep in mind its *three main divisions*:

Part One is called **The Church Age** (Chapters 1–3). We are now living in the Church Age, and it is almost over.

Part Two is called **From the Rapture to the Second Coming** (Chapters 4–19). It will be a terrible time in which to live. Many prophetic signs indicate that it is drawing closer, so we need to learn what to watch for and what to do so we can avoid it.

Part Three is called **The Millennium and Beyond** (Chapters 20–22). Some of the most precious verses in the Bible are found in these chapters. They are filled with inspiration and hope for the future.

Also keep in mind the *four ways to interpret (explain)* Revelation:

1) As a message to each one of us.
2) As a message to the entire Church.
3) As a message to seven specific churches.
4) As a message of prophecy.

Who Wrote Revelation?

John, one of the twelve disciples of Jesus, wrote Revelation under the guidance of its true author—the Holy Spirit, the third person of the Trinity. The word "**trinity**" is not found in the Bible, but it is used to explain the three different ways God reveals himself—as God the Father, his Son Jesus, and the Holy Spirit. These are three different expressions of God just as thoughts, spoken words, and written words are three different expressions of every person.

How Did We Get The Revelation We Have Today?

Revelation was originally written in the Greek language around 96 A.D. By 250 A.D. the entire Bible had been translated into what is known as *Old Latin*, but the first officially recognized Latin translation (the Vulgate) did not appear until 382 A.D. The first officially recognized English translation (the King James Bible) was circulated in 1611 A.D.

Revelation is the last book in the New Testament. It is divided into 404 verses of which at least 265 contain quotes drawn from the Old Testament, and many quotes from the New Testament. This does not mean one has to be a Bible expert to understand it, but it does mean that John had an excellent understanding of all the other books of the Bible. Therefore, it is good for all of us to have some knowledge of these books.

Symbols, Symbols, And More Symbols

Revelation is filled with symbols. John was in prison when he wrote it, and some believe he used symbols to smuggle it to the outside world. They seem to believe that he had to convince the prison authorities that these were the writings of a madman. Others believe God had John write with symbols to make us study the entire Bible to understand their meaning. Whatever the reason, the symbols make some people believe one needs a Ph.D. to understand Revelation. No one can deny the value of a good education, but people of all educational backgrounds do read it; even people who are not theologians, seminary professors, or pastors. They are just ordinary people who seem to love it and get a lot out of it. They learn about God, Jesus, the Church, and the future. I ask, "If they can do that, why can't everybody?" The answer is, "Everybody can if they want to—even the *Biblically-Inept*."

So Many Different Viewpoints

Obviously, with so many symbols there are bound to be many different interpretations. I try, as much as possible, not to take sides, and to explain each viewpoint. One of the biggest areas of discrepancy involves when the Church will go to heaven (a.k.a. the Rapture). I explain these, but take what is the most widely-accepted viewpoint—pre-Tribulation—throughout the book.

Many are tempted to date the events found in Revelation. Don't do it! Many have tried and failed. Believe what the Bible says, *No man knows about that day or hour, not even the angels in heaven, nor the Son, but only the Father* (Matthew 24:36).

I have tried to look at Revelation as the experts would, but have also tried to write it for the *Biblically-Inept*. I want it to be easy to read and understand. That's why I chose to use the *New International*

Illustration #1

The location of the seven churches which also represent the seven periods of the Church Age.

(Illustrations)

Something to Ponder

(Something to Ponder)

Remember This . . .

(Remember This)

RELATED CURRENT EVENTS

(Related Current Events)

Version (NIV) of the Bible. It is a scholarly translation that accurately expresses the original Bible in clear and contemporary English, while remaining faithful to the thoughts of the Biblical writers. That is what I want and think you, too, would want.

How To Use *Revelation—God's Word For The Biblically-Inept*

The chapter divisions in this book correspond to the chapter divisions in the Bible. There are twenty-two chapters in Revelation and twenty-two chapters in this book. First you will find each verse of Revelation. Then comes my thoughts and lots of icons and other tidbits of information to help you in the sidebar. Here's what you will see:

(Warning!)

Study Questions

(Study Questions)

CHAPTER WRAP-UP

(Chapter Wrap-Up)

Sections and Icons	What's it for?
CHAPTER HIGHLIGHTS	the most prominent points of the chapter
Let's Get Started	a chapter warm-up
Verse of Scripture	what you came for—the Bible
Commentary	my thoughts on what the verse means
GO TO:	other Bible verses to help you better understand (underlined in text)
What?	the meaning of a word (bold in text)
KEY Point:	a major point in the chapter
Key Symbols	mini-outlines to help you
What Others are Saying:	if you don't believe me, listen to the experts
Illustrations	a picture is worth a thousand words
Something to Ponder	interesting points to get you thinking
Remember This	don't forget this
RELATED CURRENT EVENTS	tidbits from today's news
WARNING	red lights to keep you from danger
Study Questions	questions to get you discussing, studying, and digging deeper
CHAPTER WRAP-UP	the most prominent points revisited

So Many Names

There are several interchangeable terms: Scripture, Scriptures, Word, Word of God, God's Word, Testimony of Jesus Christ, etc. All of these mean the same thing and come under the broad heading called the Bible. I will use each one at various times, but I will use Bible most of the time. Also, it is a common practice for many to call the last book of the Bible: The Book of Revelations, The Revelation of Saint John the Divine, Revelation, and The Revelation of Jesus Christ. We will keep it simple and call it Revelation.

One Final Tip

Prayer and meditation can be very valuable. God wants you to understand the Bible, and the Holy Spirit can do wonders to open your mind. So pray and think on the things you read. It is surprising how much you can learn and retain when you put your mind to it.

CHAPTERS AT A GLANCE

PART III: The Millennium and Beyond

Part One

THE CHURCH AGE

REVEREND FUN

Actually, your watch is working just fine . . . it is just on
God's time now, which means that one day = 1,000 years . . .
that always throws off you new angels who are used to the
24 hour scheme.

REVELATION 1

CHAPTER HIGHLIGHTS

- Read, Hear, and Keep
- Ruler of All Rulers
- Alpha and Omega
- Seven Lampstands
- Our High Priest
- He Holds the Keys

Let's Get Started

Since we will be studying Revelation, it is important to understand what a revelation is. The word **"revelation"** comes from the Greek word "apokalupsis." It means *the uncovering, the unveiling, or the disclosing*. Revelation is the disclosing of Jesus Christ. It can be taken two ways: as the revealing of the person of Jesus Christ, or as the revealing of what he intends to do starting with the "Church Age" and running through to the end of time.

The *Church Age* is that period of time that the "Church" is on earth. The *Church* consists of the followers of Jesus Christ, as opposed to a church which is a building where people meet to worship. The Church Age started fifty days after Jesus was raised from the dead on the Jewish holy day called <u>Pentecost</u> (The Feast of Weeks). It will end when the Church is **raptured**. Just as one week is divided into seven days, the Church Age is divided into seven periods (more on this later in Chapter 1).

John, one of Christ's original twelve disciples, was selected by Jesus to record Revelation. Since he knew Jesus personally, John is often called the **Apostle <u>John</u>**. He never boasted of that, but simply called himself "a **servant** of Jesus."

> **Revelation 1:1** The revelation of Jesus Christ, which God gave him to show his servants what must soon take place. He made it known by sending his angel to his servant John,

☞ **GO TO:**

Exodus 34:22, 23;
    Acts 2:1–47 (Pentecost)

I Corinthians 15:52 (rapture)

Acts 1:21–26 (Apostle John)

revelation: an uncovering of something hidden

Rapture: the Church is taken to heaven at Christ's return

apostle: someone commissioned by God to represent Christ

servant: one who follows Jesus

angel: a heavenly being that serves God

Don't Jump Ahead!

Most people who study Revelation have a tendency to rush to those hot-button topics like the *Mark of the Beast* and the *Two Witnesses* that come later. They are skipping parts of the Bible that contain many great truths. Every verse in the Bible is important, and we should want to understand what each one of them has to say.

God gave the message of Revelation to his Son Jesus. He wanted Jesus to pass it on to his servants, so Jesus gave it to an **angel**. The angel then gave it to John, who gave it to the Church.

God's purpose for giving this message was to let the Church know what was to come in the future. *Must* means it is absolutely certain that these events will take place, and *soon* means they will begin in the near future. However, remember that God's definition of *soon* is a lot different than our definition.

testimony: what Jesus told John

> **Revelation 1:2** who testifies to everything he saw—that is, the word of God and the testimony of Jesus Christ.

Who Wrote Revelation?

John wrote it. It was his task to record what he saw, and what he saw was the Word of God and the **testimony** of Jesus Christ. The things written in this book *are* the Word of God and they come from God through his Son Jesus.

☞ **GO TO:**

II Timothy 3:16 KJV (doctrine, reproof, correction, and instruction)

prophecy: what will happen in the future

heard with one's heart: freely believed and acted on

> **Revelation 1:3** Blessed is the one who reads the words of this prophecy, and blessed are those who hear it and take to heart what is written in it, because the time is near.

Read, Hear, And Keep

Revelation is more than a book of *doctrine, reproof, correction, and instruction*. It is also a book of **prophecy**. The fulfillment of this prophecy began on the first day of the Church Age (Pentecost).

God did not have John write Revelation for it to be ignored. He had John write it to be *read, heard (hear)*, and *kept (keep, take to heart)*. Yet some people won't *read* it because they are either uninterested, scared, or find it difficult to understand. All God asks is simply for us to read Revelation.

The word *hear* could simply mean to listen to someone else read Revelation. But it probably means to recognize that Revelation is the Word of God and needs to be **heard with one's heart**. The word *keep* requires obedient action to do what the Bible says. God promised a blessing to those who read, hear, and keep the Word of God.

> **Revelation 1:4** John, To the seven churches in the province of Asia: Grace and peace to you from him who is, and who was, and who is to come, and from the seven spirits before his throne,

Grace And Peace

Revelation is for all believers, but here at the beginning is a section specifically addressed to seven particular churches (see Illustration #1, page 20). The greeting is "grace" and "peace," the common need of all people. Without the **grace of God** we would perish. Without the **peace of God** we would be unsure of our <u>salvation</u>. The source of grace and peace is the eternal God; the God *who is*, *who was*, and *who is to come*.

The Holy Spirit occupies a place before the **throne of God**. He has a <u>sevenfold nature</u>. This nature is made up of *seven virtues* which are called the *seven spirits*.

The Seven Virtues (seven spirits) are:

the spirit of the Lord—the nature of Jesus

the spirit of wisdom—the ability to make the right decision

the spirit of understanding —the ability to understand everything

the spirit of counsel—the ability to give sound advice

the spirit of might—the power to do what God wants

the spirit of knowledge—the ability to know beyond human comprehension

the spirit of the fear of the Lord—the ability to respect God's will

☞ **GO TO:**

John 3:16; Romans 10:9 (salvation)

Isaiah 11:2 (sevenfold nature)

grace of God: the undeserved, saving work of God in the heart of people

peace of God: the harmony God gives to our heart because of his grace

salvation: forgiveness and cleansing

throne of God: the place where God sits in heaven

Remember This . . .

GO TO:

Luke 1:29–33 (kingdom will never end)

Word Made Flesh: the word (Jesus) was born in the flesh

sin: thoughts, acts and omissions contrary to God's will

crucifixion: execution on a cross

> **Revelation 1:5** and from Jesus Christ, who is the faithful witness, the firstborn from the dead, and the ruler of the kings of the earth. To him who loves us and has freed us from our sins by his blood

Ruler Of All Rulers

God intends to establish his kingdom here on earth, and Jesus is the Chosen One who will rule over that kingdom. Even at his birth, an angel visited his mother, the virgin Mary (see GWWB, pages 87–119), and told her she would have a son who would sit on a throne and <u>his kingdom would never end</u>. The promise that God would send his Son Jesus the first time to die on a cross was literally fulfilled. Therefore, many believe the promise that God will send his Son Jesus a second time to rule over all things will also be literally fulfilled.

Jesus is called:

1) *The Faithful Witness*—Jesus was faithful in all the things God gave him to do. He was the **Word Made Flesh**. A faithful example of the very nature of the Living God (Jesus).

2) *The Firstborn from the Dead*—Jesus was the first to die and be raised from the dead. He never died again. Others have been raised from the dead, but they eventually died again.

3) *The Prince (Ruler) of the Kings of the Earth*—This is his position in the world. World rulers do not yet realize that Jesus is in charge, but he is. The day will come when he will physically reign over every power on earth.

We are also told that Jesus loves us. He loves us with an everlasting love; a love that never fails. And the proof of his love is in the fact that he removes our **sins** through the shedding of his own blood—his **crucifixion**.

What Others are Saying:

Remember This . . .

David Breese: We should never forget that we are what we are, and we are participants in the grand scenario of history, because Jesus Christ in his own blood has given forgiveness and cleansing.[1]

The Faithful Witness—the first coming of Jesus (his physical birth and life on earth)
The Prince of the Kings of the Earth—the second coming of Jesus (the Millennium)

> **Revelation 1:6** and has made us to be a kingdom and priests to serve his God and Father—to him be glory and power for ever and ever! Amen.

☞ **GO TO:**

I Peter 2:9 (a royal priesthood)

We Are Subjects?

Jesus has made us a kingdom of priests, a _royal priesthood_. This is what he has done for us. Here is what we can do for him. We can give him **glory and dominion** throughout all eternity. Jesus is our king and we are subjects in his kingdom. Because he has exalted us, we will **exalt** him.

glory and dominion: honor Jesus and recognize his authority

exalt: honor Jesus

> **Revelation 1:7** Look, he is coming with the clouds, and every eye will see him, even those who pierced him; and all the peoples of the earth will mourn because of him. So shall it be! Amen.

☞ **GO TO:**

Acts 1:9 (Jesus went away in the clouds)

Matthew 24:30 (coming on the clouds)

Focus On This!

Jesus went away in the clouds and he is coming back in the clouds. When he does, it will not be a secret. Even those who rejected and crucified him will see him. Everyone will know who he is, and those who rejected him will mourn because they were so blind to the truth.

Q. Why will the unbelievers mourn?

A. Because they rejected him.

Remember This . . .

Alpha: *the first letter of the Greek alphabet*

Omega: *the last letter of the Greek alphabet*

> **Revelation 1:8** "I am the Alpha and the Omega," says the Lord God, "who is, and who was, and who is to come, the Almighty."

The Beginning And The End

Jesus says he is the **Alpha** and **Omega**, the beginning and the end. He is everything that can be said about God from start to finish, from A to Z. He is the creator of all things (see GWGN, page 4), and will be the final judge of all things. He is the Lord of all.

In verse four of this chapter we noted that God is the eternally existing God; the God _who is, was,_ and _is to come._ Here again in this verse he calls himself the same thing. He is equal to the Almighty God who has power over all things.

J. Vernon McGee: From an alphabet you make words, and Jesus is called the "Word of God"—the full revelation and intelligent communications of God. Jesus is the only alphabet you can use to reach God, my friend. The only language God speaks and understands is the language where Jesus is the Alpha and the Omega and all the letters in between.[2]

☞ **GO TO:**

II Timothy 3:12
(persecution)

Christian: a believer in Jesus Christ

witness: what Jesus said and did

winning crowns: rewards for doing his will

> **Revelation 1:9** I, John, your brother and companion in the suffering and kingdom and patient endurance that are ours in Jesus, was on the island of Patmos because of the word of God and the testimony of Jesus.

My Spiritual Brother

In verse 8, Jesus introduced himself. Now, John introduces himself (see GWMB, pages 261–263). He is the **Christian's** spiritual brother, a brother in Christ. He is also the Christian's companion, a companion in suffering for Christ's sake. All Christians are members of God's spiritual kingdom (the Church), a kingdom that teaches, and requires patience.

John was on the Isle of Patmos, a small island in the Mediterranean Sea (see Illustration #1, page 20), where he was imprisoned by the Roman Emperor Domitian. That explains his suffering.

What was his crime? Two things: 1) he would not deny the truth of the Bible, and 2) he would not deny the **witness** of Jesus Christ. John would rather be cast in prison and killed than reject Christ.

Becoming a servant of God will not keep a Christian out of trouble. We are not going to slide through life without problems. We are in the process of **winning crowns**. However, there are crosses to bear (persecution) before we receive them.

take control of him: to have power over him

> **Revelation 1:10** On the Lord's Day I was in the Spirit, and I heard behind me a loud voice like a trumpet,

Why Should I Worship On Sunday?

By the time John was in prison, Christians had adopted the practice of worshiping on Sunday. There are two reasons for this: 1) Jesus arose on Sunday, and 2) Pentecost falls on Sunday.

It was Sunday, the Lord's Day, and John was most likely praying when the Holy Spirit began to **take control of him**. While under the Holy Spirit's influence, John heard an unusual voice—a voice that sounded like a trumpet.

> **Revelation 1:11** which said: "Write on a scroll what you see and send it to the seven churches: to Ephesus, Smyrna, Pergamum, Thyatira, Sardis, Philadelphia, and Laodicea."

Jesus Picked Seven

The voice told John to write on a scroll what he was about to see. That scroll is Revelation. By this time in history there were probably thousands of churches in the world. Out of all of those churches, Jesus picked seven (see Illustration #1, page 20). He even identified them in a precise order.

Looking back on history, we now realize why Jesus picked these seven particular churches, and why he listed them in that order. Their good and bad qualities and the problems they faced are ideal for instructing all of God's people, and those same qualities and problems have turned out to be prophecies revealing the future history of the Church.

What Others are Saying:

Hal Lindsey: If you are going to be an interpreter of the Scripture, you have to have a **sanctified** curiosity. You cannot study the Bible without having six friends. My six friends for studying the Bible are *who, what, where, when, why,* and *so what.*[3]

> **Revelation 1:12** I turned around to see the voice that was speaking to me. And when I turned I saw seven golden lampstands,

Seven Golden Lampstands

Upon hearing the voice, John turned around to see the speaker, but the first thing he saw was seven golden **lampstands**. In verse 20, we will learn that these seven golden lampstands represent the seven churches. These seven churches represent seven different periods of the Church Age. (see Time Line #1, Appendix A).

Illustration #1

Location of the Seven Churches—Each church represents a period of the Church Age.

KEY Symbols:

Seven Golden Lampstands

seven churches/periods of the Church Age

- Ephesus
- Smyrna
- Pergamum
- Thyatira
- Sardis
- Philadelphia
- Laodicea

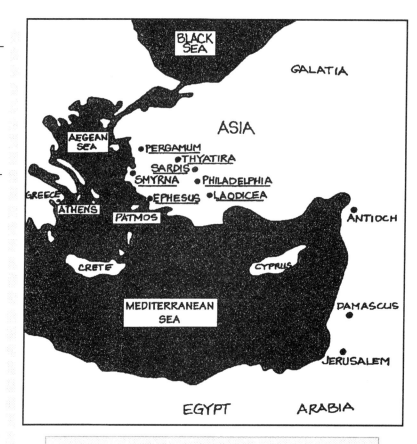

☞ **GO TO:**

Leviticus 8:7–9 (High Priest)

Hebrews 7:17–27 (Melchizedek)

high priest: *the spiritual head of Old Testament Israel*

order of Melchizedek: *the ultimate royal priesthood*

intercede: *work or pray on our behalf*

> **Revelation 1:13** and among the lampstands was someone "like a son of man," dressed in a robe reaching down to his feet and with a golden sash around his chest.

Our Great High Priest

Next, John saw where the voice came from. Someone who looked like the Son of Man was standing in the middle of the seven churches. He was wearing a long robe that went down to his feet with a golden sash around his chest.

What is the significance of this? Why this vision of Jesus standing in the middle of these seven churches dressed in the official attire of the **high priest** (see Illustration #2, page 21)? Jesus said, *For where two or three come together in my name, there I am with them* (Matthew 18:20). This vision means that Jesus will stand in the midst of the Church throughout the Church Age. He is the Great High Priest who is always with his Church; a priest after the **order of Melchizedek**; a priest who is always able to **intercede** for us.

Illustration #2

*The High Priest of Israel—
Dressed in official royal attire.
Twelve stones in breastplate
represent twelve tribes of
Israel.*

> **Revelation 1:14** His head and hair were white like wool, as white as snow, and his eyes were like blazing fire.

☞ **GO TO:**

Daniel 7:9 (hair of God)

Hair As White As Snow

When Jesus was crucified, his hair was probably a mess, so that the crown of thorns forced down on his head most likely created blood clots in his hair. Now <u>his hair is like the hair of God</u> in Daniel's vision of the **Ancient of Days** (see GWDN, page 189). It shines with the pure white brightness of heaven.

*Ancient of Days: a name
for God*

While out in the wilderness, Moses told the Hebrews, *The Lord your God is a consuming fire, a jealous God* (Deuteronomy 4:24). The eyes of Jesus were burning like a blazing fire as he looked over the seven churches. Nothing escaped his penetrating glare. He could see every good deed and every bad deed for generations to come.

> **Revelation 1:15** His feet were like bronze glowing in a furnace, and his voice was like the sound of rushing waters.

☞ **GO TO:**

Micah 4:13 (hoofs of
   bronze)

Genesis 1:1–31 (creation)

Revelation 4:1, 2 (Rap-
   ture)

Psalm 33:6–9 (authority
   over all creation)

Rise Up And Crush Your Enemies

In the Old Testament, God told the Hebrews to rise up and crush their enemies with <u>hoofs of bronze</u>. Here we see that the feet of Jesus were like burning bronze. This is a reminder that he will **judge** everyone. *We must all appear before the judgment seat of Christ* (II Corinthians 5:10).

judge: *determines our destiny and rewards*

His voice roared like the mighty waves of the ocean. It was the voice of the one who <u>spoke everything into existence (creation)</u>, the voice of the one who will <u>raise the dead (the Rapture)</u>, the powerful voice of the one who has <u>authority over all creation</u>.

- Jesus is our GOD (Revelation 1:8).
- He is our great HIGH PRIEST (Revelation 1:13).
- He is our **JUDGE** (Revelation 1:15).

Remember This . . .

What Others are Saying:

Hal Lindsey: John was put in a kind of divine time machine, shot up to the twentieth (twenty-first) century and then brought back to the first century and told to write about what he had seen. He had to use phenomenal language to describe what he saw.[4]

GO TO:

Revelation 1:20 (seven stars)

> **Revelation 1:16** In his right hand he held seven stars, and out of his mouth came a sharp double-edged sword. His face was like the sun shining in all its brilliance.

Sharper Than Any Two-Edged Sword

KEY Symbols:

Jesus

head and hair
  - white like wool
  - white as snow
  - brightness and purity of heaven

eyes like blazing fire
  - he sees everything

feet like glowing bronze
  - he will judge everything

voice like sound of rushing waters

seven stars in his right hand
  - seven angels of the seven churches

out of his mouth a double-edged sword
  - the Bible

face like the sun

Jesus tells us the <u>seven stars are the seven angels of the seven churches</u>. Whether these angels are divinely appointed spiritual leaders of the churches is much debated. Whatever they are, it is their responsibility to look after the churches. The fact that they are in the right hand of Jesus means they are his own precious, personal possession.

Scripture tells us the sharp double-edged (two-edged) sword represents the Bible. We read, *For the word of God is living and active. Sharper than any double-edged sword, it penetrates even to dividing soul and spirit, joints and marrow; it judges the thoughts and attitudes of the heart* (Hebrews 4:12). Jesus will deal with his Church through his Word. The Bible is a very efficient sword, a sword that stabs and cuts both ways. We would be wise to heed what the Bible has to say. He will judge us by its standards.

The Shekinah Glory

Jesus is also known as the Sun of Righteousness and the Light of the World. Let there be no doubt, that when John looked upon Christ's face, he was seeing the "**shekinah glory**."

> **Revelation 1:17** When I saw him, I fell at his feet as though dead. Then he placed his right hand on me and said: "Do not be afraid. I am the First and the Last."

☞ **GO TO:**

Psalm 41:13 (everlasting to everlasting)

shekinah glory: glory brighter than the noonday sun

Nothing Before Or After

What would you do if you met Jesus face-to-face? John collapsed. But Jesus did not leave him lying there. He placed his right hand upon him and said, *Do not be afraid. I am the First and the Last.* There were none before Jesus and there will be none after. Nothing came before him and nothing will come after. There never was a time when he did not exist, and there never will be a time when he does not exist. He is from <u>everlasting to everlasting</u>.

David Breese: We are going to stand in the presence of one who occupies a throne, from which the heavens and the earth flee away, and we will see Jesus Christ, not now simply as the Person of Galilee in the old days, but as the God who presides over history.[5]

What Others are Saying:

> **Revelation 1:18** I am the Living One; I was dead, and behold I am alive for ever and ever! And I hold the keys of death and **Hades**.

☞ **GO TO:**

Acts 2:31–36 (raised from the dead)

Hades: the place of the dead (hell)

resurrection: refers to the dead coming back to life

He Holds The Keys

Jesus said about himself:

- *I am the Living One.*
- *I was dead.*
- *I am alive for ever and ever.*

He has risen from the dead and will never die again. His crucifixion will not be repeated. He holds the keys, so he is in total control of death and hell. He conquered both by <u>rising from the dead</u>, (**resurrection**) so John and any other Christian need not fear death or hell.

Why are people so afraid of Revelation when it is such a book of comfort? After all, Jesus has removed the sting of death and hell for those who follow him.

Something to Ponder

☞ **GO TO:**

Revelation 1:9
(past tense—I was on)

Revelation 1:10
(past tense—I was in)

Revelation 1:12
(past tense—I turned)

Revelation 1:17
(past tense—I saw)

Tribulation Period: *seven years of God's wrath*

Millennium: *thousand year reign of Christ on earth*

KEY POINT

It is wrong to divide the Bible by shifting events from one time period to another.

KEY Symbols:

Seven Stars
angels of the seven churches

Seven Lampstands
seven churches

> **Revelation 1:19** "Write, therefore, what you have seen, what is now and what will take place later.

Past, Present, And Future

What John had seen was not for his own personal knowledge. Jesus wanted it written down for all of God's people. *What you have seen* (Chapter 1) refers to the events we have covered so far in this chapter. Notice that several of Chapter 1's verses are written in the <u>past tense</u>. *What is now* (Chapters 2–3) refers to the events of the present Church Age. They describe seven churches which actually existed when John had this vision, but they were selected for this revelation because they reveal aspects of the seven periods of the Church Age. *What will take place later* (Chapters 4–22) refers to future events that will take place after the Church Age is over. They reveal what will happen during the **Tribulation Period** plus what will happen during the **Millennium** and beyond. That is why this book is divided into three sections: 1) The Church Age, 2) From The Rapture to The Second Coming, and 3) The Millennium and Beyond (see Time Lines #1, 2, and 3, Appendix A).

The events in Revelation must be kept in their proper time periods. John's vision in Chapter 1 is of past events. They will not be repeated. The events in Chapters 2–3 are present events. They do not have anything to do with future events found in Chapters 4–22. The stage is now being set for these future events, but they will not be fulfilled until after the Church Age is over.

> **Revelation 1:20** The mystery of the seven stars that you saw in my right hand and of the seven golden lampstands is this: The seven stars are the angels of the seven churches, and the seven lampstands are the seven churches.

The Bible Interprets Itself

To avoid any misunderstanding, God often uses the Bible to interpret itself. Jesus clearly identified the seven stars in his right hand as the angels of the seven churches. Again, whether they are literal angels or great spiritual leaders is debatable, but they clearly have authority over their respective churches. The seven lampstands signify the seven churches. They also foretell the history of the Church from Pentecost to the Rapture.

A mystery is a hidden truth that has not been made known before. Until it is revealed, it is meaningless to the reader. Once it is revealed, it ceases to be a mystery and becomes a revelation.

Something to Ponder

Study Questions

1. How did Jesus make his message known to John?
2. Should we be afraid of Revelation?
3. Who will see Jesus when he returns?
4. What is the relevance of the seven churches today?
5. What is the importance of the high priest?

CHAPTER WRAP-UP

- God promised a blessing to those who *read, hear,* and *keep* the Word of God. (Revelation 1:3)

- Christ is the Ruler of All Rulers, and the day will come when he will reign over all the nations of the earth. (Revelation 1:5)

- Jesus is the Alpha and the Omega. He is everything from the beginning to the end. (Revelation 1:8)

- The seven lampstands symbolize seven churches and seven church periods. Each church represents one of the seven periods of the Church Age. (Revelation 1:12, 20)

- Jesus is the Great High Priest of the Church. He works on our behalf to reconcile our relationship with God that has been damaged by sin. (Revelation 1:13)

- Jesus holds the keys to death and hell since he conquered both through his death and resurrection. (Revelation 1:18)

REVELATION 2

CHAPTER HIGHLIGHTS

- Four Church Letters
- Second Death
- Fire and Bronze
- Jezebel
- Bright and Morning Star

Let's Get Started

Now we are about to embark on the study of seven remarkable letters to seven specifically selected churches. In one sense, they are as ancient as the Apostle John, but in another, they are as modern as today's computers. We could read them as personal messages to people who lived almost 2,000 years ago, but we would be more correct to read them as personal messages to those living today. They were **inspired** by the Holy Spirit, and their message is of the utmost importance. We should keep in mind that these seven churches represent seven time periods giving us a panoramic view of church history running from Pentecost to the Rapture.

inspired: divinely influenced

The Church Age

Author	Ephesus Period	Smyrna Period	Pergamum Period	Thyatira Period	Sardis Period	Philadelphia Period	Laodicea Period
Tim LaHaye[1]	A.D. 30 to A.D. 100	A.D. 100 to A.D. 312	A.D. 312 to A.D. 606	A.D. 606 to Trib. Per.*	A.D. 1520 to Trib. Per.*	A.D. 1750 to Trib. Per.*	A.D. 1900 to Trib. Per.*
Hal Lindsey[2]	A.D. 33 to A.D. 100	A.D. 100 to A.D. 312	A.D. 312 to A.D. 590	A.D. 590 to A.D. 1517	A.D. 1517 to A.D. 1750	A.D. 1750 to A.D. 1925	A.D. 1900 to Trib. Per.
J. Vernon McGee[3]	Pentecost to A.D. 100	A.D. 100 to A.D. 314	A.D. 314 to A.D. 590	A.D. 590 to A.D. 1000	A.D. 1517 to A.D. 1800	A.D. 1800 to Rapture	Does not say
Daymond R. Duck	Pentecost to A.D. 100	A.D. 100 to A.D. 312	A.D. 312 to A.D. 590	A.D. 590 to A.D. 1517	A.D. 1517 to A.D. 1750	A.D. 1750 to A.D. 1900	A.D. 1900 to Trib. Mid-Point

Tim LaHaye believes these 4 church periods all end with the Tribulation Period.

GO TO:

Revelation 1:16, 20
(seven stars)

Revelation 1:12, 13, 20
(seven golden
lampstands)

forsake: abandon

> **Revelation 2:1** "To the angel of the church in Ephesus write: These are the words of him who holds the seven stars in his right hand and walks among the seven golden lampstands:

I Will Never Leave You

As we just saw in Chapter 1, the <u>seven stars</u> represent seven angels and the <u>seven golden lampstands</u> represent seven churches. Since we are following the *Golden Rule of Interpretation*, we will say this letter was directed to the angel over the church in Ephesus, the same angel who presides over the Ephesus period of the Church Age.

Jesus told John to write this letter, and it is Jesus who holds the seven angels in his right hand and walks in the midst of the seven churches. Jesus is the one who controls the angels and the one who will never leave or **forsake** his Church. He is obviously a person of great power and love who has a message for the church in Ephesus and the Ephesus period of the Church Age.

What Others are Saying:

Remember This . . .

David Breese: I would like, therefore, to suggest that the Bible may be telling us that your church, my church, has an angel.[4]

Two Important Things the World Needs to Know About Jesus

1) He is all-powerful, yet loving.
2) He will never forsake his Church.

deity: a divine being

> **Revelation 2:2, 3** I know your deeds, your hard work and your perseverance. I know that you cannot tolerate wicked men, that you have tested those who claim to be apostles but are not, and have found them false. You have persevered and have endured hardships for my name, and have not grown weary.

The Eyes Of God Are Everywhere

The penetrating <u>eyes of Jesus</u> are everywhere beholding the evil and the good. He knows everything we do. He knew that the Ephesus church toiled with great difficulty, and he recognized their perseverance under trial. This church refused to tolerate evil men in their congregation that falsely claimed to have known and seen Jesus. These evil men were put on trial and found guilty of lying.

Jesus noted how the Ephesus church remained faithful, even though it was surrounded by immorality and pagan beliefs. This church stood firm against religious deception in the name of Jesus.

Jack Van Impe: Major Christian denominations have been captured by those who reject the essential truth of the Bible, and the **deity** of Jesus Christ.[5]

What Others are Saying:

Why Are These Problems Important to the Church?

- So we can learn from them.
- So we will not repeat them.

Something to Ponder

> **Revelation 2:4, 5** Yet I hold this against you: You have forsaken your first love. Remember the height from which you have fallen! Repent and do the things you did at first. If you do not repent, I will come to you and remove your lampstand from its place.

backsliding: *slipping back into sin*

first love: *original commitment to Christ*

Backsliders

In spite of all the good things about the church in Ephesus, there was a problem. There was a decline in the people's relationship with Jesus because they had stopped loving him the way they once did.

Jesus asked them to recall the relationship they once had with him, to take inventory of their lives, and to turn from the things of the world and back to him. If they did not, he warned that they would lose their right to exist as a church. They must stop **backsliding** or they will die out. The choice was theirs.

Many mistakenly believe the early Christians of the Ephesus church period got on a spiritual mountain top and stayed there. When the period began, the people's highest priority was Jesus. As time went on, they started backsliding. By the end of the period, they needed to get back to their **first love**.

KEY Symbols:

Ephesus
backsliders
the church should
  - remember
  - repent
  - return

Amos 5:15; John 15:12 (loves the person but hates the sin)

in the flesh: with the human body

the spirit: the immaterial part of man; the soul

false doctrines: beliefs contrary to God's teachings

false practices: dishonest or deceptive practices

professing Christendom: everyone who claims to be a Christian

> **Revelation 2:6** But you have this in your favor: You hate the practices of the Nicolaitans, which I also hate.

Love The Person, But Hate The Sin

Exactly who the Nicolaitans were, and what they did, is anyone's guess. Some say they were a cult that tried to create a ruling class of priests in the Ephesus church. Others say they taught that Christians could sin because what is done **in the flesh** does not affect **the spirit**. Still others say they taught that Christians needed to indulge in sin to understand it. Whoever they were, and whatever they did, the church in Ephesus hated it. And so did Jesus.

During the Ephesus period, many groups tried to introduce **false doctrines** and **false practices** into the Church. What they were doing was repulsive to Christians, and more importantly, it was repulsive to Jesus.

Jesus didn't say he hated the Nicolaitans, but he did say he hated what they were doing. This is a classic example of New Testament teaching—Jesus loves the person, but hates the sin.

What Others are Saying:

false messiahs: those who claim to be Jesus Christ but really aren't

false prophets: those who claim to speak for God but really only spread false teachings

the elect: true Christians

Remember This . . .

Ed Hindson: One of the great warnings of prophetic Scripture is that false teaching will bring deception upon **professing Christendom** in the last days. Jesus himself warned that *many will come in my name, claiming, "I am Christ," and will deceive many* (Matthew 24:5). He also predicted that *many false prophets will appear and deceive many people* (Matthew 24:11). Our Lord said this would continue throughout the Church Age, but he also spoke of a time at the end of the age in which **false messiahs** and **false prophets** would perform miracles to deceive the world and even confuse **the elect**.[6]

1) Sin is the transgression of the *Law;* breaking God's rules (I John 3:4).

2) Sin is knowing to do good but not doing it (James 4:17).

3) Sin is anything that is not of *faith;* not trusting in God (Romans 14:23).

4) Sin is all *unrighteousness;* wickedness (I John 5:17).

5) Sin is a disease of the *soul;* the inner part of man that lives forever (Psalm 41:4).

6) Sin is foolishly thinking we can ignore God (Proverbs 24:9).

> **Revelation 2:7** He who has an ear, let him hear what the Spirit says to the churches. To him who overcomes, I will give the right to eat from the tree of life, which is in the paradise of God.

Overcomers

Although this letter was specifically addressed to the church in Ephesus, the last line is addressed to anyone who will listen. He has a blessing for those who **overcome**. After Adam and Eve sinned in the <u>Garden of Eden</u> they were forbidden to eat the fruit of the tree of life. Apparently there was something on that tree that could cause a person who ate it to live forever. It amounted to a permanent cure for death. Jesus promises to give overcomers the opportunity to eat from that tree. It was located in the Garden of Eden, but now is located in **paradise**.

3 Steps to Overcoming Sin

1) **Remember** the height from which you have fallen (your first love).
2) **Repent** of your backsliding or falling away.
3) **Restore** the good deeds you did at first.

☞ **GO TO:**

I John 5:4 (overcomes)

Genesis 3:3–22 (Garden of Eden)

overcome: overcoming sin through faith in Jesus

paradise: the heavenly abode

repent: turn away from wrong

Remember This . . .

> **Revelation 2:8** "To the angel of the church in Smyrna write: These are the words of him who is the First and the Last, who died and came to life again.

Great Persecution

The church in Smyrna was experiencing great persecution, so Jesus reminded them that he is the <u>First and the Last</u>, the Alpha and Omega. He is the one who created all things, and the one who will end all things.

Just like this church, Jesus was also persecuted. His enemies falsely accused him, beat him, spit on him, ripped out his beard, crowned him with thorns, and <u>nailed him to a cross</u> where he died.

☞ **GO TO:**

Revelation 1:8 (the First and the Last)

Matthew 27:35 (nailed him to a cross)

John 20:15–18 (rose from the dead)

*Remember
This . . .*

☞ **GO TO:**

Matthew 6:19–21
(laying up heavenly
treasures)

John 10:14 (his sheep)

synagogue: *a place where
Jewish people worship*

KEY POINT

We can be either rich
in the temporary
things of this world or
rich in the permanent
things of heaven—we
can't have both.

When You're Persecuted, Remember:

- Jesus has always existed.
- Jesus will never cease to exist.
- Jesus died.
- Jesus triumphed when he <u>rose from the dead</u>.

> **Revelation 2:9** I know your afflictions and your poverty—yet you are rich! I know the slander of those who say they are Jews and are not, but are a synagogue of Satan.

Laying Up Your Treasures In Heaven

Jesus knows what his Church is facing. He knows every prayer, every hymn, every gift, every Sunday School lesson, every sermon, every visit, every good thing, and every bad thing. He knew about the poverty of the Christians in Smyrna. He knew they were serving under the most difficult of circumstances. Their property was being seized and many had no source of personal income.

Those of us who live today often think of poverty in terms of not having enough money to live comfortably. In a real sense, that is exactly what poverty is, but in a higher sense, poverty is not having an acceptable relationship with God. In that sense, these Christians were rich. They were children of God and were destined for heaven. They were <u>laying up their treasures in heaven</u>. We can be rich in the *temporary* things of this world and poor in the *permanent* things of heaven, or we can be poor in the temporary things of this world and rich in the permanent things of heaven.

Jesus also knew about a group in Smyrna who falsely called themselves Jews. They even called their place of worship a **synagogue**, inferring that it was *the synagogue of the Lord.* But Jesus called it *the synagogue of Satan.* Even today some religious pretenders call themselves members of God's Church, but Jesus knows their really members of Satan's church. It does not matter what we call ourselves because Jesus knows <u>his sheep</u>.

*What Others
are Saying:*

Wim Malgo: It was some years ago when statistics told us that more than 500 churches of Satan exist in the United states. These "churches" are dedicated to worshiping Satan.[7]

> **Revelation 2:10** Do not be afraid of what you are about to suffer. I tell you, the devil will put some of you in prison to test you, and you will suffer persecution for ten days. Be faithful, even to the point of death, and I will give you the crown of life.

GO TO:

Romans 13:1 (no power but God)

Job 1–42 (test us)

crown of life: a crown symbolizing eternal life

stood fast: did not waver

Do Not Be Afraid

Jesus knew that Satan intended to attack these Christians, so he had a word of encouragement for them; *Do not be afraid of those who kill the body but cannot kill the soul. Rather, be afraid of the One who can destroy both soul and body in hell* (Matthew 10:28).

In a sense, there is <u>no real power</u> except that which comes from God. Satan may <u>test us</u>, but only because God allows it in order that we may be strengthened.

Jesus told his people they would be persecuted for ten days. Exactly what these ten days mean is not certain, but history reveals that there were ten distinct periods of intense persecution during the Smyrna period. During this time Satan let loose all the forces of hell in an effort to stamp out the fledgling Church. Christians were beaten, jailed, tortured, and killed, yet Jesus urged faithfulness. He even promised a **crown of life** to those who **stood fast**. Many did, even unto death.

Heavenly Crowns for Overcomers

1) The Incorruptible Crown (I Corinthians 9:24–27).
2) The Crown of Rejoicing (I Thessalonians 2:19, 20).
3) The Crown of Life (James 1:12; Revelation 2:10).
4) The Crown of Righteousness (II Timothy 4:8).
5) The Crown of Glory (I Peter 5:2–4).

Remember This . . .

```
10 Periods of Persecution known by their Roman Em-
perors (dates are approximate)

1) Nero (64-68 A.D.)—burned Rome and blamed Chris-
   tians; crucified and threw Christians into pits
   with wild animals; executed Paul and possibly Peter
2) Domitian (90-96 A.D.)—killed thousands in Rome;
   banished John to the Isle of Patmos
3) Trajan (104-117 A.D.)—outlawed Christianity; burned
   Ignatius at the stake
```

RELATED CURRENT EVENTS

Smyrna

persecuted

the church should know

- that Jesus has
  always existed
- that Jesus will never
  cease to exist
- that Jesus died
- that Jesus was raised
  from the dead

☞ **GO TO:**

Revelation 20:14
(second death)

Revelation 20:14,15
(lake of fire)

John 3:3 (born twice)

born twice: *born physically
(first time) and spiritually
(second time); the second
time is also known as being
born again*

**Something
to Ponder**

☞ **GO TO:**

Revelation 1:16
(double-edged
sword)

4) Marcus Aurelius (161-180 A.D.)—tortured and beheaded Christians
5) Severus (200-211 A.D.)—burned, crucified, and beheaded Christians
6) Maximinius (235-237 A.D.)—executed Christians
7) Decius (250-253 A.D.)—tried to wipe out Christianity and executed those he could find
8) Valerian (257-260 A.D.)—tried to wipe out Christianity; executed the Bishop of Carthage
9) Aurelian (270-275 A.D.)—persecuted Christians any way he could
10) Diocletian (303-312 A.D.)—burned the Scriptures

> **Revelation 2:11** He who has an ear, let him hear what the Spirit says to the churches. He who overcomes will not be hurt at all by the second death.

A Second Death?

Once again Jesus turns from addressing a specific church to addressing anyone who will listen. No other church, and no other individual can do our listening for us.

We have already noted we can be overcomers by our faith in Jesus Christ. Now we learn that faith in Jesus is also rewarded with victory over the second death. The Bible teaches that there are two deaths: a first death and second death. The first death is physical. The second death is spiritual. But do not think of death as the end of things. Think of it as a separation. The first death is a separation of the soul and spirit from the body. The second death is a separation of the soul and spirit from God. A person would be better off having physical death be the end of things than to die this second death—being cast into the lake of fire forever and having eternal separation from God.

If we are born just once, we will die twice, but if we are **born twice**, we will die just once.

> **Revelation 2:12** "To the angel of the church in Pergamum write: These are the words of him who has the sharp, double-edged sword.

Compromise

Compromise was the big problem for those under this angel's authority. It was caused by a merging of church and state. The church in Pergamum allied itself with the world.

Jesus identified himself as the one who has the sharp double-edged sword. We know from the last chapter that the sharp <u>double-edged sword</u> is the Word of God. Jesus reminds this church that he will deal with it through the Bible. It is a book that can create or destroy, heal or afflict, soothe or trouble. And it is always successful.

What Does a Compromising Church Need to Know?

That Jesus wields a sword called the Word of God. Watch out!

Remember This . . .

> **Revelation 2:13** I know where you live—where Satan has his throne. Yet you remain true to my name. You did not renounce your faith in me, even in the days of Antipas, my faithful witness, who was put to death in your city—where Satan lives.

heathen: *an unsaved person*

idolatry: *worshiping false gods*

martyr: *one who dies for his beliefs*

Don't Back Off

Jesus knows where his Church is. This particular church was located in a city run by **heathen** intellectuals—a city given over to **idolatry** and the temple worship of: Athena, Caesar Augustus, Dionysus, Asklepios, Hadrian, and Zeus. Satan had a large power base there and his rulers of darkness were a major force to be reckoned with.

Satan's power was strong, but the power of the Holy Spirit was stronger. These Christians refused to surrender. They didn't back off, and greater words could not be spoken of anyone than was of Antipas. He was a "faithful **martyr**."

Ed Hindson: The ultimate crisis in education is spiritual and philosophical. Public universities sold their souls to secularism early in this century and have survived to reap the consequences. The void of spiritual values has led to the great ethical crises of our times. People just don't care what is right or wrong anymore. All they care about is themselves.[8]

What Others are Saying:

The faithful honor God, and God honors the faithful.

Remember This . . .

☞ **GO TO:**

Numbers 22–31
(Balaam)

children of Israel: *Jews*

fornication: *forbidden sexual sins*

KEY Symbols:

Pergamum
compromising
the church should know
- that Jesus wields a sword called the Word of God

> **Revelation 2:14, 15** Nevertheless, I have a few things against you: You have people there who hold to the teaching of Balaam, who taught Balak to entice the Israelites to sin by eating food sacrificed to idols and by committing sexual immorality. Likewise you also have those who hold to the teaching of the Nicolaitans.

Balaam

Satan's vicious attack from outside the church was failing, but he had a growing danger brewing inside the church. Within its walls were two groups of people who called themselves Christians but did not measure up. Both groups were very liberal on their view of what sin is. One espoused the teachings of Balaam. The other espoused the teachings of the Nicolaitans.

To properly understand the teachings of Balaam, we have to go back to the Old Testament. Balaam, a prophet, took money from a king named Balak to pronounce a curse on Israel. When God stopped Balaam, Balaam told Balak to have women of his country intermarry with the Jews. These women could then tempt their Jewish husbands to sin against God. Balak used these women to entice the **children of Israel** into idolatry and **fornication**. There were those in Pergamum, and also during the Pergamum period, who were doing the same thing. They were liberal on sin and were enticing others to sin.

The teachings of the Nicolaitans were more complicated. As far as we know, they believed a person's spirit is inherently good and a person's flesh is inherently evil. They also believed that it did not matter what one did in the flesh because sin in the flesh had no effect on the spirit. In essence they were saying, "Live it up; immorality doesn't matter." That tickled some people's ears. They liked the idea of loose living, but Jesus was not pleased. He knew that *a little yeast works through the whole batch of dough* (I Corinthians 5:6). A little compromise would eventually corrupt a lot of people.

> **Revelation 2:16** Repent therefore! Otherwise, I will soon come to you and will fight against them with the sword of my mouth.

☞ **GO TO:**

Numbers 31:6–8
(Balaam killed)

Our Spiritual Sword

body of Christ: those who truly believe in Jesus

lights in the world: examples of Gods' love

person of Jesus Christ: the Messiah called Jesus

Jesus warned the church in Pergamum to stop following the Nicolaitans. In the Old Testament, we learn that the children of Israel eventually <u>killed Balaam</u> (along with King Balak and his nation) with a sword. Here in the New Testament, we learn that Jesus warns loose-living members of this church that he will fight them with a spiritual sword, the Bible, if they do not change their evil ways. The Bible is the effective weapon against sin in the Church because it confronts the sinner with his sin.

Our Spiritual Sword is the Bible which:

1) Reveals all things that pertain to life and godliness (II Peter 1:3).

2) Shines the light of God on our failures (John 3:20).

3) Reveals the true will of God (I Thessalonians 4:3).

4) Convicts us of sin (John 8:7).

5) Reveals the love of God (John 3:16).

6) Reveals the judgment of God (Romans 14:10).

7) Calls for repentance (Acts 2:38).

Remember This . . .

J. Vernon McGee: What a mistake we make if we think that the Church has the authority to decide what is right and what is wrong. The true Church is made up of believers in Jesus Christ—what Scripture calls the **body of Christ**. They are to be **lights in the world**. And if we are going to be lights in this dark world, we need to be careful to identify with the **person of Jesus Christ** and to recognize, not the Church, but the Word of God as our authority.[9]

What Others are Saying:

> **Revelation 2:17** He who has an ear, let him hear what the Spirit says to the churches. To him who overcomes, I will give some of the hidden manna. I will also give him a white stone with a new name written on it, known only to him who receives it.

☞ **GO TO:**

Exodus 16 (manna from heaven)

John 6:35 (never hunger spiritually)

Manna From Heaven

The hidden manna takes us back to another Old Testament story. As the children of Israel were wandering in the wilderness they ran short of food. They began to complain, so God fed them **manna from heaven**. When the manna fell, Moses told Aaron to collect a pot full and hide it in the ark as a reminder to future generations that God had met their needs. Since we cannot see Jesus, he is our *hidden* manna. He promises that we will <u>never hunger spiritually</u> because he is always with us.

The white stone is a reference to the way votes were cast at the courts of justice in John's day. When a case was tried, the jurors voted by dropping stones into an urn: black for guilty or white for innocent. Jesus promises that overcomers will be found innocent when God judges all things. Because of the shed **blood of Jesus** overcomers are set free from the **penalty of sin**.

The new name that no one knows has many interpretations, but the most common one seems to be that overcomers will receive a white stone bearing a secret name of Jesus. It will symbolize that each one of us has a special, intimate relationship with him. We will know him by a very personal name that no one else knows.

Think about it. We will be innocent, never hunger, and have a personal relationship with Jesus. Jesus promises to take care of his people and provide for their future. Overcomers will enter God's glory with many rewards from a Lord who loves each one of us.

> **Revelation 2:18** "To the angel of the church in Thyatira write: These are the words of the Son of God, whose eyes are like blazing fire and whose feet are like burnished bronze.

Eyes Of Fire and Feet Of Bronze

Jesus is the Son of God, which reveals his relationship to the God, the Father.

Jesus goes on to further identify himself as the one *whose eyes are like a blazing fire*. His fiery eyes depict his penetrating insight, his anger, and his attitude toward the **adulterous nature** of the church in Thyatira and its church period. His eyes are burning with strong displeasure as he looks upon the wickedness of this church.

Jesus describes himself as the one *whose feet are like burnished bronze*. This is a reminder that he will judge his Church. Those who bring evil into the Church in the name of Christianity are begging to be judged by the Son of God.

> **Revelation 2:19** I know your deeds, your love and faith, your service and perseverance, and that you are now doing more that you did at first.

☞ **GO TO:**

II Corinthians 5:10 (appear before judgment seat)

Galatians 5:22 (fruit of Holy Spirit)

I John 4:7 (love is God)

James 2:17, 18 (faith produces works)

We Are What We Do?

The Bible teaches that all believers will appear before the judgment seat of Christ. This is not the **Great White Throne Judgment** where only the lost will appear. It is the judgment seat of Christ where heavenly crowns will be given. To be a Righteous Judge, Jesus must know how we lived. Concerning this church, he knew:

1) Their *deeds*. We are what we do! Christians do the works of Christians. Those who do not do the works of Christians, are not Christians.

2) Their *love*. When people turn to God they receive the Holy Spirit in their heart. The first fruit of the Holy Spirit is love. Love is of God, and God's people will love.

3) Their *service*. Service is a ministry. The purpose of the Church is not for entertainment, enhancing our image, or doctoring our sore toes. Its purpose is service to God.

4) Their *faith*. Genuine faith is something that can be seen. It produces good deeds. It is how an unbelieving world sees Christ in us.

5) Their *perseverance*. This is often called long-suffering in the Bible. It is the fourth fruit of the Holy Spirit. Many in this church endured under great pressure for long periods of time.

6) Their *last works*. This church was doing more and more. That should be the goal of every church: to grow, to do more, to reach more people, and to increase in good works.

> **Revelation 2:20, 21** Nevertheless, I have this against you: You tolerate that woman Jezebel, who calls herself a prophetess. By her teaching she misleads my servants into sexual immorality and the eating of food sacrificed to idols. I have given her time to repent of her immorality, but she is unwilling.

Great White Throne Judgment: the judgment of the unsaved

reach more people: tell them the message of salvation

depart from the faith: leave one's beliefs

inclusiveness: the tendency to accept anyone into the Church regardless of what they believe

heresies: false teachings

occult: Satanic practices

Thyatira

DEVIL'S MILLENNIUM

spiritual adultery
the church should
know

- that Jesus is the Son of God
- that Jesus sees every sin
- that Jesus will judge sin in the church

Jezebel

Something Jesus did not like was the fact that this church was using a false teacher named Jezebel. History shows that she was a priestess at a pagan temple. She was also deeply involved in fortune-telling but was passing herself off as a prophetess of God. She was enticing God's people to **depart from the faith**. Instead of teaching them to be faithful, she was teaching them to commit fornication. Instead of teaching them to avoid idolatry, she was teaching them to eat food sacrificed to idols. Instead of leading them to Jesus, she was leading them astray.

This is a good example of what **inclusiveness** does. The church leaders in Thyatira thought their inclusiveness would bring in more people. They wanted to make more people comfortable at church, so they allowed Jezebel to tickle their ears with **heresies**.

Jesus was patient with Jezebel. He gave her plenty of time to repent, but those who are caught up in the **occult** find it difficult to change. Such is the case with Jezebel who persisted in her sin.

Jesus gave the Thyatira church approximately one thousand years to turn around. This is why some call it the Devil's Millennium. Jesus held his peace while the Church cooperated with false teachers. Multitudes were led astray. Instead of repenting, some in charge of the Church often had the true servants of God killed.

RELATED CURRENT EVENTS

Examples of the Devil's Millennium

Sudan—the governing National Islamic Front murders or enslaves Christians on sight; 2,000,000 Sudanese have been massacred since 1989

China—millions of Chinese Christians have been arrested, killed, tortured, or sent to labor camps for "re-education;" eye-witnesses say pastors are regarded as more dangerous than common criminals

Nigeria and Chad—ruling Muslems incite mass riots against Christians; one riot was started when a Christian was beheaded and his head paraded down a street to shouts of "Allah Akbar!" (God is great) [10]

> **Revelation 2:22** So I will cast her on a bed of suffering, and I will make those who commit adultery with her suffer intensely, unless they repent of her ways.

☞ **GO TO:**

Matthew 7:15 (wolf in sheep's clothing)

Playing With Fire

This church is a forerunner to the harlot church in Chapter 17. When we reach that chapter we will study events that will occur during the Tribulation Period, and learn that world leaders will turn on the harlot church and destroy it with a vengeance.

Jezebel was a spiritual harlot at Thyatira. Harlots are known for committing sins in bed, so Jesus warns this church that he will make a bed for Jezebel and her adulterous followers. He will put them in bed together and cast them into intense suffering. If a church wants to play with fire, Jesus will let it play with fire. If it does not repent, he will eventually let it die out and pay for its sins. False teachings should never be tolerated.

KEY POINT

If you want to play with fire, Jesus will let you play with fire.

Hal Lindsey: Today some leaders of churches and "Christian" colleges who ought to know better are doing the same sort of thing. They invite noted fortune-tellers to speak in churches and classrooms to satisfy curiosity. These occultic mediums are Trojan horses (wolf in sheep's clothing)in the midst of God's camp. Only evil can come from listening to their poisonous doctrines.[11]

What Others are Saying:

> **Revelation 2:23** I will strike her children dead. Then all the churches will know that I am he who searches hearts and minds, and I will repay each of you according to your deeds.

KEY POINT

Everyone will receive according to what they have done on earth.

You Get What You Do

Some would argue that Jezebel was entitled to her own beliefs, but her beliefs were passed on from generation to generation. Her children followed in her footsteps and also led others astray. The Bible says, *Consider therefore the kindness and sternness of God* (Romans 11:22). Everyone needs to keep in mind these two natures of God: 1) He is good, but 2) he will judge sin. He is good, but he will be no more tolerant of spiritual adultery in our day than he was in Jezebel's day. The offspring of Jezebel's teachings will suffer the same fate as Jezebel. They will suffer the second death and be cast into the lake of fire.

When Jesus talks about being the one *who searches hearts and minds*, he is reminding us that he looks inside us to our innermost core. He looks to see what our real affections are. He looks at our emotions, desires, and thoughts. Nothing is hidden from him.

When Jesus talks about giving to everyone *according to their deeds*, he is talking about the coming judgment. Every person will be judged in the future. There will be degrees of reward in heaven and degrees of punishment in hell. Everyone will receive according to what they did on earth.

> **Revelation 2:24, 25** Now I say to the rest of you in Thyatira, to you who do not hold to her teaching and have not learned Satan's so-called deep secrets (I will not impose any other burden on you): Only hold on to what you have until I come.

Hold On

Jesus is talking to those in Thyatira who either rejected Jezebel's teachings or who were unaware of it. He promised not to place any other burdens upon them. They were already serving under difficult circumstances, so he would not ask anything more of them.

He did have some advice though. Hold on to your love, faith, ministry, patience, and ever-increasing works. Hold on to these until I return. This is another reference to the Rapture. It is also another indication that there is some overlapping of the seven church periods. It tells us that there will be some people in every church period who have characteristics of other church periods.

WARNING

Satan's Attack on the Church

1) *I know the slander of those who say they are Jews and are not, but are a synagogue of Satan* (Revelation 2:9).

2) *You remain true to my name. You did not renounce your faith in me, even in the days of Antipas, my faithful witness, who was put to death in your city—where Satan lives* (Revelation 2:13).

3) *Now I say to the rest of you in Thyatira, to you who do not hold to her teaching and have not learned Satan's so-called deep secrets* (Revelation 2:24).

> **Revelation 2:26–28** To him who overcomes and does my will to the end, I will give authority over the nations—He will rule them with an iron scepter; he will dash them to pieces like pottery—just as I have received authority from my Father. I will also give him the morning star.

A Promise

If you refuse to follow Jezebel's teachings, refuse to do her works, continue in the <u>works of Jesus</u>, persist until your death or Christ's return, you will receive a <u>position of power</u> over the nations.

Be a faithful believer and you will rule over nations with a strong, loving hand. You will break those who resist your authority like a potter breaks vessels of clay. <u>You will receive power and authority from Jesus</u> in the same way <u>he received power and authority from God the Father</u>.

The planet Venus is called the morning star because it is the brightest object in the sky just before the sun rises. It is sometimes a guide to navigators who use it to determine their location on earth. The <u>Bright and Morning Star</u> is also one of the names of Jesus, so when he promises to give the morning star to the overcomer, the gift is himself. This is a promise that Jesus will **indwell** in the believer, that he will never leave the believer, and that he will guide the believer during the dark or difficult times of life.

Believe and receive or doubt and go without.

> **Revelation 2:29** He who has an ear, let him hear what the Spirit says to the churches.

Faithful Unto Death

We have already seen this same statement four times. The fact is, Jesus ends every letter with this same **exhortation**. It is a command for all to listen and pay attention to what is in these letters. History tells us that the followers of Jezebel did not listen, just as many churches today are not listening. Yet some in Thyatira were faithful unto death, just as some today will be faithful unto death.

☞ **GO TO:**

John 6:29 (work of God)

I Corinthians 6:2 (position of power)

II Timothy 2:12 (you will receive power and authority)

Acts 1:8; Revelation 20:4 (he received power and authority)

Revelation 22:16 (Bright and Morning Star)

indwell: Christ "lives in" or "inhabits" the believer

☞ **GO TO:**

Revelation 4:1 Rapture)

exhortation: a plea to do something

Before the Tribulation Period begins, Jesus will remove his faithful from the earth. True believers will not suffer the terrible events found later in Revelation, but instead will be removed from this earth in what we know as the <u>Rapture</u>. In Revelation 13:9 we read, *He who has an ear, let him hear.* The question is, why did Jesus leave out that last part about *what the Spirit says to the churches*? Why does he say seven times, *He who has an ear, let him hear what the Spirit says to the churches*, and then suddenly shorten it by saying, *He who has an ear, let him hear*? Could it be that the Church is no longer on earth?

**What Others
are Saying:**

Hal Lindsey: I believe that (Revelation 13:9) is another one of those clear symbols that show the Church is not on earth during that (the Tribulation) period.[12]

Study Questions

1. What did God hold against the church in Ephesus?
2. What was the affliction of the church in Smyrna?
3. What was the good asset of the church in Pergamum?
4. Why was God upset with the church in Thyatira?
5. What message should Christians today get from these letters?

CHAPTER WRAP-UP

- The first four church letters are addressed to: Ephesus, Smyrna, Pergamum, and Thyatira. Each letter explains the churches' problems and offers a solution.

- Those who conquer their sinful nature can overcome the second death. Through faith in Jesus Christ one can live forever with God. (Revelation 2:11)

- Christ is described as having eyes of fire and feet of bronze. His eyes depict his ability to see everything that we do, and his feet refer to his position as judge over of all creation. (Revelation 2:18)

- Jezebel, a false priestess in Thyatira, was leading people away from God. God told this church to rid themselves of her or face punishment. (Revelation 2:20–23)

- When Christ promises to give the Bright and Morning Star to overcomers he is really promising the gift of himself to the believer. (Revelation 2:28)

REVELATION 3

CHAPTER HIGHLIGHTS

- Three Church Letters
- Lamb's Book of Life
- Key-Holder
- Lukewarm
- Standing at the Door

Let's Get Started

Chapter 3 continues with the seven letters to the seven churches in Asia Minor. We will now study the last three letters. Keep in mind the fact that these last letters are personal messages from Jesus to each one of us, and that they represent a prophetic view of Church history beginning around 1517 A.D. and running to the Tribulation Period mid-point. There are some great messages here for all who will heed what the Holy Spirit has to say.

> **Revelation 3:1** "To the angel of the church in Sardis write: These are the words of him who holds the seven spirits of God and the seven stars. I know your deeds; you have a reputation of being alive, but you are dead.

A Pretend Church

As we have seen, the <u>seven spirits</u> of God refers to the sevenfold nature of the Holy Spirit. The <u>seven stars</u> are the seven angels of the seven churches. Jesus is the one who possesses and gives the **fullness of the Holy Spirit**, but his authority is greater than that. He also controls these angels. This is an awesome amount of power. It means the destiny of the Church is in his hands.

Jesus knew the works of these churches. Sardis is not like Thyatira. In Thyatira the last works were greater than the first, but in Sardis their works were decreasing. Jesus said Sardis had a reputation of being alive, but it was actually dead. It had become a church in name only, a pretend church, one that was just going through the motions.

☞ GO TO:

Revelation 1:4 (seven spirits)

Revelation 1:20 (seven stars)

Luke 1:15; 4:1; John 20:21, 22 (fullness of Holy Spirit)

fullness of the Holy Spirit: *the indwelling and empowering of the Holy Spirit*

Ninety-Five Theses: *statements challenging Church beliefs and errors*

Reformation: *the religious movement that split the Church into two groups: Catholic and Protestant*

David Breese: What do the seven churches represent? The seven ages of Church history that bring us down to this very hour.[1]

Church historians agree that the Sardis church period began when Martin Luther nailed his **Ninety-Five Theses** to the church door in Wittenburg, Germany. This began what is commonly called the **Reformation**. The changes, however, did not dislodge the old leadership. In a short time, the Reformation stalled, complacency set in, and the Church started living off its reputation.

ministry: religious work

doctrines: teachings

> **Revelation 3:2** Wake Up! Strengthen what remains and is about to die, for I have not found your deeds complete in the sight of my God.

KEY Symbols:

Sardis
spiritually dead
the church should know
  - that Jesus possesses and gives the fullness of the Spirit
  - that Jesus controls the guardian angels of the church

Time For A Spiritual Overhaul

Jesus told the church in Sardis to, "Wake up, and stay awake." He told them that there were certain aspects of their faith and practice that were still alive, but they needed to be more serious about their worship, study, and **ministry**. He was calling on them to overhaul their relationship with God. The steps that they had already taken were good, but they had not yet reached God's standards. It is not enough for a church to hold right **doctrines** or go through a ritual or form of worship. For a church to have a valid relationship with God, it must back up its doctrines and words with devotion and works (see WBFW, pages 209, 220). When the apostle John received Revelation, it was not for his own personal knowledge. He was told to write it down for others. When a church receives a great revelation from God, it needs to put that revelation into practice. If it doesn't, it will die out. This is where the Sardis church failed.

What Others are Saying:

Ed Hindson: When we look at the trends of our times and the Biblical prophecies of the end of times, we see more and more that we may be running out of time to reach our generation for Christ. We cannot wait for somebody else to do the job. We must act now to reach the people around us. We can do it . . . we must do it . . . while there is still time.[2]

Today the average age of members of the Presbyterian church is 62. Commentator Clark Morphew says this church will be dead in 50 years and perhaps much sooner. The Episcopal church has lost one-third of its membership since 1965. The United Methodists are losing 1,500 members a week.[3]

RELATED CURRENT EVENTS

> **Revelation 3:3** Remember, therefore, what you have received and heard; obey it, and repent. But if you do not wake up, I will come like a thief, and you will not know at what time I will come to you.

☞ **GO TO:**

I Thessalonians 5:1–9 (asleep)

ecclesiastic: churchly

Surprise!

Jesus wanted his followers to recall their better days; to reflect on what they had received and heard. They had received forgiveness of their sins, salvation, eternal life, and future rewards in heaven. They had heard the preaching of the true Word of God with its clear and correct teachings. Jesus wanted his followers to recognize that they had backslid and needed to return to his teachings.

History shows that on two separate occasions, when enemy armies had surrounded Sardis, her careless guards fell asleep. Each time the opposing army slipped in and captured the embarrassed city. Jesus seems to be using this example to teach this church a great truth. If we do not return to worshiping, believing, and living the way we once did, we will not recognize the prophetic signs of his coming. The Rapture will catch them <u>asleep</u>, causing them to miss it. This is an important point.

Those who have a good knowledge of Bible prophecy will not be caught by surprise when the Rapture occurs, but those who do not understand Bible prophecy will be surprised.

John Scott: We can have a fine choir, an expensive organ, good music, great anthems, and fine congregational singing. We can mouth hymns and psalms with unimpeachable elegance, while our minds wander and our hearts are far from God. We can have pomp and ceremony, color and ritual, liturgical exactness and **ecclesiastic** splendor, and yet be offering a worship which is not perfect or "fulfilled" in the sight of God.[4]

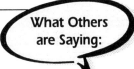

What Others are Saying:

☞ **GO TO:**

Revelation 20:12–15
(Book of Life)

Revelation 21:27
(Lamb's Book of Life)

Exodus 32:33 (name
blotted out)

KEY Symbols:

Book of Life
all who are born once

Lamb's Book of Life
only those born twice
- believers

*Remember
This . . .*

> **Revelation 3:4, 5** Yet you have a few people in Sardis who have not soiled their clothes. They will walk with me, dressed in white, for they are worthy. He who overcomes will, like them, be dressed in white. I will never blot out his name from the book of life, but will acknowledge his name before my Father and his angels.

Two Different Books Of Life

Jesus knew all his people in this church by name. Not many people in Sardis were faithful, but he could identify the ones who were. He said they were the ones who had refused to defile their garments, the ones who refused to be dirtied or influenced by the sins of those around them. He promised that they would walk with him in robes of white. Why? Because they had sincerely accepted Jesus as their Savior and, by the power of the Holy Spirit, lived holy lives.

Jesus promised never to blot out their names from the Book of Life. Many people confuse the *Book of Life* with the *Lamb's Book of Life*, but they are completely different. The Book of Life is a list of all who are born *once*; every person who ever lived. The Lamb's Book of Life is a list of all who are born *twice*; in other words, all who truly accept Jesus. It is possible to have one's name blotted out of the Book of Life for sinning against God, for denying Jesus, and for taking away from the words in Revelation. But many believe it is impossible for a saved person's name to be blotted out of the Lamb's Book of Life.

Jesus also promised to acknowledge the names of the saved before God and his holy angels. Wouldn't it be great to hear your name called out in heaven? Jesus said, *Whosoever therefore shall confess me before men, him will I confess before my Father which is in heaven. But whosoever shall deny me before men, him will I also deny before my Father which is in heaven* (Matthew 10:32, 33).

Jesus Promised:

- they would walk with him in robes of white
- he would never blot out their names from the Book of Life
- he would acknowledge the names of the saved before God and his holy angels

> **Revelation 3:6** He who has an ear, let him hear what the Spirit says to the churches.

Hear With Your Ears

It is no accident that Jesus keeps talking about **hearing**. We cannot begin to understand how important this is. It is the Bible that teaches us to remember, repent, and be righteous. To live our lives with *glorification*, *justification*, and *sanctification*. We must overcome, hold fast, and live holy lives. The great truths that sparked the Reformation started with people hearing what the Bible had to say. From the Bible they learned about the total depravity of man, justification by faith, and the authority of the Bible. When we hear the Word, we receive life, light, and truth; we learn God's commandments, judgments, and promises; we get to know his heart, mind, and will; and we find comfort, peace, and strength.

He who has an ear, let him hear. . . . Hearing is of the utmost importance. It does us no good to spend years in church without change or without hearing. We should give careful consideration to what Jesus is saying. It would be a great tragedy to think we are saved only to discover that we have made a mistake. We would never eat from the tree of life, receive the crown of life, rule over nations, dwell in the presence of God, or share in Christ's throne. If your church is almost dead, if it seems like rigor mortis has set in, Jesus says, *strengthen the things which remain.*

The Bible's 3R's are:

Remember (Revelation 2:5; 3:3; John 15:20; Jude 1:17)

Repent (Luke 13:3; Acts 2:38; 26:20)

Be **R**ighteous (I Timothy 6:11, 12)

> **Revelation 3:7** "To the angel of the church in Philadelphia write: These are the words of him who is holy and true, who holds the key of David. What he opens no one can shut, and what he shuts no one can open.

The One True God

Holy and **true** are attributes of God. He has the nature of deity. When put together, this means *Jesus is the true God.* He is not a false god like today's popular **New Age** gods such as Ishtar, Mother Earth, Gaia, Diana, and Sophia. He is the only real God.

☞ **GO TO:**

Revelation 1:3; 2:7, 11, 17, 29; 3:6 (hear)

Romans 8:17, 18 (glorification)

Romans 5:16–18 KJV (justification)

I Thessalonians 4:3, 4 KJV (sanctification)

hear: to listen, understand, and do

Remember This . . .

☞ **GO TO:**

Isaiah 22:20–25 (Eliakim)

holy: *different or separate from everyone and everything*

true: *real or genuine*

New Age: *false religious movement*

No matter what door it is, if Jesus opens it, no one can close it. If he closes it, no one can open it.

Remember This . . .

evangelistic: *declaring the Word of God to the unsaved*

revival: *renewed zeal to obey God*

Who holds the key of David takes us back to the Old Testament. There was a priest named Eliakim who held the office of *Key-holder* in King David's palace. His office gave him full authority to act on behalf of the king. If he unlocked a palace door, it remained unlocked. If he locked a palace door, it remained locked. Just like Eliakim, Jesus is the ultimate key-holder.

The Church Needs to Know:

- Jesus is the holy and true God.
- Jesus is the Key-Holder.

> **Revelation 3:8** I know your deeds. See, I have placed before you an open door that no one can shut. I know that you have little strength, yet you have kept my word and have not denied my name.

God Plus One Is A Majority

The church in Philadelphia was more like what the Church should be than any of the other churches. It was a working, **evangelistic**, Bible-believing church.

Jesus is the one who opens and closes doors. We are totally dependent upon him. We cannot evangelize or expect God to send **revival** without Jesus. Satan cannot stop revival if Jesus is on our side. Jesus told this small church in Philadelphia, *I know that you have little strength*. All they needed was him behind them. God plus one faithful Church member is a majority.

RELATED CURRENT EVENTS

In the mid 1800's, people began to be converted at the rate of 10,000 a week in New York City. The movement spread throughout New England. Church bells would bring people to prayer at eight in the morning, twelve noon, and six in the evening. The revival went up the Hudson and down the Mohawk. Baptists had so many people to baptize, they couldn't get them into their churches. They went down to the river, cut a big square in the ice, and baptized them in cold water. In one year (1857), more than one million people were converted. The revival crossed the Atlantic, broke out in Northern Ireland and Scotland and Wales and England, South Africa, South India—anywhere there was an evangelical cause, there was revival—and its effect was felt for 40 years.[5]

———

Iron Curtain—When the Soviet Union was founded, it created the Iron Curtain. It closed its doors to missionaries, spied on the church, killed millions of Christians, built nuclear weapons, and raised one of the largest armies in the world. Then it collapsed almost overnight. The Iron Curtain fell and new leaders opened the doors, allowing missionaries and pastors to go in and preach the gospel with multitudes accepting Christ.

———

Bamboo Curtain—When the Communists took over in China, they created the Bamboo Curtain to keep the non-Communists out. China has 330 million men of military age, and is spending billions to modernize its army. In spite of rapid growth in its economy and living conditions, China is increasingly *cracking down* on Christians and closing its doors to missionaries.

> **Revelation 3:9** I will make those who are of the synagogue of Satan, who claim to be Jews though they are not, but are liars—I will make them come and fall down at your feet and acknowledge that I have loved you.

The Synagogue Of Satan

There were those who wanted the church in Philadelphia to deny the name of Jesus. These citizens of Philadelphia refused to believe in Jesus or the gospel. They worshiped at a **synagogue** and said they were Jews, but Jesus called them imposters. He called their place of worship the synagogue of Satan.

Jesus assured the Philadelphia church that these pretenders would pay for their misdeeds. He said they would be forced to bow down and worship at their feet acknowledging that Jesus is Lord of this church.

KEY Symbols:

Philadelphia
evangelistic
*the church should
know*
- that Jesus is the true God
- that Jesus has the keys to lock or unlock doors, and
- that Jesus controls the door to heaven, evangelism, etc.

☞ **GO TO:**

I John 2:18 (Antichrist)

I John 3:10 (child of God)

synagogue: Jewish house of worship

This prophecy was fulfilled in Philadelphia when the Romans tried to wipe out the Jews. However, some also believe it is a prophecy that will be fulfilled during the Tribulation Period. Then, the <u>Antichrist</u> will turn against the Jews. Many will be killed, and a remnant will flee into the wilderness before they realize that Jesus is indeed the Messiah.

— — —

More than 8 of every 10 Americans today believe that it's possible to be a good Christian or Jew even without attending a church or synagogue.[6]

Something to Ponder

People are not always what they claim to be. Jesus told a group of Jews who said God was their Father, *You belong to your father the devil* (John 8:44). Even the Apostle Paul said, *Not all who are descended from Israel are Israel* (Romans 9:6). Many people fail to live up to their spiritual claims. That was true of the Jews in Philadelphia, and it is still true of the Church today. Not everyone who claims to be a <u>child of God</u> truly is.

☞ **GO TO:**

Revelation 17:12 (hour of trial)

Hour of Trial: a period of testing, another name for the Tribulation Period

> **Revelation 3:10** Since you have kept my command to endure patiently, I will also keep you from the hour of trial that is going to come upon the whole world to test those who live on the earth.

An Hour Of Trial

This church was following God's commandments in two ways: 1) it was working in the name of Jesus, and 2) it was patiently waiting for his return. Because of this, Jesus promised to keep these believers out of the **Hour of Trial** that would come in the future to test everyone. He will not permit this church or any who follow in their footsteps to go through the Tribulation Period. It will be a time of literal hell on earth, replete with famine, natural disasters, epidemic sickness, war, and murder.

What Others are Saying:

John Hagee: The Rapture is the literal, physical "snatching away" of those who have placed their faith in Jesus Christ. The Rapture could come at any moment, and it will occur without warning. Every single member of the corporate body of Christ, the genuine believers, will be taken alive to *meet him in the air* (I Thessalonians 4:17). Those who have suffered physical death will be resurrected with incorruptible, supernatural bodies.[7]

> **Revelation 3:11** I am coming soon. Hold on to what you have, so that no one will take your crown.

Twinkling Of An Eye

Some think Jesus was telling the Philadelphia church he would come soon. That is not the case. He was telling them that when he comes back, it will happen very fast. *For as lightning that comes from the east is visible even in the west, so will be the coming of the Son of Man* (Matthew 24:27). Both the Rapture and Second Coming will take place in the <u>twinkling</u> of an eye.

Hold on to what you have—do not abandon your doctrines and deeds, keep believing the Bible, keep evangelizing, and keep sending out missionaries to tell the world about Jesus. *So that no one will take your crown*—let no one else have your **reward**. God's work will still be accomplished.

☞ **GO TO:**

I Corinthians 15:52 (twinkling)

II John 1:8 (reward)

reward: *a crown given to Christians for their faithful service*

Ed Hindson: Rather than possessing an escapist mentality, prophecy students have an earnest desire to be ready at all times to meet the Lord, who could come at any moment to call us home. We want to be watching, ready, and serving.[8]

What Others are Saying:

> **Revelation 3:12, 13** Him who overcomes I will make a pillar in the temple of my God. Never again will he leave it. I will write on him the name of my God and the name of the city of my God, the new Jerusalem, which is coming down out of heaven from my God; and I will also write on him my new name. He who has an ear, let him hear what the Spirit says to the churches.

☞ **GO TO:**

Revelation 9:4 (Seal of God)

Revelation 21:9–22:6 (New Jerusalem)

Revelation 22:4 (name of Jesus)

A New Jerusalem

Jesus' promises for those who overcome:

1) *I will make you a pillar in the temple of my God*—Jesus will make his followers strong, durable and stable in the house of God.

2) *Never again will he leave it*—Jesus will make his followers secure. They will desire to stay forever, and no one will move them.

3) *I will write on him*—Jesus will write three things upon the foreheads of his followers:
   a) the <u>Seal (name) of God</u> to designate them as a child of God;

b) the name of his eternal home which is <u>New Jerusalem</u>;

c) and a new <u>name of Jesus</u> signifying their personal relationship to the Lord of lords and King of kings. Those who overcome will belong to God. They will be citizens of the New Jerusalem and will have a special relationship with Jesus.

Once again, the entire Church is asked to pay attention to these things. The faithful will escape the terrible judgments, but the unfaithful will not unless they repent of their sins and fix their relationship with God.

☞ **GO TO:**

John 14:6 (true)

John 1:3; Colossians 1:16, 17 (creation)

> **Revelation 3:14** "To the angel of the church in Laodicea write: These are the words of the Amen, the faithful and true witness, the ruler of God's creation.

The Great Amen

The Laodicea church period is the last period of the Church Age, and the last letter to the Church before the Rapture. We are living in the Laodicea church period today.

Jesus is the *Amen,* the Truth, the one we can trust. There is no greater person to believe in, no greater one to lean on.

Jesus is the *faithful and <u>true</u> witness,* the one who faithfully serves God. His deeds and words accurately testify to God.

Jesus is *the ruler of God's <u>creation</u>,* the one who is the source of all things. Some people theorize that the universe began as an explosion that took place billions of years ago. Some think we came into being through evolution. But Jesus says he created all things.

Something to Ponder

If you search the entire Bible, examine every leader of every religion, and scour every period of history, you will find that Jesus is the *only* perfect and truly righteous man who ever lived.

> **Revelation 3:15, 16** I know your deeds, that you are neither cold nor hot. I wish you were either one or the other! So, because you are lukewarm—neither hot nor cold—I am about to spit you out of my mouth.

Hot, Cold, Or Lukewarm?

Church members in Laodicea were neither *cold* nor *hot*, but *luke-warm*. Any church or church member can find itself in one of these three states: cold, lukewarm, or hot. Cold signifies formal or without spiritual life, lukewarm means indifferent or straddling the fence, and hot expresses passionate or zealous.

The church in Laodicea had become complacent. Its people were not being persecuted, but were comfortable, prospering, and self-satisfied. They were doing nothing to evangelize, grow, or glorify Jesus.

According to Jesus, this is the worst state of all. It would be easier to judge a cold or dead church and easier to bless a hot or spiritual church. But what do you do with an indifferent church that claims Christ's name? Jesus wished they would be hot or cold, but since they were neither, he would spit them out of his mouth.

KEY Symbols:

Laodicea
lukewarm
the church should
know

- that Jesus is the truth
- that the deeds and words of Jesus are reliable, and
- that Jesus is the Creator

John Hagee: There is a tomorrow that will usher in events that will completely change this planet and that will radically change your life and future. This is not the time to procrastinate. This is not the time for complacency. This is not the time to be luke-warm. This is the time to realize that one day time will be no more and the choices you have made in life will be irrevocably ratified for all eternity.[9]

What Others are Saying:

The heir apparent to the British throne is Prince Charles. He will ultimately be the head of the Anglican church, the Church of England, and probably the most well-heeled Protestant church in the world. But the Anglican church is becoming increasingly liberal, and Prince Charles is a committed New Ager. Recently, his oldest son Prince William, also heir to the leadership of the Anglican church, made news around the world when he asked his dad what religion he was.[10]

RELATED CURRENT EVENTS

The New Age movement came into being in the United States during the 1960's, but it is now a worldwide phenomenon. It originated as the umbrella for several groups: hippies, feminists, environmentalists, and others. New Agers are involved in many "consciousness raising" techniques such as channeling, transcendental meditation, astrology, and developing psychic powers. Basically,

WARNING

they see man as the sole designer and maker of his future. The movement dominates the United Nations and is greatly influencing public education, many politicians, corporations, and the U.S. military. Its greatest danger lies in its rejection of Jesus as the Savior, its promotion of false religions and doctrines, its corruption of the Church, and its support of "peace at any price." It is a major force behind the one-world religion movement that will help trigger the judgment of God on the world.

☞ **GO TO:**

Matthew 6:33 (his kingdom)

Matthew 6:21 (treasure)

Daniel 5 (writing on the wall)

Colossians 1:19; 2:9 (fullness of Jesus)

Romans 11:21, 22 (didn't spare Jews)

> **Revelation 3:17** You say, 'I am rich; I have acquired wealth and do not need a thing.' But you do not realize that you are wretched, pitiful, poor, blind, and naked.

All The Money In The World Won't Save Your Soul

This church did not have a realistic view of itself. It saw itself in one light, but Jesus saw it in another. It prided itself in its bank accounts, buildings, and members of high standing. It said we have money and material things, so why do we need anything else. Obviously, they had lost sight of Jesus and what it means to be in <u>his kingdom</u>.

It is not enough to build showy sanctuaries, great gymnasiums, and paved parking lots. Worldly <u>treasure</u> is not God's measuring stick. The church in Laodicea thought they were high on the social register, but Jesus said they were wretched. They thought they were happy, but Jesus said they were miserable. They thought they were rich, but Jesus said they were poor.

It is unfortunate, but many churches today are making the same mistake. They do not recognize the <u>writing on the wall</u> (see GWDN, pages 130–143). Unfortunately, they will never know the <u>fullness of Jesus</u> if they don't wake up. God <u>did not spare the Jews</u> when they abandoned him, so he will not spare churches that do the same.

What Others are Saying:

Hal Lindsey: There is this health and wealth gospel that is out today that is a flat out error . . . that's leading many astray . . . that says that God is going to make you rich, and if you are not, you are just not believing God.[11]

> **Revelation 3:18** I counsel you to buy from me gold refined in the fire, so you can become rich; and white clothes to wear, so you can cover your shameful nakedness; and salve to put on your eyes, so you can see.

☞ **GO TO:**

I Peter 1:7 (refined)

I Timothy 6:3–10 (came with nothing)

John 3:1–21 (Nicodemus)

righteousness of Christ: the nature or qualities of Christ (his purity, love, kindness, etc.)

God's Furnace

Mined gold is placed into a red-hot furnace not to destroy it, but to purify it. The ore is melted, the impurities are drawn out, and the residue is left—pure gold. We are put into God's furnace of testing not to destroy our faith, but to refine it. Trials humble us, our sins are drawn out (through repentance), and the residue is left—an improved Christian.

If we really want to be rich, we must buy from Jesus, with a spiritual currency, a faith that grows stronger with every test. Without this spiritual currency, we are paupers. We came into this world with nothing, and apart from a faith in Jesus, we will leave this world with nothing.

This church was naked and had no covering for their sins. He told them they should put on spiritual garments—*white clothes*—the **righteousness of Christ**. The finest earthly clothes cannot hide the tiniest sin from God's eyes. When we stand before the judgment throne, the only thing that will hide our spiritual nakedness is the righteousness of Jesus.

Jesus said this church is blind and has no spiritual discernment. He desired that they seek him for the salve to cure their spiritual blindness. To Nicodemus, he said, *I tell you the truth, no one can see the kingdom of God unless he is born again* (John 3:3). The Apostle Paul said, *The man without the Spirit does not accept the things that come from the Spirit of God, for they are foolishness to him, and he cannot understand them, because they are spiritually discerned* (Corinthians 2:14).

> **Revelation 3:19–22** Those whom I love I rebuke and discipline. So be earnest, and repent. Here I am! I stand at the door and knock. If anyone hears my voice and opens the door, I will come in and eat with him, and he with me. To him who overcomes, I will give the right to sit with me on my throne, just as I overcame and sat down with my Father on his throne. He who has an ear, let him hear what the Spirit says to the churches."

☞ **GO TO:**

Hebrews 12:5–8 (discipline)

free will: the ability to choose

Open Your Heart

The Lord will not allow anyone he loves to <u>escape discipline</u>. Even the harshest discipline is a sign of his love. It is done for two reasons: 1) to cause people to be honest about their sins, and 2) to bring them to repentance.

Jesus could have demanded that the church in Laodicea come to his door. He could have required them to knock, beg, cry, and plead for salvation, but instead, *he* was the one who knocked, begged, and pleaded. He gave them their own **free will** to accept or reject him. He did not force them to open the door.

Here lies the final promise to the overcomer: Just as Jesus overcame Satan by his life of obedience to God and his ultimate sacrifice on the cross, and just as he now sits in an exalted position on his Father's throne, the overcomer will sit on the throne of Jesus and reign with him. And for a seventh and last time, all are invited to hear what the Holy Spirit has to say to the churches.

What Others are Saying:

David Reagan: Receiving Jesus into your life is not just a way of preparing for his soon return. It will have an impact upon your life here and now. He will give you the gift of his Holy Spirit (Romans 5:5), and the Spirit will begin to empower and strengthen you for victorious living as an "overcomer."[12]

Something to Ponder

There is a famous painting by the artist Holman Hunt of Jesus standing at the door and knocking. People say when he painted it, he asked friends to come by and critique it. One friend told him he left out something very important, the door handle. Holman Hunt replied, "This door is a picture of the human heart, and the handle is on the inside."

Study Questions

1. What false reputation did the church at Sardis have?
2. Why was the church at Philadelphia so weak?
3. What was the admonition to the church at Laodicea?
4. Which letter probably applies to today's church?
5. How does one avoid being lukewarm?

- The last three church letters are to Sardis, Philadelphia, and Laodicea. Each letter explains further problems for the Church and offers solutions.

- Jesus promises to keep the names of overcomers in the Lamb's Book of Life, and he will acknowledge the believers' names before God. (Revelation 3:4, 5)

- Christ holds the keys to our lives. What doors he opens for us cannot be shut and those he shuts can't be opened. (Revelation 3:7)

- For a Christian, the worst state to be in is lukewarm—neither on fire for the Lord nor ignorant of him. Indifference leads to Christ's anger. (Revelation 3:15, 16)

- Jesus comes to us (our door) and knocks to be let in. Those who let him in will be allowed to eat (fellowship) with him. (Revelations 3:20)

Part Two

FROM THE RAPTURE TO THE SECOND COMING

REVEREND FUN

Great troubles will come to you and your people: your crops will perish, your rivers will dry up, and your descendents will all be computer illiterate.

REVELATION 4

CHAPTER HIGHLIGHTS

- Rapture
- God's Throne
- Approaching Storm
- Four Living Creatures
- Twenty-four Elders

Let's Get Started

Here in Chapter 4, we come to a major turning point. Chapters 1–3 revealed John's vision of Jesus and the Church Age. Most of this is now past and the Church Age will soon be over. Now every chapter beginning with Chapter 4 reveals what is to come in the future.

Revelation is one of the most sequence-oriented books in the Bible. We must understand this before going any further. Revelation 4:1 reveals the Rapture, Revelation 6:2 reveals the appearance of the **Antichrist**, and Revelation 6:17 reveals the beginning of the Tribulation Period.

Notice that this sequence of events indicates a period of time between Revelation 4:1 (the Rapture) and Revelation 6:17 (the Tribulation Period). The Bible does not tell us how long that period of time will be. We only know that the Antichrist must have enough time to rise to power in Europe, take over the world government, and negotiate a covenant to protect Israel (more on these events later). It is also important to note that there are three different theories regarding the sequence of these events. They are called:

☞ GO TO:

Daniel 2:41–43; 8:23–25; 9:26 (European Confederacy)

Daniel 9:27 (the covenant)

Genesis 1:1–2:3 (God creating)

Antichrist: against the Christ

Roman Antichrist: another name for the Antichrist

Messianic: reference to the expected delivery of the Jews by the Messiah

Christian Era: another name for the Church Age

Pre-Tribulation Rapture—The Church is raptured before the Tribulation Period:

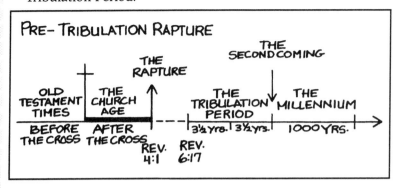

Mid-Tribulation Rapture—The Church is raptured during the Tribulation Period (at its mid-point):

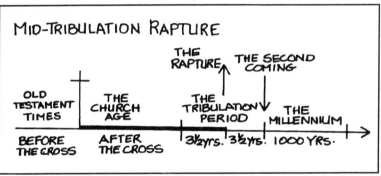

Post-Tribulation Rapture—The Church is raptured after the Tribulation Period:

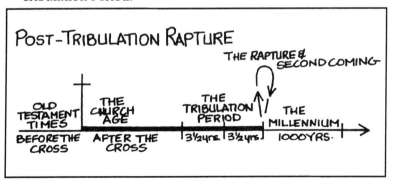

GOD'S WORD FOR THE BIBLICALLY-INEPT

The New King James Version Prophecy Bible: Sometime after the Rapture, a seven-year period will begin which is called the Tribulation. It is nowhere specified that the Tribulation will immediately follow the Rapture, so there may be some interval between the two events.[1]

Hal Lindsey: The **Roman Antichrist** must have time to be revealed, take over the <u>ten-nation European Confederacy</u> and establish himself as a world leader before he can have a power base from which to make <u>the covenant</u> with the Israeli leader.[2]

David Hocking: We may be in heaven for many years until the Tribulation actually starts. The Rapture could happen many years ahead of that. From my perspective, the Rapture could happen tonight and it still may be 20 years until the Tribulation.[3]

David Reagan: The pre-Tribulation concept of the Rapture has often been condemned as "escapism." I think this criticism is unjustified. The Bible itself says that Christians are to *comfort one another* with the concept of the Rapture (I Thessalonians 4:18).[4]

The 7,000 Year Theory of Mankind

As we draw closer to the 21st Century and a new millennium, there is a sense of change in the air with mounting anticipation about the Rapture and the Second Coming of Jesus Christ. Today, **Messianic** expectations are rampant among Jews in Israel, predictions of the Rapture and the Second Coming are widespread among Christians, and doomsday prophecies are flourishing among cults.

The 7,000 Year Theory is one of the oldest theories dating from the earliest days of the Church. It begins with <u>God creating the heavens and the earth</u> in six days and resting on the seventh. It rationalizes that God will deal with mankind for six days and rest on the seventh. It also assumes that all the days of the week are of equal length. Knowing three other Scripture verses will help in understanding: 1) II Peter 3:8 teaches one day with the Lord is 1,000 years, 2) Hebrews 4:4–11 presents the Millennium as a day of rest, and 3) Revelation 20:1–9 gives us the idea of a 1,000 year Millennium. The theory states that God will deal with mankind for six of his days (6,000 of our years) and rest on the seventh day (the 1,000 year Millennium). According to the Jewish calendar, 3,760 years after Creation the **Christian Era** began (1 A.D. on our calendar). That is almost four of God's days. Since its beginning, the Christian Era has lasted almost 2,000 years or two more of God's days. This means mankind is approaching the seventh God-day (the Millennium). But before the Millennium occurs two things must take place—the Rapture and the Tribulation Period.

☞ **GO TO:**

I Thessalonians 4:16; I Corinthians 15:52 (rapture)

> **Revelation 4:1** After this I looked, and there before me was a door standing open in heaven. And the voice I had first heard speaking to me like a trumpet said, "Come up here, and I will show you what must take place after this."

Come In

John first saw a door opening to heaven. He then heard a voice, that sounded like a trumpet, inviting him to come in and see the things that will take place *after this* (the Church Age). John *looked* and *heard.* What we see with our own eyes and hear with our own ears is real to us, but what John saw was a world that the natural eye cannot see and the natural ear cannot hear. The voice John heard was like a trumpet. It was the same kind of voice the Bible says will <u>rapture the Church</u>. For that and other reasons, many prophecy experts believe John represents the whole Church, and his ascending into heaven is symbolic of the Rapture. When the Rapture occurs, the Church will ascend into heaven at the sound of a trumpet just as John did.

Confusion over whether or not there will be a Rapture does exist. One reason for this is that the word *rapture* is not in the Bible. This is correct, but only to a point. The word rapture is not in English translations of the Bible. It is an English version of a word that appears in Latin translations. Keep in mind that most of the New Testament was written in Greek which was then translated into Latin and then to English. Saint Jerome completed most of the Latin translation in 405 A.D. His translation eventually was translated into the English Bible we know today. Several verses of the Bible in the Latin translation contain the word "rapere" or one of its derivations. It means to be *caught up*, *plucked up*, or *taken by force*. Christians translate this Latin word to mean Rapture. Christians will be both *called up* and *caught up* to heaven just as John was.

KEY POINT

The Bible was translated from Greek to Latin to English.

Grant R. Jeffrey: The early Christian writer and poet, Ephraem the Syrian, (who lived from 306 to 373 A.D.) was a major theologian of the early Byzantine Eastern Church. Ephraem's fascinating teaching on the Antichrist has never been published in English until now. This critically important prophecy manuscript from the fourth century of the Church era reveals a literal method of interpretation and a teaching of the pre-millennial return of Christ. More importantly, Ephraem's text revealed a very clear statement about the pre-tribulation return of Christ to take his elect saints home to heaven to escape the coming Tribulation.[5]

Examples of the Rapture

Remember This . . .

1) Enoch (Genesis 5:24)—Enoch went to heaven without first dying. *Enoch was taken from this life, so that he did not experience death* (Hebrews 11:5). (For more about Enoch, see GWGN, pages 59, 63–64.)

2) Elijah (II Kings 2:11)—Elijah was walking on earth when he was suddenly taken up into heaven. (See GWMB, page 139 to learn more about his disappearance.)

3) Jesus (Acts 1:9)—Jesus was taken up into the clouds to heaven.

4) Philip (Acts 8:39)—Philip was taken away, but then reappeared in another location.

5) Paul (II Corinthians 12:1–4)—Paul was caught up into heaven, and then later returned to earth. (Read more about Paul in GWMB, pages 227–336.)

6) Two Witnesses (Revelation 11:3–12)—After being killed, they will rise from the dead and ascend into heaven.

The Four Doors of Revelation

Something to Ponder

1) The **Door of Opportunity** for evangelism and missionary activity (Revelation 3:8).

2) The **Door of One's Heart** for salvation (Revelation 3:20).

3) The **Door of Heaven** for the Rapture (Revelation 4:1).

4) The **Door of Heaven** for the Second Coming (Revelation 19:11).

☞ **GO TO:**

Philippians 3:21 (glorified)

Romans 8:10 (righteousness)

John 1:7 (cleansed from sin)

glorified: *transformed into a resurrected body*

☞ **GO TO:**

Exodus 28:15–20 (breastplate)

Genesis 9: 8–17 (Noah)

I John 5:11, 12 (eternal life)

> **Revelation 4:2** At once I was in the Spirit, and there before me was a throne in heaven with someone sitting on it.

In The Spirit

John saw the door, heard the voice, and suddenly he was *in the Spirit. In the Spirit* means his spirit left his body. It was changed by the Holy Spirit into a sort of spiritual rocket ship. His body could not enter heaven because it had not yet been **glorified**. However, his spirit could enter because of the righteousness of Christ and the cleansing or purifying of his sins.

> **Revelation 4:3** And the one who sat there had the appearance of jasper and carnelian. A rainbow, resembling an emerald, encircled the throne.

Jasper and Carnelian

The one on the throne, Jesus, had the appearance of white and red light flashing off of two precious stones, jasper and carnelian. These are the first and the last stones in the breastplate of the High Priest. They remind us that the one on the throne is our High Priest forever and ever. Jasper (the white flashing light) is opaque or translucent like a diamond and represents the purity or holiness of Jesus. Carnelian (the red flashing light) is fiery red like the blood Jesus shed on the cross.

In the Old Testament God promised Noah he would never destroy the earth with a flood again. He placed a rainbow in the sky as a reminder of that promise. When the Church enters heaven, there will be a rainbow surrounding God's throne promising he will not destroy the earth during the Tribulation Period. The rainbow is a reminder that God is a God of grace, a God who keeps his promises. Where Jesus had the appearance of jasper and carnelian, the throne has the appearance of emerald green. Green is the color of life, the eternal life which comes from God as a result of the shed blood of Jesus and the grace of God.

Remember This . . .

Human words cannot describe what John saw so he used symbols to help us understand. Notice how he uses the following phrases to tell us everything about what he saw: *on the throne* (vs. 2); *surrounding the throne* (vs. 3, 4, 6); *from the throne* (vs. 5); and *before the throne* (vs. 5, 6). We will see these same things when the Church is raptured into heaven.

> **Revelation 4:4** Surrounding the throne were twenty-four other thrones, and seated on them were twenty-four elders. They were dressed in white and had crowns of gold on their heads.

☞ **GO TO:**

Revelation 3:5 (dressed in white)

II Corinthians 5:21 (righteousness of God)

Revelation 2:10 (crown of life)

The Twenty-four Elders

The number twenty-four occurs six times in the Old Testament. In every case, it is associated with the priests of Israel. On one occasion, the entire nation of Israel was represented by twenty-four special priests. Just as these priests represented all of Israel, twenty-four elders will one day represent all believers from Pentecost to the Rapture. They will surround the throne of God as representatives of a nation of kings and priests. They will stand in for all overcomers.

Just as these elders were <u>dressed in white</u>, in heaven we will all be clothed in white representing the <u>righteousness of Christ</u>. We will wear golden <u>crowns</u>—rewards for our earthly deeds. These elders will stand in for all those who love the Lord. It is very important to note that the Church will receive its robes and crowns, and it will begin its reign with Jesus in heaven before the Tribulation Period begins. There can be no doubt that God is showing us the *pre-tribulation* Rapture.

> **Revelation 4:5** From the throne came flashes of lightning, rumblings, and peals of thunder. Before the throne, seven lamps were blazing. These are the seven spirits of God.

A Storm Is Approaching

Think of the last time you saw lightning and heard thunder in the distance. You turn on the television and the weatherman says a storm is approaching. He obviously appears to be right. In the same way the lightning and thunder from the throne of God is also a signal that a storm is coming. God's patience with those on earth is wearing thin. The Tribulation Period is approaching.

We learned in Revelation 1:4 that the Holy Spirit has a *sevenfold* nature, and that the *seven spirits of God* are the *seven virtues of the Holy Spirit*. Following the Rapture, the Holy Spirit will occupy a place in the presence of God.

KEY Symbols:

Seven Lamps:
seven spirits of God
seven virtues of the Holy Spirit

KEY POINT

The Holy Spirit is everywhere, even in the presence of God.

seraphim, cherubim: angels that guard the throne of God

Remember This . . .

> **Revelation 4:6** Also before the throne there was what looked like a sea of glass, clear as crystal. In the center, around the throne, were four living creatures, and they were covered with eyes, in front and in back.

A Glassy Sea

In front of the throne was something that was so calm that it looked like a beautiful, crystal, glassy sea. Prophecy experts suggest this sea of glass is: 1) the Church because the sea is a Biblical symbol for the masses of humanity, 2) the water of the Word, and 3) the water of baptism. Whatever it is, it indicates that all is calm in front of the throne of God. Nothing is present that could cause turbulence or unrest. The Church will be at peace with God when it goes before him.

Around the throne were four unusual creatures with many eyes in front and in back. These creatures are some type of angelic beings who possess characteristics of the **seraphim** and the **cherubim**. Their many eyes indicate they can see all that is happening in every direction. They could be the highest and greatest of all heavenly beings.

The Water of Baptism

Jesus was baptized with water and he told his disciples to baptize others in the same way. For that reason, the Church uses *water baptism* as an outward sign or symbol that a change has taken place in the believer's heart. Upon being baptized, a new believer is added to the list of members of his church.

Water baptism by immersion symbolizes the death, burial, and resurrection of Jesus. Being put under water (immersed or buried in water) symbolizes the death and burial of Jesus. Being brought up out of the water symbolizes his resurrection. When a new believer is baptized by immersion he is also announcing that his old self has died, his old ways have been buried, and he has been raised to live a new life in Christ.

Some churches pour water over the new believer as a form of baptism. This may symbolize the baptism of the Holy Spirit or the pouring out of the Holy Spirit. Other churches sprinkle water over the new believer. This symbolizes the cleansing work of God in our hearts and the sprinkling of the blood of Jesus.

> **Revelation 4:7** The first living creature was like a lion, the second was like an ox, the third had a face like a man, the fourth was like a flying eagle.

☞ **GO TO:**

Revelation 5:5 (Lion of Judah)

Matthew 2:2; 21:5; 27:11 (King of Jews)

Mark 10:45 (servant)

Luke 5:24; 6:5; 7:34 (Son of Man)

John 1:3 (creator)

The Four Gospels

The first angelic being is like a lion—Jesus is the <u>Lion of the Tribe of Judah</u>. The lion is the king of beasts and Jesus is the King of Kings. The Apostle Matthew describes Jesus as the <u>King of the Jews</u>. The second angelic being is like an ox—<u>Jesus came as a servant</u>. Just like the ox, a beast that carries its burden, Jesus carried our sins. The Apostle Mark describes Jesus as a servant. The third angelic being is like a man—Jesus was human. The Apostle Luke describes Jesus as the <u>Son of Man</u>. The fourth angelic being is like an eagle—Jesus is God. Just as the eagle rules the skies, Jesus rules the heavens and reigns over all things. The Apostle John describes Jesus as <u>the creator</u> of all things. These four living creatures remind us of the qualities of Jesus that are found in the Four Gospels: Matthew (King of kings), Mark (servant), Luke (Son of Man), and John (Son of God).

The Four Living Creatures

1) Lion (king of beasts)—The Gospel of Matthew calls Jesus the King of the Jews.
2) Ox (beast of burden)—The Gospel of Mark calls Jesus a Servant.
3) Man (human)—The Gospel of Luke calls Jesus the Son of Man.
4) Eagle (rules the skies)—The Gospel of John calls Jesus God.

Remember This . . .

> **Revelation 4:8** Each of the four living creatures had six wings and was covered with eyes all around, even under his wings. Day and night they never stop saying: "Holy, holy, holy is the Lord God Almighty, who was, and is, and is to come."

Holy, Holy, Holy

Their <u>six wings</u> are characteristic of the seraphim. Their eyes are like the <u>eyes of the Lord</u>: they are everywhere, beholding everything. Their stamina is like the stamina of the Lord: they never stop singing, and they <u>never sleep</u>. They are there to <u>exalt the name of Jesus</u>, the one *who was, and is, and is to come*.

☞ **GO TO:**

Isaiah 6:2 (six wings)

II Chronicles 16:9 (eyes of Lord)

Psalm 121:4 (never sleep)

Isaiah 24:14, 15 (exalt)

Revelation 1:8 (who was)

> **Revelation 4:9** Whenever the living creatures give glory, honor, and thanks to him who sits on the throne and who lives for ever and ever,

Glory, Honor, And Thanks

The purpose of the four living creatures is to worship and give glory, honor, and thanks to the one on the throne. In doing so, they acknowledge that he is eternal and almighty. But each time they glorify the Lord, something else happens.

☞ **GO TO:**

I Corinthians 14:25 (fall down)

falling down: *drop on one's knees or lie prostrate on the ground*

> **Revelation 4:10** the twenty-four elders fall down before him who sits on the throne, and worship him who lives for ever and ever. They lay their crowns before the throne and say:

Fall On Your Knees

The twenty-four elders always follow the lead of the four living creatures. Whenever the four living creatures worship the one on the throne, the twenty-four elders also worship him by **falling down** and exalting him. This falling down is a deliberate act of humility. The elders remove their crowns and place them before the throne. Even these kings, high priests and leaders recognize that he is their power and their source.

What Others are Saying:

David Hocking: When they *fall down before him* (Revelation 4:10) they give recognition to his authority and position. It is a lesson to all believers; we need to submit to his authority as a daily principle in our lives. That's why it is a good thing to kneel when we pray to indicate our submission to the Lord.[6]

☞ **GO TO:**

Isaiah 40:28 (creator)

> **Revelation 4:11** "You are worthy, our Lord and God, to receive glory and honor and power, for you created all things, and by your will they were created and have their being."

This has been called the *song of creation*. The twenty-four elders proclaim his worthiness and acknowledge him as the creator of all things, the one who holds all things together. *By your will* expresses the desire of Jesus to create all things. We may not understand a great deal about his marvelous creation, but we can understand that it was brought into existence because Jesus wanted it to exist. And it continues to exist because it is his will.

David Hocking: God the Father is worthy of praise and worship because of two basic things we should always remember: It was *his power* that created all things, and it is *his purpose* (will) that brought everything into existence and gives meaning to it all.[7]

What Others are Saying:

Study Questions

1. What did the trumpet voice say to John?
2. What stones describe the appearance of the one on the throne?
3. What will the twenty-four elders wear in heaven?
4. What do the blazing lamps before the throne represent?
5. Following the symbolic act of the twenty-four elders, what crowns should we lay before the throne?

CHAPTER WRAP-UP

- When John goes to heaven *in the spirit* it is symbolic of the Rapture of the Church. (Revelation 4:1, 2)

- God's throne is surrounded by a rainbow, the twenty-four elders, seven lamps, a sea of glass, and the four living creatures. (Revelation 4:2–6)

- The flashes of lightning, rumblings and peals of thunder coming from the throne of God are symbolic of the approaching storm known as the Tribulation Period. (Revelation 4:5)

- The four living creatures have six wings and are covered with eyes. Each creature resembles a different animal: lion, ox, man, and eagle. (Revelation 4:7, 8)

- When the four living creatures glorify God, the twenty-four elders will lay their crowns before the throne and proclaim God's worthiness. (Revelation 4:9–11)

REVELATION 5

CHAPTER HIGHLIGHTS

- Seven-Sealed Scroll
- Lion of Judah
- Worship of the Lamb
- Praise from All Creatures

Let's Get Started

Revelation is a book of symbols. Under the inspiration of the Holy Spirit, John recorded God's message using these symbols to make it easier for us to understand. Unfortunately, now we have the task of deciphering what is the meaning of these symbols. To do that we look to the Old Testament book of the prophet Jeremiah.

Jeremiah 32 explains the <u>law for redemption of land</u>. Its purpose was to help those in Israel who fell behind in their debts. Those who got behind lost their land but were not without hope. They still had the right to buy their land back in the future. Even if they did not, or could not buy their land, after a prescribed period of time their heir or next of kin could buy it. In this way, their land remained in their family.

On one occasion, God told Jeremiah that his cousin would ask him to redeem his land. His cousin had fallen in debt, lost his land, and been sentenced to prison. It wasn't long before Jeremiah went to see his cousin in prison. There the cousin asked Jeremiah to buy his land and told him <u>it is his right to redeem it and possess it</u>. Understanding that it was God's law, Jeremiah bought the land.

Even this wasn't enough. Jeremiah had not yet met all of the requirements of the law. When his cousin lost the land, two scrolls (contracts) containing terms for redeeming the land were drafted. One scroll became a public record and was displayed unsealed for all to read. The other was rolled up and sealed with seven seals and placed in storage at the temple. It was brought out only when someone showed proof of their right to **redeem** the land.

After this redeemer presented the necessary proof of ownership, the temple priest would retrieve the seven-sealed scroll from

☞ **GO TO:**

Leviticus 25:8–24, Jeremiah 32:1–25 (law for redemption)

Jeremiah 32:8 (his right to redeem)

Isaiah 63:16 (Kinsman Redeemer)

Romans 3:23, 24; I Peter 1:18,19; Ephesians 1:7; I John 2:2 (qualifies to redeem)

redeem: to buy back

joint heir: one who shares in the inheritance of others

storage. He would then unseal the scroll and read it. If everything was in order, the redeemer would receive all ownership to the land.

When God created all things, he gave earth to man, but Adam sinned and lost it to Satan. However, Adam is still a **joint heir** with Jesus, an adopted child of God. He is a <u>Kinsman Redeemer</u>— one who can buy back the earth and mankind.

In Chapter 5 the Church is now in heaven, and we are in that period of time between the Rapture and the Tribulation Period. The question before us is, <u>who qualifies to redeem Adam's lost property</u>?

Hal Lindsey: Sealing a scroll was a common and important practice in Biblical times. The wills of both Emperor Vespasian and Caesar Augustus, for example, were secured with seven seals. For such a document, a scribe would procure a long roll of parchment and begin writing. After a period of writing he would stop, roll the parchment enough to cover his words, and seal the scroll at that point with wax. Then he would resume writing, stop again, roll the scroll, and add another seal. By the time he was finished, he would have sealed the scroll seven times. The scroll would be read a section at a time, after each seal was opened.[1]

☞ GO TO:

Genesis 6 and 7 (the flood)

Genesis 18:16: 19:29 (Sodom and Gomorrah)

Daniel 9:21, Luke 1:19 (Gabriel)

archangel: a leader among angels

> **Revelation 5:1, 2** Then I saw in the right hand of him who sat on the throne a scroll with writing on both sides and sealed with seven seals. And I saw a mighty angel proclaiming in a loud voice, "Who is worthy to break the seals and open the scroll?"

Safely Out

John is still in heaven and beside God's throne at the opening of Chapter 5. He sees a scroll in God's right hand that is sealed seven times with writing on both sides. Whatever this scroll is, there is no doubt that it is important. Why would God reveal this scroll to his Church? Could it be that he has the destiny of all mankind in his hands? Could it be that he is in charge of all that happens on earth? We know that God did not allow the earth to be destroyed by <u>the flood</u> until Noah and his family were safely in the ark. We also know that God would not allow <u>Sodom and Gomorrah</u> to be destroyed by fire and brimstone until Lot and his family were safely out of the city. Could it be that God will not allow this scroll to be opened until his church is safely in heaven?

John also saw a powerful angel. What made this angel appear

to be so strong is not revealed, but he had the authority to speak in the presence of God. We do not know who this angel is, but because the name <u>Gabriel</u> means *strength of God,* some believe he is indeed the **archangel** Gabriel. *Who is worthy to break the seals and open the scroll?* is a gripping question. Who could ever qualify as a redeemer for Adam and our fallen world?

> **Revelation 5:3–5** But no one in heaven or on earth or under the earth could open the scroll or even look inside it. I wept and wept because no one was found who was worthy to open the scroll or look inside. Then one of the elders said to me, "Do not weep! See, the Lion of the tribe of Judah, the Root of David, has triumphed. He is able to open the scroll and its seven seals."

The Root Of David

No one in heaven or earth, either living or dead, will be able to open the scroll and look inside. Obviously John was heartbroken because he desired to know what the scroll contained. He had a great love for all mankind and had hoped the scroll would provide the answers to its problems, but that was not to be. The message of the scroll would have to wait.

Suddenly, one of the twenty-four elders told John to stop crying. Someone worthy to open the scroll had been found. It is the Lion of the tribe of Judah, the Root of David. These two Old Testament names of God remind us of the first and second coming of Jesus.

<u>Judah</u>, one of the twelve sons of <u>Israel</u> (also called Jacob), was also the first leader of one of <u>the twelve tribes of Israel</u>. God promised the <u>Messiah</u> would come from that tribe whose symbol was a lion. Jesus, a descendant of the tribe of Judah, is the Messiah— <u>the Lion of the tribe of Judah</u>. At the end of the Tribulation Period Jesus will return with the strength of a lion.

Jesus is also the <u>Root of David</u>. God promised David that one of his descendants would be the Messiah. Jesus is a fulfillment of that prophecy. His earthly mother was Mary, a descendant of David. Jesus came as a lamb the first time.

Wim Malgo: Why was it necessary for one of the elders to comfort John, who already knew that Jesus had overcome? Because John did that which we so easily do. He lost sight of the victory of the Lamb and this always results in hopelessness and tears. How

☞ **GO TO:**

Genesis 35:23–26 (Judah)

Genesis 32:28 (Israel)

Genesis 49:28 (twelve tribes)

Genesis 49: 9,10; II Samuel 7 (Messiah)

Genesis 49:9 (Lion of Judah)

Isaiah 11:1, Revelation 22:16 (Root of David)

Romans 3: 10, 23 (none righteous)

What Others are Saying:

very often do we insult the Lord with our weeping and discouragement. We are often ready to resign in spite of the fact that he has achieved the great and wonderful victory.[2]

When we get to heaven, it will <u>not be because we are righteous</u> or because we are worthy redeemers, but because we have been redeemed by the grace of God.

> **Revelation 5:6** Then I saw a Lamb, looking as if it had been slain, standing in the center of the throne, encircled by the four living creatures and the elders. He had seven horns and seven eyes, which are the seven spirits of God sent out into all the earth.

Sacrifice The Lamb

When Jesus walked upon this earth, <u>John the Baptist</u> introduced him by saying, *Look, the Lamb of God, who takes away the sin of the world* (John 1:29). When the John of Revelation saw him in heaven, he described Jesus as *a Lamb, looking as it had been slain.* Jesus is our sacrificial lamb. The Old Testament prophet Isaiah foretold that he would be as a <u>lamb led to the slaughter</u>.

Jesus looked like he had been killed, but he was not lying on an altar, in bed, or in a casket. He was standing in the center of the throne, surrounded by the four living creatures and twenty-four elders.

Seven is the number of perfection in the Bible, and horns are symbols of power. Seven horns means that Jesus had **omnipotent**, perfect power. He may have looked like a little lamb, but he had all the power of God. After being raised from the dead, Jesus said, *All authority in heaven and on earth has been given to me* (Matthew 28:18).

The seven eyes are defined as the seven spirits of God sent out to all the earth. He looked like he had been slain, but his eyes were not closed. He had the all-seeing **omniscient** vision of the Holy Spirit. He sees and knows all.

The seven virtues of the Holy Spirit are, the nature of Jesus, wisdom, understanding, counsel, might, knowledge, and respect for God's will. Jesus also possessed these same virtues—and the Holy Spirit continually spreads them over all the earth. Not everyone is willing to receive them, but they still are everywhere.

Something to Ponder

☞ **GO TO:**

Matthew 3:1–17 (John the Baptist)

Isaiah 53:7 (led to slaughter)

omnipotent: *all powerful*

omniscient: *all knowing*

KEY Symbols:

Seven Horns
  omnipotent

Seven Eyes
  omniscient (seven spirits of God)

Something to Ponder

> **Revelation 5:7, 8** He came and took the scroll from the right hand of him who sat on the throne. And when he had taken it, the four living creatures and the twenty-four elders fell down before the Lamb. Each one had a harp and they were holding golden bowls full of incense, which are the prayers of the saints.

From Lamb To Lion

Keep in mind that John was seeing those things that will take place after the Church is raptured. The Rapture is a very significant event because it marks a distinct change in the way Jesus deals with mankind. Up until now he has dealt with us as a lamb, but from this point on through the Tribulation Period, he will deal with those who are left behind as a lion.

John watched as Jesus took the scroll from the right hand of God. All of creation has waited almost six thousand years for this pivotal moment. Adam lost the title deed to earth for all mankind, but Jesus has proven himself a worthy redeemer and will get the deed back.

When Jesus took the scroll, the four living creatures and the twenty-four elders fell down and worshiped him each with a harp and a golden bowl. The harps are musical instruments that will accompany the singing in heaven. The golden bowls will contain the prayers of the saints. Who and what will we be praying for? We will be praying for our loved ones on earth who are being persecuted. We will pray for the defeat of the **Satanic trinity**, and we will pray for the Second Coming and subsequent reign of Jesus.

The Godhead is thought of as trinity. Father, Son, and Holy Spirit. Satan seems to try to duplicate that with his own trinity called the Satanic trinity. Satan tries to replace God, the Antichrist tries to replace Christ, and the False Prophet tries to replace the Holy Spirit. Satan will indwell the Antichrist and False Prophet, so they will be pure evil. When the Antichrist supposedly dies and is resurrected some think he will come back to life because Satan has possessed his body.

Satanic trinity: consists of Satan, the Antichrist, and the False Prophet

KEY Symbols:

Harps
musical instruments

Bowls
the prayers of the saints

Something to Ponder

☞ **GO TO:**

Acts 10:34 (no re-specter)

John 3:16 (loves the world)

Revelation 20:6 (reign with him)

Matthew 28:19 (disciples)

Calvary: the site in Jerusalem where Jesus died

transgressions: sins

iniquities: sins

atonement: Jesus' crucifixion that restored our relationship with God

commissioned: authorized

> **Revelation 5:9, 10** And they sang a new song: "You are worthy to take the scroll and to open its seals, because you were slain, and with your blood you purchased men for God from every tribe and language and people and nation. You have made them to be a kingdom and priests to serve our God, and they will reign on the earth."

A New Song

The four living creatures and the twenty-four elders sang a new song with a new form of praise. Their song speaks of what Jesus is to do, and what he has already done. It tells why Jesus is worthy to take the scroll and open the seals.

Jesus is worthy because he was slain on the cross at **Calvary**. The Old Testament prophet Isaiah said, *Surely he took up our infirmities and carried our sorrows, yet we considered him stricken by God, smitten by him and afflicted. But he was pierced for our **transgressions**, he was crushed for our iniquities; the punishment that brought us peace was upon him, and by his wounds we are healed. We all, like sheep, have gone astray, each of us has turned to his own way; and the Lord has laid on him the **iniquity** of us all* (Isaiah 4:6).

Jesus is worthy because with his blood he purchased our sins. He paid the price of our redemption. *For you know that it was not with perishable things such as silver or gold that you were redeemed from the empty way of life handed down to you from your forefathers, but with the precious blood of Christ, a lamb without blemish or defect* (I Peter 18:19). The blood of Jesus was precious. God said, *For the life of a creature is in the blood, and I have given it to you to make **atonement** for yourselves on the altar* (Leviticus 17:11) It was the blood of Jesus that makes atonement for our sins.

Jesus is worthy because he is no respecter of persons. He died for the sins of all the world—*every tribe and language and people and nation*—because he loves the world.

Jesus is worthy because he made us a royal priesthood to serve and reign with him. He **commissioned** his Church to go and make disciples of all nations. And when he returns in his Second Coming at the end of the Tribulation Period, we will reign with him on earth for a one thousand years (the Millennium).

What Others are Saying:

J. Vernon McGee: The "new song" is the song of redemption. The "old song" is the song of creation.(The Old Testament praises God for his creation, but the New Testament praises God for his love.)[3]

Iniquity is a type of sin. It is a sin of commission such as theft or murder. *Sin* is wrongdoing of any kind. It can be an act of omission (not doing something) or of commission (doing something).

Remember This . . .

> **Revelation 5:11, 12** Then I looked and heard the voice of many angels, numbering thousands upon thousands, and **ten thousand times ten thousand**. They encircled the throne and the living creatures and the elders. In a loud voice they sang: "Worthy is the Lamb, who was slain, to receive power and wealth and wisdom and strength and honor and glory and praise."

☞ **GO TO:**

Daniel 7:10 (ten thousand times ten thousand)

ten thousand times ten thousand: *too many to count*

obeisance: *respect or reverence*

Worthy Is The Lamb

John looked and he saw a multitude of angels gathered around the living creatures, the twenty-four elders, and the throne of God. Then he heard them singing declaring the worthiness of God. Who is to receive:

Power—the authority to do whatever he wants (forgive sins, give eternal life, and command angels)

Wealth—the riches of God (everything belongs to him)

Wisdom—the natural wisdom of God (his counsel, his understanding, and the ability to create, uphold, govern, judge, and redeem)

Strength—the physical strength to do whatever he wants (perform miracles, conquer, create, destroy, cast into the lake of fire)

Honor—rewards (the rewards of God and his people)

Glory—the image of God (God's glory, God's magnificence, God's splendor, the royal dignity and the royal majesty)

Praise—worship, acknowledgment and commendation

Tim LaHaye: In a day when humanistic men are unwilling to acknowledge Jesus Christ as more than a "good man" or a "model example," we should hear what the angels of heaven, who know him best, say of him. They proclaim him worthy to receive seven things—power, riches, wisdom, might, honor, glory, and blessing—which far outshadows any **obeisance** due to mortal men. I joyfully accept the description of the angels as the only authentic portrait of Christ.[4]

What Others are Saying:

☞ **GO TO:**

Philippians 2:9–11
(God has exalted
the Son)

days of Adam: beginning
of Creation

> **Revelation 5:13, 14** Then I heard every creature in heaven and on earth and under the earth and on the sea, and all that is in them, singing: "To him who sits on the throne and to the Lamb be praise and honor and glory and power, for ever and ever!" The four living creatures said, "Amen," and the elders fell down and worshiped.

Every Creature

John heard every creature praise God and his son Jesus. Every creature in heaven, under the earth, and on the sea. Every creature that is alive or dead. Every creature who has been judged, and or will be judged. *Every creature* from the **days of Adam** to the Rapture will praise him.

The four living creatures responded to the praise by saying, *Amen*, signifying that they were in agreement with the praise of every other creature. They affirmed their praise and worship. Then the twenty-four elders responded by falling down and worshiping the Father and the Son. Praise and worship is due the <u>Father and the Son</u> throughout all eternity. Both were involved in the redemption of all things and both should be praised as long as anything exists.

What Others are Saying:

David Hocking: Can there be any doubt as to the grand and ultimate objective for the believer? Is not the worship and praise of Almighty God our primary goal? We will one day participate in that heavenly scene, but even now we can enjoy the privilege of exalting Him. As Paul exhorts us, whatever we do, let us do it to the glory of God (I Corinthians 10:31).[5]

Study Questions

1. What is the implied significance of the scroll?
2. How are the two comings of Jesus symbolized in John's vision?
3. How does this chapter explain the seeming injustice of God letting sin go unpunished?
4. Why is the Church a royal priesthood?
5. How do we know that Jesus was more than just a good man, or a prophet?

- God will hold a seven sealed scroll in his right hand as an angel asks, who is worthy to open the scroll? John will cry when no one steps forward. (Revelation 5:1–4)

- Jesus is the Lion of Judah, and he is the only one worthy to open the scroll. He is worthy because he was slain for the sins of the world. (Revelation 5:5–7)

- Once Jesus takes the scroll, the four living creatures and twenty-four elders will sing a new song; the angels will also join in proclaiming Christ's worthiness. (Revelation 5:8–12)

- When heaven is singing to Jesus, all creatures on earth and under the sea will also sing praise to him. (Revelation 5:13)

REVELATION 6

CHAPTER HIGHLIGHTS

- First Seal
- Four Horsemen
- Tribulation Saints
- Great Earthquake
- Fear

Let's Get Started

In Chapter 6, the scene shifts from future events in heaven to future events on earth. We have looked at what will happen in *heaven* between the Rapture and the Tribulation Period. Now we turn our attention to what will happen on *earth* during this same period of time. There is much debate about how long this period will last, but three years is a good possibility.

The Seven Jewish Feast Days

God gave the Jews <u>seven feast days</u> to observe forever (see Time Line #4, Appendix A). It can be shown that:

1) Jesus was crucified on Passover (the first feast day)

2) Jesus was in the grave on Unleavened Bread (the second feast day)

3) Jesus arose from the dead on First Fruits (the third feast day)

4) the church began on Pentecost (the fourth feast day)

5) there is reason to believe the Church will be raptured on Trumpets (the fifth feast day)

6) there is reason to believe the Second Coming will occur and the Tribulation Period will end on Atonement (the sixth feast day)

7) there is reason to believe the Millennium will begin on Tabernacles (the seventh feast day)

☞ **GO TO:**

Leviticus 23 (seven feast days)

Revelation 6:17 (Tribulation Period)

II Thessalonians 2:6–8 (restrained)

eschatology: *teachings or beliefs about end time events*

Something to Ponder

Interestingly enough, between Trumpets (the Rapture) and Atonement (the Second Coming and the end of the Tribulation Period) there is a ten-day period called the "ten days of awe," "the awesome days," or the "ten days of repentance." Since the seventieth week (or the <u>Tribulation Period</u>) corresponds to seven years (one day of the seventieth week = one year of the Tribulation Period), it is reasonable to assume that the ten days of awe will correspond to ten years. This period of time will give people, Gentiles and Jews, an opportunity to grieve, mourn, repent and accept Jesus as Messiah before the Second Coming occurs and their fate is sealed forever. It will also allow three years for the Antichrist to come on the scene and rise to power before the Tribulation Period begins.

The Number Seven

Something to Ponder

During the tribulation Period Jesus will start to deal with the Satanic trinity and man's rebellion on earth. His course of discipline will be directed from heaven, but the terrible events will take place on earth. The Holy Spirit has divided these events into three sets of seven: *seven seal judgments, seven trumpet judgments*, and *seven bowl judgments*. It would be easy to say that twenty-one judgments will occur, but that is not the case. The first six seals will be broken one at a time and each seal will produce a judgment for a total of six judgments. The seventh seal will not produce a seventh judgment. Instead it will produce the seven trumpets. The first six trumpets each produce a judgment for a total of six. But the seventh trumpet will produce seven bowls. When the seventh bowl is poured out, the Tribulation Period will come to an end.

A small number of prophecy experts suggest that these judgments will occur simultaneously. This can't be. The seven trum-

KEY Symbols:

Seven Seal Judgments	Seven Trumpet Judgments	Seven Bowl Judgments
Seal 1—Judgment	Trumpet 1—Judgment	Bowl 1—Judgment
Seal 2—Judgment	Trumpet 2—Judgment	Bowl 2—Judgment
Seal 3—Judgment	Trumpet 3—Judgment	Bowl 3—Judgment
Seal 4—Judgment	Trumpet 4—Judgment	Bowl 4—Judgment
Seal 5—Judgment	Trumpet 5—Judgment	Bowl 5—Judgment
Seal 6—Judgment	Trumpet 6—Judgment	Bowl 6—Judgment
Seal 7—Seven Trumpet	Trumpet 7—Seven Bowl	Bowl 7—Judgment
Judgments	Judgments	**End of Tribulation**

pets do not begin until the seventh seal is opened, and the seven bowls do not begin until the seventh trumpet is blown.

Over the centuries people have always tried to figure out the Antichrist's identity, since he will probably be alive when the Church is raptured. But the problem with this is he will be restrained and will not be revealed until the proper time. When the true Church is raptured, it will be time to start watching for the Antichrist. He will not stand out at first, so the best thing to look for will be a popular and powerful person. When he signs a seven-year treaty to protect Israel, his identity will be known.

What Others are Saying:

John Hagee: The Antichrist will be a man who makes his debut upon the stage of world history with hypnotic charm and charisma. He will probably come from the European Union or a country or confederation that was once part of the Roman Empire, which stretched from Ireland to Egypt and included Turkey, Iran, and Iraq.[1]

Noah Hutchings: The consistent interpretation by pre-millennial scholars of **eschatology** in reference to Daniel 9:27 and Matthew 24:15–21 is that a dictator will rise up out of the Revived Roman Empire and confirm, or add the prestige and power of his empire, to a peace treaty that will involve Israel. This same dictator is thought by the same scholars to become the Antichrist. . . . On page 11 of . . . *The European* (Nov. 15, 1995), Israel is hailed by the European Union (E.U.) as a new ally. Therefore, the assassination of Prime Minister Rabin actually hastened a comprehensive peace agreement in the Middle East, and now the E.U. states that within a few months this final peace process instrument will be confirmed by (its member) nations.[2]

> **Revelation 6:1** I watched as the Lamb opened the first of the seven seals. Then I heard one of the four living creatures say in a voice like thunder, "Come!"

Like A Tiny Snowball Rolling Down A Hill

The terrible judgments will not begin like a nuclear explosion, but rather like a tiny snowball rolling down a long hill. They will not appear that bad at first but they will gain strength and momentum with each roll. Things will eventually get out of control and become so bad that mankind would destroy the earth were it not for the Second Coming of Jesus.

☞ GO TO:

Genesis 6, 7 (Noah)

Genesis 18:16–19:29 (Sodom and Gomorrah)

KEY Symbols:

First Four Seal Judgments

the Four Living Creatures

four horses and riders

Remember This . . .

☞ **GO TO:**

Revelation 13:2, 4, 5, 14, 15 (gift)

Daniel 9:27 (peace treaty)

II Chronicles 36:15, 16 (prophets of Israel)

Matthew 21:1–10 (donkey)

Revelation 19:11 (white horse)

Notice who opens the seals. Jesus! He is in charge of the judgments and their timing. He once said, *Moreover, the Father judges no one, but has entrusted all judgment to the Son, that all may honor the Son just as they honor the Father* (John 5:22, 23). When he opens the first seal, one of the four living creatures will speak in a voice like thunder.

In each of the first four seals a horse and rider are released by one of the four living creatures of Chapter 4. Each horse is waiting in its stall ready to charge, as if in a race, when the command is given. They will not, however, all race out at once. Each horse must wait for its command, and its command will be given by a different living creature when Jesus breaks a seal. When all four living creatures have commanded their horses to come forth, all four horses will have been released. Each living creature summons its horse by speaking just one word—*Come!*

As long as <u>Noah</u> (see GWMB, pages 107–112) was on the earth, God did not send the flood, but when Noah entered the ark, God did send the flood and judged the world. As long as Lot and his family were in <u>Sodom and Gomorrah</u>, God did not send fire and brimstone to destroy the cities. But likewise, when Lot and his family were safely out of Sodom and Gomorrah (see GWGN, page 155), God did not hesitate to judge these cities. Today, as long as the Church is in the world, God will not send these terrible judgments. But as soon as the Church is taken to heaven, God will not hesitate to pour out his wrath.

> **Revelation 6:2** I looked, and there before me was a white horse! Its rider held a bow, and he was given a crown, and he rode out as a conqueror bent on conquest.

A White Horse

Chapter 19 also speaks of a rider on a white horse—Jesus. For this reason, a few experts suggest that this rider will also be Jesus. But most experts disagree, believing this rider to be none other than the counterfeit Christ, or Antichrist.

He will come forth with a bow. A bow was an effective weapon in John's day; a symbol of military power. However, nothing is said about arrows, so many think this rider will come forth as a man of peace.

Crowns were worn by heads of state. Those who wore them usually earned or inherited the right to wear their crown. But this man will receive his crown as a <u>gift</u>, meaning he will not earn or inherit it.

The world will be looking for such a ruler who can put an end to nuclear weapons, environmental and economic problems, poverty, etc. He will go forth *as a conqueror bent on conquest*, thereby abandoning his peace program in an attempt to dominate the world. But his use of force to attain his goal of world domination will be a disaster, resulting in the persecution and death of all those who oppose him. The earth will have a charismatic leader negotiating <u>peace treaties</u> that are a fake.

prophets of Israel:
Testament prophets

Apocalypse: *the vision of a great world upheaval*

last days: *days prior to the end of any period in history*

What Others are Saying:

John Hagee: In the surge of advocates for peace, voices of dissent will be shouted down or ignored. The peace process will cease to become a political action; it will become a spiritual mandate for a nation. Based on the words of the **prophets of Israel**, I believe this peace process will lead to the most devastating war Israel has ever known.[3]

Grant R. Jeffrey: When the inner circle of five European nations expands to include ten states, the white horseman of the **Apocalypse** (as prophesied by John in Revelation) will arise to seize power over this alliance. This horseman, the Antichrist, will make a seven-year treaty with Israel as part of his strategy to *destroy the mighty, and also the holy people* (Daniel 8:24 NKJV). Daniel's prophecy that *the people of the prince who is to come shall destroy the city and the sanctuary* (Daniel 9:26 NKJV) spoke of two distinct destructions of Jerusalem within this single prophecy. The first destruction occurred in 70 A.D. when the Roman Empire and its armies burned Jerusalem and destroyed the Temple. Daniel's prophecy also foretold a final attack on Jerusalem at the end of the seven-year treaty in the **last days**. *The people of the prince who is to come* reveals that the future *prince who is to come* will come out of the revived Roman Empire. This future Roman emperor will rule the ten-nation European confederacy of the last days.[4]

KEY Symbols:

First Seal
   the First Horse (white)
   Antichrist

John Hagee: He (the Antichrist) is going to turn the streets of the world into a blood-bath. According to the prophets, one-third of all humanity is going to be massacred under this monster who is going to make Adolf Hitler look like a choir boy.[5]

John Hagee: Israel has yet to endure her darkest night. I believe the peace process now under way will prove alas to be a Trojan horse. Instead of bringing the long-sought-for peace, it will bring the Antichrist and the most horrible war the Holy Land has ever known.[6]

RELATED CURRENT EVENTS

Israel and the PLO signed Phase I of the Oslo Peace Accords, called the Declaration of Principles, at the White House on September 13, 1993. Less than three years later, Israel accused the PLO of violating the accords by:

1) Opening fire on Israeli forces.
2) Failing to confiscate illegal arms and disband illegal militia.
3) Failing to extradite suspected terrorists to Israel.
4) Failing to change the PLO charter.
5) Incitement of violence against Israel.
6) Opening PLO offices in Jerusalem.
7) Recruiting terrorists to serve in the PLO police.
8) Exceeding the limit of 2 to 1 on the number of PLO police.
9) Abuse of human rights and the Rule of Law.
10) Conducting foreign relations.[7]

What kind of peace can there be when only one side is sincere and forthright. When both parties do not negotiate in good faith, the end result is disaster. This is the kind of peace the Antichrist will negotiate.

Remember This . . .

When Jesus made his triumphal entry into Jerusalem as a man of peace, he did not ride in on a conqueror's white horse, but on a <u>donkey</u>. When he returns as a conqueror at the end of the Tribulation Period, he will ride on a <u>white horse</u>. Notice that the Antichrist does not ride in on a donkey in peace, but rather on a horse in conquest.

> **Revelation 6:3, 4** When the Lamb opened the second seal, I heard the second living creature say, "Come!" Then another horse came out, a fiery red one. Its rider was given power to take peace from the earth and to make men slay each other. To him was given a large sword.

 **GO TO:**

Ezekiel 38, 39 (attack Israel)

Ezekiel 38:21–23 (against brother)

A Fiery Red Horse

The Antichrist will barely have his peace program off the ground when Jesus breaks the second seal. This time it will be the second living creature who speaks the command, *Come*!

A fiery red horse will go forth and its rider will have an unusual power. He will take peace from the earth and cause men to slay each other. This rider will charge forth with a great sword in his hand, signifying that he will go forth with many powerful weapons of war.

Some experts associate this rider on a red horse with Communism. The prophet Ezekiel foretells the rise of a dictator from *the far north* (possibly Russia) who will go forth to <u>attack Israel</u> in the last days. He will advance with a great army carrying swords and riding horses, but will meet defeat when many of his own troops slay each other because God will turn <u>each man against his brother</u> so that God's glory may be shown.

KEY Symbols:

Second Seal
Second Horse (fiery red) sword

Hal Lindsey: I believed that the peace process that Yitzhak Rabin (former Prime Minister of Israel) started would never bring peace, but would lead ultimately to nuclear holocaust in the Middle East, because they're giving away absolutely essential land assets that are indispensable for defending Israel in return for a treaty that doesn't remove the basic cause of war in the first place.[8]

What Others are Saying:

```
In spite of all the emphasis on peace, this century
has given us WW I, WW II, the Vietnam War, the Ko-
rean War, the Persian Gulf War, etc. There were 84
armed conflicts in the world during the first three
years of the nineties.
```

RELATED CURRENT EVENTS

The Prince of Peace—The Prince of War

The Antichrist will be a false prince of peace. God will show the world he is a fake by causing his phony peace programs to fail. Jesus is the true Prince of Peace. When world leaders reject him, they reject the only solution to their problems.

Remember This . . .

☞ **GO TO:**

John 6:31–35 (Bread of Life)

KEY Symbols:

Third Seal

Third Horse (Black)

scales

> **Revelation 6:5, 6** When the Lamb opened the third seal, I heard the third living creature say, "Come!" I looked, and there before me was a black horse! Its rider was holding a pair of scales in his hand. Then I heard what sounded like a voice among the four living creatures, saying, "A quart of wheat for a day's wages, and three quarts of barley for a day's wages, and do not damage the oil and the wine!"

A Black Horse

Peace without the Prince of Peace is no peace. The end result can only be war. War will rule the whole world after the Rapture. The wars of foolish and deceitful men will kill farmers, destroy land and crops, and cause the collapse of social, physical, and political structures. These wicked men will destroy, confiscate, and hoard food supplies causing despair, misery, poverty, and death.

When Jesus opens the third seal, the third living creature will give the same command as the first two, *Come!* This horse will be black, the color of grief and mourning. Its rider will hold a pair of scales that symbolize economic disaster and famine. The scales will be used to weigh food which will sell for a ridiculously-high price. A small quart of wheat will cost the equivalent of a day's wages, but many will not be able to survive on this, so they will be forced to buy barley, a cheaper food that is usually fed to animals. Three quarts of barley will still cost the equivalent of a day's wages, so no money will be left for clothes, housing, or automobiles. In spite of all this, the rich will still be able to afford luxury items such as oil and wine.

What Others are Saying:

Billy Graham: I have no doubt that a financial judgment day is coming for the United States before the end of this century unless our financial problems are addressed.[10]

Jack Van Impe: America, the world's sole remaining superpower, does not seem to play a significant role in the end-time scenario as described by the prophets. Why? Some scholars suggest America will be severely weakened—even neutralized—by the time the critical events, leading up to the Lord's return, occur.

Economic collapse? Moral decay? Poor leadership? Nuclear attack? All are possibilities.

The situation in Russia worsens with each passing day: a loaf of bread costs 1,500 rubles—about 8 percent of some monthly salaries. The average prices for rent, heat, and electricity often increase as much as 250 percent in one month. The fee for public transportation has increased 2,000 percent since 1994. And to make matters worse, workers are simply not being paid in some enterprises.[11]

Grant R. Jeffrey: I am not a prophet so I cannot predict when the governments of both the United States and Canada will "hit the wall" financially. That moment will occur when the national debt and its compounding interest charges have risen so high that the total tax revenue of the country will not be enough to pay the interest on the national debt. . . . A nation cannot continue to borrow forever, going deeper and deeper in debt each year. Finally, they "hit the wall" and economic collapse or hyper-inflation is the only remaining option.[12]

Ed Hindson: Despite the initial success of global economic unity, a worldwide economic disaster will occur, increasing the need for further global economic controls, including a personalized insignia.[13]

John Hagee: People ask, "Why would God allow a financial collapse in America?" I'll tell you why. Because the First Commandment says, *Thou shalt have no other gods before me* (Exodus 20:3 KJV). And in America, money is god.[14]

RELATED CURRENT EVENTS

> Today, we have famine in Angola, Ethiopia, Mozambique, Rwanda, Somalia, Sudan, the Democratic Republic of Congo, and North Korea. More people have died from famine in the last 150 years than in all of human history combined. More than 25 million people who are alive today are threatened. Almost one-half of the world's population is underfed.[15]

> The world grain harvest (1995) was the smallest since 1988 and grain reserves (the grain available to the world if all production stopped) were at an all time low of just 48 days of consumption.[16]

> World population, as it does every year, reached new heights, growing by 87 million to 5.732 billion. with more than 80 million added in developing (third-world) countries.[17]

U.S. Public Debt:

- 1980 $907.7 billion
- 1985 $1,823.3 billion
- 1990 $3,233.3 billion
- 1995 $4,974.0 billion[18]

Something to Ponder

eternal damnation: *when unbelievers are cast into hell*

KEY Symbols:

Fourth Seal

the Fourth Horse (pale) Death

Jesus is the <u>Bread of Life</u>, but the Antichrist will be a false bread of life. The Antichrist will prove to be a fake when his food programs result in famine.

> **Revelation 6:7, 8** When the Lamb opened the fourth seal, I heard the voice of the fourth living creature say, "Come!" I looked, and there before me was a pale horse! Its rider was named Death, and Hades was following close behind him. They were given power over a fourth of the earth to kill by sword, famine and plague, and by the wild beasts of the earth.

A Pale Horse

The world will have a false peace, then war, and then economic collapse and famine. Things will grow progressively worse. This obviously contradicts those who say things will get better and better, or those who teach that the Church will eventually bring in a perfect society. The Bible says, *There will be terrible times in the last days* and *evil men and impostors will go from bad to worse* (II Timothy 3:1, 13).

When Jesus opens the fourth seal, it will be the fourth living creature's turn to command a horse by saying, *Come!* This horse will surge forth creating an eerie sight because of its pale color. In the Greek translation of the Bible, the word used for pale is "chloros," meaning pale green like chlorophyll. This horse is the color of spoiled meat and rotting flesh. His rider and the creature following him are personified by Death and Hades. This rider won't be looking for the saved who have been raptured or the few who have accepted Jesus during the Tribulation Period. Instead, he will be hunting the great mass of people who are destined for an eternity in hell. Sadly, this horse and rider will go forth to harvest the souls of unbelievers to fuel the fires of hell.

Notice the progression: The rider on the white horse will be only partially armed. He will have a bow but no arrows. The rider on the red horse will carry a single large sword. The rider on the black horse will have two weapons—economic collapse and famine. This rider will have four weapons—a sword, famine, plagues, and wild animals. Things will get worse and worse, not better.

The sword signifies continuing war and bloodshed; famine signifies starvation; plague signifies diseases; and wild beasts signify the animals of the earth. This last weapon will be a strong signal to the "politically correct" who worship Mother Nature and value the life of animals over unborn babies. God will show the world that it's wrong to worship Mother Nature. Hungry animals will turn on the unbelieving world and add to the death and **eternal damnation** of more than one billion people.

Billy Graham: It is not God's intent that any should perish, but when people defiantly refuse God's plan, the consequence of this disobedience is death. The rider on the pale horse is only taking his due.[19]

Hal Lindsey: It staggers the imagination to realize that one-fourth of the world's population will be destroyed within a matter of days. . . . When I think about this awful judgment that awaits the Christ-rejecting world, it gives no satisfaction to my heart; it fires me up to get out the message that God has provided an alternative in Jesus.[20]

Jack Van Impe: The number of people who die every two days of hunger and starvation is equivalent to the number who were killed instantly by the bombing of Hiroshima. And there's no sign of better days to come.[21]

Grant R. Jeffrey: The dreaded plague known as AIDS may well be the beginning of the fulfillment of the prophecy of the Fourth Horseman of the Apocalypse.[22]

"We are standing on the brink of a global crisis in infectious diseases. . . . During the past 20 years, at least 30 new diseases have emerged to threaten the health of hundreds of millions of people. For many of these diseases there is no treatment, cure, or vaccine."—Hiroshi Nakajima, Director General of the World Health Organization [23]

What Others are Saying:

RELATED CURRENT EVENTS

According to the World Health Organization between 300 and 500 million people will contract malaria in 1997 with as many as 5 million dying.[24]

— — —

Largely unknown to the outside world, we (the U.S.) now have information that the Russian military, in defiance of its own president, has been secretly developing biological weapons of mass destruction, including a "super-plague" for which the West has no antidote.[25]

**GO TO:**

Matthew 24:9 (death)

> **Revelation 6:9** When he opened the fifth seal, I saw under the altar the souls of those who had been slain because of the word of God and the testimony they had maintained.

KEY Symbols:

Fifth Seal
under the altar the souls of the Tribulation Saints

Tribulation Saints

Following the Rapture, multitudes will accept Jesus. They are usually called the Tribulation Saints. World leaders will say these Christians are a threat to world government, world peace, world religion, and the environment. Therefore they must be dealt with. Followers of the New Age Movement teach that the earth must go through a cleansing in order to proceed to perfection. This cleansing they envision will include the <u>death of all who turn to Jesus</u>.

The opening of the fifth seal switches attention from the death of unbelievers to the death of believers; from the pit of Hades to under the altar in heaven. The four living creatures will summon no more horses. The last three seals will be different from the first four.

Jesus obviously will not forget his people because he showed John the souls of these slain believers gathered in a special place. They will have died because of the Word of God and because of the testimony they maintain. Many of these will be from families of Christians who left in the Rapture. Others will be Jews who realize the mistake they made in not accepting Jesus. Some will have heard the Word of God for the first time. Others will finally come to grips with their sin and turn to Jesus who said, *Do not be afraid of those who kill the body but cannot kill the soul. Rather, be afraid of the one who can destroy both soul and body in hell* (Matthew 10:28). These believers will realize that the Antichrist can do nothing worse than kill their body, for God will raise them from the dead. They will choose to die one death (physical), rather than two (physical and spiritual).

> **Revelation 6:10** They called out in a loud voice, "How long, Sovereign Lord, holy and true, until you judge the inhabitants of the earth and avenge our blood?"

Glorified Bodies

The souls of the Tribulation Saints are under the altar crying out instead of rejoicing and praising God around the throne with the rest of the Church. Unlike those who received their **glorified bodies** in the Rapture, these saints will have to wait until later for theirs. Because of this they will be fully conscious and able to rationalize the persecution, torture and murder they have endured. They will have a sense of justice and want to be raised, vindicated, and given glorified bodies.

They will cry out with a loud voice which is reminiscent of Psalm 94:1–3: *O Lord, the God who avenges, O God who avenges, shine forth. Rise up, O Judge of the earth; pay back to the proud what they deserve. How long will the wicked, O Lord, how long will the wicked be jubilant?* They will utter the prayer Jesus prayed, *Father, forgive them, for they do not know what they are doing* (Luke 23:34). They will appeal to God's sovereign nature and to his sense of justice and fairness when they ask to be avenged.

Hal Lindsey: It's a sobering fact that if people will not give their hearts to Christ now, while it is still easy and small cost is involved, when the Tribulation judgment sets in, although they can still be saved, it will be *so as by fire* (I Corinthians 3:15 KJV).[26]

What Others are Saying:

> **Revelation 6:11** Then each of them was given a white robe, and they were told to wait a little longer, until the number of their fellow servants and brothers who were to be killed as they had been was completed.

Be Patient

These martyrs will not be rebuked for asking to be vindicated. They will receive white robes signifying the righteousness of Jesus. Some experts suggest these robes may indicate some type of intermediate body, but whatever the case, we know that the martyrs will be able to hear, understand, and converse because Jesus tells them to be patient.

The Tribulation Saints will be told to wait until other believers are killed, indicating Jesus has a specific plan for the rest of the world.

Billy Graham: We learn two important facts from this mysterious moment. First, there will be a point at the end of time when God will judge the inhabitants of the earth. Second, before that moment can come, other men and women equally dedicated to God and his kingdom will be martyred for the Word of God and for the testimony they maintain. Are you prepared for the risk such words describe?[27]

David Jeremiah with C.C. Carlson: As I write this, I long for everyone to give their hearts to Christ now, when it is comparatively easy to be a Christian. During the Tribulation, the fate of believers will be worse than what happened in the Nazi concentration camps during World War II.[28]

☞ **GO TO:**

Isaiah 17:1 (Damascus)

Ezekiel 29:9–12; 30:3–6 (Egypt)

day of the Lord: another name for the Tribulation Period

KEY Symbols:

Sixth Seal
earthquakes

> **Revelation 6:12** I watched as he opened the sixth seal. There was a great earthquake. The sun turned black like sackcloth made of goat hair, the whole moon turned blood red,

Definitely Not A Harvest Moon

When Jesus opens the sixth seal, the whole earth will shake. John calls this shaking a great earthquake, but the description sounds more like a nuclear explosion. It may be a great earthquake triggered by one or more nuclear explosions. Whatever it is, it will be massive. The whole earth will go into convulsions, and the appearance of the sun and moon will be changed.

While the earth is going through tremendous vibrations, the sun will be darkened as if almost black, and the moon will turn blood red. It could be that one or more nuclear explosions will take place, causing the earth to shake violently and spew tons of debris into the atmosphere. The resulting atmospheric pollution will cause darkness to cover the land and the moon to appear red. The cataclysmic effects of Mount St. Helens and El Niño will be dwarfed in comparison.

Today the Middle East is brimming over with weapons of mass destruction. There are unsubstantiated reports that now Israel and Iran both have the nuclear bomb. Couple this with unfulfilled prophecy and we can understand why the prophet Isaiah said Damascus will be turned into a ruinous heap and the mountains of Lebanon will be on fire. The prophet Ezekiel said Egypt will turn to utter waste and desolation for forty years. It is easy to see the possible results of atomic or nuclear weapons.

The prophet Joel said *The sun will be turned to darkness and the moon to blood before the coming of the great and dreadful **day of the Lord*** (Joel 2:28–31). According to Ezekiel, the sword will come upon Egypt when the day of the Lord is near.

What Others are Saying:

Hal Lindsey: The earthquake described in this sixth judgment will be of a magnitude never before known by mankind. It will be "the grand daddy of them all." The particular Greek word used here actually means "a violent, catastrophic shaking." This meaning, coupled with the darkening of the sun and the moon, leads me to believe that the Apostle John is describing an earthquake set off by many nuclear explosions.[29]

RELATED CURRENT EVENTS

```
(Egyptian President Hosni) Mubarak's words were not
the only ones that upset (Israeli Prime Minister
Benjamin) Netanyahu. Egyptian Defense Minister
Mohammed Hussein Tantawi earlier told the Egyptian
Al-Gomhuriyyah (a Cairo newspaper) that Egypt's
military was training in the event of a nuclear attack
by Israel.[30]
```

> **Revelation 6:13** and the stars in the sky fell to earth, as late figs drop from a fig tree when shaken by a strong wind.

Star Wars

The *Golden Rule of Interpretation* (see Introduction) states, "When the plain sense of Scripture makes common sense, seek no other sense." This, however, is one of those instances where the plain sense does not seem to fit because most stars are bigger than the earth. No star could fall to the earth *as late figs drop from a fig tree* without decimating the planet.

Since the word *stars* in the Greek translation could also be translated "meteors," this could indicate a meteor shower. It could also mean a missile attack. During the Persian Gulf War nights were filled with cruise missiles and laser-guided smart bombs One can easily see how someone living almost 2,000 years ago would describe scenes like this as falling stars. Whatever this is, stars, meteors, or missiles, they will fall to earth like overripe figs dropping from a fig tree in a mighty wind.

☞ **GO TO:**

Isaiah 34:1–10 (sky rolls up)

> **Revelation 6:14** The sky receded like a scroll, rolling up, and every mountain and island was removed from its place.

A Giant Tidal Wave

This seems to be another indication of a coming nuclear war. During a nuclear blast the wind is rapidly pushed out (displaced) for several miles, creating a vacuum at the center of the blast site. Suddenly, this wind, like a giant tidal wave, rushes violently back into the vacuum. The sky actually rolls up on itself. This explosion will be so great it will cause every mountain and island on earth to move.

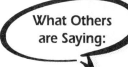
What Others are Saying:

Billy Graham: Pope John Paul II has stated, "Our future on this planet, exposed as it is to nuclear annihilation, depends on one single factor: humanity must make a moral about-face."[31]

Ed Hindson: The threat of a global nuclear holocaust will push the world to the brink of disaster and leave people crying for peace. This crisis will probably be centered in the Middle East.[32]

☞ **GO TO:**

Isaiah 24:1–13 (panic)

KEY POINT

Survival will be man's only concern.

> **Revelation 6:15** Then the kings of the earth, the princes, the generals, the rich, the mighty, and every slave and every free man hid in caves and among the rocks of the mountains.

Run For Your Life

There will be worldwide panic. Regardless of one's status in life, all people will try to hide. Multitudes will leave everything behind and rush into caves and bomb shelters. Multitudes will flee the cities to hide in the mountains. Kings and princes will flee their palaces. Great generals and mighty men will turn and run in fear of their lives. People of every class will flee and hide. Survival will be man's only concern.

What Others are Saying:

David Breese: The love of God is eternal. His patience is not.[33]

> **Revelation 6:16** They called to the mountains and the rocks, "Fall on us and hide us from the face of him who sits on the throne and from the wrath of the Lamb!

☞ **GO TO:**

Acts 4:12 (call)

Nothing Will Escape

Will these panic-stricken people <u>call on Jesus</u>? No! They will call on Mother Nature. They will call on the rocks and mountains to fall on them, because they will want to hide from the face and wrath of God.

Multitudes will finally admit the existence of God. They will even admit that it is possible to anger Jesus, but they will not turn to him. Instead they will try to hide, but to no avail since nothing can escape the sight of God.

David Jeremiah with C.C. Carlson: What a prayer meeting! The people will shout out to anything—even the mountains—for help. Their first instinct is to hide—get away from God. Isn't that what sin does to a man? He covers up what he has done, thinking that he can escape the consequences. He turns his back on God's provision for sin and seeks help elsewhere.[34]

What Others are Saying:

J.H. Melton: We are not accustomed to connecting the thought of wrath with the lamb, which has always been the accepted symbol of gentleness, but after the grace of the Lamb of God is rejected, his indignation and wrath must be faced. The Lord Jesus Christ will either be your Savior or your Judge. Your sins will either be judged in Jesus Christ or they will be judged by Jesus Christ. Now he offers his mercy to save you. If you reject his mercy he will judge you in absolute justice and wrath.[35]

> **Revelation 6:17** For the great day of their wrath has come, and who can stand?"

☞ **GO TO:**

Zephaniah 1:14–16 (Day of Wrath)

Daniel 9:20–27 (Daniel)

Matthew 24:15 (future events)

A Day Of Wrath

The <u>Day of Wrath</u> is another name for the Tribulation Period (see GWDN, pages 249–257). The multitudes will recognize the beginning of that day when the first seal is opened. Sadly, we read nothing about people repenting and accepting Jesus—only the realization that the dreaded Tribulation Period has come. And there is the question: *Who can stand?* The answer is in Revelation 7:3–8.

literally fulfilled: *happened as predicted*

Something to Ponder

David Hocking: Our present generation has no desire to hear of these things or to believe them. We want to be stroked and reminded of our self-worth and potential for success. The real issue has not changed—heaven and hell, life and death. Where will you spend eternity?[36]

A Tribulation Yet To Come

1) In <u>Daniel's 70-Weeks Prophecy</u>, the first sixty-nine weeks of Daniel's prophecy is the period of time (69 weeks x 7 years/week = 483 years) between the decree for the captive Jews in Babylon to return to Israel to restore and rebuild Jerusalem, and the triumphal entry of Jesus into Jerusalem. Since these first sixty-nine weeks of Daniel's prophecy were literally fulfilled, we can only assume that the seventieth week (the last week of seven years) will also be literally fulfilled.

2) Some people do not understand why prophecy teachers say there is a gap between the first sixty-nine weeks of Daniel's prophecy and the seventieth week (the Church Age—the period between the triumphal entry of Jesus into Jerusalem and the Tribulation Period). A careful study of the prophecy reveals that Jesus would be killed, and Jerusalem and the Temple would be destroyed after the sixty-ninth week. That happened in 70 A.D. when the Romans overran Israel, burned Jerusalem, tore down the Temple, and killed 5 million Jews. Part of the prophecy has been fulfilled. But a careful study also reveals that the seventieth week will not begin until the Antichrist signs a seven-year covenant to protect Israel, that he will break that covenant and stop all animal sacrifices. For this to happen, Israel had to be restored as a nation (which happened in 1948) and the Temple must be rebuilt (which has yet to happen). Part of the prophecy is yet to come.

3) Some believe the Church will succeed in establishing the Kingdom of God on earth without the world going through the Tribulation Period. But the angel Gabriel told Daniel the Jews would go through the entire seventy weeks before the kingdom of righteousness is brought in. Since the earth has never experienced some of the things prophesied for that time, it must go through them before the Kingdom of God can be established.

4) Some people believe that the seventieth week of Daniel had been fulfilled by the time Jesus arrived, but Jesus spoke of these things as <u>future events</u>, not events of the past.

Study Questions

1. What weapon did the rider on the white horse carry?
2. What power was given to the rider on the red horse?
3. How much will a quart of wheat cost during the Tribulation Period?
4. What was the name of the rider on the pale horse and who was following him?

CHAPTER WRAP-UP

- The judgments of the Tribulation Period begin when Christ opens the first of the seven seals. (Revelation 6:1)
- The four horsemen will bring about: the Antichrist, war, economic ruin, famine, and death. (Revelation 6:2–8)
- During the Tribulation Period people will still turn to Christ and be killed for their faith. These people will be known as the Tribulation Saints, and they will ask to be avenged. (Revelation 6:9, 10)
- An earthquake will wrack the earth affecting the sun, moon, sky, land, and sea. (Revelation 6:12–14)
- Following the sixth seal fear will grip everyone on earth as they try to hide from the wrath of God. (Revelation 6:15–17)

REVELATION 7

CHAPTER HIGHLIGHTS

- Mark of God
- 144,000
- Great Multitude
- A Great Worship Service
- Never Again!

Let's Get Started

Today Christians are spreading the Word of God throughout the world by short wave radio, television, and the Internet. The Bible has been translated into almost every language of every nation. The world has repeatedly heard the message of salvation, and yet following the Rapture, there will be multitudes who have rejected the Bible and its message.

Jesus said, *This gospel of the kingdom will be preached in the whole world as a testimony to all nations, and then the end shall come* (Matthew 24:14). Everyone will hear his message and have the opportunity to accept salvation before they die or take the Mark of the Beast.

☞ **GO TO:**

Revelation 13:17 (Mark)

> **Revelation 7:1** After this I saw four angels standing at the four corners of the earth, holding back the four winds of the earth to prevent any wind from blowing on the land or on the sea or on any tree.

Hold Back The Wind

After the first six seals are opened, four angels will stand at the earth's four corners to prevent any wind from blowing. This does not mean that the earth will become square. It is simply a symbolic expression meaning the angels will be standing at the four points of the compass: north, south, east, and west. They will control the winds of the earth. Without these angels the airborne plagues from the previous seals would spread around the world.

☞ **GO TO:**

Romans 11:4–6 (turning)

KEY Symbols:

Four Angels
hold back the winds

J. Vernon McGee: I do not think that God would permit any period to continue on this earth in which there were not some of the <u>human family turning to God</u>, because that is his purpose. I do not think he would continue to keep this world running; I think he would shut it down, turn it off, and speak it out of existence if there were not folk turning to him.[1]

Tim LaHaye: The greatest revival the world has ever known is yet to come. It will not occur within the Church Age but during the Tribulation Period.[2]

KEY Symbols:

Angel from the East
seal of the Living God

> **Revelation 7:2** Then I saw another angel coming up from the east, having the seal of the living God. He called out in a loud voice to the four angels who had been given power to harm the land and the sea:

The Angel From The East

Christians have always believed in angels. It would be impossible to believe the Bible without believing in angels. They play a prominent role in God's plan for mankind. This is especially true of the stories about Jesus and the judgments of Revelation.

Angels are divided into different categories or ranks. Some rank higher than others, and some serve Satan and not God. We do not know who this angel from the east is, but we do know that he will have authority over the other four angels. The four angels will have the power to harm the earth and sea, but just before they unleash their great power, the angel from the east will intercede with a loud voice and stop them. He will have the seal of the Living God in his hand, and it will be used to mark a group of special messengers.

Hal Lindsey: Although the subject of angels is usually associated with fairy tales or myths, these creatures are spoken of very matter-of-factly in the Bible and they play a very important part in the predicted judgments of God on earth.[3]

**RELATED
CURRENT
EVENTS**

```
El Niño, the weather phenomenon that turns up in the
tropical Pacific every three to five years, is ex-
pected to have a massive impact on weather patterns
around the world the coming year. Climatologists warn
that current El Niño could be the worst in 150 years,
as the mass of warm water in the Pacific Ocean grows
```

to 1½ times the size of the continental United States. That's much stronger than the 1982-1983 El Niño, which left an estimated 2,000 dead and $13 billion in damages around the world, according to the World Meteorological Organization, the weather agency for the United Nations.[4]

> **Revelation 7:3** "Do not harm the land or the sea or the trees until we put a seal on the foreheads of the servants of our God."

☞ **GO TO:**

Ephesians 1:13 (sealed)

Ezekiel 9:4; Genesis 4:15 (God marks)

The Mark Of God

The four angels will be commanded to hold back their destructive forces until God's servants can be <u>sealed</u>. Nothing will happen to the land, sea, or trees until these special messengers are protected.

The Bible does not say what this seal will be. We are told only that these believers will be protected by some type of mark. Since the beginning of creation <u>God has been marking</u> his people. God's mark will be placed on their foreheads. It will be an actual mark that will show others that these are God's people.

What Others are Saying:

Dennis Pollock: Nowhere in the Scriptures are we given a picture of a God who contemplates his creation with an unruffled, distant, purely logical view. The God of the Bible is an emotional God—he rejoices, he becomes grieved, he takes delight in his people, and he becomes very angry when his creatures default, rebel against the commands he has given them.[5]

RELATED CURRENT EVENTS

The world's top atmospheric scientists are now in agreement that the recent rapid climate changes are at least partially caused by human factors. (Intergovernmental Panel on Climate Change, Second Assessment Report, 1995). A recent report predicts increase of tropical diseases, a rise in sea level, more destructive weather patterns, extinction of plant and animal species, and crop failure in many parts of the world. The report continues to suggest that unless drastic changes in emissions levels occur, the rate of global warming will escalate.[6]

☞ **GO TO:**

Judges 18:30; I Kings 12:28–30 (Dan)

Hosea 4:17 (Ephraim)

Genesis 49:17 (False Prophet)

Deuteronomy 10:8, 9 (tribe of priests)

Numbers 13:11; 36:5 (tribe of Joseph)

KEY Symbols:

144,000
marked men from the twelve tribes of Israel

WARNING ▶

> **Revelation 7:4–8** Then I heard the number of those who were sealed: 144,000 from all the tribes of Israel. From the tribe of Judah 12,000 were sealed, from the tribe of Reuben 12,000, from the tribe of Gad 12,000, from the tribe of Asher 12,000, from the tribe of Naphtali 12,000, from the tribe of Manasseh 12,000, from the tribe of Simeon 12,000, from the tribe of Levi 12,000, from the tribe of Issachar 12,000, from the tribe of Zebulun 12,000, from the tribe of Joseph 12,000, from the tribe of Benjamin 12,000.

144,000

God will seal 144,000 of his servants, but they will not come from the Church or any particular denomination. Instead, all 144,000 will come from the twelve tribes of Israel—the Jews.

The list of tribes is unusual in that two of the original twelve tribes of Israel—Dan and Ephraim—will be left out. (To learn more about the beginnings of the twelve tribes, see GWGN, pages 253–254 and 291–293.) Most experts believe these two tribes will be skipped because they were both guilty of idolatry, thus disqualifying them as special servants of God. Some even believe the False Prophet mentioned in Chapter 5 will come from the tribe of Dan.

The tribes of Levi and Joseph will be added to make the twelve marked tribes of the Tribulation Period. As the tribe of priests, Levi was not counted among the original twelve tribes of Israel. The tribe of Joseph was also not one of the original twelve. Joseph was Ephraim's father, and it looks like he will replace his idolatrous son.

> Even though these verses are clear and straightforward, some people still want to spiritualize them. The Jehovah's Witnesses, for example, believe this refers to 144,000 of their members. However, the verse clearly states that the 144,000 will come from the twelve tribes of Israel which excludes all Gentiles. It is best to ignore the mental gymnastics and accept the literal interpretation.

> **Revelation 7:9** After this I looked and there before me was a great multitude that no one could count, from every nation, tribe, people and language, standing before the throne and in front of the Lamb. They were wearing white robes and were holding palm branches in their hands.

Listen To The Gospel

Once God has sealed his 144,000, the whole world will hear his message. Multitudes will believe and be saved. The Antichrist and his False Prophet will be furious and try to stop the revival by forcing new believers to <u>turn away from the faith</u>. They will deny people food and medicine. Executions will be frequent and numerous. The number of **martyrs** will be more than any man can count.

These martyrs will be given white robes, symbolizing the righteousness of Jesus. They will also receive palm branches, symbolizing their triumphal entry into heaven. You may remember Jesus was also given palm branches when he <u>entered the city of Jerusalem</u> before his death. The martyrs will stand in the presence of Jesus before the throne of God.

☞ **GO TO:**

Matthew 24:9–14 (turn away)

John 12:12, 13 (entered Jerusalem)

martyrs: those who died for their beliefs

 *KEY Symbols:*

Multitude Before the Throne
martyrs (Tribulation Saints)

RELATED CURRENT EVENTS

> According to a report by George Otis of High Adventure Ministries, over 1,500,000 Christians in Sudan have been murdered and another 1,000,000 have disappeared. . . . More than 100 Christian pastors from Southern Sudan have been killed by crucifixion at Moslem hands.[7]

> 1996 will be recorded as one of the most violent years for Christian persecution. The secular human rights group Freedom House has just completed a report proving that religious persecution is still a harsh fact heading into the 21st century. The Freedom House's Puebla Program on Religious Freedom studied eight countries with the worst records of religious persecution. Specific examples cited in the report included China's circulation of arrest warrants for 3,000 evangelical preachers. In Sudan, Christian children are apprehended in the southern part of the country, then sold at open-air slave markets for as little as $15. Saudi Arabia has decreed there will be no public expression of Christianity.[8]

☞ **GO TO:**

Ephesians 4:5 (way to
   heaven)

KEY POINT:

God, the author of
salvation, has given us
only one way to
heaven—his Son.

Saints: those who are truly
saved

> **Revelation 7:10** And they cried out in a loud voice:
> "Salvation belongs to our God, who sits on the throne,
> and to the Lamb."

One Choice

This is a great worship service of victory and rejoicing whose
central theme is salvation. The glory of salvation that belongs to
God and his Son Jesus. God is the author of salvation and has
narrowed the <u>way to heaven down to one</u>—the Lamb of God.

> **Revelation 7:11** All the angels were standing around
> the throne and around the elders and the four living
> creatures. They fell down on their faces before the
> throne and worshiped God,

Worship Before The Throne

This may well be the greatest worship service ever. When this
multitude of Tribulation **Saints** stand before the throne praising
and glorifying the Father and Son, all the angels of heaven will
join in; followed by the twenty-four elders and four living creatures.

Notice all the different groups: the Tribulation Saints, the
twenty-four elders (representing the Church), the angels, and the
four living creatures. Everyone in heaven will participate in this
service.

> **Revelation 7:12** saying: "Amen! Praise and glory and
> wisdom and thanks and honor and power and strength
> be to our God for ever and ever. Amen!"

Sevenfold Worship

Amen indicates that the angels will agree with the Tribulation
Saints. Salvation belongs to God and his Son, and they deserve
the credit for getting this great multitude to heaven. Then the
angels will break forth with a sevenfold declaration of worship:
praise, glory, wisdom, thanks, honor, power, and strength all belong to God forever and ever.

What Others are Saying:

Hal Lindsey: Perhaps you've heard it said that the angels in heaven rejoice when one sinner is saved. I'm sure they're happy for the sinner who has been redeemed, but I have a suspicion that the real reason for their joy is that it gives them another opportunity to fall down on their faces and praise the one who made the sinner's salvation possible.[9]

> **Revelation 7:13** Then one of the elders asked me, "These in white robes—who are they, and where did they come from?"

blood of the Lamb: *blood of Jesus*

Two Questions

One of the twenty-four elders will ask two questions: Who are they, and Where did they come from? He already knows the answer, but he will ask them anyway to make sure everyone else does.

What Others are Saying:

Tim LaHaye: These "Tribulation Saints" constitute a distinctive category, just as the Church and Israel or Old Testament Saints form a special company. Each group has its own relationship to Christ, depending on the period of time in which these individuals were converted. That these are believers is unquestionable in view of the fact that they have *washed their robes and made them white in the* **blood of the Lamb** (Revelation 7:14).[10]

> **Revelation 7:14** I answered, "Sir, you know." And he said, "These are they who have come out of the great tribulation; they have washed their robes and made them white in the blood of the Lamb.

☞ **GO TO:**

Ephesians 1:7; Hebrews 9:22 (blood)

The Blood Of The Lamb

This great multitude before the throne of God will come out of the Tribulation Period. They will be saved people; people clothed in the righteousness of Jesus; people who trusted in the <u>shed blood of the Lamb</u>.

The elders' answer tells us what the 144,000 will be preaching. They will preach *the blood of the Lamb*. The fact that these 144,000 are Israelites will not alter their message.

When most prophesy experts talk about the Great Tribulation, they are talking about the last three and one-half years of the seven-year period. But in this verse, the term refers to *all those* who have come out of the entire seven-year Tribulation Period.

☞ **GO TO:**

II Corinthians 5:8 (with Jesus)

I John 5:18; Psalm 121 (protected by God)

> **Revelation 7:15** Therefore, "they are before the throne of God and serve him day and night in his temple; and he who sits on the throne will spread his tent over them.

Suddenly

This is a very special promise. On earth, the saved will not be safe anywhere. They will either starve, die of disease, or be murdered. There will be no way to escape the clutches of the Antichrist. Suddenly, they will find themselves in the throne room of God, <u>face-to-face with Jesus</u>, surrounded by angels, clothed in white robes, and <u>protected by God</u>.

☞ **GO TO:**

Psalm 91:1–16; Psalm 46:1–11 (fortress)

> **Revelation 7:16** Never again will they hunger; never again will they thirst. The sun will not beat upon them, nor any scorching heat.

A Covering Of Protection

KEY POINT

God promises in heaven we will never suffer again.

The Tribulation Saints will face hunger, thirst, death from starvation and poisoned water, burning by the blazing sun, and suffocation by scorching heat. Once they arrive in heaven, though, it will never happen again. They will be in the <u>fortress</u>, the place a refuge of the Almighty God. It is a place of constant protection that cannot be breached. This is God's promise.

What Others are Saying:

Jack Van Impe: The World Watch Institute recently reported that carbon emissions, deforestation, and soil erosion are worsening. Birds are disappearing. Destructive insects are developing resistance to pesticides. The seas are producing fewer harvests of edible fish. Grain stocks are down. Tropical rain forests are dwindling.[11]

Grant R. Jeffrey: During the last thirty days another ten million hungry humans arrived on earth. Every month another five thousand animal and plant species become extinct as they succumb to the relentless population pressures on their precious and endangered habitat.[12]

Some of the possible effects of global warming:

- Higher temperatures
- More droughts
- Agricultural growing areas shift north in Northern Hemisphere; south in Southern Hemisphere
- More severe tropical storms
- Flooding of low coastal areas and islands [13]

☞ **GO TO:**

Revelation 2:7 (tree of life)

> **Revelation 7:17** For the Lamb at the center of the throne will be their shepherd; he will lead them to springs of living water. And God will wipe away every tear from their eyes.

No More Tears

The Lamb, who stands in the midst of the throne of God, will preserve the Tribulation Saints. He will feed the saints from the tree of life and let them drink from fountains of living water.

This also tells us the saints are destined for a great deal of weeping before they depart this earth. They will face incredibly harsh living conditions, terrorizing circumstances, and the loss of loved ones. Their tears will have reason to fall, but when they get to heaven, God will wipe them away.

Study Questions

1. What will the first four angels do? Why are they doing it?
2. What will the 144,000 preach? Why is their message so important?
3. What seven things do the angels say belong to God? Why do they belong to him?
4. What is the difference between the twenty-four elders and the Tribulation Saints?
5. Will God let people die for their faith?

- An angel will place the Mark of God on the foreheads of God's servants so that his judgments do not harm them. (Revelation 7:2, 3)

- God is not finished with Israel. He will seal 144,000 of them with his mark of protection. 12,000 will come from each of the twelve tribes of Israel. (Revelation 7:4–8)

- During the Tribulation multitudes will be killed on earth. These martyrs will find themselves in heaven standing before Jesus. (Revelation 7:9)

- A Great Worship Service will start in heaven when the Tribulation Saints, followed by the rest of heaven inhabitants, start worshiping God for being the author of salvation. (Revelation 7:10, 11)

- God promises that the martyrs will *never again* endure the hardships they suffered on earth, and he promises to wipe their tears away. (Revelation 7:15–17)

REVELATION 8

Let's Get Started

Chapter 6 described the opening of the first six seals, but it ended before reaching the seventh seal. Chapter 7 covered the sealing of the 144,000 but likewise, failed to mention the seventh seal. It is not until Chapter 8 that we learn about this final seal. The opening of the seventh seal reveals the appearance of seven angels with seven trumpets (see Time Line #2, Appendix A).

Note the pattern being established. The seven seals were broken down into two sets: the four horsemen followed by three additional judgments. Likewise, the seven trumpet judgments will be broken down into two sets: four judgments followed by three judgments called "woes."

> **Revelation 8:1** When he opened the seventh seal, there was silence in heaven for about half an hour.

worthiness: *the merit, or qualifications of Jesus to open the seals*

KEY Symbols:

Seven Seal Judgments		*Seven Trumpet Judgments*
Seal 1—Judgment	White horse, Antichrist	Trumpet 1—Judgment
Seal 2—Judgment	Red horse, sword of war	Trumpet 2—Judgment
Seal 3—Judgment	Black horse, scales of economic collapse and famine	Trumpet 3—Judgment
Seal 4—Judgment	Pale horse, death	Trumpet 4—Judgment (woe)
Seal 5—Judgment	Many believers die	Trumpet 5—Judgment (woe)
Seal 6—Judgment	Earthquake	Trumpet 6—Judgment (woe)
Seal 7—Seven Trumpet Judgments		Trumpet 7—Seven Bowl Judgments (woe)

The Seventh Seal

When this seal is broken, the scroll will be completely open. Nothing will remain to restrain the carrying out of the remaining judgments. Before they can begin, though, there will be silence in heaven for about half-an-hour.

The flashes of lightning, rumblings, and peals of thunder coming from the throne of God will cease. The four living creatures will cease their talk about the holiness of God. The twenty-four elders will suspend their declarations about the **worthiness** of the Lamb. The heavenly hosts will stop their singing, and the Tribulation Saints will cease their praise. An eerie silence will move across heaven.

Everyone will wait in anticipation of what is to come next. Will people be given time to repent? Will God destroy the earth? Something will be on the horizon—something of tremendous importance.

> **Revelation 8:2** And I saw the seven angels who stand before God, and to them were given seven trumpets.

Seven Archangels

The Tribulation Period carries many names: the Time of Jacob's Trouble, the Seventieth-Week of Daniel, and the Day of the Lord's Vengeance. The prophet Zephaniah gives it seven different names, and it is significant to notice that the last one is *a day of trumpet and battle cry* (Zephaniah 1:14–16).

Out of all the angels in heaven only seven particular angels constantly stand in the presence of God. They are known as archangels. The names of these archangels is a mystery, except for two—the angels Michael and Gabriel. These seven archangels, who make announcements of great significance, will each be handed a trumpet on this *day of trumpet and battle cry*.

> **Revelation 8:3** Another angel, who had a golden censer, came and stood at the altar. He was given much incense to offer, with the prayers of all the saints, on the golden altar before the throne.

An Eighth Angel?

Even though this eighth angel is not identified, some experts believe he is Jesus. He could be Jesus, but he is probably just an-

☞ **GO TO:**

Jeremiah 30:7 (Jacob's Trouble)

Daniel 9:24–27 (Seventieth-Week)

Isaiah 34:8 (Lord's Vengeance)

Daniel 10:13 (Michael)

Luke 1:19 (Gabriel)

KEY Symbols:

Seven Trumpets
held by seven archangels

☞ **GO TO:**

Exodus 30:1–8 (golden altar)

II Chronicles 4:22 (censer of gold)

Illustration #3

Golden Altar—Made by King Solomon for God's Temple. Symbolizes the altar of God, where an angel will mix incense with the prayers of the Tribulation Saints.

other powerful angel. We do know this angel holds a special position of service before the <u>golden altar</u> (see Illustration #3, this page) of God.

This <u>golden censer</u> (see Illustration #4, this page) is similar to the one used in the Old Testament Jewish Temple. It contained charcoal that was burned under a layer of incense. When the hot charcoal warmed the layer of incense, a sweet fragrance was produced. This fragrance or aroma may be that of the spice <u>frankincense</u>, one of the gifts the wise men gave to the baby Jesus. Frankincense was also one of the spices <u>burned</u> in the censer at the Jewish Temple. Its fragrance reminds God of his Son who came and <u>died for the sins</u> of the world.

☞ **GO TO:**

Matthew 2:11 (frankincense)

Exodus 30:7–10, 34–38 (burned)

I Peter 2:24 (died for sin)

Psalm 141:2 (incense)

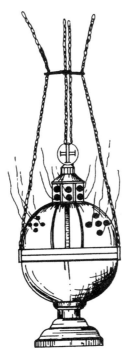

Illustration #4

Golden Censer—Similar to the censer used in the Old Testament Jewish Temple for burning incense.

The eighth angel will come with a golden censer and stand before the altar of God. He will be given a great quantity of <u>incense to mix with the prayers</u> of the saints. Then he will place the censer on the golden altar before the throne of God.

☞ **GO TO:**

James 5:16 (prayers)

> **Revelation 8:4** The smoke of the incense, together with the prayers of the saints, went up before God from the angel's hand.

No Other Choice

KEY POINT

When all options fail, God's judgment will fall.

Revelation 8:3 told us that the eighth angel will be given the prayers of all the saints. We may never know what all those requests may be, but Revelation 6:10 identifies one of them as a prayer of the Tribulation Saints: *How long, Sovereign Lord, holy and true, until you judge the inhabitants of the earth and avenge our blood?* Judgment is not God's first choice, but patience is. He is patient and will hold off his judgment longer than any man. Nevertheless, when all options fail, his judgment will fall.

The angel will take the censer containing the hot incense and the prayers of the saints, and wave it around causing the smoke to drift toward the throne of God. The Almighty God will smell the incense, <u>hear the prayers, and prepare an answer</u>.

☞ **GO TO:**

Psalm 82:8 (whole earth)

> **Revelation 8:5** Then the angel took the censer, filled it with fire from the altar, and hurled it on the earth; and there came peals of thunder, rumblings, flashes of lightning, and an earthquake.

futurist: a person who uses data, science, and technology to try to predict future events

Answered Prayers

When the incense and all the prayers of the saints have been consumed in the censer, the angel will take the empty censer, go back to the altar, fill it with fire, and hurl it down on the earth. The prayers will go up to God and the answers will come down to earth. God will avenge the death of the Tribulation Saints with fiery trials on earth.

Try to visualize this great scene. The Antichrist and False Prophet will rise to power leading the inhabitants of the earth to worship Satan, while at the same time, God's people will be hunted down, persecuted, and killed. These martyred saints will arrive in heaven praying to be avenged. At first, they will be told to wait until the number of saved is increased, but then after a brief time,

God will hear their prayers and respond by having his angel hurl the burning censer (possibly in the form of a meteor) to earth. This will be a clear statement of God's wrath. It will be followed by loud thunderclaps, flashes of lightening, and an earthquake. The earnest prayers of God's hurting people will finally reach into his wrath and cause a response that will be <u>felt by the whole earth</u>.

What Others are Saying:

***Jack Van Impe:* Futurist** Gordon-Michael Scallion, editor of *Earth Changes Report,* has been suggesting for months that a frightening global killer earthquake pattern is emerging. He is predicting that a series of magnitude 10.0 quakes will rip up America's West Coast in the next few years.[1]

RELATED CURRENT EVENTS

```
The following major earthquakes occurred during the
first six months of 1996:

January 1 ..... Indonesia—7.7 on the Richter Scale
February 3 .... China—7.0
February 7 .... Kuril Islands—7.0
February 17 ... Indonesia—7.5
February 25 ... Mexico—6.6
April 29 ...... Solomon Islands—7.5
June 10 ....... Aleutian Islands (2)—7.2 and 7.7
June 11 ....... Philippines—7.0
June 17 ....... Indonesia—7.5 [2]
```

> **Revelation 8:6** Then the seven angels who had the seven trumpets prepared to sound them.

Thus It Begins

Once the burning censer has hit the earth the archangels will prepare to sound their trumpets. The prayers of the saints will be heard, and the whole world will be ripe for judgment. God's wrath will be kindled to unleash the next set of judgments, and the archangels will prepare to sound the alarm.

☞ **GO TO:**

Exodus 9:18–2 (plague)

Genesis 18:16–19:29 (Sodom)

Joel 2:30 (hail, fire)

KEY Symbols:

First Trumpet

FIRST TRUMPET ANGEL

hail, fire, and blood
1/3 of earth and trees,
all grass burned up

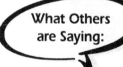

What Others
are Saying:

RELATED
CURRENT
EVENTS

Something
to Ponder

> **Revelation 8:7** The first angel sounded his trumpet, and there came hail and fire mixed with blood, and it was hurled down upon the earth. A third of the earth was burned up, a third of the trees were burned up, and all the green grass was burned up.

Destruction Of The Earth

Some Bible experts will not accept a literal fulfillment of this verse. However, prophecy experts have little difficulty believing this will happen. The <u>seventh plague on Egypt</u> in the days of Moses was a rain of grievous hail mixed with fire that smote the cattle, herbs, and trees. It was a plague directed against Egypt's false goddess, Isis. God also rained hail, fire, and brimstone on <u>Sodom and Gomorrah</u>. There is no reason to believe he will not do it again.

The result of <u>hail, fire, and blood</u> being hurled down upon one-third of the earth in a furious storm is almost unimaginable. Not only will it cause immediate and indescribable destruction, it will also bring many other terrible consequences. Much of the lumber needed to build houses will be gone, along with much of the grain used for food. The entire balance of nature will be upset and the loss of life will be horrendous.

Hal Lindsey: With this massive loss of vegetation will come soil erosion, floods, and mudslides. Air pollution will be immense; the smoke of the fire will fill the atmosphere, and the remaining vegetation will be unable to adequately absorb the hydrocarbons from automobiles and industry. Ecology will be thrown chaotically out of balance.[3]

Jack Van Impe: Comet Shoemaker-Levy 9's impact on Jupiter grabbed the attention of the entire world. Was it a sign? Enormous explosions, hundreds of times more powerful than all the earth's nuclear warheads, made people realize just how vulnerable our planet is to a similar occurrence.[4]

```
Destruction of the world's rain forests contributes
to global warming by destroying trees and other plant
life that absorb carbon dioxide from the atmosphere.[5]
```

If God opposed the false goddess Isis, would he not oppose any other false god or goddess?

> **Revelation 8:8, 9** The second angel sounded his trumpet, and something like a huge mountain, all ablaze, was thrown into the sea. A third of the sea turned into blood, a third of the living creatures in the sea died, and a third of the ships were destroyed.

Destruction Of The Sea

The first trumpet will signal judgment upon the earth. This trumpet will signal judgment upon the sea. It reminds us of the first plague on Egypt in the days of Moses that turned the <u>waters into blood</u>. It was a plague directed against Egypt's false goddess Hika that killed the fish and frogs, and made the water unfit for consumption.

Pay close attention to the wording in this verse. It does not say a burning mountain will be thrown into the sea. It says, something like a huge burning mountain will be thrown into the sea. Some think it will be a nuclear missile. Others think it will be a burning meteor. Whatever it is, it will be big, blazing, and cause the sea to turn into blood. It will kill one-third of sea life and destroy one-third of the ships. Those who depend upon the sea for jobs, food, defense, or cargo transport will suffer. As a result of this "mountain" hitting the sea, it is likely that everything close to the sea will probably be damaged or destroyed by a great tidal wave.

> "If you've gotta go, go with a bang." That's what Comet Shoemaker-Levy 9 did last July (1994). Nearly two dozen mountain-size chunks of this fragmented interplanetary wanderer slammed into Jupiter, creating 2,000-mile-high fireballs and sooty smudges on the planet's cloud tops that were visible from backyard telescopes.[6]
>
> — — —
>
> They are a cosmic accident waiting to happen: Astronomers revealed new evidence that the solar system is encircled by a 90 billion-mile-wide, disk-like cloud of at least 200 million mountainous chunks of dirt and ice, some of which occasionally come hurtling through the solar system as starry-tailed comets.[7]
>
> — — —
>
> Astronomers forecast a meteorite storm between 1997–2001 that will produce more than 250,000 meteorites in one evening.[8]

☞ **GO TO:**

Exodus 7:14–25 (waters to blood)

KEY Symbols:

Second Trumpet
SECOND TRUMPET ANGEL

a huge mountain thrown into the sea
1/3 of sea turned to blood, living sea creatures die, ships destroyed

RELATED CURRENT EVENTS

☞ **GO TO:**

Deuteronomy 29:18;
Lamentations 3:15
(Wormwood)

Wormwood: *a bitter, intoxicating, and poisonous herb*

KEY Symbols:

Third Trumpet
THIRD TRUMPET ANGEL

a poisonous ball
1/3 of earth's fresh
water contaminated

What Others are Saying:

RELATED CURRENT EVENTS

More than 200 asteroids measuring as much as a half mile in diameter are drifting around the solar system. Scientists believe that some of them could cross the Earth's orbit.[9]

> **Revelation 8:10, 11** The third angel sounded his trumpet, and a great star, blazing like a torch, fell from the sky on a third of the rivers and on the springs of water—the name of the star is Wormwood. A third of the waters turned bitter, and many people died from the waters that had become bitter.

Wormwood

Some believe this star *blazing like a torch* will be a meteor. Others suggest a nuclear missile. While they hold different opinions about what it is, they usually agree about what it will do.

A great blazing object containing some type of pollutant or poisonous substance will fall out of the sky. It will be named after a bitter herb called **Wormwood** in the Bible. It will contaminate one-third of earth's fresh water supply, causing many people to die from drinking the tainted water. Although the Bible does not say, it is reasonable to assume that many others will die from thirst. With one-third of the fresh water tainted, most people will be unable to obtain drinkable water before extreme thirst sets in. Adults will survive without water for about three days while the sick and infants will have fewer.

David Hocking: This tragic judgment, affecting the water supply of the world and bringing about the death of many, is a consequence upon those who refuse to submit to God's authority in their lives. We all need water; it is basic to human survival. One can only imagine what sort of additional tragedies will occur because of the terrible pollution caused by this third trumpet judgment.[10]

According to a former Soviet scientist, Russia has developed extremely deadly biological weapons, including a strain of bacteria that could produce a "superplague" capable of wiping out tens of thousands of people within a week.[11]

— — —

As the Clinton White House recklessly plunges head-first into the chemical and biological warfare ban

agreement, critics warn the treaty is full of loop-
holes that will allow the Russians to continue developing and producing their new weapons. . . . The
new weapons, referred to as Novichok, Russian for
"newcomer," can be "toxic like a chemical agent or
cause diseases like a biological agent. It can be
lethal or debilitating."[12]

> **Revelation 8:12** The fourth angel sounded his trum-
> pet, and a third of the sun was struck, a third of the
> moon, and a third of the stars, so that a third of them
> turned dark. A third of the day was without light, and
> also a third of the night.

Lights Out

The fourth trumpet judgment will affect the heavenly bodies: the
sun, moon, and stars. Pagan religions worship these objects. Astrologers, fortune tellers, and witches rely on them to predict the
future. A few bizarre interpretations of this judgment exist, but
the generally accepted meaning is that the light of the sun, moon,
and stars will be diminished by one-third. We can be sure that
smoke from the burning of one-third of the earth will block out a
lot of the light from the sun, moon, and stars. Nuclear winter
brought on by smoke, dirt, and debris being hurled into the atmosphere is also a possibility.

How long this will continue is not said, but there is no question that a reduction of the earth's sunlight will affect the weather,
crops, and all of life in general. Major winter storms will sweep
the earth causing multitudes to freeze to death.

World Book Encyclopedia: Nuclear winter refers to the deadly
worldwide environmental effects that could result from a major
nuclear war. Such a war could bring on nuclear winter by causing
disastrous changes in the earth's atmosphere and climate.

Nuclear winter could begin to develop from city fires created by
the extreme heat of nuclear explosions. Large amounts of smoke
from these fires could spread and cover at least half the earth's surface. The smoke could prevent most sunlight from reaching the
ground. Temperatures could drop substantially, and rainfall could
be reduced. These conditions might last for several months or years.
With greatly reduced sunlight, less rain, and lower temperatures,
farming could stop, and worldwide famine could result.[13]

KEY Symbols:

Fourth Trumpet

FOURTH TRUMPET ANGEL

*1/3 of sun, moon and
stars are struck
causing 1/3 darkness*

**What Others
are Saying:**

☞ GO TO:

Numbers 22:21–30
(Balaam's donkey)

Pilate's hall: where Jesus
was condemned to die

KEY POINT

The three trumpet
woes will be worse
than any prior judg-
ment.

**What Others
are Saying:**

> **Revelation 8:13** As I watched, I heard an eagle that was flying in midair call out in a loud voice: "Woe! Woe! Woe to the inhabitants of the earth, because of the trumpet blasts about to be sounded by the other three angels!"

Trumpet Woes

Who or what is this eagle? Some say it will be the Raptured Church. Others say it will be an angel, while still others say it will be a literal eagle. One thing is for sure: If God could make Balaam's donkey talk, he can make an eagle talk.

This eagle will fly through the air pronouncing three woes upon the inhabitants of the earth. These three woes correspond to the last three trumpets. Some even call them the "trumpet woes." It is hard to imagine, but these woes will be worse than any judgment previously mentioned.

J.H. Melton: Long was the old world left to drive its crimes, jeer at Noah's odd notions, and fling defiance into the face of God; but presently the earth broke down beneath their feet, and their lifeless bodies dashed upon each other amid the waves of an ocean world. The trampled law will assert its rightful honour, and Christ will not endure the smiting, taunts, and wrongs of **Pilate's hall** forever. And when these trumpets once give out their clangour, the vibrations will run through the universe, and everything created for human blessedness shall turn into a source of disaster and trouble to them that know not God and obey not the Gospel of Christ.[14]

Study Questions

1. What is the reason for the heavenly silence?
2. The fragrance of the incense reminds God of what?
3. Why would God call for an earthquake?
4. What is the correlation between the plagues of Egypt, Sodom and Gomorrah, and the judgment of thirds?

- Silence fills heaven for a half hour upon the opening of the seventh seal. (Revelation 8:1)

- The aroma coming from the incense mixed with the prayers of the saints will elicit a response from God when an angel takes the Golden Censer filled with fire and hurls it to earth. (Revelation 8:3–5)

- The first four trumpet judgments will: burn a third of the earth, turn a third of the seas to blood, pollute a third of all drinkable water, and diminish a third of the light from heavenly bodies. (Revelation 8:7–12)

- After the first four trumpets have sounded an eagle will fly through the air proclaiming three woes upon the earth. These woes correspond to the last three trumpet blasts. (Revelation 8:13)

REVELATION 9

CHAPTER HIGHLIGHTS

- Opening the Abyss
- Demon-Possessed Locusts
- Four Bound Angels
- 200 Million Troops
- Unrepentant Hearts

Let's Get Started

Interpreting the symbols is one reason why Chapter 9 is considered one of the most difficult chapters in Revelation. Unlike other chapters where many of the symbols are explained, this chapter offers few explanations for the symbols used.

John used symbols to describe events that will take place centuries after he lived. Some of these symbols are unusual, but that should not keep us from trying to understand this chapter's prophecy.

> The mystery of the seven stars and lampstands is this: *The seven stars are the angels of the seven churches, and the seven lampstands are the seven churches* (Revelation 1:20).

Remember This . . .

> **Revelation 9:1** The fifth angel sounded his trumpet, and I saw a star that had fallen from the sky to the earth. The star was given the key to the shaft of the Abyss.

Come Blow That Trumpet, Gabriel

This is not a literal star. This is not even a star that will fall, but one that has already fallen—Satan. Revelation 9:2 refers to this star as a *he*. The prophet Isaiah said, *How you have fallen from heaven, O morning star* (Satan)*, son of the dawn! You have been cast down to the*

☞ **GO TO:**

Luke 8:30, 31 (Abyss)

subterranean: *beneath the earth's surface*

Abyss: *a deep pit where demons are kept*

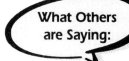
What Others are Saying:

earth (Isaiah 14:12). Satan will be cast down indeed. He will be given the key to his **subterranean** home called the **Abyss**. The Abyss is a place of torment where the worst of his demonic spirits are held and from where the Antichrist will come forth.

Some people think Jesus was referring to the Abyss when he said, *for as Jonah was three days and three nights in the belly of a huge fish, so the Son of Man will be three days and three nights in the heart of the earth* (Matthew 12:40).

David Jeremiah with C.C. Carlson: The "pit" that has been the home of the demons is the Greek word for "abyss." We have a picture of a vast depth approached by a shaft, whose top is covered. It is a sobering thought to realize that many of the demons of hell are not free to hurt us in this present age. Satan is managing to do a good job of destruction today without his entire war corps to back him up.[1]

> **Revelation 9:2** When he opened the Abyss, smoke rose from it like the smoke from a gigantic furnace. The sun and sky were darkened by the smoke from the Abyss.

Darkness Over The Earth

Satan will descend and open the Abyss. When he does, a thick black smoke will rush out, covering the earth in darkness. The sky will be blackened, and the sun will be obscured.

> **Revelation 9:3** And out of the smoke locusts came down upon the earth and were given power like that of scorpions of the earth.

Locusts Will Come

Locusts will come out of the smoke, but not locusts as we know them. They will not be the short-horned grasshoppers that have plagued people around the world. Instead they will be demon-possessed and have horrible features—part-animal and part-human.

These locusts will be like scorpions. They will have stingers to stab and poison their victims. Victims rarely die from the sting of a scorpion, but often turn black and blue and go into convulsions. The pain is unbearable. What could be worse than millions of demon-possessed locusts dive-bombing us like mosquitoes.

☞ **GO TO:**

Luke 8:26–33 (herd)

Gerasenes: descendants of the Jewish tribe Gad

Many locusts can make a sound by rubbing their ridged hind legs on their front wings. This causes the wings to vibrate, which makes the noise. . . . Plagues of crop-destroying locusts have been known since ancient times. One swarm by the Red Sea was believed to cover an area of 2,000 square miles. . . . Swarms of migrating locusts are sometimes so large they shut out the sunlight. They interfere with railroad trains, airplanes, and make automobile travel dangerous.[2]

RELATED CURRENT EVENTS

Jesus once visited the **Gerasenes** where he encountered a demon-possessed man living among the tombs. The demons begged Jesus not to cast them into the Abyss, so he <u>cast them into a herd of pigs</u> instead. The demons would rather be cast into the pigs than cast into the Abyss.

Remember This . . .

> **Revelation 9:4** They were told not to harm the grass of the earth or any plant or tree, but only those people who did not have the seal of God on their foreheads.

Demon-Possessed Locusts

As intelligent as these demon-possessed locusts will most likely be, it's ironic that they will still be under God's control. They will only harm those *who do not have <u>the seal of God on their foreheads</u>* (the 144,000 Jews).

Even though locusts eat plants, God commands these locust not to harm the grass, plants, or trees. We may wonder why, but can only speculate how locusts would not eat their most staple foods. Perhaps it will be because the earth may be in such ecological chaos that any further damage by locusts would destroy it altogether. If the grass, plants, and tress were gone, the earth could no longer produce oxygen, and if there were no oxygen, God's people would not survive during the Millennium.

☞ **GO TO:**

Ephesians 4:30;
 II Corinthians 1:21,
 22 (seal of God)

> **Revelation 9:5** They were not given power to kill them, but only to torture them for five months. And the agony they suffered was like that of the sting of a scorpion when it strikes a man.

A Scorpion's Sting

These locusts will not kill but only torture for a period not to exceed five months. They will be the masters of suffering by inflicting pain similar to a scorpion's sting.

What Others are Saying:

David Hocking: While a scorpion sting is usually not fatal (although children often die from such a sting), it is painful. The venom affects the veins and nervous system. Normally the pain and discomfort last for several days. This plague lasts for five months.[3]

> **Revelation 9:6** During those days men will seek death, but will not find it; they will long to die, but death will elude them.

Begging To Die

During these five months of the Tribulation Period, people will hurt so much they will want to die. Their nervous systems will become infected, parts of their bodies will swell and hurt, and other parts will fail to function altogether. Some will suffer seizures and convulsions and others will lose consciousness. Many will take medicines that fail to provide relief. Because of this torture, many will try to commit suicide, but God will not let them find death to end their suffering.

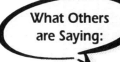

What Others are Saying:

J. Vernon McGee: It is not a laughing matter to reject Jesus Christ; it is not a simple thing to ignore him. People say there are so many important things in this life—I am willing to grant that many things take second, third, and fourth place—but the most important thing is your decision concerning Jesus Christ.[4]

> **Revelation 9:7–10** The locusts looked like horses prepared for battle. On their heads they wore something like crowns of gold, and their faces resembled human faces. Their hair was like women's hair, and their teeth were like lions' teeth. They had breastplates like breastplates of iron, and the sound of their wings was like the thundering of many horses and chariots rushing into battle. They had tails and stings like scorpions, and in their tails they had power to torment people for five months.

A Grasshopper? No, A Locust

How would you describe a locust? I'm sure you wouldn't say it has a body shaped like a horse, hair like that of a woman, and two eyes like a man? Of course you wouldn't, but that's what John saw.

The word *like* appears seven times and the word *resembled* appears one time in these verses. Obviously, John is using comparisons and symbolic language to describe what these demon-possessed locusts will look like.

They will have bodies shaped like a horse with a breastplate of iron. Something similar to a crown of gold will adorn their heads, and their faces will resemble that of a human. Their manes will be long like a woman's hair, and their teeth will be small and sharp like a lion's. They will have tails like a scorpion, and their wings will sound like an army of chariots.

Oliver B. Greene: In Italy and some other foreign countries locusts are called "little horses" and some of them resemble a horse.[5]

J. Vernon McGee: Dr. Vincent makes this comment in his *Book on Revelation*: The likeness of a locust to a horse, especially to a horse equipped with armor, is so striking that the insect is named in German *heupferd (hay-horse),* and in Italian *cavaletta (little horse).*[6]

> **Revelation 9:11** They had as king over them the angel of the Abyss, whose name in Hebrew is Abaddon, and in Greek, Apollyon.

A Demon Army

This <u>unnatural army</u> of locusts will be under the direction of an angelic king. Some say this angelic king will be Satan, but it seems more likely he will be one of Satan's powerful assistants. Satan will not be one of the demons confined in the Abyss. He is the Fallen Star who opens the pit to let this angelic king and his ungodly army loose.

This must be one of Satan's top *henchmen.* His Hebrew name will be **Abaddon**, meaning *destruction*, and his Greek name **Apollyon**, meaning *destroyer*. Since his name is given in both Hebrew and Greek, he will probably be permitted to attack both Jew

KEY Symbols:

Locust
*shaped like a horse
with a breastplate of
iron
crown of gold on their
heads
hair of a woman
teeth small and sharp
like a lion
tails like a scorpion
wings that sound like
an army of chariots*

**What Others
are Saying:**

☞ **GO TO:**

Proverbs 30:27 (unnatural)

Abaddon: *destruction*
Apollyon: *destroyer*

and Gentile alike. His name is given twice, so it is a double warning of his destructive powers.

What Others are Saying:

J.H. Melton: Most Bible students underestimate the power of the devil. To do so is a grievous error. The misery Satan has wrought in God's creation and in mankind should be reason enough to recognize his power and mind.[7]

> **Revelation 9:12** The first woe is past; two other woes are yet to come.

One Down And Two To Go

This verse is further proof that Revelation is sequence-oriented. The trumpet woes will not overlap. They will come in sequence. It is obvious why the angel called them *woes*—tormented people, losing their minds and begging to die.

> **Revelation 9:13** The sixth angel sounded his trumpet, and I heard a voice coming from the horns of the golden altar that is before God.

The Sixth Trumpet Angel

This is the altar of Chapter 8. It is where the angel mixes the incense with the prayers of the Tribulation Saints. The mixture rises to God and kindles his wrath. Then the sixth angel will stand up and sound his trumpet, and a voice will be heard coming from the horns of the altar that will speak for the martyred saints.

☞ **GO TO:**

Exodus 27:1, 2 (four corners)

I Kings 1:49, 50; 2:28–34 (grabbing the horns)

Something to Ponder

The horns of the golden altar refer to horns like animal horns that were extensions or spires that were <u>placed at the four corners of the altar</u> of burnt offerings. Sometimes sacrificial animals were tied to the horns, and there are even two instances of men <u>grabbing hold of the horns</u> when they thought they were going to be killed. They hoped to receive mercy.

> **Revelation 9:14** It said to the sixth angel who had the trumpet, "Release the four angels who are bound at the great river Euphrates."

The Great River

The Euphrates River first appears in Genesis. It was close to the Garden of Eden where Adam sinned and Cain slew Abel. It is where the flood began, where the Tower of Babel stood, where Babylon was built, and where world government and world religion began. It has long been associated with astrology, idolatry, demon worship, witchcraft, and other sordid sins. It is also widely recognized as the boundary between East and West.

Who are these four angels? The fact that they are bound indicates that they are four more fallen angels. Why they fell and are bound we are not told, but they appear to be powerful cohorts of Satan who may have had a part in the many sins committed along the Euphrates. In any case, the voice coming from the golden altar will tell the sixth angel to release these four angels.

> **Revelation 9:15** And the four angels who had been kept ready for this very hour and day and month and year were released to kill a third of mankind.

Four Fallen Angels

These four fallen angels will be restrained and kept ready for the precise month, day, and year of God's choosing. God's precise timing for the seven year Tribulation Period is laid out to the exact hour, minute, and second. When these four angels are released, the earth will lose one-third of its population. Since we have not witnessed such speedy and cataclysmic loss of life, it is safe to say Revelation has not yet been fully fulfilled.

David Jeremiah with C.C. Carlson: Not since Noah has such a substantial proportion of the earth's population come under God's righteous judgment.[8]

1) A few hundred million will leave in the Rapture.
2) One-fourth of those who remain on earth (more than one billion people) will die when the fourth seal (the horseman called Death) is opened (Revelation 6:8). Others

☞ **GO TO:**

Genesis 2:14 (Euphrates River)

Genesis 4:8 (Cain and Abel)

Genesis 11:1–9 (Tower of Babel)

KEY Symbols:

Sixth Trumpet Judgment

SIXTH TRUMPET ANGEL

four fallen angels
- from the Euphrates River
- powerful cohorts of Satan

What Others are Saying:

Remember This . . .

(number unknown) will die from war, natural disasters, and poisoned water.

3) Then one-third of the remainder will die when these four angels are released (Revelation 9:15).

This is why Jesus said, *If those days had not been cut short, no one would survive* (Matthew 24:22).

> **Revelation 9:16** The number of the mounted troops was two hundred million. I heard their number.

KEY Symbols:

Mounted Troops
200 million

An Army Of 200 Million

This army of mounted troops must be a future army since it numbers more than the entire population of the earth in John's day. It is significant to note that today only one nation has the capability of fielding a 200 million man army—China.

The leaders of this army will be seduced by the four angels that will be released from the Euphrates River. God will allow these evil angels to convince the army's leaders to go on the rampage and kill a third of mankind. However, without God's permission, these angels would still be bound at the great river.

What Others are Saying:

Jack Van Impe: China is a huge country, with a population of some 1.2 billion. However, the magnitude of this nation is also a two-edged sword for its leaders: the masses must be fed, clothed, and put to work. On the other hand, the sheer numbers of men, women, and children also make the country a loose cannon that could aim virtually any of its desires at anyone, anywhere, at any time. Chairman Mao once said that China could easily lose half its population and still win its battles with the enemy.[9]

Hal Lindsey: I believe these 200 million troops are Red Chinese soldiers accompanied by other Eastern allies. It's possible that the industrial might of Japan will be united with Red China. For the first time in history there will be a full invasion of the West by the Orient.[10]

J. Vernon McGee: China, India, and Japan could easily put that many in the field tomorrow.[11]

The Associated Press carried an article by John H. Hightower on April 28, 1964 saying Red Chinese leaders estimate they have "200 million armed and organized militiamen." [12]

> **Revelation 9:17** The horses and riders I saw in my vision looked like this: Their breastplates were fiery red, dark blue, and yellow as sulfur. The heads of the horses resembled the heads of lions, and out of their mouths came fire, smoke, and sulfur.

Like Fire-Breathing Dragons

This great force will have 200 million mounted troops. These troops and their horses (possibly machines) will have breastplates that will be fiery red, dark blue, and sulfur yellow. The heads of these horses will resemble the heads of lions, and out of their mouths will come fire, smoke, and sulfur (possibly explosions, projectiles, or missiles).

It is interesting to note that China's flag is red and yellow; that many of China's army wear dark blue uniforms; that China is commonly called *the yellow peril*; and that fire-breathing dragons with large heads are a favorite Chinese symbol.

Hal Lindsey: I believe he (John) is describing main battle tanks . . . rocket launchers . . . and a tremendous, horrible invasion.[13]

No matter how much you learn about Revelation, never think you know it all. John's use of the words *like* and *resembled* indicate he is using symbols to describe the future, so how can anyone claim to know for certain when and how things will come to pass?

RELATED CURRENT EVENTS

KEY Symbols:

Riders and Horses
breastplates of fiery red, dark blue, and yellow like sulfur

Horses
heads resembling the heads of lions

out of their mouths came fire, smoke, and sulfur

What Others are Saying:

WARNING

> **Revelation 9:18** A third of mankind was killed by the three plagues of fire, smoke and sulfur that came out of their mouths.

Where Is The Antichrist?

He promised world peace? But in reality, without the Prince of Peace, there will be no peace. This army of 200 million will do what the demon-possessed locusts couldn't do—kill, until a third of mankind is gone.

What Others are Saying:

Hal Lindsey: John describes the means by which one-third of mankind will be annihilated as *fire, smoke, and brimstone* (KJV). All of these things are a part of a thermonuclear war; smoke represents the immense clouds of radioactive fallout and debris, while brimstone is simply melted earth and building materials.[14]

J. Vernon McGee: This terrible decimation of the earth's population seemed incongruous with all of history until the atomic bomb fell upon Hiroshima. Since then men have been using more frightening language than that of Revelation. They now talk of the total decimation of earth's inhabitants.[15]

> **Revelation 9:19** The power of the horses was in their mouths and in their tails; for their tails were like snakes, having heads with which they inflict injury.

What Are They?

What these will be is anyone's guess. Some believe they are horses as we know them. Others think they are demon monstrosities, and still others think they are tanks, helicopters, or some type of future weapon. We can only speculate on what they really are, but one thing is for sure, they will be deadly.

What Others are Saying:

Ed Hindson: The Apostle John had been transported, in the Spirit, down through the canyon of time and the halls of human history to witness an event so distant in the future that it was difficult for him to describe what he saw.[16]

WARNING These things are of the future. They may already exist, but they are unlike anything we would recognize today.

> **Revelation 9:20** The rest of mankind that were not killed by these plagues still did not repent of the work of their hands; they did not stop worshiping demons, and idols of gold, silver, bronze, stone, and wood—idols that cannot see or hear or walk.

☞ **GO TO:**

Psalm 9:17 (forget God)

Deuteronomy 18:10–11 (conversations)

The First Two Sins

Those remaining on earth at this time will persist in their sins, refusing to repent, and continuing to reject Jesus. Two of the six sins that will be prominent during the Tribulation Period are demon worship (Satanism) and idolatry. The Satanic Bible will be widely read, and the Church of Satan will fill its pews. Goddess worship and witchcraft will be the rage of the politically correct. Statues and images of the Antichrist will be common, and multitudes will bow before them. These nations will soon learn what happens to those who <u>forget God</u>.

animism: the belief that trees, stones, and other objects have souls

What Others are Saying:

Hal Lindsey: Ten years ago I couldn't imagine how people with today's education and enlightenment could do such a thing. But in the last few years we've seen the greatest turning to witchcraft, Satan worship, and occultism since the days of ancient Rome.[17]

John Hagee: Hillary Clinton has brought witchcraft into the White House, lending her name and influence to medium and so-called "psychic spiritualist" Jean Houston.

Hillary and Jean have met together on numerous occasions in numerous places including several meetings in the private quarters of the White House. Houston claims to have a mystical link with the ancient Greek goddess Athena. The remarkable relationship between Jean and Hillary received national publicity when the news leaked that Jean Houston was leading Hillary into "<u>imaginary conversations" with the dead</u>, while the President of the United States sat by looking on approvingly.[18]

Jack Van Impe: There is widespread—even rampant—interest in and acceptance of Eastern religions, extrasensory perception, astrology, witchcraft, and false prophets.[19]

According to the January 23, 1995 edition of *Time*, in order to revive and improve his political image after the November 1994 election, President Clinton is

RELATED CURRENT EVENTS

evidently consulting with several New Age gurus. The New Age religion encompasses many things including: that God is us, situation ethics, holistic health, Jesus Christ is just one of many messiahs, **animism** and nature worship, and reincarnation . . .[20]

According to *Signs of Our Times* a federal judge has ruled that a convicted kidnapper can perform satanic rituals in his prison cell. The prisoner, Robert James Howard, is serving a ten-year sentence in a federal prison for auto theft and abduction. The judge, U.S. District Judge Edward Nottingham who declared the federal prison rule that bars devil worship to be unconstitutional, wrote in his recent decision, "We ought to give the devil his due."[21]

☞ **GO TO:**

Hosea 9:10 (Baal)

> **Revelation 9:21** Nor did they repent of their murders, their magic arts, their sexual immorality, or their thefts.

Four More Sins

Four more sins of the Tribulation Period are murder, magic arts, sexual immorality, and theft. It is apparent that unbelievers will be determined to trample on the laws of God and refuse to repent.

Depraved men and women will kill God's children without fear of punishment. Drug abuse, astrology, fortune telling, signs and omens, and theft will be worldwide. The world will move from an over-tolerance of perversion and sexual immorality to a blatant promotion of these sins.

What Others are Saying:

John Hagee: Instead of seeking God's wisdom, the "New Age" religions search for spiritual answers from alien beings, fortune tellers, and demons. Environmental pagans are now worshiping Mother Earth. Increasingly they call on Gaia, the ancient earth goddess who is only a recycled version of <u>Baal</u>, the pagan god of Biblical history.[22]

Grant R. Jeffrey: Modern criminologists, sociologists, and liberal politicians claim that the crime wave is caused by society, poverty, and poor career opportunities. This premise underlies the appalling short prison sentences handed out to violent criminals. Rather than demanding that individuals take responsibility for their choices and actions, criminal behavior is blamed on social problems.[23]

Jack Van Impe: Moral chaos in America is tearing apart the fabric of our society—with no end in sight. Drug addiction, physical, emotional, and sexual abuse are becoming enemies in America, and throughout the world—West and East. Crime, riots, unemployment, poverty, illiteracy, mental illness, illegitimacy, and other social problems are also on the rampage.[24]

RELATED CURRENT EVENTS

The National Center for Policy Analysis reports that crime in the United States has increased 300 percent in 30 years, making our nation the most violent one in history. In 1992, 24 million Americans were victims of crime. There is now a rape every five minutes, a robbery every 46 seconds, and a murder every 21 minutes. Gang violence (a prelude to anarchy) is increasing, as well as domestic violence (a prelude to moral degeneration). But what about justice? Punishment for major crimes meted out by our courts is as follows:

- Rape—average jail time, 60 days
- Armed robbery—average jail time, 23 days
- Arson—average jail time, 6 days and 17 hours
- Car theft—average jail time, one day and 12 hours
- Murder—average jail time, 20 months [25]

The Greatest Mass Killings of History:

China (Mao's Cultural Revolution, 1966-76)	20 million
U.S.S.R. (Stalin's reign of terror, 1933-45)	20 million
Europe (the Holocaust, 1933-45)	11 million
Pakistan (reprisals against Bengalis, 9 months in 1971)	3 million
Cambodia (the Khmer Rouge killing fields, 1975-79)	1.6 million
Rwanda (Tutsis, 3 months in 1994)	1 million
Indonesia (killings of Communists and Chinese, 1965-66)	500,000
Bosnia (ethnic cleansing, 1992-4)	200,000 [26]

As FBI Director Louis J. Freeh puts it: "the ominous increase in juvenile crime coupled with population trends portend future crime and violence at nearly unprecedented levels."[27]

Study Questions

1. For what purpose would God allow an invasion of demon-possessed locusts?
2. What will be the human characteristics of the demon-possessed locusts?
3. What is the meaning and the significance of the locust king's Hebrew and Greek names?
4. Who asked for the release of the four angels at the river Euphrates?
5. What are some of the Tribulation Period sins?

CHAPTER WRAP-UP

- When the fifth trumpet is sounded Satan will be given the key to the Abyss. The sun and sky will be darkened from the smoke pouring out of the Abyss. (Revelation 9:1, 2)

- Demon-possessed locusts will come out of the Abyss to torment mankind for five months. The pain from the locusts will be so bad that men will seek death, but God will not let them find it. (Revelation 9:3–6)

- After the sixth trumpet is sounded the four angels that have been bound at the Euphrates will be released to kill a third of mankind. (Revelation 9:13–15)

- An army of 200 million mounted troops will kill a third mankind through the three plagues of fire, smoke, and sulfur that will come out of their horses' mouths. (Revelation 9:16–19)

- Those who are not killed by these plagues will still refuse to repent of their sins. Instead, they will cling to their idols and demon worship. (Revelation 9:20, 21)

REVELATION 10

CHAPTER HIGHLIGHTS

- A Mighty Angel
- No More Delay!
- Be a Doer
- Eat the Book
- A Commission

Let's Get Started

In Chapter 1 John was given a message by one *like a son of man.* He was told to write down what he saw and pass it on to the seven churches. This vision became known as Revelation. Now at the start of Chapter 10, John will see a mighty angel who will present him with a book that will contain another message for him to another pass on.

> **Revelation 10:1** Then I saw another mighty angel coming down from heaven. He was robed in a cloud, with a rainbow above his head; his face was like the sun, and his legs were like fiery pillars.

He Will Wear A Cloud

John saw a mighty angel in Revelation 5:2. Now we read that he will see another mighty angel. We do not know the identity of this angel, but we do know that he will have great authority. He will be allowed to stand in the presence of God and will speak for God. He will probably be an archangel who will come down from heaven wearing some unusual garments.

First, this mighty angel will be clothed in a cloud. In the Bible, clouds have been associated with at least two things: the presence of God and the return of Jesus. God came down to Mt. Sinai in a cloud and led the Israelites with a pillar of cloud; Jesus **ascended to heaven in a cloud** and will return in the clouds. This mighty angel's clothing could be a reminder that he will be a messenger

☞ **GO TO:**

Exodus 19:9–11 (Mt. Sinai)

Exodus 13:21 (pillar)

Acts 1:8–11 (ascended)

Matthew 24:30 (return)

Genesis 9:11–16 (rainbow)

Revelation 4:3 (around the throne)

Exodus 34:29–33 (face shined)

Revelation 1:9–16 (Isle of Patmos)

ascended: going up from
the earth into heaven

KEY Symbols:

A Mighty Angel
robed in a cloud
rainbow above his
head
his face like the sun
legs like fiery pillars

from God, or it could also be a reminder that Jesus will be return-ing soon.

Second, this mighty angel will either wear a "hat" that looks like a rainbow or he will have a rainbow circling his head. The rainbow is a reminder that God promised to never destroy the world with a flood again. He even placed a rainbow around his throne as a reminder. We can only speculate about the rainbow on the mighty angel's head, but it probably will symbolize that God is a God of grace, a God who keeps his promises, a God who will not let the world destroy itself, and a God whose Son is coming back.

Third, this mighty angel's face will shine like the sun. When Moses came down from Mt. Sinai with the Ten Commandments, his face shined from being in the presence of God. When John saw Jesus on the Isle of Patmos, Christ's face shined like the sun. The shekinah glory of God on this mighty angel's face will indicate he has been in the presence of God.

Fourth, this mighty angel's legs will be as pillars of fire. When John saw Jesus on the Isle of Patmos, his feet were like burning bronze—a symbol of judgment. This angel's fiery legs will rep-resent God's plan to take control of the earth through divine judgment.

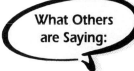

**What Others
are Saying:**

David Hocking: In the book of Revelation, angels are angels, not symbols of events, things, places, or persons.[1]

J. Vernon McGee: All of these features of identification are his credentials and connect him to the person of Christ as his special envoy.[2]

God('s)

Remember
This . . .

is a God of grace.

will keep his promises.

will not let the world destroy itself.

Son, Jesus, is coming back.

> **Revelation 10:2** He was holding a little scroll, which lay open in his hand. He planted his right foot on the sea and his left foot on the land,

In The Name Of My King

The mighty angel will carry a small open book in his hand. While he is holding it, he will plant his right foot on the sea and his left foot on dry land. This is a symbolic gesture that has been played out in the movies many times. The main character sails to some new island or far-off country. When he arrives he leaves his ship, gets into a rowboat, and his sailors row him to land. Then he steps out of the rowboat onto dry land, and claims that island or country in the name of his ruler. The same is true of this angel. He will have one foot on the sea and one foot on the land as he stakes a claim in the name of his King because the earth is the Lord's.

> **Revelation 10:3** and he gave a loud shout like the roar of a lion. When he shouted, the voices of the seven thunders spoke.

He Speaks With Thunder

This mighty angel will shout with a loud voice *like the roar of a lion* to speak on behalf of the King of kings. At the same time he speaks, a voice in heaven will roar like the seven thunders. The seven thunders is a symbol for the voice of God. The Almighty will make a strong statement when this angel speaks.

David Hocking: Such "thunders" do come forth from the throne of God (Revelation 4:5) and dramatically emphasize the importance of God's message and purposes (Revelation 8:5).[3]

David Jeremiah with C.C. Carlson: This is like a seven-gun salute in the skies.[4]

☞ GO TO:

Psalm 24:1 (earth is Lord's)

🔑 KEY Symbols:

A Mighty Angel
a little scroll in his hand
one foot on sea and
one on land
claims earth for his king

☞ GO TO:

Psalm 29:3; Job 37:5 (thunders)

🔑 KEY Symbols:

A Mighty Angel
a voice like the roar of a lion

Seven Thunders
the voice of God

What Others are Saying:

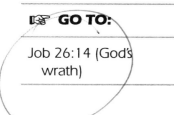

☞ **GO TO:**

Job 26:14 (God's wrath)

> **Revelation 10:4** And when the seven thunders spoke, I was about to write; but I heard a voice from heaven say, "Seal up what the seven thunders have said and do not write it down."

Seal It Up

God will make an emphatic remark in his voice of seven thunders that even John will be able to hear. Unfortunately, John will be told not to write it down. No one knows why John was prevented from recording what he heard, but just remember that thunder is also <u>a symbol of God's wrath</u>, and what he utters will probably coincide with divine judgment.

What Others are Saying:

Hal Lindsey: It must be something so potent that the world simply can't take it at this point. Whatever it is, I think it won't be long before we can ask the angel personally what this unmentionable message is.[5]

Tim LaHaye: Since the Apostle John was commanded by the voice to *seal up* their utterances, it is foolish to conjecture any further.[6]

Oliver B. Greene: Already set before us are blood, tears, famine, heartache, and heartbreak; killing, misery, hail, fire, burning mountains, demon monstrosities, men begging to die and unable to do so. Surely what John was forbidden to write must have been beyond human imagination and understanding.[7]

KEY POINT

When it is time, it is time. God will not be delayed.

KEY Symbols:

A Mighty Angel
right hand raised to heaven
There will be no more delay!

> **Revelation 10:5, 6** Then the angel I had seen standing on the sea and on the land raised his right hand to heaven. And he swore by him who lives for ever and ever, who created the heavens and all that is in them, the earth and all that is in it, and the sea and all that is in it, and said, "There will be no more delay!

The Time To Act Is Now!

Just as a witness raises his right hand to take the oath to tell the whole truth in a courtroom, this angel will raise his right hand toward heaven to swear to tell God's truth. His oath will emphasize the fact that he has the authority and power of God behind him.

There will be no more delay! It will be the answer the martyred Tribulation Saints have been waiting for. God will no longer delay his vengeance for their persecution and death. To the believers on earth who have been running, hiding, and waiting, these words will mean they will no longer have to wait for God to move against the wicked. And to the unbelievers on earth, they will mean God is now going to fulfill his wrath with no more delay.

This message should be a word of consolation to the saved and a word of terror to the lost. In a moment, the awesome, final judgments of God will start falling and nothing will stop them.

David Hocking: Although at times we wonder if God knows or cares about what is taking place on earth, the Bible assures us that he does.[8]

The Tribulation Saints asked in Revelation 6:10, 11: *How long, Sovereign Lord, holy and true, until you judge the inhabitants of the earth and avenge our blood?* Then each of them was given a white robe, and they were told to wait a little longer, until the number of their fellow servants and brothers who were to be killed was completed. Now that the time of vengeance has come. There will be no more delay!

> **Revelation 10:7** But in the days when the seventh angel is about to sound his trumpet, the mystery of God will be accomplished, just as he announced to his servants the prophets."

God's Mystery Accomplished

Jesus has now opened all seven seals, and six of the angels have sounded their trumpets. The last trumpet will bring the seven bowl judgments. But before the seventh angel blows his trumpet, a voice from heaven will declare, *the mystery of God will be accomplished, just as he announced to his servants the prophets.* One of God's great secrets will unfold during the seventh trumpet judgment exactly as the <u>prophets predicted</u>.

The Bible identifies several mysteries. One of them is called the mystery of iniquity or the <u>mystery of lawlessness</u>. It is a mystery why God allowed Satan to cause the fall of mankind, a mystery why he allowed sin to do so much damage in the world, a mystery why he will allow his people to be persecuted and martyred in the Tribulation Period, and a mystery why he will

What Others are Saying:

Remember This . . .

☞ **GO TO:**

Jeremiah 51:25; Isaiah 13:19, 20 (prophets predicted)

II Thessalonians 2:7 (mystery of lawlessness)

allow the Antichrist and the False Prophet to reign. All of these mysteries will finally be answered when we reach heaven.

J. Vernon McGee: As this passage of Scripture indicates, the fact that there is something that we don't know about because it has been sealed means that God has a whole lot to tell us yet. When we get into his presence, we will find out.[9]

Something to Ponder

So Many Things We Do Not Know:

1) The mystery of the Rapture—I Corinthians 15:51
2) The mystery of Israel's blindness—Romans 11:25
3) The mystery of God's wisdom—I Corinthians 2:7
4) The mystery of Christ and the Church—Ephesians 5:31, 32
5) The mystery of Christ in us—Colossians 1:26, 27
6) The mystery of the kingdom of heaven—Matthew 13
7) The mystery of godliness—I Timothy 3:16

☞ **GO TO:**

James 1:22 (listener/doer)

> **Revelation 10:8** Then the voice that I had heard from heaven spoke to me once more: "Go, take the scroll that lies open in the hand of the angel who is standing on the sea and on the land."

Be A Doer Of The Word

Now John must be <u>more than just a *listener*, he must also be a *doer*</u>. The same voice of the seven thunders tells John to go and take the open book out of the mighty angel's hand. The same is true for all believers. Serving God requires doing, not just listening. The Word of God should be like a cavalry bugle blowing for an attack—sparking believers to action.

☞ **GO TO:**

Mark 16:14–20 (go and preach)

Jeremiah 15:16 (ate words)

Ezekiel 3:1–15 (ate scroll)

> **Revelation 10:9** So I went to the angel and asked him to give me the little scroll. He said to me, "Take it and eat it. It will turn your stomach sour, but in your mouth it will be as sweet as honey."

Eat The Book?

Whether John will move from heaven to earth or whether he will already be on earth is a matter of debate, but he will go to the mighty angel and request the little book. This is a form of receiving a **commission** or special task from God. John was switched from being a spectator of these amazing things to being a participant in them. God does that with all of his people. Before Jesus ascended to heaven he instructed his disciples to <u>go and preach the good news to everyone</u>. Christians are not saved to be waited on; they are saved to serve.

The angel tells John to take the book and eat it. This may sound off-the-wall, but it's not new to the Bible. Jeremiah <u>ate the words of God</u>. Ezekiel <u>ate a scroll</u> from God. The implied idea is that the Word of God must <u>be taken to heart (not left outside one's body)</u>. The Bible will profit us little unless it becomes part of us, so it must be brought inside of one's self and **assimilated**. We need to *read* the Bible, and then <u>*obey* its instructions</u>.

The instruction to eat the little book will come with a warning that the <u>Word of God will taste sweet</u> but will turn sour once digested. Learning the Word of God with its plans and mysteries can be enjoyable and exciting, but understanding the reality of its judgments is sickening. Isn't it sweet to know that Satan will soon be bound and chained, but bitter to contemplate what people will go through beforehand? Isn't it sweet to know that final victory is assured, but bitter to contemplate the plagues, pain, loss of life, and eternal destiny of the lost? It was pleasant for John to receive the message from God, but painful for him to contemplate the steps toward fulfillment.

Ezekiel 3:10 (take to heart)

Romans 2:13 (obey)

Psalm 119:103 (taste sweet)

commission: *a special assignment from God*

assimilate: *become part of us*

KEY POINT

We need to read the Bible, and then obey its instructions.

David Jeremiah with C.C. Carlson: Preaching the prophetic truth is a bitter-sweet experience.[10]

David Hocking: Perhaps the full impact of what John experienced is a reminder to all who proclaim God's wonderful Word and speak of his coming judgment and wrath. We must speak it with a measure of sorrow and bitterness. A broken heart is a prerequisite to the proclamation of God's judgment and wrath.[11]

What Others are Saying:

John was called up into heaven in Chapter 4, but in this chapter he saw an angel coming down from heaven. The angel planted his feet on the land and sea, and John even took a book out of his hand. Some experts seem to think John had a vision of this in heaven, while others are not sure he did not come back to earth. This apparent discrepancy is still debated today.

Remember This . . .

☞ **GO TO:**

Ezekiel 2:1–9 (Ezekiel)

Jeremiah 1:3–19
(Jeremiah)

> **Revelation 10:10** I took the little scroll from the angel's hand and ate it. It tasted as sweet as honey in my mouth, but when I had eaten it, my stomach turned sour.

Get The Word

John did what he was instructed to do. He took the little book and ate it. It tasted good at first, but later it was sickening. But there's more to this verse.

True prophets hear the voice of God just like John did. What did John do? He got the Word of God (took it from the angel). This is the only place to find a prophetic message. Go and get the Word of God. Digest it. Here is a test. If everything comes up roses, you have eaten the wrong thing. True prophets prophesy because God loves the lost. He cares about what will happen to them.

Something to Ponder

When the <u>prophet Ezekiel was called</u> he was told to stand on his feet while God spoke to him. Then the Spirit raised him up and spoke to him. He told Ezekiel, *I am sending you to the Israelites, to a rebellious nation that has rebelled against me; they and their fathers have been in revolt against me to this very day. The people to whom I am sending you are obstinate and stubborn.* Ezekiel was told to speak God's words whether the people listened or not.

• • •

When the <u>prophet Jeremiah was called</u> he was told God had appointed him to be a prophet before he was born. Jeremiah did not want the assignment and said he was too young. But God told him he would tell Jeremiah what to say. Even though Jeremiah was only about twenty, he still obeyed.

> **Revelation 10:11** Then I was told, "You must prophesy again about many peoples, nations, languages, and kings."

For Them To Read

When John was told to eat the book, he was also given a commission from God. He was told to prophesy *about many peoples, nations, languages, and kings.* This was his great privilege, his great calling, and his great responsibility.

John was not told to deliver the message *to* many peoples, nations, languages, and kings but *about* many peoples, nations, languages, and kings. This is what John does in the remaining chapters of Revelation. During the Tribulation Period, many peoples, nations, languages, and kings will open these last chapters and read what John had to say about them.

Study Questions

1. What will the glow on the mighty angel's face indicate?
2. Who has the voice of seven thunders?
3. What are some of the mysteries that will not be answered until we reach heaven?
4. What are the two commissions God gave to all Christians through John?

CHAPTER WRAP-UP

- Another mighty angel will come down from heaven adorned in strange garments and holding a little scroll. He will claim the land and sea for God. (Revelation 10:1, 2)

- The angel standing on the sea and land will raise his right hand and declare that there will be no more delay for the judgment of earth. (Revelation 10 :5, 6)

- John will be told to take the scroll from the angel which signifies a Christian's duty to act upon God's Word and not just listen to it. (Revelation 10:8)

- When John eats the scroll it will taste sweet at first but will turn his stomach sour. This exemplifies that learning God's Word can be exciting, but understanding the realities of the judgments is sickening. (Revelation 10:9)

- God assigned John the task of prophesying about many peoples, nations, languages, and kings. (Revelation 10:11)

REVELATION 11

CHAPTER HIGHLIGHTS

- Two Witnesses
- The Antichrist Retaliates
- A Severe Earthquake
- The Seventh Trumpet
- God's Heavenly Temple

Let's Get Started

At the close of Chapter 10, we learned that John was commissioned to prophesy about many peoples, nations, languages, and kings. In Chapter 11 we see the beginning of John's commission by looking at Israel and the Temple. Also discussed are the actions of the Gentiles, Antichrist, God, and the two witnesses for God. We will also learn about the reactions of the nations and the residents of heaven.

Another point needs to be examined—a very important one. In Revelation 10:6 we learned that God will start to finalize his wrath upon the world—there will be no more delays. It is extremely significant that when God begins this, he will focus his attention on Israel and the Temple. In connection with this it is good to recall Old Testament prophecies. From these we learn:

1) Israel will become the storm center of the world during the Tribulation Period. Zechariah 12 and 14 reveal some of God's judgments upon Israel and her enemies. We read that God will make Jerusalem a cup that will send all the nations **reeling**. In Zechariah's time drinking from a cup was a metaphor similar to the expression, "take your medicine." In this case the nations opposing Jerusalem will be sent reeling when they drink the concoction Jerusalem has prepared for them.

The nations of the earth will <u>gather against Jerusalem</u>. She will be captured and half of her Jews will flee into exile. Remember: Anyone who harms Israel will actually be harming themselves, because they will be setting themselves against God. This struggle

☞ **GO TO:**

Zechariah 12:1–3; 14:1–3 (gather nations)

Jeremiah 51:19–23 (shatter nations)

Daniel 9:27, 28 (rebuild the Temple)

reeling: *send the nations into turmoil and confusion*

over Jerusalem will trigger the Second Coming and the Battle of Armageddon. Israel is God's weapon of battle and he will use her to shatter the nations.

This struggle is already underway. Israel has made Jerusalem its Capitol. The Palestinian Liberation Organization says Jerusalem will be the capital of their new Palestinian state. And the Pope has asked that it be designated an international city so he can move his headquarters there. All of this is a thorn in the flesh for the United Nations, and there is a great desire to move against the Jews. When they do, they will bring certain destruction down on themselves.

2) The Jews want to rebuild the Temple, the heart and soul of their religion. They want it rebuilt on the same site as their Old Testament Temple. However, the Palestinians want to keep this same site as holy ground for their existing mosque. They do not want their mosque torn down or moved. For the Jews to rebuild their Temple on this site would be like putting a gun to the Palestinians. It would be a great insult to their religion and to their god.

The Middle East conflict is really a struggle between two religions—Judaism and Islam. It raises the question, "Whose god is God, and who worships the true God?" Neither side dare give in because the reputations of both their god and their religion are at stake.

☞ **GO TO:**

II Chronicles 4:19 (golden)

I Kings 8:64 (bronze)

Leviticus 1:4 (atonement)

Hebrews 10:4 (sins)

Hebrews 10:1 (shadow)

Hebrews 9:12; 10:12 (permanent solution)

John 3:36; Acts 4:12 (only sacrifice)

> **Revelation 11:1** I was given a reed like a measuring rod and was told, "Go and measure the temple of God and the altar, and count the worshipers there."

None Were Found

John was given a reed and told to measure the Temple (see Illustration #5, page 153), measure the altar, and count the worshipers. This is significant because in the last days the Temple, and one of its two original altars will be rebuilt. The altar that will be rebuilt was called the golden altar (see Illustration #3, page 117), or the altar of incense. It was located *inside* the Temple. The altar that will not be rebuilt was called the bronze altar. It will not be rebuilt because, as Revelation 11:2 says, it was located *outside* in the outer court. The Gentiles will rule the outer court.

God will evaluate (count) the worshipers to see how many people on earth are truly worshiping Jesus. He will find none. The Jews will rebuild the Temple so they can re-establish their

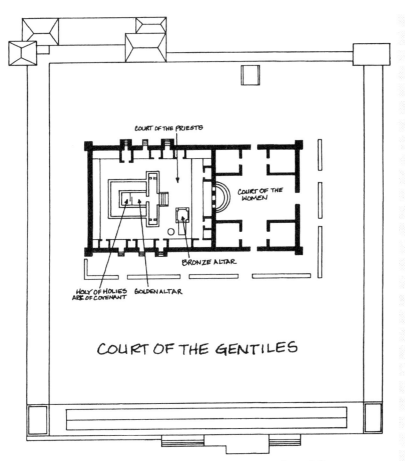

COURT OF THE PRIESTS

COURT OF THE WOMEN

BRONZE ALTAR

HOLY OF HOLIES
ARK OF COVENANT

GOLDEN ALTAR

COURT OF THE GENTILES

old way of worship—sacrificial worship. In the Old Testament, God accepted animal sacrifices as a temporary <u>atonement for sin</u>. The New Testament, however, teaches that those animal sacrifices did not permanently <u>take away the sins of people</u>. These sacrifices were inadequate to truly cover the sins of the people which is why they had to offer *the same sacrifices repeated endlessly year after year* (Hebrews 10:1). The reason God had the Jews sacrifice those animals was because it was a <u>shadow of the things</u> to come. It reminded the people of their sins and pointed them to the time when the Messiah would come to permanently take away their sins through his death on the cross.

Because animal sacrifice only brought temporary forgiveness another method was needed for making atonement for sin. A permanent method was required. Christ's sacrifice on the cross is this <u>permanent solution</u>. His death so thoroughly pleased God that it will never need to be repeated. In fact, no other sacrifices will ever be needed again.

Animal sacrifices are no longer acceptable because the death of

Jesus is the <u>only sacrifice that God will accept</u>. Jesus even spoke about this when he said, *I am the way and the truth and the life. No one comes to the Father except through me* (John 14:6). It is only through Christ's offering of himself for our sins that we can gain <u>eternal life</u>. During the Tribulation Period, when the Jews rebuild the Temple and resume animal sacrifices, their sacrifices will not be accepted which is why God will not find any worshipers in his Temple.

What Others are Saying:

Charles H. Dyer: Work goes on to breed the red heifer and to prepare the necessary articles and clothing to rebuild the Temple. Some erroneous reports have said that Israel is secretly stockpiling marble and limestone blocks for the building, but those reports appear to be groundless. Still, some groups, though they represent a small minority, are making serious preparations to rebuild the Temple and resume its worship.[1]

Hal Lindsey: I believe this very problem (the violent reaction of the Arabs to a Jewish Temple being rebuilt) may be the reason for the "strong covenant" which the Prophet Daniel says the Jewish people will make with the Roman Antichrist. In return for certain concessions from the Jews, he will guarantee protection for them so that they can rebuild their Temple and reinstate animal sacrifice. The religious Jews will push for this and accept the False Prophet as the Messiah because he helps to secure the rebuilding of the Temple.[2]

RELATED CURRENT EVENTS

The **yeshivas** on **Mt. Moriah** are training priests and Levites for resuming sacrificial worship. Other yeshivas are weaving priests' clothing out of pure linen, while silversmiths and metal workers fashion vessels for the Temple, and musical instruments are made to announce the Messiah's appearance.[3]

— — —

Within 48 hours of the **Hasmonean Tunnel's** opening, Yassar Arafat urged the Arab League to issue a declaration claiming the opening to be "part of an Israeli **Zionist** plot to destroy the **Aqsa Mosque** (and) set up the <u>Temple of Solomon</u>."[4]

According to Numbers 19, the blood of a red heifer, without spot or blemish, must be sprinkled in front of the Temple before God will accept a service there.

1) Daniel implied that the <u>Temple will be rebuilt</u> and in use by the middle of the Tribulation Period.
2) Jesus authenticated Daniel's prophecy in his **Olivet Discourse**.
3) Paul verified that the Temple will be rebuilt when he said the <u>Antichrist will defile it</u>.

Remember This . . .

> **Revelation 11:2** But exclude the outer court; do not measure it, because it has been given to the Gentiles. They will trample on the holy city for 42 months.

What About The Wall?

John will be told not to measure the outer court of the Temple. This may signify that only the **Holy Place** and the **Holy of Holies** will be rebuilt. Some architects and prophecy experts say these could be rebuilt without disturbing the **Dome of the Rock** or the Aqsa Mosque. Such an arrangement would allow the various religions to share the Temple Mount. Sharing that religious sight or sharing sovereignty over it could mean there may not be a wall around the outer court. Without the outer court wall the Jews and **Moslems** would be able to share the Temple Mount.

John is told not to measure the outer court *because it has been given to the Gentiles* (see Illustration #5, page 153). *They will trample on the holy city for 42 months.* This coincides with what Jesus taught. <u>Gentiles will control Jerusalem</u> and the Temple during the last three and one-half years of the Tribulation Period.

☞ **GO TO:**

Luke 21:24 (Gentiles)

Genesis 17:19–22 (Ishmael and Isaac)

Holy Place: *the large room just inside the door of the Temple building*

Holy of Holies: *innermost sanctuary of the Temple; housed the Ark of the Covenant*

Dome of the Rock: *a Moslem shrine on the Temple Mount*

Moslem: *one who practices the religion of Muhammad which is called Islam*

What Others are Saying:

Hal Lindsey: The importance of the Temple Mount site in Jerusalem to two faiths (Judaism and Islamism) make it the most strategic and potentially explosive piece of real estate on the face of the earth.[5]

David Hocking: It is possible the instruction to measure the Temple suggests what the last part of verse 2 reveals. The Gentiles will once again take control of Jerusalem and its holy sites.[6]

Charles H. Dyer: In a remarkable article in *Biblical Archaeology Review* Asher Kaufman argues that the ancient Holy of Holies was not located over the Dome of the Rock. Instead, he suggests that the Holy of Holies stood approximately a hundred yards farther north on the Temple Mount. . . . No major archaeologist in Israel finds Kaufman's views convincing, but the point here is not to argue whether Kaufman's views are correct. Many Orthodox Jews are poring over every scrap of data, trying to find where the Temple stood. If they conclude that Kaufman's position fits the evidence, then they will build the Temple where he suggested.[7]

RELATED CURRENT EVENTS

```
The report (a secret report commissioned by the Israeli
Foreign Ministry on possible solutions to the Jerusa-
lem problem) recommends that Palestinians be allowed
to set up their own police force in eastern Jerusalem,
and that the holy places in the Old City become "au-
tonomous areas" controlled by the different religions.
Sources involved said a central recommendation is that
Israel and the Palestinian Authority suspend their
claims for sovereignty, and instead talk about the
possibilities of division of power.[8]
```

Something to Ponder

Islam is a rapidly growing religion with almost one billion followers worldwide. About fifteen percent live in the Middle East and the remainder are spread around the world with the largest populations in Indonesia, Bangladesh, Pakistan, India, and China.

. . .

The Islamic religion is dominated by fundamentalists who try to impose the beliefs of Muhammad on the rest of the world. Extremists believe in spreading their religion by conquest. The more radical members deny basic freedoms such as human rights, civil rights, and women's rights. They will kill people of other religions in the name of their god Allah. Moslems believe:

1) Allah is the same God Christians worship, although he was a moon god in Muhammad's day.
2) Muhammad received revelations from God which prove that he was a prophet.
3) Muhammad wrote a book called the Koran (the Moslem's holy book).
4) The Koran contains God's latest revelations and supersedes all other revelations.

5) God exists, but his name is Allah not Jehovah.

6) Jesus existed, but he was a great prophet or messenger, not the Son of God who was crucified.

7) They are the true inheritors of the covenants of God as descendants of Abraham's son Ishmael, even though the Bible says the Jews are the inheritors of the covenants of God as descendants of Abraham's son Isaac. This one point has sparked a never-ending conflict between the Arabs and the Jews since the days of Abraham.

Jerusalem is considered the Holy City by Christians, Jews, and Moslems. Among other things Christians consider it holy because Jesus was crucified there, Jews consider it holy because their Temple was located there, and Moslems consider it holy because they believe Muhammad ascended into heaven there.

Remember This . . .

> **Revelation 11:3** And I will give power to my two witnesses, and they will prophesy for 1,260 days, clothed in sackcloth.

Two Witnesses

In the Old Testament the **Mosaic Law** required two witnesses to validate matters pertaining to Jewish religion. In the same way God will send two witnesses to prophesy and validate the world's sin and blasphemy during the Tribulation Period.

The identities of these witnesses are unknown, but most experts agree that one of them will be Elijah. The main reason for this agreement is a verse found in the Old Testament: *I will send you the prophet Elijah before that great and dreadful day of the Lord comes* (Malachi 4:5, 6). Currently, Elijah is in heaven, but he will return to earth *before* the Tribulation Period.

Elijah and the second witness will stay and prophesy for 1,260 days or three and one-half years. Experts agree that this will be the first three and one-half years of the Tribulation Period.

The two witnesses will wear sackcloth. This type of attire undoubtedly seems strange to us but can be explained with help from the Old Testament. Old Testament prophets wore **sackcloth** when they were ministering to people who were deeply involved in sin. Sackcloth, however, is also worn as a garment of mourning. Most likely the Jews of the Tribulation Period will be grieving over their sins and their relationship with God.

☞ **GO TO:**

Exodus 20:1–17 (Law)

Deuteronomy 17:6; 19:15 (witnesses)

II Kings 2:1 (Elijah)

Isaiah 20:2; Joel 1:13 (sackcloth)

Genesis 37:34; Esther 4:1–4 (mourning)

Genesis 5:22–24; Hebrews 11:5, 6 (Enoch)

John 1:29–36; 5:33 (John the Baptist)

Mosaic Law: the Ten Commandments

sackcloth: a coarse cloth worn as a sign of mourning

What Others are Saying:

KEY Symbols:

Two Witnesses

Elijah and ??? (no one knows)

WARNING

KEY Symbols:

Two Witnesses

olive tree

- filled with the Holy Spirit

lampstand

- light of God to the world

KEY Symbols:

Two Witnesses

fire from mouths

John Hagee: The two witnesses, who many theologians believe to be Elijah and Enoch, will appear on the earth during the Tribulation. They will wear the traditional clothing of mourning, and their mission will be to call men to repentance.[9]

J. Vernon McGee: Let us say with some assurance that Elijah is one of the witnesses. As to who the other one is, your guess is as good as mine.[10]

Most people want to know who the two witnesses will be. Some say Elijah and <u>Enoch</u>. Others say Elijah and <u>John the Baptist</u>. Still others suggest Elijah and Moses. I believe they will be Jews, but no one knows for sure. It may possibly be that God does not tell us because it is not important.

> **Revelation 11:4** These are the two olive trees and the two lampstands that stand before the Lord of the earth.

Oil And Light

Each witness is represented by one olive tree and one lampstand. It takes two symbols to represent one person.

To understand this passage we need to know what these symbols mean. The answer to the olive trees is found in Zechariah 4:3–6—two olive trees stand by a lampstand and provide oil to the lampstand. This oil represents the Holy Spirit. The two witnesses will be olive trees because they will be filled with the Holy Spirit.

Zechariah 4:11–14 explains what the lampstands represent—the lampstands hold pots of burning oil that provide light. The two witnesses will be lampstands because they will provide light to a dark world.

Now, combine the two symbols. Each witness will be one olive tree filled with the Holy Spirit and one lampstand giving off the light of God. They will be two witnesses, filled with the Holy Spirit, counteracting the forces of darkness in the world.

> **Revelation 11:5** If anyone tries to harm them, fire comes from their mouths and devours their enemies. This is how anyone who wants to harm them must die.

They Speak With Fire

God told Jeremiah, *I will make my words in your mouth a fire and these people the wood it consumes* (Jeremiah 5:14). Those who reject the Word of God will be like wood when it is consumed by fire.

The two witnesses will be invincible. They will have the supernatural power of the Word of God in their mouths. When their enemies try to harm them they will merely speak to consume their enemies.

> **Revelation 11:6** These men have power to shut up the sky so that it will not rain during the time they are prophesying; and they have power to turn the waters into blood and to strike the earth with every kind of plague as often as they want.

I Don't Want To Be Here

These two men will have unlimited power. They will be able to stop the rain from falling, turn water to blood, and smite the earth with many different kinds of **plagues**. Without rain for three and a half years the ground will be cracked and dry like old leather, and the dust will be ankle deep. When the waters turn to blood, they will be unfit to drink, and uninhabitable for fish. There is no telling what the other plagues will do, but one thing is for sure, this will not be the same planet we know today.

John Hagee: The seven seas of the earth will be turned into blood. Every river (and) stream will become as blood. Every basin in your home will run with hot and cold blood. This plague will produce mind–numbing thirst from which there will be no relief.[11]

David Jeremiah with C.C. Carlson: (The two witnesses) will tell men to their faces about their human wickedness; they will stab hearts with warnings of future judgments, even worse than the past. The hatred this pair arouses will be intense.[12]

plagues: afflictions or calamities that are sometimes viewed as an act of God

KEY Symbols:

Two Witnesses
> power to shut up the sky so that it will not rain
>
> power to turn the waters into blood
>
> power to strike the earth with every kind of plague

What Others are Saying:

Something to Ponder

Do You Want to be Around?

First Trumpet:	1/3 of trees and grass will burn up
Second Trumpet:	1/3 of sea will become blood
Third Trumpet:	1/3 of fresh water will be polluted
Fourth Trumpet:	1/3 of sunlight and moonlight will be diminished
Fifth Trumpet:	a plague of demon locusts will infest the land
Sixth Trumpet:	war will ravage the nations

> **Revelation 11:7** Now when they have finished their testimony, the beast that comes up from the Abyss will attack them, and overpower and kill them.

☞ **GO TO:**

Revelation 13:1 (Antichrist)

Revelation 13:11 (False Prophet)

beast: in Revelation a beast is a person who is full of evil

KEY Symbols:

First Beast

ANTICHRIST

Second Beast

FALSE PROPHET

☞ **GO TO:**

Isaiah 1:1–10 (days of Isaiah)

Ezekiel 16:1–62 (days of Ezekiel)

Exodus 32 (calf)

Isaiah 1:11–17 (not what God wanted)

The Beasts

The two witnesses will be supernaturally protected. Nothing will harm them. However, when they have finished their assignment of providing light to a dark and evil world, they will be killed.

Revelation mentions two **beasts**: the _Antichrist_ and the _False Prophet_. The Antichrist will hate the Two Witnesses. He will fail to cope with their condemnation of his world government, religion, social principles, and economic system, and will be infuriated when he hears them preaching about Jesus. He will be jealous of their number of converts, so he will throw all the power of his Satanic government into an attack against them. The witnesses will be overpowered and killed.

> **Revelation 11:8** Their bodies will lie in the street of the great city, which is figuratively called Sodom and Egypt, where also their Lord was crucified.

Not Even A Burial Plot

Several cities are called "great cities" in the Bible. This great city, however, is clearly identified as the city where the Lord was crucified, which can only be Jerusalem.

In the days of Isaiah, Jerusalem was a wicked place. Things were so bad that Isaiah compared Jerusalem to the cities of Sodom and Gomorrah. That was strong language, considering God destroyed those cities with fire and brimstone.

In the days of Ezekiel, Jerusalem played the harlot and chased after idols and false gods. God said they acquired their adulterous and idolatrous ways in Egypt. Remember the golden calf the Israelites built on their way from Egypt to the promised land.

In Christ's day, Jerusalem was full of sin again. The leaders falsely accused him; tried him; and had him beaten and crucified. They offered daily sacrifices at the Temple that were not what God wanted.

Jerusalem will be full of sin again in the Tribulation Period. It will become even more sinful after the Temple is rebuilt. Worship of the Antichrist will flourish while worship of Jesus will be condemned. God's two witnesses will be killed in Jerusalem and no one will bother to bury them.

> **Revelation 11:9** For three and a half days men from every people, tribe, language and nation will gaze on their bodies and refuse them burial.

Seen By The Whole World

The dead bodies of the witnesses will lie in the street for three and a half days. The whole world will see they are dead. No one will accept their remains. Multitudes from every people, tribe, and nation will see their corpses and refuse them burial.

What Others are Saying:

Ed Hindson: We are living in the most incredible times the world has ever known. Live reports via satellite beam the latest events from around the globe into our living rooms every day. This technology has allowed us, for the first time in human history to actually watch developments of great significance as they unfold.[13]

John Hagee: Prophecy states that the whole world will, at the same time, be able to see the two witnesses in the streets of Jerusalem. My father's generation could not explain that. How could the whole world see two dead men lying in the streets of Jerusalem at one time? It was a mystery. Then came television, followed by international satellites, the Internet, and wireless communication.[14]

☞ **GO TO:**

Matthew 2:1–12 (wise men)

> **Revelation 11:10** The inhabitants of the earth will gloat over them and will celebrate by sending each other gifts, because these two prophets had tormented those who live on the earth.

Antichristmas

When Jesus was born, <u>wise men</u> traveled from the East to see him. When they arrived, they fell down and worshiped him with great joy, and presented him with extravagant gifts. We, too, celebrate the birth of Jesus by worshiping him and exchanging gifts at Christmas.

When the bodies of the two witnesses are lying in the street, the inhabitants of the earth will gloat. They will be proud of their Antichrist, proud they are following him, and proud of his great power because no one else could harm the two witnesses. They will praise his victory, worship him, and exchange gifts. The celebration will be like an Antichrist Christmas. Call it the first "Antichristmas."

> **Revelation 11:11** But after the three and a half days a breath of life from God entered them, and they stood on their feet, and terror struck those who saw them.

Let There Be Life

This incredible scene is beyond human comprehension: The two witnesses will be killed. Television cameras (or something similar) will broadcast pictures of their bodies lying in the street around the world. No one will move them. The cameras will remain focused on the corpses while the whole world begins to celebrate. Food will probably be scarce, but parties will abound. Festivities will continue for three days or more. Then God will suddenly step in. He will breathe life into the two witnesses, causing them to move. The partying will stop; the revelry will end. The whole world will watch in terror as the two witnesses stand to their feet.

What Others are Saying:

J. Vernon McGee: While the world is celebrating in jubilation the death of these witnesses and while the television cameras are focused upon them, the witnesses will stand on their feet. All of the networks will regret that they had their cameras pointed to (the witnesses), because (the networks) will not really want to give the news as it is.[15]

> **Revelation 11:12** Then they heard a loud voice from heaven saying to them, "Come up here." And they went up to heaven in a cloud, while their enemies looked on.

☞ **GO TO:**

Acts 1:9 (ascension)

Matthew 28:12, 13; I Corinthians 15:12 (unbelievers)

Revelation 4:1 (come)

Believe What You See

Following the death, burial, and resurrection of Jesus, skeptics tried to explain away his resurrection by blaming his disciples for carrying out an elaborate hoax. However, the world will not be able to claim a hoax when the two witnesses rise from the dead and disappear into heaven. Everyone will know they died because their bodies will lie in the street for three and a half days. Everyone will also know the witnesses were raised from the dead when they stood up.

Then, while some are wondering what to do, a great voice from heaven will call the two witnesses to heaven. None of their enemies will be able to harm them as they disappear into heaven in a cloud. They will only be able to look on in amazement.

When Jesus ascended into heaven, many did not believe. When the Church is raptured, the world will not believe. Excuses will abound to save people from the harsh reality of the truth. But when the two witnesses ascend to heaven many will change their mind about Jesus and the Rapture.

What Others are Saying:

David Jeremiah with C.C. Carlson: Meanwhile, back in the executive suite, the Beast (Antichrist) will attempt to explain the (resurrection) of the prisoners he killed, but he will not be able to duplicate this miracle.[16]

Remember This . . .

When John went up to heaven, he also heard a voice say, *Come up here*.

> **Revelation 11:13** At that very hour there was a severe earthquake and a tenth of the city collapsed. Seven thousand people were killed in the earthquake, and the survivors were terrified and gave glory to the God of heaven.

Finally Some Will Believe

When the two witnesses stand to their feet, panic will spread around the world. Then as people are wondering what will happen next, the two witnesses will ascend to heaven. They will still be staring at the sky when the ground will begin to shake. Ten percent of the buildings in Jerusalem will collapse, killing seven thousand people. The fear of God will enter the hearts of the survivors. Many will change their minds about the two witnesses, praise the God of heaven, and begin a Jewish revival.

RELATED CURRENT EVENTS

Over ninety major earthquakes have taken place in Israel in the last 2,000 years, with an average of 27 years between each. In this century alone, over 1,000 earthquakes of all measurable intensities have been recorded. Scientists predict another major earthquake in Israel but they are not prepared to say whether it will be next week, or next century. Complete buildings, including the Dome of the Rock in 1546, and even whole cities (Safed in 1837) were totally destroyed in past centuries.[17]

Something to Ponder

- When Jesus died, the earth shook (Matthew 27:51, 52).
- When Jesus arose, there was a violent earthquake (Matthew 28:2).

> **Revelation 11:14** The second woe has passed; the third woe is coming soon.

Strike Two!

This earthquake in Jerusalem will mark the end of the second woe or the sixth trumpet. The seventh trumpet will sound soon and bring the third woe.

> **Revelation 11:15** The seventh angel sounded his trumpet, and there were loud voices in heaven, which said: "The kingdom of the world has become the kingdom of our Lord and of his Christ, and he will reign for ever and ever."

KEY Symbols:

Seventh Trumpet
a heavenly declaration of praise

The Seventh Trumpet

When the seventh trumpet sounds there will be a heavenly declaration that God and his Son, Jesus, will be taking over. The Apostle Paul talked about this when he said, *the end will come, when he (Jesus) hands over the kingdom to God the Father after he has destroyed all dominion, authority, and power* (I Corinthians 15:24).

Satan is the head of those dominions, authorities, and powers. They are organized and influence the nations to do evil. However, before the Tribulation Period ends, God and his Son will do away with them.

> **Revelation 11:16, 17** And the twenty-four elders, who were seated on their thrones before God, fell on their faces and worshiped God, saying: "We give thanks to you, Lord God Almighty, the One who is and who was, because you have taken your great power and have begun to reign.

Fall On Your Knees

The announcement that God and Jesus will be taking over will cause a tremendous reaction in heaven. The Church will fall down on their faces and worship God. They will thank him because he is alive and will be exercising his great power by starting his earthly reign.

From this point on Satan's days will be drawing quickly to a close. Jesus will begin to exercise the <u>authority over nations</u> that became his when he died on the cross. He will go forth to <u>conquer the forces of evil</u> and usher in the Millennium.

The <u>twenty-four elders</u> represent the Church from Pentecost to the Rapture.

> **Revelation 11:18** The nations were angry; and your wrath has come. The time has come for judging the dead, and for rewarding your servants the prophets and your saints and those who reverence your name, both small and great—and for destroying those who destroy the earth."

The Time Has Come

Satan will know his day will soon end, so he will stir the anger of the nations. At the same time he does that, God's wrath will burn brighter, which will put Satan and Jesus on a collision course.

☞ GO TO:

Psalm 2:9; Revelation 2:27; 12:5 (authority)

Psalm 37:9–17 (evil)

Revelation 4:4, 5 (twenty-four elders)

KEY Symbols:

Seventh Trumpet
the Church gives thanks

Remember This . . .

Battle of Armageddon:
the last and greatest war before the Millennium

KEY POINT

The righteous will be rewarded for reverencing the name of Jesus, and the wicked will be destroyed for their sin.

Satan will unite the nations against Jesus. The ensuing conflict is referred to as the **Battle of Armageddon**.

Everyone is accountable to God. No one will escape his judgment. Even the dead will be judged. But the righteous will be rewarded for reverencing the name of Jesus, and the wicked will be destroyed for their unrepented sin.

☞ **GO TO:**

Hebrews 8:1–5 (temple)

Exodus 25–27 (Moses)

Leviticus 16:15 KJV (mercy seat)

Exodus 25:10–22 (Ark)

> **Revelation 11:19** Then God's temple in heaven was opened, and within his temple was seen the ark of his covenant. And there came flashes of lightning, rumblings, peals of thunder, an earthquake, and a great hailstorm.

Mercy

Following the heavenly worship service (described in the three preceding verses), when the elders declare that Satan will stir the nations against God's people, God will open his <u>heavenly temple</u>. He has a temple similar to the <u>tabernacle Moses</u> constructed in the wilderness.

Gods' heavenly temple houses the Ark of the Covenant. The <u>mercy seat</u> rests on top of the Ark where the blood of sacrificial goats was sprinkled for the sins of God's people. The Ark, with its mercy seat, will be a reminder that God has always shown mercy to his people.

Satan will stir the nations against Israel. The lightening, rumbling, thunder, earthquakes, and hailstorms will be signs of God's wrath to come, but God will show mercy by protecting Israel.

Remember This . . .

The <u>Ark of the Covenant</u> (see Illustration #6, page 167) was a rectangular shaped box made of acacia wood and overlaid with gold. It had two rings on each side so that staves could be inserted to carry it. It had a gold lid on top called the mercy seat. On the gold lid were two cherubim with their wings spread over the mercy seat and looking down at the box which contained the earthly presence of God. The Ark was kept in the Holy of Holies inside the Temple. The High Priest would go in there, pour blood of sacrificial animals on the mercy seat as an atonement for sin, and God would communicate with him. The Ark was a symbol of God's presence with his people, his protection of them, his mercy, and his forgiveness.

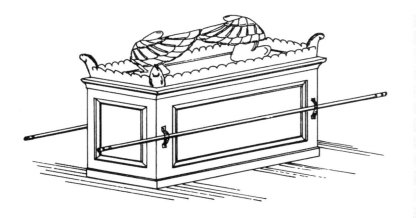

Study Questions

1. Why will God tell John not to measure the outer court of the temple?
2. What symbols will be used to represent the two witnesses? What do they symbolize?
3. Why will God figuratively refer to Jerusalem as Sodom and Egypt?
4. What will cause the world to rejoice during the Tribulation Period?
5. What are the similar patterns of events God uses to prove his authority?

CHAPTER WRAP-UP

- God will empower his two witnesses to prophesy for 1,260 days during which time they will be able to smite the earth with plagues and consume their enemies with fire. (Revelation 11:3–6)

- After prophesying for 1,260 days the two witnesses will be killed by the Antichrist in Jerusalem. Their bodies will lie in the street while unbelievers celebrate. (Revelation 11:7–10)

- Three and a half days after the witnesses are killed God will resurrect them, call them home to heaven, and destroy a tenth of Jerusalem with an earthquake. (Revelation 11:11–13)

- A heavenly declaration proclaiming that Jesus will soon start his earthly reign will follow the seventh trumpet blast. (Revelation 11:15)

- God will open his heavenly temple revealing the Ark of the Covenant which serves as a reminder that he has always shown Israel mercy. (Revelation 11:19)

REVELATION 12

CHAPTER HIGHLIGHTS

- The Woman
- A Red Dragon
- War in Heaven
- Satan's Army
- Earth's Mouth

Let's Get Started

At the close of Chapter 10, we learned that John was told to prophesy about many peoples, nations, languages, and kings. Chapter 11 began this prophecy which now continues into Chapter 12. Here we will learn more about Israel, Jesus, Satan, the archangel Michael, and the inhabitants of the earth.

> **Revelation 12:1** A great and wondrous sign appeared in heaven: a woman clothed with the sun, with the moon under her feet and a crown of twelve stars on her head.

The First Great Sign From Heaven

The symbols in this first **sign** take us back to the Old Testament to one of the <u>dreams</u> of <u>Joseph</u>. Joseph's father, a man named Jacob, interpreted the dream like this: the sun represented himself (Jacob, whose name was later changed to Israel), the moon represented his wife (whose name was Rachel), and the crown of twelve stars represented their twelve children (the twelve tribes of Israel). This family was the beginning of the nation of Israel.

Notice that the three symbols in Joseph's dream (the sun, moon, and twelve stars) are all associated with this woman in Chapter 12. She is clothed with the sun (a symbol of Israel), has the moon (a symbol of Rachel) under her feet, and has a crown of twelve stars (a symbol of the twelve tribes of Israel) on her head. This woman represents the nation of Israel at its beginning.

☞ GO TO:

Genesis 37:9–11 (dreams)

Genesis 30:22–24; 37:3, 4 (Joseph)

sign: a symbol for something else

KEY Symbols:

First Sign in Heaven— a Woman

ISRAEL

clothed with the sun
- Jacob
- Israel

the moon under feet
- Rachel
- Israel's wife
- a crown of twelve stars on her head
- Jacob's twelve sons Israel's twelve tribes

Harper's Bible Dictionary: Historians see in Jacob, who was renamed "Israel" after his experience wrestling with an angel (Genesis 32:28; 35:10), the personification of the national Israel.[1]

Charles H. Dyer: In the Apostle John's vision the woman clothed with the sun, the moon, and the twelve stars represents the nation of Israel.[2]

travail: *groans, pain, and suffering*

seed of Israel: *the descendants of Israel*

KEY Symbols:

A Woman
   pregnant in pain
   captive Israel before
   Christ

> **Revelation 12:2** She was pregnant and cried out in pain as she was about to give birth.

A Nation In Travail

Verse 5 of this chapter tells us that Israel is pregnant with *a male child, who will rule all the nations.* Her pregnancy is a reference to her condition just before the birth of Jesus. John says she cried out in pain as she was about to give birth.

Before Christ's birth, Israel was a captive nation to the Roman Empire. She had to submit to Roman leaders, pay Roman taxes, and obey Roman laws. She was a nation in **travail**.

Ed Hindson: The woman, then, has to symbolize Israel because Christ was born of the **seed of Israel**.[3]

☞ GO TO:

John 8:44 (killed)

Revelation 17:10 (heads)

Revelation 17:12 (horns)

Daniel 7:8, 24 (three)

divisions: *groups of nations*

KEY Symbols:

Second Sign In Heaven—
   Red Dragon

SATAN

   enormous
   ▪ great power

> **Revelation 12:3** Then another sign appeared in heaven: an enormous red dragon with seven heads and ten horns and seven crowns on his heads.

The Second Great Sign From Heaven

The first sign in heaven was a sun-clothed woman (the nation of Israel). The second sign in heaven is an enormous red dragon (Satan) that is explained further in Revelation 12:9. He is enormous because of his great power; red, since he has <u>killed multitudes</u>; and a dragon due to his fierce nature.

This fierce, powerful, murderous dragon will appear in heaven with <u>seven heads</u> (symbols of world governments), <u>ten horns</u> (symbols of powerful kings), and seven crowns (symbols of the seven **divisions** controlled by the ten powerful kings).

The dragon will have seven heads symbolizing the seven Gentile world governments that Satan has led since the beginning of creation. It will also have ten horns, symbolizing the ten kings that will reign with him during the entire Tribulation Period. The Bible teaches that these ten kings will rise to power, and that the Antichrist will come on the scene in a unified Europe (The European Community). The <u>Antichrist will subdue three</u> of those ten kings so that their power will ultimately be concentrated into seven crowns (or seven divisions) of the last world government.

This must not be taken lightly. A one-world government empowered and controlled by Satan is a terrible thought. Some say it will make what Adolf Hitler did during WWII look like a Sunday picnic.

red
- the blood of multitudes

dragon
- fierce nature

seven heads
- seven gov'ts

ten horns
- ten powerful kings

seven crowns
- seven divisions

Hal Lindsey: The seven Gentile world governments are:

1) Assyrian
2) Egyptian
3) Babylonian
4) Medo-Persian
5) Greek
6) Roman
7) The current European Community (Revived Roman Empire)[4]

What Others are Saying:

> **Revelation 12:4** His tail swept a third of the stars out of the sky and flung them to the earth. The dragon stood in front of the woman who was about to give birth, so that he might devour her child the moment it was born.

Falling Stars

Stars are symbols of angels. The fact that Satan swept a third of the stars out of the sky means that he caused one-third of the <u>angels to fall</u>. Satan's mutiny was a tremendous rebellion involving millions of angels.

Satan has tried to destroy Jesus (or at least Jesus' mission of dying on the cross) many times while Jesus was on earth:

1) Satan waited for the birth of Jesus because he <u>wanted to destroy Jesus</u>. When Jesus was born, he stirred the wrath of Herod, King of Judea, to have all the male babies in and around Bethlehem killed. God, however, sent an angel to warn Jesus' father, Joseph, to take Mary and flee with Jesus to Egypt.

2) At the beginning of Christ's ministry Satan offered Jesus the <u>kingdoms of the world</u> if he would bow down and worship Satan.

☞ **GO TO:**

Daniel 8:10; II Peter 2:4; Jude 1:6 (angels)

Matthew 2:13–18 (Jesus)

Matthew 4:8, 9 (kingdoms)

Luke 22:39–46 (Mount of Olives)

KEY POINT

Many times Satan tried to devour the Messiah—but to no avail.

KEY Symbols:

Red Dragon

SATAN

tail swept a third of the stars (angels) out of the sky

wants to devour the child (Jesus)

3) Later, when Jesus told his disciples he would die, Peter disagreed and Jesus answered, *Get behind me, Satan* (Matthew 16:23). Satan was working through Peter to tempt Jesus to by-pass the cross.

4) Before Jesus was crucified he went to the <u>Mount of Olives</u> to pray. There Satan came against him with such power that God sent an angel to strengthen him. Jesus was put under such agony and temptation that he sweat drops of blood, but he still prevailed.

5) When Jesus was hanging on the cross the chief priests, scribes, and elders mocked him saying, *Let him come down now from the cross, and we will believe in him. He trusts in God. Let God rescue him now if he wants him* (Matthew 27:42, 43). Satan was doing everything he could to keep Jesus from dying on the cross.

6) Satan even used the thieves who were crucified with Jesus. *In the same way* (with insults and taunting) *the robbers who were crucified with him also heaped insults on him* (Matthew 27:44).

What Others are Saying:

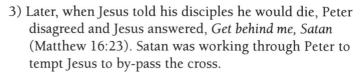

Remember This . . .

☞ **GO TO:**

Psalm 2:2–9 (Anointed One)

Revelation 19:15, 16 (Lord of lords)

Acts 1:9 (ascension)

Luke 23:26–24:12 (resurrection)

iron scepter: *a rod or staff a ruler carries to demonstrate his authority*

Charles H. Dyer: Satan tried to short-circuit God's plans for the earth by eliminating God's Messiah.[5]

The <u>seven stars</u> are angels.

> **Revelation 12:5** She gave birth to a son, a male child, who will rule all the nations with an iron scepter. And her child was snatched up to God and to his throne.

Snatched Up

The woman will give birth to a son who will rule all the nations with an **iron scepter**. The second Psalm identifies the one who will do this as God's <u>Anointed One</u> (Jesus). Chapter 19 calls him the King of kings and <u>Lord of lords</u>.

Her (Israel's) *child was snatched up to God* is a reference to the <u>ascension of Jesus</u>. He ascended to heaven following his <u>death and resurrection</u>.

Notice that Jesus will not rule the nations with love but with an iron scepter. The world is full of people who are in rebellion against God because they follow false teachings or religions (i.e. atheists, communists, Moslems). However, when Christ returns he will crush these rebellions with an iron scepter.

David Jeremiah with C.C. Carlson: The identification of the child could not be clearer, even in symbolic terms. Christ was born, he was resurrected, and when he comes again he will rule the nations with a rod of iron.[6]

John saw a Lamb (Jesus), looking as if it had been slain, standing in the center of God's throne (Revelation 5:6).

> **Revelation 12:6** The woman fled into the desert to a place prepared for her by God, where she might be taken care of for 1,260 days.

Flee Away

We are now at the midpoint of the seven year Tribulation Period. 1,260 days (three and one half years) have past. Now there are 1,260 more days before Christ's Second Coming.

Jesus taught that the <u>Temple would be defiled</u> by an image of the Antichrist at the Tribulation Period midpoint. He told those who live in Judea to <u>flee into the mountains</u> when that happens.

Where will they go? The woman (Israel) will flee into the desert to a place prepared for her by God. Most prophecy experts believe the Jews will flee to a mountainous area in the Jordan desert called Petra. It is an abandoned city that was carved into the rocks of the mountains centuries ago. It has only one entrance, so the Jews will be able to hide in those caves and barricade themselves in for protection. They will hide there for 1,260 days (three and one half years), the last half of the Tribulation Period.

Recently, Israel's (former) Prime Minister Yitzhak Rabin toured Petra with his wife, children, and grandchildren. According to reports in *The Jerusalem Post* (May 13, 1995), Rabin expressed awe at the beauty of the site saying it was "indescribable." His wife's most notable comment was her surprise at the size of the city.[7]

—— —— ——

Jordan now allows 1,400 (Jewish tourists) a day to enter the country and this has increased the number of visitors daily going into Petra. Also, according to a news item on page 24 of the October 28, 1995,

Remember This . . .

☞ **GO TO:**

Matthew 24:15 (Temple defiled)

Matthew 24:16 (flee)

KEY Symbols:

The Woman
a male child (Jesus)
rules with an iron scepter
snatched up to God and his throne

RELATED CURRENT EVENTS

Jerusalem Post, the Jews will soon be allowed to drive their own cars and busses into Jordan and right up to El Ciq, the narrow entrance to Petra.[8]

The ancient city of Petra (see Illustration #7, this page) lies in a mountainous area about 20 miles south of the Dead Sea in the country of Jordan. These white and red sandstone mountains are simply a great volcanic crater where the Edomites lived about 500 B.C. These people carved temples, houses, and businesses directly out of the rock face. The name Petra means "the rock" and the city is often called the "Rose Red City" because of its red stone buildings and the red cliffs they are cut out of. The city was long deserted and is still difficult to reach because of the narrow passages that serve as the only entrances. Due to the narrow passages it would be easy for a small force to defend the city against a larger army.

Illustration #7

Petra—Was hidden at the end of a mile-long, 1,000 foot-deep gorge. As you entered the city, through this corridor, you could see the columns of rose-red sandstone cut into the cliff.

> **Revelation 12:7** And there was war in heaven. Michael and his angels fought against the dragon, and the dragon and his angels fought back.

 **GO TO:**

Daniel 12:1 (Michael)

Charge!

As soon as Israel flees, a great war will erupt in heaven. God's angels will be led by the archangel <u>Michael</u> in the fight against Satan and his angels. It will be a fierce spiritual battle, since the last thing Satan wants is to be cast out of heaven again.

 **KEY Symbols:**

Michael
God's head archangel in battle

Charles H. Dyer: These spiritual beings fall into two classes—angels and demons. Angels are those beings who, after their creation, remained true to God. Demons are spirit beings who were created perfect but who chose to rebel against their Creator.[9]

 **What Others are Saying:**

Some of Satan's Names are:

- the prince (Matthew 9:34)
- the prince of this world (John 12:31)
- the prince of the powers of the air (Ephesians 2:2 KJV)
- the god of this world (II Corinthians 4:4 KJV)

Remember This . . .

> **Revelation 12:8** But he was not strong enough, and they lost their place in heaven.

Banished Forever

Satan and his angels will fight to no avail. They will lose their place in heaven forever.

John Hagee: At the midpoint of the Tribulation, the Antichrist makes his play to control the earth. Simultaneously, Satan makes his play to control heaven. But while the Antichrist appears to be successful at first, Satan's all-out war against the archangel Michael for control of heaven results not only in a stunning defeat, but in banishment from heaven as well.[10]

 **What Others are Saying:**

> **Revelation 12:9** The great dragon was hurled down—that ancient serpent called the devil, or Satan, who leads the whole world astray. He was hurled to the earth, and his angels with him.

Bittersweet

There is no mistaking that the great dragon is Satan. He is also called that old serpent and the devil. This verse is bittersweet: *Bitter* because Satan and his demon angels will thrown down to earth. *Sweet* because Satan and his angels will lose the war in heaven.

What Others are Saying:

Tim LaHaye: Today the world is prepared for a one-world governmental philosophy. That philosophy, **propagated by Satan** and advocated by the intellectual, godless, **atheistic** leading of world governments today, is rapidly spreading across the world.[11]

John Hagee: Not powerful enough to prevail in heaven, Satan lashes out on the earth against everything God holds dear.[12]

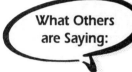

Something to Ponder

Satan has always persecuted God's people. He especially hates the Jews because Jesus was a Jew. He and his demons will come to the earth with great wrath, but God will have Israel flee into the mountainous desert before they arrive.

Examples of Jewish Persecution:

1) The Holocaust
2) Special taxes were imposed on them by Europeans during the Middle Ages
3) They were placed in ghettos during the Middle Ages in Europe
4) They were driven out of Spain in 1492
5) In the 1800's Poland and Russia killed them in massacres called pogroms

☞ **GO TO:**

I John 2:1 (defending)

> **Revelation 12:10** Then I heard a loud voice in heaven say: "Now have come the salvation and the power and the kingdom of our God, and the authority of his Christ. For the accuser of our brothers, who accuses them before our God day and night, has been hurled down.

For The Defense

When Satan is cast out, heaven will rejoice because: 1) our salvation will be complete and Satan will be banished from our presence forever; 2) all power will belong to Jesus, and there will be no more evil (Satan) in heaven; 3) the kingdom of God will come to earth; and 4) Jesus will finally exercise the authority over earth that he won at the cross.

Today, Satan is the accuser of believers. He parades before the throne of God day and night pointing out the sins of God's people. Jesus, too, is there—defending us. But his defense will end when Satan is cast out of heaven. Satan will never accuse us again.

> **Revelation 12:11** They overcame him by the blood of the Lamb and by the word of their testimony; they did not love their lives so much as to shrink from death.

We Have The Power

Believers will have the power to overcome Satan during the Tribulation Period by: 1) trusting in the blood of the Lamb, because through the blood, atonement was made for our sins; 2) testifying to our faith, because if we acknowledge Jesus before men, he will acknowledge us before God; and 3) not fearing death, because a physical death is far better than being cast into hell.

> **Revelation 12:12** Therefore rejoice, you heavens and you who dwell in them! But woe to the earth and the sea, because the devil has gone down to you! He is filled with fury, because he knows that his time is short."

The Seventh Trumpet—The Third Woe

Heaven will celebrate its great triumph after Satan and his angels have been cast out. But watch out earth and sea. Satan and his demons are on their way filled with fury, knowing that their days are numbered.

When Satan is cast out of heaven, Jesus will exercise his authority over the earth. He will declare that the Kingdom of God will come to earth. Because of this, Satan will do all the damage he can with the time he has left.

KEY Symbols:

Red Dragon
SATAN

hurled down from heaven

☞ **GO TO:**

Matthew 10:32 (acknowledge)

KEY POINT

Trust in the sacrifice of Jesus. Express your faith, and do not fear.

KEY Symbols:

Seventh Trumpet
THIRD WOE

Satan is on his way

Remember This . . .

☞ **GO TO:**

Matthew 24:17–22
(flee)

☞ **GO TO:**

Exodus 19:4 (eagles'
wings)

Deuteronomy 32:11,
12 (escaped)

Exodus 16:13–15
(manna and quail)

Exodus 15:22–27;
Exodus 17:1–7
(water)

Deuteronomy 29:5
(wear out)

Jeremiah 30:7 (Jacob's
trouble)

Jacob's trouble: *another
name for the Tribulation
Period*

KEY Symbols:

The Woman
*given two wings of a
great eagle*

> **Revelation 12:13** When the dragon saw that he had
> been hurled to the earth, he pursued the woman who
> had given birth to the male child.

Flee

Israel will <u>flee</u> when Satan is cast down to the earth, because his
rage will burn against the nation of Israel for bringing forth Jesus.
The quicker the Jews escape the better.

> **Revelation 12:14** The woman was given the two wings
> of a great eagle, so that she might fly to the place pre-
> pared for her in the desert, where she would be taken
> care of for a time, times and half a time, out of the
> serpent's reach.

The Wings Of An Eagle

Israel will escape Satan's grasp on the *wings of a great eagle*. Some
believe the United States is the wings of a great eagle. They believe she will rapidly airlift the Jews to safety. This is probably not
the case.

By letting Scripture be our guide, we learn that God says he
brought Israel out of Egypt on <u>eagles' wings</u>. The Jews interpret
this to mean they <u>escaped by the grace of God</u> because they could
not deliver themselves. This is most likely the way it will happen
during the Tribulation Period. God will intervene to help them
escape.

Notice that Israel will flee to *the place prepared for her*. God
knows everything. He knows what Satan will try to do to Israel
during the Tribulation Period, so he has already devised an escape route to safety. God will prepare this place of safety, so it will
be ready when needed.

When Israel arrives, God will take care of her. He will supernaturally provide food, water, clothing, protection, and anything
else she needs. It will be like it was during the days of Moses
when they were wandering in the wilderness. God fed them <u>manna
and quail</u>, <u>provided water</u>, and did not allow their <u>clothes or san-
dals to wear out</u>.

This will go on for three and one half years. It is the meaning of
a time, times and half a time. God will sustain this remnant of
Israel in her special place for the entire second half of the Tribulation Period.

Noah Hutchings: As we (Hutchings and other tourists) were walking into Petra we observed a new, wide road being constructed right up the Ciq entrance. The article (p. 24 *The Jerusalem Post* Oct. 28, 1995) also indicates that a new wide bridge will be constructed at the Allenby checkpoint. Our Jordanian guide also pointed out plans for utility improvements. Another item of information of great interest was that this next year (1996) Petra will come under United Nations supervision as the United Nations Educational, Scientific, and Cultural Organization (UNESCO) has invested millions in excavation and improvement projects.[13]

J. Vernon McGee: This is the Time of **Jacob's Trouble**, and this is the reason I cannot rejoice in the present return of Israel to that land. Some people seem to think they are going back for the Millennium. They are not—they are going back for the Great Tribulation Period if they are going back for any purpose at all, according to the Word of God.[14]

Even in Biblical Times Efforts to Eliminate the Jews Failed:

1) The king of Egypt could not diminish the Jews (Exodus 1:9–12).

2) The Egyptian army could not recapture them (Exodus 14:13–31).

3) Balaam could not curse them (Numbers 23:7, 8).

4) The nations of the world could not assimilate or destroy them (Esther 3:8–9:17).

5) The dictators of the nations cannot annihilate them (Isaiah 14:1–5; Zechariah 8:22, 23).[15]

> **Revelation 12:15** Then from his mouth the serpent spewed water like a river, to overtake the woman and sweep her away with the torrent.

Like A Flood

In the Old Testament, God used the flood waters of a river as a symbol to represent an attack by the <u>King of Assyria</u> on Judah. The <u>flood waters</u> represented enemy troops pouring into the tiny nation.

This verse uses that same type of symbolism. When Satan sees Israel fleeing into the wilderness, he will probably speak through

What Others are Saying:

Remember This . . .

☞ **GO TO:**

Isaiah 8:7, 8 (Assyria)

Jeremiah 46:7, 8; Jeremiah 46:13–47:3 (flood)

KEY Symbols:

Red Dragon

SATAN

spewed water like a river

the Antichrist or his False Prophet, using their mouths to incite an attack on the terrified Jewish people. It will be his intent to pour many troops into the wilderness, and drown the woman (Israel) with an overwhelming force.

David Jeremiah with C.C. Carlson: The Antichrist, indwelt by Satan, is going to be furious that the believers have escaped his grasp, so he will send his henchmen after them like a flood.[16]

KEY Symbols:

Earth
opened its mouth (an earthquake) and swallowed the river

> **Revelation 12:16** But the earth helped the woman by opening its mouth and swallowing the river that the dragon had spewed out of his mouth.

Into The Pit

God will intervene. A supernatural catastrophe will befall Satan's pursuing army. The earth opening its mouth probably symbolizes another great earthquake with the earth splitting open. Satan's troops will suddenly drop into the pit.

This is why the Jews should not go back after anything when they see the Antichrist defile the Temple. Instead they should escape the enemy troops and stay ahead of the great earthquake.

> **Revelation 12:17** Then the dragon was enraged at the woman and went off to make war against the rest of her offspring—those who obey God's commandments and hold to the testimony of Jesus.

Pick Your Target

The escape of Israel will infuriate Satan. Since he failed to wipe out Israel, he will pick another target—those *who obey God's commandments and hold to the testimony of Jesus.*

Notice two things:

1) we have now started reading about things that will happen during the second half of the Tribulation Period, and

2) there will be Gentile believers on earth at that time. Israel's offspring is a reference to Gentile believers. Satan will go on a rampage against God's people in the second half of the Tribulation Period. He will do everything he can to destroy the elect.

Study Questions

1. What are the two signs in heaven and what do they represent?
2. What is the meaning of the number 1,260 and what will happen now?
3. Who is the angel that will cast Satan out of heaven?
4. Where will Satan go when he is cast out of heaven? Why will he be so angry?
5. What powers do believers have for overcoming Satan?

CHAPTER WRAP-UP

- Israel, represented as a woman clothed with the sun, is the first sign in heaven. She is pregnant with a child. (Revelation 12:1, 2)

- A great red dragon, symbolic of Satan, is the second sign in heaven. He will cause a third of the angels to fall to earth due to rebellion. (Revelation 12:3, 4)

- Satan will war against God in heaven, but God's angel will overpower him, expel him, and throw him to earth. (Revelation 12:7–9)

- After Satan's heavenly defeat he will try to attack God's people on earth, so he will send an army to drown them. (Revelation 12:15)

- The earth, however, will help God's people by swallowing these troops in an earthquake. (Revelation 12:16, 17)

REVELATION 13

CHAPTER HIGHLIGHTS

- Antichrist
- A Fatal Wound
- False Prophet
- Image of the Beast
- Mark of the Beast

Let's Get Started

At the close of Chapter 10 John was told to eat the little book and to prophesy *about many peoples, nations, languages, and kings.* In Chapter 11 John wrote about the rebuilding of the Temple, the two witnesses, and the impact they will have on the world. In Chapter 12 he wrote about Satan being cast out of heaven, and how it will affect Israel and the other believers in the world. Now in Chapter 13 John will tell us about the two powerhouses of the Tribulation Period—the Antichrist (the political powerhouse) and the False Prophet (the religious powerhouse). These two end-time dictators will merge church and state. The results will be disastrous.

> **Revelation 13:1** And the dragon stood on the shore of the sea. And I saw a beast coming out of the sea. He had ten horns and seven heads, with ten crowns on his horns, and on each head a blasphemous name.

The Beast From The Sea

The *dragon*, Satan, will stand on the shore of the masses of humanity in the last days. The *beast*, <u>the Antichrist</u>, will rise up out of this <u>sea of wickedness</u> that will reign when the Church is gone. The *ten horns are ten rulers* who will reign with the Antichrist during the Tribulation Period. The *seven heads* have a double meaning: 1) they are <u>seven world governments</u>, and 2) they are <u>seven hills</u> where the world religion will be located for a short

☞ **GO TO:**

Revelation 12:9 (dragon)

I John 2:18 (Antichrist)

Revelation 17:15; Isaiah 57:20 (sea)

Revelation 17:12 (horns)

Daniel 7:24; Revelation 17:10 (seven gov'ts)

Revelation 17:9, 10 (seven hills)

Revelation 12:3; 17:3 (seven heads)

KEY Symbols:

Beast from the Sea

ANTICHRIST (FIRST BEAST)

sea
- wicked people

seven heads/hills
- seven governments
- seven religions

ten horns
- ten rulers

ten crowns
- ten divisions of seventh world government

time during the Tribulation Period. The *ten crowns* are the ten divisions of the last world government. It will be divided into ten divisions with each division having its own ruler and set of false religions.

According to the Bible, mankind will go through seven heads—the heads of seven world kingdoms or seven world governments. Each of the seven heads will have a **blasphemous** name, because all seven world governments and their corresponding false religions will be noted for their wickedness. The seventh head (seventh world government) will be run by the Antichrist. His world government will be subdivided into ten crowns (ten major divisions) with each division having its own wicked ruler.

Seven Heads/Hills (seven world governments)	**Ten Horns/Crowns** (ten divisions/rulers)
1 **Assyrian**	
2 **Egyptian**	
3 **Babylonian**	
4 **Medo-Persian**	
5 **Greek**	
6 **Roman (Old Roman Empire)**	
7 **Revived Roman Empire** (run by the Antichrist)	1 2 3 4 5 6 7 8 9 10

Jack Van Impe: In man's search for international leadership, there has always been the drive to find the one who is destined to hold it all together. Are people today really ready to accept a "devil" as the new CEO of world affairs?[1]

What Others are Saying:

Grant R. Jeffrey: The Ten Regions (Divisions) of the New World Government:

Region	1	Canada and the United States of America
Region	2	European Union—Western Europe
Region	3	Japan
Region	4	Australia, New Zealand, South Africa, and Pacific Islands
Region	5	Eastern Europe
Region	6	Latin America—Mexico and Central and South America
Region	7	North Africa and Middle East (Moslems)
Region	8	Central Africa
Region	9	South and Southeast Asia
Region	10	Central Asia [2]

Ed Hindson: Most Bible commentators understand the beast of the sea to be the Antichrist. Whether he is a specific person, a political system, or both is a matter of debate. Since he is associated with the same symbol given to Rome (seven heads and ten horns), it is assumed that he represents the revived Roman Empire of the last days. Some people speculate this could be in the process of being formed even now in the European Economic Community (EEC).[3]

WARNING

The prophet Daniel teaches that the Antichrist will come up among the ten horns and uproot three of them (Daniel 7:7, 8, 23–25). There is some debate as to whether the Antichrist is one of the ten or whether he is an eleventh person who arises while the ten are in power. I personally do not think he is one of the ten. I think he rises while they are in power. He takes over the power of one, then a second, a third, and finally the remaining seven give him their power. He is then the head of the world government which started with ten divisions and was whittled down to seven.

I wish I could say what happens to America, but I would only be speculating. All that can be said is that Europe is going to replace America as the dominant power in the world.

☞ **GO TO:**

Ezekiel 38, 39 (invasion)

II Thessalonians 2:9, 10 (Satan)

parrot: mimic

incarnation: the Antichrist will become Satan in the flesh

KEY POINT

The Antichrist will be the incarnation of Satan.

KEY Symbols:

First Beast

ANTICHRIST

resembled a leopard
feet like those of a bear
mouth like that of a lion

> **Revelation 13:2** The beast I saw resembled a leopard, but had feet like those of a bear and a mouth like that of a lion. The dragon gave the beast his power and his throne and great authority.

Three Groups

The word "beast" (see GWDN, page 177) can represent either the Antichrist or his world government. In this verse, it represents his world government. This government will begin as a mixture of three groups of nations.

The Antichrist will have complete control of these groups at the beginning of his reign. He and the group known as the *leopard* will act as one body on all critical issues (Israel, Jesus, believers, etc.). He and the *bear* group will stand for the same things while the *lion* group will **parrot** the Antichrist. The Antichrist's final world government will begin as a composite world government. At the start, three groups of nations will give the Antichrist his strongest support, but eventually his control will encompass the whole world.

In my opinion the interpretation of this beast is as follows:

1) *Resembled a leopard* refers to a future Arab coalition. The Antichrist and a group of Arab nations will act as one body. Leopards are native to Africa, and have been used at various times as a symbol of African nationality.

2) *Feet like those of a bear* refers to Russia and her allies. The Antichrist will be supported by what is left of the Russian Empire (the Russian Bear) following the first <u>Russian invasion of Israel</u>.

3) *A mouth like a lion* refers to England and those nations established out of England. The symbol of England is the lion. The Antichrist, England, and those nations coming out of England will speak with the same voice. They will parrot or mimic each other.

His power, office, and authority will come from Satan. Jesus was the incarnation of God in the world. The Antichrist will be the **incarnation** of Satan. Whoever he is and whatever he does comes from the pits of hell.

Charles H. Dyer: The Bible paints a complex portrait of this individual who will take the world by storm and lead the final rebellion against God.[4]

William S. McBirnie: Is Satan cruel? The Antichrist will be cruel. Is Satan a liar? The Antichrist will be a liar. Is Satan treacherous, blood thirsty, contemptuous, unreliable? The Antichrist will be all that. That's why I'm urging you to go in the Rapture. Don't be on this earth after we Christians leave.[5]

Speaking at Mikhail Gorbachev's "The State of the World Forum" in San Francisco recently, Zbigniew Brzenzinski (a Harvard professor) noted, "We cannot leap into world government in one quick step. . . . In brief, the precondition for eventual globalization—genuine globalization—is progressive regionalization, because thereby we move toward larger, more stable, more cooperative units."[6]

— — —

The Bilderberg (a secretive group of rich and powerful Globalists who influence decisions affecting the whole world) interest in war is to establish a world army to serve under a United Nations world government.[7]

— — —

Our (United States) reduced armed forces are being trained to merge into a United Nations army to help enforce a world government (that is not for the protection of our nation).[8]

— — —

Nobel Prize-winning economist Jan Tinbergen, says, "Mankind's problems can no longer be solved by national governments. What is needed is world government."[9]

RELATED CURRENT EVENTS

☞ **GO TO:**

Revelation 13:12
    (wounded head)

Revelation 13:14
    (sword)

> **Revelation 13:3** One of the heads of the beast seemed to have had a fatal wound, but the fatal wound had been healed. The whole world was astonished and followed the beast.

Up From The Dead

Remember that the heads represent seven world governments. Also understand that the Bible speaks of the Antichrist and his world government interchangeably. The Antichrist will be given so much power that he will be the world government and the world government will be the Antichrist.

This verse tells us that one of the seven heads will seem to have a fatal wound. Other verses of Scripture tell us which head it is and how it will be wounded. The wounded head will be the Antichrist. He will appear to be fatally wounded with a sword. But something amazing will happen. His seemingly fatal wound will be healed. It will appear that the has been killed with a sword and miraculously raised from the dead. Obviously, this is another attempt to copy Jesus and make the world believe the Antichrist can do anything Christ can do.

What Others are Saying:

Hal Lindsey: John says that he saw one of the Beast's heads *as if* it had been killed. When this apparently mortal head wound is somehow miraculously healed by Satan, the whole world will follow after the Beast in amazement.[10]

J. Vernon McGee: There are many who have taken the position that the Beast is actually raised from the dead by Satan. This cannot be because Satan does not have the power to raise the dead; that power has not been given to him. The Lord Jesus Christ is the only one who can raise the dead. . . . I believe the Beast is a man who will exhibit a counterfeit and imitation resurrection. This will be the great delusion, the big lie of the Great Tribulation Period. We are told that God will give them over to believe the big lie (II Thessalonians 2:11) and this is part of the big lie.[11]

John Hagee: Lulled into a sense of complacency by both his arrogance and the ease of his victories, the Antichrist's security breaks down. An assassin will exploit the opportunity and strike a lethal blow to the head of the Antichrist, a wound so grievous that those attending to him might as well take him directly to the coroner, bypassing the hospital and the EMT's altogether—the Antichrist is dead. I believe that upon death he will descend directly into Hades or Sheol—the hellish holding tank where those who have rejected the Messiah wait for their ultimate and irreversible consignment to the eternal lake of fire.[12]

> **Revelation 13:4** Men worshiped the dragon because he had given authority to the beast, and they also worshiped the beast and asked, "Who is like the beast? Who can make war against him?"

How Can They Be So Blind

This will be a pivotal moment for Satan and his Antichrist. Every unbeliever in the world will be amazed. They will believe they have a new superhero. They will be encouraged to exalt him even higher, to follow him even more. At this point, they will be willing to go to war with him, to walk through fire with him, to do whatever he bids.

Satan has <u>always wanted to be worshiped</u>. His pride has been the root of all his problems and what caused removal from heaven in the beginning. This resurrection of the Antichrist will boost Satan's stock and make Satanic worship the worldwide rage. It will dominate the one-world religion. Such blasphemy is hard to imagine, but the **occult** will be in charge of this blind and corrupt world.

The Antichrist will also desire to be worshiped. Satan will have no problem with that since the Antichrist will receive his power from Satan. Those who worship the Antichrist will actually be worshiping Satan.

This adoration will lead to question, "Who is like the Antichrist?" and "Who can defeat him?" They will recall his meteoric rise to power, his great victories in other wars, his overwhelming personality, and of course, his miraculous healing. They will believe this man is invincible. Even the rulers of the other divisions of the world will be impressed and will <u>turn their authority over to him</u>.

Jesus said, *if a blind man leads a blind man, both will fall into a pit* (Matthew 15:14).

☞ **GO TO:**

Isaiah 14:13, 14 (Satan worshiped)

Revelation 17:13 (authority)

occult: anything dealing with the mystic arts like Satanism, black magic, witchcraft, etc.

WARNING

☞ **GO TO:**

Daniel 7:8, 11, 20, 25
(blasphemies)

II Thessalonians 2:4
(calls himself God)

> **Revelation 13:5** The beast was given a mouth to utter proud words and blasphemies and to exercise his authority for forty-two months.

Half Way There

The search for a charismatic world leader will be over. This man will know it all, and his heart will be filled with pride. He will boast of his great achievements, power, and world government. He will make long spell-binding <u>speeches filled with passion and the vilest of blasphemies</u>.

The Tribulation Period will last seven years being divided into two, three and a half year periods. When this miraculous healing occurs, the end of the Tribulation Period will be exactly forty-two months away. It will take place about the time the Antichrist sits in the Temple and <u>declares that he is God</u>.

**What Others
are Saying:**

**Something
to Ponder**

Jack Van Impe: Revelation 13:5–7 makes it even clearer that war with the saints will be rampant, and that power will be given to those who oppose the Church.[13]

Notice the words *gave* and *given* in Chapter 13. Everything the Antichrist does is given to him.

VERSE 2: gave . . . his power . . . his throne
VERSE 4: given authority
VERSE 5: given a mouth
VERSE 14: given power
VERSE 15: given power

> **Revelation 13:6** He opened his mouth to blaspheme God, and to slander his name and his dwelling place and those who live in heaven.

slander: *defame or talk falsely about*

anti-Semitic: *prejudice or hostility against the Jews*

Watch Out If You're For God

Four kinds of blasphemy that will come from the Antichrist: 1) He will blaspheme God. 2) He will **slander** the name of God. 3) He will slander the dwelling place of God (the Church), and 4) He will slander those who live in heaven. He will be anti-God, anti-Church, **anti-Semitic**, anti-anything that has to do with God the Father. The mere mention of things like Jesus, the cross, and redemption will send him into a rage.

According to (Ishmael) Amat, who speaks for (China's) State Security Bureau, missionaries in China will be "criminalized," meaning that any proselytizing, or approaching any Chinese citizen with a religious message outlawed by the state, will result in criminal punishment. Criminal punishment in China means imprisonment or execution.[14]

— — —

In September (1996), the Senate and the House of Representatives adopted resolutions urging the Clinton administration to deal with the issue of global religious persecution, particularly against Christians. But the Clinton administration decided in favor of a broad-based committee approach.[15]

> **Revelation 13:7** He was given power to make war against the saints and to conquer them. And he was given authority over every tribe, people, language, and nation.

Bow Down Or Die

The Tribulation Saints will face the most intense persecution (see GWDN, page 74) the world has ever known. In the short-term, their future will be bleak, but in the long-term, their future will be bright.

Satan will give the Antichrist power to conquer all who turn to God. He will go forth with a vengeance to wipe out all Christians. Multitudes will be slaughtered in his effort to establish a one-world Satanic religion. No place on earth will be safe. The Antichrist will extend his domain to include every tribe, people, and nation on earth. Everyone must submit to him or be killed.

What Others
are Saying:

David Jeremiah with C.C. Carlson: When we talk about the judgment of God upon our sinful, unbelieving world, we may not be popular, but lives will be saved for eternity. . . . As I write this, I long for everyone to give their hearts to Christ now, when it is comparatively easy to be a Christian.[16]

Hal Lindsey: That's why it is so important for everyone who hears these messages now to put their faith in Jesus Christ and accept the gift of forgiveness that he died to make free to us, to invite him into our lives, to accept the gift of pardon, and simply to express to him that you're willing for him to change your life.[17]

Ed Hindson: All resistance to the world system will be crushed by a massive *worldwide persecution*. Men, women, and children will be slaughtered in the name of the World State.[18]

**Remember
This . . .**

A parallel of the Antichrist can be found in the Book of Daniel 3:1–30:

> As the head of a world kingdom, King Nebuchadnezzar was like the Antichrist in at least two ways: 1) he was given authority over every tribe, people, language, and nation, and 2) he built a great image and ordered people to worship it. People from all over the world obeyed the command except for three Jews—Shadrach, Meshach, and Abednego. Nebuchadnezzar was furious and ordered them thrown into a fiery furnace unless they changed their mind. They did not know whether or not God would deliver them and they preferred death over worshiping the image so they refused again. The angry king had them cast into the blazing furnace, but God protected them and they came out unharmed.

☞ **GO TO:**

Romans 8:35–39 (not separated)

> **Revelation 13:8** All inhabitants of the earth will worship the beast—all whose names have not been written in the book of life belonging to the Lamb that was slain from the creation of the world.

One Willing To Die For The Godly, The Other Willing To Kill The Godly

It is difficult to imagine a world filled with Satan worshipers, but that is the way it will be. The only ones who will not worship the Antichrist will be those whose names have been written in the Book of Life. This is one of the few bright spots in this chapter. There are some who <u>cannot be separated from the love of Jesus</u>. Satan can rage, but God is still in control.

The Book of Life belongs to the Lamb that was slain. He is omniscient (all-knowing). He knows who will worship the Antichrist and who will not. He has already entered the names of those who will not fall in his book. Before the world was created, he planned to die for them. What a difference between the Christ and the Antichrist—one willing to die for the godly, the other willing to kill the godly.

Ed Hindson: Secularism is giving way to New Age mysticism as the do-it-yourself religion of our times. The end result will be the watering down of religious beliefs so that they are more palatable to the general public.[19]

What Others are Saying:

Tim LaHaye: A man's name is written in the Lamb's Book of Life because he chooses to ask God to place it there. Jesus Christ offers men eternal life if they will receive him—if they will invite him into their life.[20]

> **Revelation 13:9** He who has an ear, let him hear.

Open Your Ears And HEAR!

Everyone has ears and <u>everyone should listen</u> to the things from our all-knowing God. No one has to go through the Tribulation Period. God loves everyone. He is warning everyone. Will anyone commit his/her life to Jesus before it is too late to leave in the Rapture?

This phrase about hearing has been mentioned earlier in Chapters 2 and 3. However, those times it was followed by the phrase *let him hear what the Spirit says to the churches.* The omission of that phrase here proves that the Rapture of the Church occurs *before* the Tribulation Period.

> **Revelation 13:10** If anyone is to go into captivity, into captivity he will go. If anyone is to be killed with the sword, with the sword he will be killed. This calls for patient endurance and faithfulness on the part of the saints.

Believe, Trust, and Look

In my opinion, there is a double meaning here. If a Tribulation Saint kills someone, even in self-defense, he will be killed in a similar manner. If an unbeliever kills a Tribulation Saint, he will be killed in a similar manner. Sin will have its own reward. This is the way it was in Old Testament days. It is commonly called an <u>eye for an eye</u> and a tooth for a tooth. The New Testament says it like this, *a man reaps what he sows* (Galatians 6:7). If you sow corn, you get corn, and if you sow wheat you get wheat. During the Tribulation Period, if you kill, you will be killed.

☞ **GO TO:**

Romans 10:17 (listen)

Something to Ponder

☞ **GO TO:**

Leviticus 24:17–22 KJV (eye for an eye)

I Peter 1:21 (believe)

John 14:1 (trust)

II Corinthians 4:18 KJV (look)

KEY POINT

Believe in God, *trust* in Jesus, and *look* to the resurrection of the dead.

This will require patience and faith. It will be the only way to stand up under the terrible persecution of the Tribulation Period. _Believe_ in God, _Trust_ in Jesus, and _Look_ to the time when you will live again. Leave revenge to the Almighty.

Something to Ponder

The world seems to be going in a circle. In the Old Testament a person who killed someone was put to death. That worked quite well in Israel for several hundred years. It taught people to value human life, and there were few murders. America was founded on tough Bible-based laws and there were relatively few violent crimes, but things have changed in this century. Now murderers usually serve less than seven years with the average sentence being about 20 months. This leniency will not last, though, because God is going to do what society will not—kill those who kill others.

☞ **GO TO:**

Revelation 17:15; Isaiah 57:20 (sea)

Psalm 25:13 (earth)

John 1:29 (Lamb)

> **Revelation 13:11** Then I saw another beast, coming out of the earth. He had two horns like a lamb, but he spoke like a dragon.

The Beast From The Earth

John saw a second beast (the False Prophet). The first beast will come out of the sea, but this beast will come from the earth. The sea is a symbol of the masses of humanity while the earth is a symbol of the land of Israel.

KEY Symbols:

Beast
FALSE PROPHET

from the earth
- land of Israel

two horns like a lamb
- wolf-in-sheep's clothing

spoke like a dragon
- deceit

It is important to remember that the focus of the world will be mainly upon two places during the Tribulation. One pivotal location point will be the revived Roman Empire (see Revelation 6, 17, and 18) with its one-world government. The other will be the land of Israel with its Jewish religion, Temple, 144,000 sealed Jews, and two witnesses.

The first beast will have ten horns. The second will have two. Lambs do not have horns, so except for his two horns, the second beast will look like a lamb. This suggests that he will try to imitate the Lamb of God, but he will be a wolf-in-sheep's clothing.

The first beast will get his power _from_ the dragon. The second will speak _like_ a dragon. He will do a lot of talking about loving, accepting, diversity, gender equality, etc. He will condemn racism, sexism, poverty, and all forms of discrimination. Underneath, though, he will be a slithering monster.

Hal Lindsey: While the first beast emerged from the sea (the unrest of troubled nations), the second beast emerges from the land. (*Earth* in verse 11 could just as well be translated "land.") When the Bible uses the word "land" symbolically, it usually refers to the land that belongs to Israel. So the second beast will come from the region of the Middle East, and I believe he will be a Jew.[21]

Dave Weber: The leading candidate to succeed Pope John Paul II is Jean Marie Lustiger. This crusading cardinal is a personal friend of the pope. He is an interesting figure in the intrigue of France's religion and politics. Lustiger was born to a Jewish mother, who died in the Auschwitz death camp. After his conversion to Roman Catholicism, he rose swiftly through the ranks as an outspoken leader against racial inequality.[22]

One of the big words today is rights: civil rights, human rights, children's rights, gay rights, etc. Our modern society is overdosing on inclusiveness. We are told to accept same-sex marriages for our adults and homosexuals as our pastors. Almost anything goes—except Christianity. When Christians say this inclusiveness is wrong, according to the Bible, they are told that is unacceptable. Many times it is also considered unacceptable when Christians want to read their Bibles in school, pray in school, set up religious displays in the city park, or even post the Ten Commandments in the courtroom.

> **Revelation 13:12** He exercised all the authority of the first beast on his behalf, and made the earth and its inhabitants worship the first beast, whose fatal wound had been healed.

Words Sweeter Than Honey

The second beast, the False Prophet, will hold as much authority as the first beast, the Antichrist. He will be the third member of the Satanic trinity, but he will not use his great authority to exalt himself. He will use it to exalt the Antichrist.

His deeds will betray his sweet-sounding words. Instead of loving and accepting everyone, he will try to change everyone's beliefs. He will attempt to merge religion and politics by promoting a world religion and world government. He will order everyone to worship the Antichrist and will not hesitate to use force.

Whose fatal wound had been healed refers back to Revelation 13:3. It reveals that the False Prophet will claim to be a healer and miracle worker. He will be what Jesus said, *For false Christs and false prophets will appear and perform great signs and miracles to deceive even the elect . . .* (Matthew 24:24).

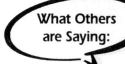

What Others are Saying:

Grant R. Jeffrey: It is an open secret in Italy and Europe that many of the present priests, cardinals, and bishops are no longer true believers in the inspiration of the Scriptures and the historical credibility of the gospel of Christ. Just like the growing apostasy in the Protestant denominations many of these modern Catholic leaders have rejected the fundamentals of the New Testament faith such as the virgin birth and the resurrection of Jesus Christ. Pope John Paul II fears that, following his death, the conclave of cardinals who will choose the next pope will elect someone who will not uphold historic Christianity.[23]

Jack Van Impe: We see a serious movement toward a one-world religion system, with Pope John Paul II himself fearing the rise of the Antichrist and an "anti-pope" in the near future.[24]

☞ **GO TO:**

Exodus 7:11, 12 (rods became serpents)

Job 1:12, 16 (Satan sent fire)

Daniel 12:11 (abomination of desolation)

Revelation 13:13, 14 And he performed great and miraculous signs, even causing fire to come down from heaven to earth in full view of men. Because of the signs he was given power to do on behalf of the first beast, he deceived the inhabitants of the earth. He ordered them to set up an image in honor of the beast who was wounded by the sword and yet lived.

The Image Of The Beast—How Vain Can We Get

In the Old Testament Book of Genesis, God had Moses cast his rod down before Pharaoh and it <u>turned into a serpent</u>. Then Pharaoh's magicians did the same thing with their rods. And in the Book of Job, <u>Satan sent fire</u> from heaven to destroy Job's sheep, and the people thought it was the work of God. Satan can perform what appears to be miraculous signs and wonders. The Apostle Paul tells us, *The coming of the lawless one will be in accordance with the work of Satan displayed in all kinds of counterfeit miracles, signs and wonders, and in every sort of evil that deceives those who are perishing* (II Thessalonians 2:9, 10).

One of the most impressive signs the False Prophet will perform is that of causing fire to fall from heaven before a great multitude. This in itself will not prove he is from God, but yet many will believe he is. He will order his followers to honor the Antichrist by setting up an image (see GWDN, page 70) or a statue of the first beast. They will gladly do what he commands. When they do, emphasis will be placed on the Antichrist's wound and what appears to be a miraculous healing and resurrection.

The image of the first beast, the Antichrist, will be built in the Temple at the mid-point of the Tribulation Period (see Time Line #2, Appendix A). Jesus said, *So when you see standing in the holy place "the abomination that causes desolation," spoken of through the prophet Daniel—let the reader understand—then let those who are in Judea flee to the mountains* (Matthew 24:15, 16). Jesus was undoubtedly referring to the Holy Place in the Temple that will be rebuilt before the mid-point of the Tribulation Period arrives.

> **Revelation 13:15** He was given power to give breath to the image of the first beast, so that it could speak and cause all who refused to worship the image to be killed.

It Speaks

The False Prophet will be given the power to impart breath to the image of the Antichrist. When he does, the image will appear to come to life. This will be a reminder that the Antichrist was once dead but is alive again. How the False Prophet will accomplish this is a matter of speculation, but there is no doubt that it will be an incredible event; one that will catch the world's attention.

After the image begins breathing, it will also speak. Whether that will be an act of ventriloquism, demonic possession, computers, or something else is left unsaid, but nevertheless, we know that it will be a convincing performance.

The image will proclaim that all who refuse to worship it will die. Jesus warned of this kind of persecution when he said, *Then you will be handed over to be persecuted and put to death, and you will be hated by all nations because of me* (Matthew 24:9). Paul warned us about it too when he said, *But mark this: There will be terrible times in the last days* (II Timothy 3:1).

The False Prophet sure doesn't sound like the lamb he first appeared as. He now sounds more like a satanically-inspired roaring lion. That's why he's called the False Prophet. He is a religious

KEY Symbols:

Image of the Beast
ANTICHRIST

built by the followers of the False Prophet
bow down in worship or die

pretender who will not hesitate to break God's laws. The False Prophet will be responsible for the unwarranted death of multitudes of Christians even though God said, *You shall not murder* (Exodus 20:13). God also said, *You shall have no other gods before me. You shall not make for yourself an idol in the form of anything in heaven above or on the earth beneath or in the waters below. You shall not bow down to them or worship them* (Exodus 20:3–5). Instead of putting the Bible into practice, the False Prophet will make every attempt possible to set it aside.

What Others are Saying:

Tim LaHaye: As we approach the end of the age and these signs in their initial stages begin to come to pass, we should not let miraculous power deceive us, but judge everything according to the Word of God.[25]

John Hagee: Satan knows the prophecy that one day every knee will bow before Jesus Christ, but so great is his hatred toward God that he's determined to lash out at God by keeping as many from salvation as possible.[26]

☞ **GO TO:**

Genesis 4:15 (Cain)

Deuteronomy 6:6–8 (phylacteries)

Revelation 14:1 (foreheads)

Ephesians 4:30 (Holy Spirit)

Leviticus 19:28 (marks)

Revelation 14:9, 10 (wrath)

> **Revelation 13:16, 17** He also forced everyone, small and great, rich and poor, free and slave, to receive a mark on his right hand or on his forehead, so that no one could buy or sell unless he had the mark, which is the name of the beast or the number of his name.

The Mark Of The Beast

In addition to building the Image of the Beast, the False Prophet will also mandate that everyone be given a mark known as the Mark of the Beast.

People will be allowed to select one of two different places for the mark: their right hand or their forehead. When Cain slew Abel, God put a <u>mark on Cain</u> to protect him. Since the days of Moses, pious Jews have worn small leather pouches called <u>phylacteries on their left hand</u> and on straps tied around their forehead. The phylacteries (see Illustration #8, page 199) contain small pieces of parchment with important passages of Scripture written on them. When they wear them, they are symbolically placing the Word of God on their hand (with their arm bent it is over their heart) and on their forehead (in front of their mind).

In Revelation 7:2–4, we read about an angel of God that will

Illustration #8

Phylacteries—These were strapped to the foreheads and left arm for morning prayer. These small leather boxes contained folded slips of parchment with four passages from the Bible, including the Ten Commandments.

KEY Symbols:

Mark Of The Beast

ANTICHRIST

instituted by the False Prophet
on the forehead or hand
needed to buy and sell

mark 144,000 Jews on their foreheads. In Chapter 14, we will see that they have the <u>names of Jesus and the Father on their foreheads</u>. Just as Christians are <u>sealed by the Holy Spirit</u>, so will the False Prophet seal his servants.

No one will be exempt. Laws will be enacted to identify and punish those who do not support the world government. To have food and medicine will be a privilege. Those who co-operate will receive these privileges. Those who refuse will be denied.

Taking the Mark will be like buying a license to transact business. Merchants will need it to sell their goods. Those who want to visit a doctor or specialist will need it to get treatment. Control over the necessities of life amounts to control over people. With these in his grasp, the False Prophet will force people to worship the Image of the Beast. In this way, he will merge church and state.

Many prophecy experts see the ultimate result of the Mark of the Beast as a "cashless society." Today the governments of the world want to eliminate coins and paper money so all transactions can be tracked electronically. In this way computers will have the ability to track all buying and selling.

John Hagee: The Antichrist's economy will be a cashless society in which every financial transaction can be electronically monitored. . . . My bank today offers a debit card; even today I don't need money to go to the grocery store. Everything is scanned these days, from library cards to thumb prints, and it doesn't re-

What Others are Saying:

quire a great leap of imagination to see how this cashless, computerized system of buying and selling will be placed into operation. A day is coming when you will not even be able to buy Rolaids without the proper approval, without having a mark upon your hand or forehead scanned.[27]

Jack Van Impe: Could information embedded in tiny biochips be the personal end-time ID code we are warned of in the Bible? Scripture tells us that in the future, a one-world system of government will require every person to receive a "mark" in his or her right hand or in their foreheads. Without this "Mark of the Beast," no one will be permitted to buy or sell. In years past, few could envision such a system in operation. The technology simply did not exist. But today, with what amounts to virtually daily breakthroughs in biometric technology, these advances now make such a system not only viable, but plausible.[28]

Jack Van Impe: Meanwhile, the *Wall Street Journal* reported a record trading day for the NASDAQ stock exchange on May 6, 1996 as stock for a high-tech company, whose main asset is new biometric ID technology, soared overnight. The *Journal* said, "Comparator says the burst in trading volume is due to pent-up demand from plugged-in investors who knew that the release of the company's new line of 'biometric identity verification systems' was imminent." The above secular sources confirm that the means now exist to usher in the infamous "Mark of the Beast" in which no human will be able to buy or sell without a "mark" or traceable implant.[29]

Hal Lindsey: The False Prophet will perfect a way to expose everyone who believes in Jesus Christ. All Beast-worshipers will be compelled to receive a distinguishing mark (perhaps a tattoo visible only under ultraviolet light) on their right hand or their forehead. Everyone who refuses the Mark will be cut off from economic survival.[30]

Tim LaHaye: Physically speaking, it will be necessary for men to have the Mark of the Beast. Spiritually speaking, it will be fatal. For we have repeatedly seen that those who are redeemed by the Lamb, those who have the seal of God, do not have the Mark of the Beast. But those who receive the Antichrist's mark will have made the final decisions for eternity to reject Christ and worship his archenemy.[31]

Ed Hindson: Clearly this prophecy speaks of the religious, political, and economic control of the world at the end of the age by a combination of political and religious powers.[32]

Reasons for the Mark

1) To counterfeit the mark God will give to the 144,000 Jews.
2) To extend favors to those who support the world government.
3) To identify and eliminate opposition to the world government.
4) To track and control commerce.
5) To force people to stop worshiping God
6) To force people to worship the Antichrist.
7) To permanently tie people to the kingdom of the Antichrist.

Do not put <u>marks on your body</u>.

Those who take the mark will face the <u>wrath of God</u>.

Remember This . . .

> **Revelation 13:18** This calls for wisdom. If anyone has insight, let him calculate the number of the beast, for it is man's number. His number is 666.

666—Not That Number Again

The first thing we need to note is that this verse calls for wisdom. Many are so caught up trying to figure out who the Antichrist is, that they lose all sight of using any **wisdom**. The Antichrist could not exist until after Israel became a nation because he will <u>sign a covenant with them</u>, so obviously those who believed he was Hitler or Mussolini overlooked this important detail. In my opinion, the Antichrist will rise to power in Europe because Daniel told of the destruction of Jerusalem by the Romans and the <u>Antichrist will come out of those people</u>. This is why he cannot be an American. Those who identified the American Secretary of State, Henry Kissinger, overlooked this. The Antichrist will not be revealed until <u>after the Rapture</u>. Those who think they can identify him now are overlooking this. People eventually *will* be able to identify him in the future, but wisdom will be needed. All pieces of the puzzle will have to fall together.

WARNING

☞ **GO TO:**

Daniel 9:27 (covenant)

Daniel 9:26 (Antichrist)

II Thessalonians 2:1–8 (after the Rapture)

Genesis 1:27–31 (sixth day)

Genesis 2:2 (seventh day)

Mark 16:9 (eighth day)

wisdom: *the right use of knowledge*

modern world: *the world we live in*

ancient world: *the people in Israel at the time of Christ*

alphanumeric: *letters that have a numerical value*

This verse tells us that those with insight who will want to identify the Antichrist after the Rapture can calculate his number. It is the number of a man, and it equals 666. Two things are important here: how to calculate the number, and why it is 666.

To calculate the number one needs to know that things have changed since John wrote Revelation. The **modern world** has two sets of symbols—the alphabet and numbers. We use two systems. A letter is a letter, and a number is a number. But the **ancient world** did not do this; they used a single set of symbols to represent both letters and numbers. Such a system is called an "**alphanumeric** system." Every number is a letter, and every letter is a number.

In an alphanumeric system, every word has a numeric value, every sentence has a numeric value, every paragraph has a numeric value, etc. The same is true of every name. Every name has a numeric value. For example, let A = 100, B = 101, C = 102, etc. Now calculate the number for the name "Hitler." Here is another example, 6 is the number of man so let A = 1 x 6 or 6, B = 2 x 6 or 12, C = 3 x 6 or 18, etc. Now calculate the number for the name "Kissinger." This is how to calculate the number of the name of Antichrist. It will be 666 in somebody's alphanumeric system (Hebrew, Greek, computer, etc.). Many scientists are now studying the mathematical structure of the Bible with computers. All of them are finding remarkable mathematical patterns. It is quite possible that someday someone will unlock this mystery with a computer by the time the Antichrist arrives.

Concerning why the Antichrist's name will equal 666 is another matter of speculation. The most common answer centers around the fact that 6 is the number of man, 7 is the number of God, and 8 is the number of Jesus; man was created on the sixth day, the Creator rested on the seventh day, and the Redeemer of creation rose on the eighth day. These numbers in their triplicate are 666, 777, and 888.

What Others are Saying:

John Hagee: This information about how to identify the Antichrist is of no practical value to the Church since we will be watching from the balconies of heaven by the time he is revealed.

This cryptic puzzle is not intended to point a finger at some unknown person. It is, however, intended to confirm to the world someone already suspected as being the Antichrist. And in the idolatry of the end time, "the number of a man" is fully developed and the result is 666.[33]

Study Questions

1. Will people be saved during the Tribulation Period?
2. What part will miracles play in this?
3. What two spiritual things will the saints need to endure the Tribulation Period? Why?
4. Is the Mark your social security number, credit card number, or driver's license number?

CHAPTER WRAP-UP

- The dragon will give his power and authority to the Antichrist, so the world will be deceived and worship the dragon. (Revelation 13:1–4)

- The Antichrist will receive what appears to be a fatal wound that will be healed. The world will marvel at this "miracle" and follow him. (Revelation 13:3, 4)

- The False Prophet will perform miracles to deceive the earth's inhabitants into worshiping the Antichrist. (Revelation 13:11–13)

- The False Prophet will have the people erect an image of the Antichrist and worship it. Anyone who doesn't will be killed. (Revelation 13:14, 15)

- Everyone who wishes to buy or sell will be forced to take the Mark of the Beast. This mark is a man's number, 666. (Revelation 13:16–18)

REVELATION 14

CHAPTER HIGHLIGHTS

- Sealed by the Lamb
- The Gospel Preached
- Fall of Babylon
- An Angelic Warning
- Harvests of the Earth

Let's Get Started

This chapter continues to tell us about peoples, nations, languages, and kings that will exist during the Tribulation Period. We will learn more about the 144,000 Jewish witnesses, the Tribulation Saints, the city of Jerusalem, and those who take the Mark of the Beast. We will also learn about Armageddon and Babylon.

> **Revelation 14:1** Then I looked, and there before me was the Lamb, standing on Mount Zion, and with him 144,000 who had his name and his Father's name written on their foreheads.

Preserve And Protect

After having the rise of the Antichrist and the False Prophet revealed to him, John now sees Jesus standing on Mount Zion in Jerusalem, with his 144,000 Jewish witnesses gathered around him. These 144,000 are those believers who will have the name of Jesus and his Father <u>written on their foreheads</u>.

☞ **GO TO:**

Revelation 7:3 (fore-heads)

Proverbs 2:8 (preserve)

Revelation 13:16, 17 (Antichrist)

II Samuel 5:6, 7 (Jebusites)

I Chronicles 11:4–8 (Jerusalem)

first magnitude miracle: one of the greatest miracles

Hal Lindsey: This is a **first magnitude miracle**, since more than half the earth's population, including many thousands of the evangelists' converts will be wiped out during the horrors of the Tribulation Period.[1]

What Others are Saying:

Jesus will seal the 144,000 Jewish witnesses between the opening of the sixth and seventh seal. After this, when the seventh seal is opened and the seven trumpets sound:

- one-third of the earth and trees will burn up
- one-third of the sea will turn to blood
- one-third of all ships will be destroyed
- one-third of the fresh water will be polluted
- one-third of the light of the sun and moon will be diminished and multitudes will die

KEY POINT

Jesus knows how to preserve and protect his own.

The Antichrist and his False Prophet will slaughter even more multitudes, and cause the Jews to flee from Jerusalem, but none of the dead will include the chosen 144,000. Jesus and his 144,000 will not be afraid to stand in the middle of the city, for he knows how to <u>preserve and protect</u> himself and his own.

• • •

The 144,000 will have the name of Jesus and the Father on their foreheads. The followers of the False Prophet will have the <u>name of the Antichrist</u> on their foreheads.

• • •

Mount Zion was the name of an ancient fortified hill controlled by the <u>Jebusites</u>. King David captured the hill and took up residence in the fortress at the top. He then built a city around the fortress which was called by two names: 1) the city of David, and 2) <u>Jerusalem</u>. Today, Jerusalem is the political and religious capital of Israel.

☞ **Go To:**

Psalm 144:9; 147:7; 149:3; 150:3 (harps)

> **Revelation 14:2** And I heard a sound from heaven like the roar of rushing waters and like a loud peal of thunder. The sound I heard was like that of harpists playing their harps.

Heavenly Harps

Singing will be heard in heaven for the 144,000 who stand unhurt on Mount Zion. They alone have survived the disasters of the Antichrist and False Prophet.

What Others are Saying:

David Hocking: The idea of people <u>playing harps</u> in heaven is not foreign to the Bible.[2]

> **Revelation 14:3** And they sang a new song before the throne and before the four living creatures and the elders. No one could learn the song except the 144,000 who had been redeemed from the earth.

You Would Have Had To Been There

The heavenly multitude will sing a new song before the throne of God, the four living creatures, and the twenty-four elders. No one will understand their song except the 144,000.

Often we sing songs without really understanding what the writer went through or is trying to convey. We would have needed to be there to understand what inspired them. The next two verses will give us an idea of the demands placed on the 144,000 that enabled them to understand this new song.

David Hocking: They alone, having experienced deliverance through their suffering and death, are able to sing its praise.[3]

What Others are Saying:

celibate: *abstaining from sexual activity*

spiritual fornication: *worshiping any god(s) other than the God of the Bible*

> **Revelation 14:4** These are those who did not defile themselves with women, for they kept themselves pure. They follow the Lamb wherever he goes. They were purchased from among men and offered as firstfruits to God and the Lamb.

True To The End

This is a controversial verse. Some say the 144,000 will be **celibate**, while others claim they will either not break their marriage vows, or will remain unmarried. Still others believe they will not commit **spiritual fornication** by worshiping idols and teaching false doctrines. It is difficult to say who is right, but we can be sure of some things: 1) during the Tribulation Period, it will be difficult for these men to be married and be good husbands and fathers, and 2) they will remain pure in spite of living in a world filled with immorality and spiritual fornication.

They follow the Lamb wherever he goes means they will abide in his presence. They will not stray from the will or teachings of Jesus. *They were purchased from among men* means they have been bought with the blood of Jesus. *Offered as firstfruits to God and the Lamb* means they will be the first Jews saved during the Tribulation Period with more fruit to follow.

Tim LaHaye: The Bible does not teach celibacy; in fact, no hint of it is found in Scripture. The Bible everywhere advocates that Christians be holy and virtuous, undefiled by the world. Misuse of sex has always been one of man's greatest problems; infidelity and immorality one of man's greatest temptations.[4]

Hal Lindsey: Most Bible commentators agree that the celibacy of these men refers not so much to *sexual* purity (although this is important) but to separation from *spiritual* fornication and adultery (James 4:4).[5]

J. Vernon McGee: Therefore, the comment, *These are they which were not defiled with women for they are virgins* (KJV), is probably referring to chastity in both the literal sense and the spiritual sense. And this makes good sense, by the way.[6]

> **Revelation 14:5** No lie was found in their mouths; they are blameless.

Faithful And True

Truthfulness will also characterize the 144,000. They will have nothing to do with the lies of the Antichrist, or the counterfeit doctrines of the False Prophet. They will be faithful to God and clothed in the righteousness of Christ.

Remember This . . .

The 144,000

stand with Jesus on Mount Zion	they are victorious with Jesus
marked on their foreheads	the names of Jesus and his Father
understand the heavenly new song	understand because of their trials
kept themselves pure	avoid immorality and idolatry
follow the Lamb wherever he goes	abide in his presence
purchased from among men	bought with the blood of Jesus
offered as firstfruits to God and the Lamb	first Jews saved during the Tribulation
no lie was found in their mouths	faithful and true

> **Revelation 14:6** Then I saw another angel flying in midair, and he had the eternal gospel to proclaim to those who live on the earth—to every nation, tribe, language, and people.

Proclaim The Gospel

Today, the Church is responsible for the **proclamation of the gospel**. But that will change after the Rapture. Jesus said, *This gospel of the kingdom will be preached in the whole world as a testimony to all nations, and then the end will come* (Matthew 24:14). Because the Church will be in heaven, God will use the 144,000 Jews, the two witnesses, and even an <u>angel</u> to spread his message. He will go to great lengths to give the world one last chance to be saved.

What gospel will the angel preach? The fact that it is called *the eternal gospel* is indication that it is identical to the gospel the Church preached. Some try to separate the gospel into different categories: the gospel of grace, the gospel of the kingdom, the gospel of judgment, the eternal gospel, Paul's gospel, etc. But all of these are part of the same gospel.

> **Revelation 14:7** He said in a loud voice, "Fear God and give him glory, because the hour of his judgment has come. Worship him who made the heavens, the earth, the sea, and the springs of water."

Death Or Life—That Is The Choice

People will have two choices: 1) believe the Antichrist, believe his lie, and worship him, or 2) **fear God** alone and give him all the glory. Choosing to follow the Antichrist can only lead to spiritual death, but choosing to follow God will surely lead to spiritual life.

What does it mean to fear God? Satan would have us believe it means to be afraid of God, but that is incorrect. To fear God means to have a holy respect for him, believe he exists, and believe he reigns and will judge all mankind. This kind of fear is the beginning of wisdom and it pleases God. (For more about the connection between the fear of the Lord and wisdom, see WBFW, pages 15 and 154.)

proclamation of the gospel: *the declaring, preaching, or teaching of the Bible*

KEY POINT

There is only *one* Gospel.

KEY Symbols:

The First Angel
proclaims the eternal gospel to all people

fear God: *to respect God for who he is, what he has done, and what he can do*

☞ **GO TO:**

Isaiah 47:9–13 (birth-place)

Luke 8:26–36 (possession)

Isaiah 13:4–6, 19, 20; Jeremiah 51:7, 25, 26 (prophets)

maddening wine: *a symbol of evil spirits or demon possession*

one-world harlot religion: *the set of religious and social values of the Antichrist and False Prophet*

KEY Symbols:

Second Angel
declares the fall of Babylon

> **Revelation 14:8** A second angel followed and said, "Fallen! Fallen is Babylon the Great, which made all the nations drink the maddening wine of her adulteries."

Babylon The Harlot

Babylon (see Illustration #9, page 211) is known as the city of Satan because of its long history of idolatry, astrology, witchcraft, and other occult practices. It is the <u>birthplace of many false doctrines</u> and religions such as goddess worship.

In Acts 2:3 the new believers of Christ were accused of being drunk on new wine, but they were actually being filled with the Holy Spirit. In that chapter wine is a symbol of the Holy Spirit. In this chapter, **maddening wine** is a <u>reference to demon possession</u>. Making the nations drink this wine is a reference to Babylon forcing her Satanic-inspired false religion on the world.

The ancient city died out many centuries ago, but during the 1980's and 90's Saddam Hussein poured hundreds of millions of dollars into rebuilding it.[7] The Persian Gulf War eventually slowed him down, but the rebuilt city will become a great center of religion and trade during the Tribulation Period. The False Prophet will locate the headquarters of his false religion there.

In verses 6 and 7, we learned that God will send the first angel of Chapter 14 to proclaim the gospel to all people. That angel will also proclaim the arrival of God's judgment. Then a second angel will declare the fall of Babylon. This is a judgment the <u>Old Testament prophets</u> predicted and it must come to pass. Babylon's fascination with the occult and her spread of a **one-world harlot religion** will bring a world-class fall.

The word *Fallen* is repeated twice to mean two separate falls or judgments. The false religious system will fall first when the Antichrist turns on it just after the mid-point of the Tribulation Period. The rebuilt city of Babylon will fall again when it is burned to the ground in one hour near the end of the Tribulation Period (more on this later in Chapter 17).

What Others are Saying:

J. Vernon McGee: I believe the ancient city of Babylon will be rebuilt though not at the same location, and that judgment upon it, which is predicted in the Book of Isaiah, is yet to come.[8]

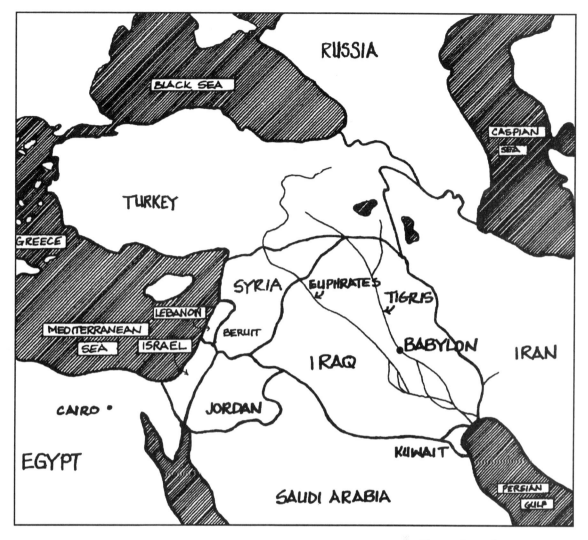

Illustration #9

Babylon—Modern day map of the Middle East showing location of the city of Babylon and the Tigris & Euphrates Rivers.

J.H. Melton: Many religious leaders of the present day are very enthusiastic about what they call "Christian unity." Millions of professing Christians are being swept by sentimental appeals into the ecumenical monster, the World Council of Churches, the one-world church. Again and again people are heard to exclaim, "Wouldn't it be wonderful if we just had one great big church?" They will have their one great big church, but it will not be so wonderful. It will be a federation of God-defying, Christ-denying, apostate religious leaders.[9]

Third Angel
warns not to worship the Antichrist or take the Mark of the Beast

> **Revelation 14:9** A third angel followed them and said in a loud voice: "If anyone worships the beast and his image and receives his mark on the forehead or on the hand,

Do Not Take The Mark

A third angel will fly through the air with a third announcement. This announcement will concern those who worship the Antichrist, worship his image, and take his Mark. The first angel will preach the gospel and plead with people to worship God. The second angel will announce the fall of Babylon. This angel will warn people not to worship the Antichrist or take the Mark of the Beast.

cup of his wrath: a symbol meaning judgment is coming when God's cup is full

wine of God's fury: a symbol meaning they will be cast into the Lake of Fire

> **Revelation 14:10** he, too, will drink of the wine of God's fury, which has been poured full strength into the **cup of his wrath**. He will be tormented with burning sulfur in the presence of the holy angels and of the Lamb.

Tormented By Fire

This is one of those "you will reap what you sow" verses. Babylon will make *all the nations drink the maddening wine of her adulteries.* Those who drink her wine will then be made to *drink the **wine of God's fury*** which will be unimaginable torment with burning sulfur. We know that burning sulfur increases the temperature of a fire, and therefore, in this case, would raise the level of suffering.

Everyone should heed this warning. Following the Antichrist and worshiping him will stir the wrath of God.

What Others are Saying:

J. Vernon McGee: If you believe that the Church is going through the Great Tribulation, you also believe that the Lord Jesus Christ is going to subject his own to the mingled, unmixed cup of his anger. I simply cannot believe that Christ would do this to the Church which he has redeemed.[10]

J.H. Melton: There are those who mock and jeer at the idea of an eternal hell for the wicked. Shall we believe our modern, sentimental philosophers, or abide by the Word of our God and his holy angels?[11]

> **Revelation 14:11** And the smoke of their torment rises for ever and ever. There is no rest day or night for those who worship the beast and his image, or for anyone who receives the mark of his name."

No End To It

The smoke will roll up as if from a great volcano. Anyone who worships the beast, his image, or who receives the Mark will never rest.

What Others are Saying:

Oliver B. Greene: There are those today who tell us that the wicked will be burned up . . . that there is no such thing as an everlasting hell. I would like for these fellows to explain to me why, if God is going to burn up the wicked, he does not put out the fire. Why does the smoke ascend up forever and ever?[12]

David Hocking: But does God punish people forever? It appears that his holiness, justice, and righteous character demand it. If we refuse his offer of salvation from sin, death, and hell, what else could he do and remain a holy God? His love, mercy, and forgiveness become totally meaningless if there is no retribution for our rebellion and sin. If there is eternal life for the believer then there is also eternal punishment for the unbeliever.[13]

Tim LaHaye: It is well to remember that even matter cannot be annihilated, as any scientist will confirm. Elements can be changed, but they cannot be annihilated. If matter cannot be annihilated, how much less the immortal soul of man.[14]

> **Revelation 14:12** This calls for patient endurance on the part of the saints who obey God's commandments and remain faithful to Jesus.

☞ **GO TO:**

Matthew 24:13; Luke 21:19 (remain faithful)

Remain Faithful

God has decreed that the Tribulation Period will come and the Antichrist will be given power over the world for seven years. When the Antichrist goes on his rampage, there will not be much that believers can do. God cannot go back on his Word. His prophecies must be fulfilled. Believers will have to endure, keep his commandments, and remain faithful.

☞ **GO TO:**

II Timothy 2:11, 12 (die)

Matthew 6:20 (follow)

> **Revelation 14:13** Then I heard a voice from heaven say, "Write: Blessed are the dead who die in the Lord from now on." "Yes," says the Spirit, "they will rest from their labor, for their deeds will follow them."

A Blessing To Die

This is a message of assurance and hope to those who will be trying to endure the trials of the Tribulation Period. God does not want believers to be afraid to die. It is a blessing to die in the Lord, but still, most of us do not want to die before our time.

A time will come during the Tribulation when it will be <u>better for the saved to die</u> than to live. They will leave their grief and torment behind, enter heaven, and rest in the presence of God where their deeds <u>will follow them</u>. This, obviously, is far better than taking the Mark and suffering eternal damnation in hell.

What Others are Saying:

John Hagee: Some Christians and Jews who are unable to flee to the Jordanian wilderness will be sheltered from the genocide by caring individuals (Matthew 25:31–46). Others will be captured and put to death, and these saints will receive a special blessing from God for their courageous devotion to him in the midst of horrific persecution and torture.[15]

☞ **GO TO:**

Daniel 7:13 (clouds)

> **Revelation 14:14** I looked, and there before me was a white cloud, and seated on the cloud was one "like a son of man" with a crown of gold on his head and a sharp sickle in his hand.

harvest: the gathering of the wicked nations for judgment

KEY Symbols:

Crown Of Gold
  Jesus is king

Sharp Sickle
  the harvest is coming

The Harvest

A day is coming when Jesus will take a <u>seat in the clouds</u>. He will wear a gold crown and hold a sharp sickle. The crown will identify him as a king, and the sickle will signify a coming **harvest**.

The Scriptures teach that Jesus will come back in the clouds as the King of kings and Lord of lords. He said, *The harvest is the end of the age, and the harvesters are angels. As the weeds are pulled up and burned in the fire, so it will be at the end of the age. The Son of Man will send out his angels, and they will weed out of his kingdom everything that causes sin and all who do evil. They will throw them into the fiery furnace, where there will be weeping and gnashing of teeth* (Matthew 13:39–42). It will be a terrible day for the lost because not only will it be their last day on earth, but their destiny will be sealed for eternity as well.

David Hocking: Jesus was called "the Son of Man" throughout the Gospels. It was the title he most often used for himself. It is a reminder that our coming Judge is one who knows what we are like. His humanity gives him valid credentials for judging mankind. John 5:27 (NKJV) says the Father *has given Him authority to execute judgment also, because He is the Son of Man.*[16]

Wim Malgo: The sharp sickle is raised in preparation for the harvest. This term is never used for the gathering of good grain, and therefore it means something terrible: He is coming here as the Judge of the world.[17]

> **Revelation 14:15** Then another angel came out of the temple and called in a loud voice to him who was sitting on the cloud, "Take your sickle and reap, because the time to reap has come, for the harvest of the earth is ripe."

KEY Symbols:

Fourth Angel

take your sickle and reap because the harvest is ready

Not Too Soon

As Jesus appears in the clouds, an angel will come forth from the heavenly temple. He will urge Jesus to take his sickle and reap because the time of judgment has arrived and the harvest is ready.

The Greek word for "ripe," *xeraino*, means totally ripe, rotten, or withered. *The harvest of the earth is ripe* shows us that God will withhold his judgment until the last minute. When his judgment falls, the Church will have been raptured, most of the Tribulation Saints and Jews will have been killed, and the world will be totally corrupt. No one will be able to truthfully claim that Jesus acted too soon.

> **Revelation 14:16** So he who was seated on the cloud swung his sickle over the earth, and the earth was harvested.

Swoosh

Jesus will <u>swing his sharp sickle</u> over the earth. Many of the remaining unbelievers will be filled with terror and try to run and

☞ GO TO:

Joel 3:13, 14 (sickle)

Matthew 25:41 (eternal fire)

hide. Others will beg, cry, and plead, but it will be too late. They will have wasted their last chance, and he will take multitudes and <u>cast them into the eternal fire</u> (Lake of Fire).

J. Vernon McGee: The Lord Jesus Christ is the Savior of the world, but he is also the *Judge* of all the world.[18]

KEY Symbols:

Fifth Angel
a second sickle from God

> **Revelation 14:17** Another angel came out of the temple in heaven, and he too had a sharp sickle.

Mercy, Not Another Angel

This angel will come directly from the presence of God with a sharp sickle just like the one Jesus will have.

☞ **GO TO:**

John 15:1 (True Vine)

KEY Symbols:

Clusters Of Grapes
fruit of the Antichrist (his followers)

Earth's Vine
Antichrist

The Sixth Angel
tells the fourth angel to take his sharp sickle and gather the clusters of grapes

> **Revelation 14:18** Still another angel, who had charge of the fire, came from the altar and called in a loud voice to him who had the sharp sickle, "Take your sharp sickle and gather the clusters of grapes from the earth's vine, because its grapes are ripe."

And Yet Another Angel

Yet another angel will come forth—this time from the altar in the heavenly temple. We read about this altar before in Revelation 8:3. It is where the Tribulation Saints call upon God to avenge their blood. Now this angel will urge the angel with the sharp sickle (the fourth angel of Chapter 14) to *gather the clusters of grapes from the earth's vine, because its grapes are ripe.* Since Jesus is the <u>True Vine</u>, it is likely that the *earth's vine* is a reference to the Antichrist. The clusters of grapes will be the fruit of the earth's vine or those nations that follow the Antichrist.

This indicates two things: 1) God will eventually answer the prayers of the Tribulation Saints who cried out for revenge, and 2) the wickedness of the earth will be great. God does not always answer prayers right away, but he will not let them go unanswered forever. Neither will he let wicked nations or individuals deny him forever.

David Hocking: All true believers are designed by God to bear the fruit of God's righteousness (Galatians 5:22–23; Philippians 1:9–11). In a similar manner, unbelievers are described as a vine that bears fruit, not the fruit of God's character, but the fruit of wickedness and rebellion.[19]

The souls of the martyred Tribulation Saints under the altar asked, *How long, Sovereign Lord, holy and true, until you judge the inhabitants of the earth and avenge our blood* (Revelation 6:9, 10)?

> **Revelation 14:19** The angel swung his sickle on the earth, gathered its grapes and threw them into the great winepress of God's wrath.

Cast Them Out

The fourth angel will use his great sickle to gather the wicked nations of the earth. He will then cast them into the *winepress of God's wrath*. This is a symbol to help us understand what is going to happen. When farmers go into their vineyards to harvest the grapes they cast them into the winepress and squeeze the juice out of them. In this process the grapes are practically destroyed. The same thing will happen to the wicked when this angel harvests the earth. They will be like a grape being squashed in a winepress.

J.H. Melton: This is, in reality, a war scene, a gathering of armies, the bringing together of the kings of the earth and of the whole world to the battle of the great day of God Almighty. . . . They are assembled on the battlefield of Megiddo.[20]

J.R. Church: I believe that Christians will not be forced to endure the wrath of God's judgment. We will be raptured to meet our Lord in the air at some point prior to the beginning of that dreadful time.[21]

Two reasons why many believe the Church will be raptured before the Tribulation Period are:

1) Jesus will rescue us from the <u>coming wrath</u>.
2) God did not appoint us to <u>suffer wrath</u>.

Remember This . . .

☞ **GO TO:**

I Thessalonians 1:10 (coming wrath)

I Thessalonians 5:9 (suffer wrath)

What Others are Saying:

Remember This . . .

☞ GO TO:

Isaiah 34:1–8 (wrath)

Revelation 1:15
   (bronze)

1,600 stadia: about 180 miles

horse's bridle: about four feet high

valley of Megiddo: the valley where the Battle of Armageddon will be fought

> **Revelation 14:20** They were trampled in the winepress outside the city, and blood flowed out of the press, rising as high as the horses' bridles for a distance of **1,600 stadia**.

As High As A Horse's Bridle

This is a reference to the Battle of Armageddon. The ripe grapes (wicked nations) will be trampled in the winepress of <u>God's wrath</u>. People will be crushed by the burning bronze feet of Jesus like small grapes under the weight of a large man.

Since the blood will rise as high as the **horses' bridles** for approximately 180 miles we know that millions will die. Before it happens, though, God will preach the gospel through the 144,000 Jews, the two witnesses, and his angel (the first angel of Chapter 14). He will also send an angel (the third angel of Chapter 14) to warn those who follow the Antichrist. He will give the world many chances to repent before he destroys it.

What Others are Saying:

Hal Lindsey: Apparently this whole valley (**valley of Megiddo**, or Armageddon, see Illustration #10, page 240) will be filled with war materials, animals, bodies of men, and blood.[22]

David Hocking: God's righteous anger is unleashed against all unbelievers, the nations of the world who have lived in opposition to his purposes and rejected his Messiah. Now, at the end of the Tribulation, they will taste his personal wrath. The consequences are awesome.[23]

Peter and Paul Lalonde: Despite their rebellion, the knee of every person at Armageddon shall indeed bow and the tongue of each shall indeed confess that Jesus Christ is Lord![24]

KEY POINT

God will give the world many chances to repent before he destroys it.

When John saw Jesus, Christ's feet were like <u>bronze glowing in a furnace</u>.

Remember This . . .

Study Questions

1. What sounds did John hear in heaven and what do they mean?
2. What is significant about "dying in the Lord?"
3. Who will send harvesters to the earth during the Tribulation Period, who will do the harvesting, and what will they harvest?
4. What does "trampled in the winepress" imply?

CHAPTER WRAP-UP

- The 144,000 will stand with Jesus on Mount Zion and sing a new song since they will be redeemed from the earth and offered as firstfruits. These are also the ones who kept themselves pure during the Tribulation. (Revelation 14:1–5)

- An angel will fly through the air proclaiming the Gospel to all the earth's inhabitants and warning them that the hour of God's judgment is near. (Revelation 14:6, 7)

- A second angel will follow the first and proclaim the fall of Babylon because she caused the nations of the earth to sin. (Revelation 14:8)

- A third angel will follow the first two and warn the people of earth to not worship the Antichrist or receive his Mark. Those who do follow the Antichrist will suffer God's fury forever. (Revelation 14:9–12)

- Two harvests of the earth will occur. The first one will be by Christ and the second by an angel who will throw his harvest into the winepress of God's wrath. (Revelation 14:14–20)

REVELATION 15

CHAPTER HIGHLIGHTS

- Third Great Sign
- Second Glassy Sea
- Song of the Lamb
- Under the Law
- Seven Angels with Seven Plagues

Let's Get Started

Chapter 15 is the shortest chapter in Revelation. Most scholars believe it should be combined with the next chapter because it is the introduction to the seven bowl judgments of Chapter 16. It predicts what will go on in heaven just before the final judgments fall.

> **Revelation 15:1** I saw in heaven another great and marvelous sign: seven angels with the seven last plagues—last, because with them God's wrath is completed.

The Third Great Sign From Heaven

This will be the third of three great signs in heaven: first, the sun-clothed woman (Israel); second, the great red dragon (Satan); now, seven angels with seven last plagues. This sign will be great and marvelous because of its terrible nature and amazing result. It will bring on the full wrath of God which will cause the fall of Satan and his devilish crew.

Wim Malgo: This is the complete fulfillment of prophecy. When this last unimaginable judgment of the bowls of wrath has passed over the earth, the seventh angel proclaims its accomplishment, *It is done* (Revelation 16:17).[1]

What Others are Saying:

Tim LaHaye: Revelation becomes much more understandable when one recognizes that the word "sign" really means a "symbol of revelation." That is, it is a symbol or picture or prophetic event that conveys some great truth or principle of God which he wants to convey to his people.[2]

The Three Great Signs from Heaven

1) the sun-clothed woman (Israel)—Revelation 12:1
2) the great red dragon (Satan)—Revelation 12:3
3) seven angels with seven plagues—Revelation 15:1

> **Revelation 15:2** And I saw what looked like a sea of glass mixed with fire and, standing beside the sea, those who had been victorious over the beast and his image and over the number of his name. They held harps given them by God.

The Second Glassy Sea

This will be the second glassy sea to appear in heaven. The first glassy sea will be <u>clear as crystal</u>. This one will be mixed with fire. The <u>sea symbolizes the masses</u> of humanity, and the fire represents judgment.

The Tribulation Saints will come up out of the sea of humanity. They will have been in a fiery persecution. They are *those who had been victorious over the beast and his image and over the number of his name.* They will not be deceived by the Antichrist or his False Prophet. They will be tracked down and ordered to take the Mark of the Beast but will refuse. For their refusal they will face retaliation in the form of torture and death. <u>Victory</u>, however, will still be theirs because they will lose their earthly life but will <u>gain</u> an eternal one.

When they reach heaven God will give them harps. Their earthly trials will have caused a lot of crying, but when they get to heaven they will sing and play.

Tim LaHaye: Death at the hands of a murderous dictator or anti-Christian persecutor is only defeat as man looks upon the situation. People living during the Tribulation will think the Antichrist is overcoming the saints, but in reality he is sending them out into eternity to be with the Lord. . . . If man does not incur blessings in this life, he considers that defeat, not realizing that what

Remember This . . .

☞ **GO TO:**

Revelation 4:6 (crystal)

Revelation 17:15 (sea)

I Corinthians 15:55–57 (victory)

Philippians 1:21 (gain)

KEY Symbols:

The Second Glassy Sea

sea of glass
- masses of humanity

mixed with fire
- judgment

What Others are Saying:

man gains in this life is inconsequential in comparison to what he gains in the life to come.[3]

Hal Lindsey: Real victory is not found in seeking to avoid conflicts and living a don't-rock-the-boat kind of life. The cemetery is full of people who fit that category. The kind of triumph these martyrs of the Tribulation will experience will be deliverance *through* fire, not *out* of it.[4]

> **Revelation 15:3** and sang the song of Moses the servant of God and the song of the Lamb: "Great and marvelous are your deeds, Lord God Almighty. Just and true are your ways, King of the ages.

☞ **GO TO:**

Exodus 15:1–19
(Moses)

The Song Of The Lamb

The Tribulation Saints will sing two songs: 1) the song of Moses, and 2) the song of the Lamb. The <u>song of Moses</u> is found in the Old Testament. It celebrates the victory God gave Israel when he brought her out of Egypt. Pharaoh's army chased after the Hebrews to recapture them, but his troops were drowned in the Red Sea.

The *song of the Lamb* is found in this verse. It celebrates God's reign and victory over all the nations. The deeds of Jesus are *great and marvelous* because he died for the sins of the world and will defeat Satan. The ways of Jesus are *just and true*. He is never unjust, never untruthful. His judgments are righteous. His words are accurate and reliable. Jesus is the *King of the ages*. He is the eternal King. The one who has reigned, is reigning, and always will reign.

J.R. Church: Just prior to the seven vial judgments, the saints in heaven will sing the song of Moses. They await the victory. Soon, Satan will be bound and the Messianic kingdom will be established.[5]

What Others are Saying:

Peter and Paul Lalonde: Those who reject God will grow closer and closer to a very subtle but real decision to join forces with the spirit of Antichrist, blaspheme God, and fight against Christ in this hopeless battle. You are already on one of only two roads. There is no other option.[6]

> **Revelation 15:4** Who will not fear you, O Lord, and bring glory to your name? For you alone are holy. All nations will come and worship before you, for your righteous acts have been revealed."

Fear And Glory

Today, few people speak of having a **reverential** fear of the Lord or of giving glory to him. We seem to think there is something wrong with these. However, these are of the utmost importance now and in heaven for three reasons:

1) Jesus should be feared and glorified because *he alone is holy.* He is the only one to live by all of God's standards, the only one worthy of our worship, the only one who never sinned. He has been hallowed or set apart for God's special purpose: an atonement for our sin.

2) Jesus should be feared and glorified because *he will be worshiped by all nations.* The day will come when he will deal with the godless leaders of this world. He will do away with them, and every nation will worship him.

3) Jesus should be feared and glorified because *his righteous acts will be revealed.* The terrible judgments of the Tribulation Period will be righteous acts of Jesus. He will deal with those who do not accept his mercy.

**What Others
are Saying:**

Peter and Paul Lalonde: According to opinion polls, an overwhelming majority of North Americans believe they will spend eternity in heaven (about 93 to 95 percent). Yet it is obvious from the moral decay and decadence in the West that such a majority do not have the love of Christ in their hearts.[7]

☞ GO TO:

Exodus 20:2–17 (Ten Commandments)

KEY POINT

Those who will not accept Jesus will be judged *under* the Law.

> **Revelation 15:5** After this I looked and in heaven the temple, that is, the tabernacle of the Testimony, was opened.

Under The Law

The Temple in heaven will be opened. Then the Holy of Holies (see Illustration #5, page 153) inside the Temple will be opened, followed by the Ark of the Covenant (see Illustration #6, page 167) inside the Holy of Holies. The Ark of the Covenant contains the Ten Commandments, which are sometimes called the Law or the Testimony.

Those who reject the grace and mercy God offers through the death, burial, and resurrection of his Son will be judged uner the Law (the Ten Commandments). In rejecting what God offers, they also reject Jesus. Many, including the Jews, do not realize this most important point. By rejecting Jesus, they reject God, and leave themselves open to be judged under the Law of Moses in the Old Testament.

> **Revelation 15:6** Out of the temple came the seven angels with the seven plagues. They were dressed in clean, shining linen and wore golden sashes around their chests.

Seven Angels With Seven Plagues

Seven angels will come out of the Temple. They will be dressed in clean, shining linen signifying their righteousness. They will wear golden sashes around their chests (see Illustration #2, page 21) signifying their royal priesthood.

These seven angels will move away from the Temple and the **mercy seat**. They are royal and powerful priests preparing to pour out the wrath of God. Those on earth will receive judgment without mercy. Because they have flouted God, followed the Antichrist, took the Mark, worshiped his image, and rejected Jesus, they will face the full fury of God.

> **Revelation 15:7** Then one of the four living creatures gave to the seven angels seven golden bowls filled with the wrath of God, who lives for ever and ever.

The Seven Angels Of God's Wrath

The four living creatures will hand the seven angels seven bowls filled with the wrath of God. Some Bible translations call these bowls "vials," but that does not do justice to the meaning of this verse. When a vial is turned upside down the liquid bubbles out slowly, but when a bowl is upset the liquid is suddenly dumped out. That is the picture we have here. God's wrath will be suddenly dumped out on the inhabitants of earth.

In the Old Testament, once a year on the Day of Atonement, the high priest would take a bowl of blood from a sacrificial ani-

☞ GO TO:

Hebrews 10:31 (fury)

mercy seat: *the gold lid on the Ark of the Covenant*

KEY Symbols:

Seven Angels
seven plagues
- the wrath of God

clean, shining linen
- righteousness

golden sashes
- royal priesthood

☞ GO TO:

Leviticus 16:14, 15 KJV
(Day of Atonement)

Revelation 6:1–8
(creatures)

KEY Symbols:

Seven Angels
seven golden bowls
- seven plagues

mal into the Holy of Holies and dump it on the mercy seat over the ark of the covenant. God had him do that to offer atonement for the sins of the people. Since the Antichrist and his followers will not accept the blood of Jesus as an atonement for their sins, these priestly angels will be given bowls filled with God's wrath instead of the blood of Jesus. And instead of dumping the bowls on the mercy seat, they will dump them on the earth.

What Others
are Saying:

Remember
This . . .

J. Vernon McGee: Notice, they are not filled with the *love* of God but with God's *wrath*.[8]

First, the <u>four living creatures</u> summon the four horsemen.

Now the four living creatures summon the seven angels of God's wrath.

☞ **GO TO:**

Isaiah 6:4 (smoke)

> **Revelation 15:8** And the temple was filled with smoke from the glory of God and from his power, and no one could enter the temple until the seven plagues of the seven angels were completed.

No More!

KEY POINT

There will be no more mercy, no more delays, and no more opportunities to repent until the seven plagues are over.

Things just keep getting worse for those who reject God. When the priestly angels leave the Temple, it will be <u>filled with smoke</u> from the glory and power of God. No one will be able to go back in or enter the Holy of Holies. No one can change their mind and pour blood on the mercy seat. There will be no more mercy, no more delays, and no more opportunities to repent until the seven plagues have passed.

This is a warning to those on earth who won't listen to the pleas of God made through his messengers—the 144,000 Jews, the two witnesses, the angel, and others. At some point in the Tribulation Period, God will say, "It's over. The destiny of those who keep rejecting my Son is sealed forever." He will pour out his wrath, keep people away from the mercy seat, and refuse to hear the pleas of those crying out for one more chance.

Study Questions

1. How are the actions of angels in this chapter contrary to our concept of angels?
2. Is God unjust or unrighteous for sending the Tribulation Period?
3. What is meant when the Bible says, *You alone are holy*?
4. What will the golden bowls contain?
5. Why will smoke fill the Temple?

CHAPTER WRAP-UP

- The third great sign John will see will be seven angels carrying the seven last plagues which will complete God's wrath. (Revelation 15:1)

- Standing beside the sea of glass mixed with fire will be those who will be victorious over the Antichrist. They will receive harps and sing about the deeds of Christ. (Revelation 15:2–4)

- Those who overcome the Antichrist will sing the song of the Lamb. They will sing about: his marvelous deeds, his just and true ways, and his holiness. (Revelation 15:3, 4)

- Anyone who rejects Christ and his gift of eternal life will be judged according to the Law of Moses (the Ten Commandments). (Revelation 15:5)

- When the heavenly temple opens, the seven angels with the seven last plagues will come out of it. Once the angels leave the temple smoke from God's glory will fill the temple preventing anyone from seeking mercy and obtaining one last chance. (Revelation 15:5–8)

REVELATION 16

CHAPTER HIGHLIGHTS

- Seven Bowls of Wrath
- Just and True
- Euphrates River
- Armageddon
- A Great Earthquake

Let's Get Started

We put the introduction to this chapter behind us when we studied Chapter 15. Now we move on to see what will happen when the seven bowls of God's wrath are poured out on a sinful world. The severity of these judgments indicate the extent of God's wrath toward those who steadfastly refuse to acknowledge him. They also indicate the extent of God's love by showing how far he will go to get unbelievers to repent. He loves the wicked and wants them to change before he has to remove them from the earth to set up his kingdom of righteousness.

> **Revelation 16:1** Then I heard a loud voice from the temple saying to the seven angels, "Go, pour out the seven bowls of God's wrath on the earth."

KEY Symbols:

Seven Trumpet Judgments		Seven Bowl Judgments
Trumpet 1—Judgment	Hail, fire, and blood hurled to earth *1/3 of plants burned up*	Bowl 1—Judgment
Trumpet 2—Judgment	Burning mountain hurled into sea *1/3 of seas polluted, fish killed, ships sunk*	Bowl 2—Judgment
Trumpet 3—Judgment	Blazing object fall to earth *1/3 of fresh water polluted*	Bowl 3—Judgment
Trumpet 4—Judgment	Heavenly bodies struck *1/3 of sun, moon, and stars darkened*	Bowl 4—Judgment
Trumpet 5—Judgment (woe)	Abyss opened *Demon-possessed locusts released*	Bowl 5—Judgment
Trumpet 6—Judgment (woe)	Four angels released at Euphrates *1/3 of mankind killed*	Bowl 6—Judgment
Trumpet 7—Seven Bowl Judgments (woe)		Bowl 7—Judgment

Seven Bowls

*seven angels given
seven portions of
God's wrath*

Seven Bowls

In Chapter 15 we read that the heavenly Temple will be filled with smoke so that no man will be able to enter in. However, the Father, Son, and Holy Spirit will already be inside which is where this voice originates. Remember that God has committed all judgment to Jesus which means Jesus will order the seven angels to, *Go, pour out the seven bowls of God's wrath on the earth.* Each angel will be given a portion of God's wrath.

**What Others
are Saying:**

Peter and Paul Lalonde: Armageddon is coming. . . . Who in their right mind would choose to fight with the Antichrist against God? Yet millions are making such a decision each day when they reject so great a salvation as that offered by God through his Son, Jesus Christ. For this is the heart of what Armageddon is all about. It is the world saying, "We will not bow our knee to anyone. We are too proud. We are too mighty. We are too important."[1]

GO TO:

Exodus 9:8–12 (sixth plague)

> **Revelation 16:2** The first angel went and poured out his bowl on the land, and ugly and painful sores broke out on the people who had the mark of the beast and worshiped his image.

KEY Symbols:

First Bowl Judgment

ugly and painful sores

The False Physician

The first bowl judgment will cause ugly and painful sores. Some Bible commentators say these sores will have a very offensive odor. Only those who take the Mark of the Beast or worship his image will be afflicted. When the Antichrist is unable to heal his own people, the world will know he is a false physician.

This plague will be similar to the sixth plague in Egypt when Moses was trying to have the Hebrews set free. At that time, God afflicted the Egyptian people with tumors, festering sores, and itching skin. The whole land, all the Egyptians, and even the animals were affected.

**What Others
are Saying:**

J.R. Church: In the end-time there will be several world-wide epidemics raging out of control.[2]

Peter and Paul Lalonde: Diseases like tuberculosis, once thought to have been totally eradicated, are now resurfacing. Other strange new diseases are also appearing. There's streptococcus A, the flesh-eating virus, and there was also the Ebola outbreak in (former) Zaire. Doctors are now finding themselves losing the battle as microbes are becoming immune to all the antibiotics that we have. . . . World travel, changing sexual habits, and increasing numbers of refugees have made it possible for many of these diseases to become pandemic, rapidly spreading across the entire planet almost overnight.[3]

> **Revelation 16:3** The second angel poured out his bowl on the sea, and it turned into blood like that of a dead man, and every living thing in the sea died.

Seas of Blood

The second bowl judgment will be worse than the second trumpet judgment. It will pollute the sea by turning it into blood and killing everything in it. One can easily imagine the repercussions of such a horrible event.

J. Vernon McGee: I wonder if we realize how much we are dependent upon God today?[4]

In the second trumpet judgment, one-third of the <u>sea creatures</u> were killed.

> **Revelation 16:4** The third angel poured out his bowl on the rivers and springs of water, and they became blood.

Rivers of Blood

The third bowl judgment will be worse than the third trumpet judgment. This plague will be similar to the <u>first plague</u> in Egypt. Back then, God turned all the waters of Egypt into blood. The fish died, the water smelled, and the people could not drink it. This plague will be far worse because all the earth's water will be polluted causing worldwide suffering and death.

☞ **GO TO:**

Revelation 8:8, 9 (sea)

KEY Symbols:

Second Bowl Judgment
sea turned to blood; everything in it dies

What Others are Saying:

Remember This . . .

☞ **GO TO:**

Exodus 7:17–25 (first plague)

Revelation 8:10, 11 (waters)

KEY Symbols:

Third Bowl Judgment
rivers and springs of water turn to blood

Remember This . . .

In the third trumpet judgment one-third of the <u>waters turned bitter</u>.

☞ **GO TO:**

Revelation 7:1 (wind)

Psalm 89:14 (justice)

Deuteronomy 33:27 (eternal existence)

Psalm 99:4, 5 (holy nature)

> **Revelation 16:5** Then I heard the angel in charge of the waters say: "You are just in these judgments, you who are and who were, the Holy One, because you have so judged;

The Water Angel

We probably do not realize the important role angels play in managing God's creation. We have already encountered <u>the four wind angels</u>, those angels in charge of holding back the earth's wind. Now we learn that God has a water angel in charge of the earth's water. Were it not for these angels man would not have survived as long as he has.

The angel in charge of earth's waters will look at this judgment and declare it to be a judgment deserved. He will express <u>the justice of God</u>, <u>the eternal existence of God</u>, and <u>the holy nature of God</u>.

John saw four angels standing at the four corners of the earth, holding back the four winds of the earth.

Remember This . . .

☞ **GO TO:**

Genesis 4:10 (Abel)

fundamentalist: someone who only accepts the literal interpretation of the Bible

> **Revelation 16:6** for they have shed the blood of your saints and prophets, and you have given them blood to drink as they deserve."

A Round of Blood Please

The bloody waters will be God's response to the shedding of the blood of the Tribulation Saints and the Old Testament prophets. The Old Testament plainly says, *You shall not murder* (Exodus 20:13), and Jesus clearly said, *all who draw the sword will die by the sword* (Matthew 26:52). It is a hard truth, but these unbelievers will get what they have coming to them. It is bad enough to ignore the Bible, but it is even worse, to turn one's back on the mercy of God at the same time.

What Others are Saying:

Wim Malgo: We can only grasp the full extent of this judgment when we consider the reason for it. If the voice of the blood of one single person who was murdered (<u>Abel</u>) cries to the Lord, how much louder must the blood of all the innumerable murdered people cry to heaven?[5]

Peter and Paul Lalonde: Today, through the power of television, a world is being fed an anti-Christian agenda. It has been so successful that a recent poll showed that Americans would least like to live next door to a cult member. Number two was a **fundamentalist**.[6]

Redneck web-site

☞ **GO TO:**

Revelation 6:9–11
(Saints)

> **Revelation 16:7** And I heard the altar respond: "Yes, Lord God Almighty, true and just are your judgments."

Just And True

The Antichrist and his followers will shed the blood of saints all over the world. God will eventually respond by turning their drinking water into blood. When he does, the martyred Tribulation Saints will declare that God's judgments are just and true.

At the opening of the fifth seal, the martyred <u>Tribulation Saints</u> under the altar will ask God how long it will be until he judges the inhabitants of the earth and avenges their blood. God will tell them to wait until more of their fellow servants and brothers are killed.

Remember This . . .

> **Revelation 16:8** The fourth angel poured out his bowl on the sun, and the sun was given power to scorch people with fire.

A Hot Time In The Old Town

The fourth bowl judgment will cause the sun to scorch people with fire. According to the prophet Malachi a day is coming when the earth will <u>burn like a furnace</u>. Many evildoers will be reduced to stubble.

☞ **GO TO:**

Malachi 4:1 (furnace)

KEY Symbols:

Fourth Bowl Judgment
the sun scorched people with fire

What Others are Saying:

Hal Lindsey: Already the thinning ozone layer is being blamed for severe sunburns in the southern end of Chile.[7]

John Hagee: The sun will scorch the earth and men with fire. Major uncontrollable fires will break out all over the world, spontaneously destroying homes, vegetation, and livestock.[8]

RELATED CURRENT EVENTS

What also makes current climate change different from earlier episodes (time periods) is the speed with which temperatures are rising. Creation will not be able to adapt to changes that occur so quickly. Scientists are predicting serious consequences of the rapid climate change such as the spread of infectious disease, rise in sea level, changes in weather patterns, and contamination of water supplies.[9]

> **Revelation 16:9** They were seared by the intense heat and they cursed the name of God, who had control over these plagues, but they refused to repent and glorify him.

Still Cursing

The strong heat of the sun will bear down on them with a vengeance. They will sweat and thirst but will have nothing to drink except blood. They will get sunburned on top of the painful sores caused by the first bowl judgment. Blisters, sunstroke, and extreme thirst will be like God's punishment to the unbelievers.

These afflictions will cause them to finally admit that God exists, and that he controls these plagues. But even with that in mind, they will still not fall on their sunburned faces and sore knees to ask for mercy. Instead, they will curse his name.

> **Revelation 16:10** The fifth angel poured out his bowl on the throne of the beast, and his kingdom was plunged into darkness. Men gnawed their tongues in agony

Darkness Over All The Land

The fifth bowl judgment will mark a turning point. God will begin to focus his attention on one of his biggest adversaries on

☞ **GO TO:**

Exodus 10:21, 22 (Egypt)

Matthew 27:45 (cross)

Isaiah 60:2; Joel 2:1, 2, 31 (prophecies)

earth—the Antichrist. Total darkness will cover the planet. People will not be able to see the stars or moon or even the sun.

This darkness will be similar to the <u>darkness that covered the land of Egypt</u> when Moses was trying to free the Hebrews. The last time darkness covered the earth was when <u>Jesus hung on the cross</u>. The next time it will happen will be to fulfill several <u>Old Testament prophecies</u>.

People will become anxious and nervous. They will begin to ponder their future. Some will have misgivings about taking the Mark of the Beast and following the Antichrist. Others may be tormented by insanity and chew their tongues in agony.

KEY Symbols:

Fifth Bowl Judgment
darkness over all the earth

John Hagee: Mighty men, kings, and men of power will gnaw their tongues in pain and crawl into caves and beg God to kill them.[10]

What Others are Saying:

Something to Ponder

1) It was so dark in Egypt the people could not see each other and they were afraid to move from the place they were in for three days.

2) When Jesus, who is the Light of the World (John 8:12), died, God plunged the world into darkness for three hours. Because the world cannot survive without light many preachers understand this to mean that the world cannot survive without Jesus.

3) The prophet Joel says the Tribulation Period darkness will be unlike anything the world has ever experienced. The agony and fear will be indescribable.

> **Revelation 16:11** and cursed the God of heaven because of their pains and their sores, but they refused to repent of what they had done.

blaspheme: cursing, or directing false accusations against God

It Ain't My Fault

God is great and good. He is the God of heaven. He deserves praise and exaltation, but these people will curse and **blaspheme** everything he is and does. They will not blame themselves for their sins or admit that these judgments are fair retribution for their wrongdoing. Instead of repentance, they will choose continued blasphemy. And, in spite of their misgivings, they will continue to follow the Antichrist and his False Prophet.

☞ **GO TO:**

Revelation 9:14–16
(200 million)

KEY Symbols:

Sixth Bowl Judgment
the Euphrates River will dry up

Revelation 16:12 The sixth angel poured out his bowl on the great river Euphrates, and its water was dried up to prepare the way for the kings from the East.

The Way Is Clear

The Euphrates River (see Illustration #9, page 211) is mentioned more than twenty-five times in the Bible and is often referred to as the "great river." Nevertheless, this great river will dry up during the Tribulation Period. Why? Because it is a barrier that divides East from West. It prevents the kings of the East from moving their great army into the West (the Middle East).

When the sixth angel pours out his bowl, the river will dry up, the barrier will be gone, and the kings of the East will be able to move their 200 million man horde against Israel in the Battle of Armageddon (see GWDN, page 184). Notice the word "kings" is plural. This will likely be an alliance of Eastern nations.

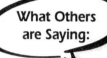

What Others are Saying:

Charles H. Dyer: The world powers will come together, and the drying up of the Euphrates hastens their arrival.[11]

J.R. Church: The Battle of Armageddon will be a worldwide attempted genocide of the Jew. Israel will have no friends in that day, and the armies of the world will converge upon Israel to slaughter every Jew on the face of the earth.[12]

Peter and Paul Lalonde: Today, China and India alone comprise 40% of the world population. With 2 billion citizens, an army of 200 million is not all that hard to imagine.[13]

RELATED CURRENT EVENTS

```
Turkey today (through the installation of the Ataturk
Dam) will cut off the flow of the Euphrates River—
the lifeblood of ancient Mesopotamia—in a move that
could lead to tensions with arid neighbors Syria and
Iraq.[14]
```

— — —

```
China's own military buildup is already alarming its
neighbors.[15]
```

— — —

According to the CIA, Red China has 330,353,665 men of military age, and boasts a standing army of 184,515,412 (1994 estimates).[16]

———

The Clinton administration, as part of its drive for the so-called New World Order, has pulled out all of the stops to make Red China the future world's most powerful economic power.[17]

———

Asia's need for oil will accelerate drastically and force Asia to focus more attention on the Middle East beginning in 1996.[18]

> **Revelation 16:13** Then I saw three evil spirits that looked like frogs; they came out of the mouth of the dragon, out of the mouth of the beast, and out of the mouth of the false prophet.

☞ **GO TO:**

I Kings 22:20–37 (Ahab)

Exodus 8:1–15 (second plague)

A Frog In Your Throat

In the Old Testament, God was looking for someone to lure the wicked king Ahab into a death trap. An evil spirit stepped forward and volunteered to be a lying spirit in the mouths of Ahab's false prophets. God said that would work and sent the lying spirit forth. Shortly after that, Ahab asked his prophets if he should battle the Arameans at Ramoth Gilead. His prophets, influenced by the lying spirit, said he would win. Instead, he was killed.

John tells us that three evil spirits will come forward during the Tribulation Period: one from the mouth of Satan, one from the mouth of the Antichrist, and one from the mouth of the False Prophet.

We can only speculate about the frog-like appearance of these demons. We know that the Egyptians worshiped Heka, a frog-headed goddess. She is one of the oldest goddesses who was said to have demonic powers. The second plague on Egypt during the days of Moses was a plague of frogs. We know too, that frogs are connected with the occult. Witches are often portrayed with frogs and use them in their spells. Frogs breed in mire and muck and are a symbol of uncleanness.

One more point. There are other Scriptures on this subject. For example, the Apostle Paul said, *The Spirit* (Holy Spirit) *clearly*

KEY POINT

This verse is where we get the term "False Prophet."

KEY Symbols:

Three Evil Spirits
looked like frogs
they came out of the mouth of the dragon (Satan)
out of the mouth of the beast (the Antichrist)
and out of the mouth of the False Prophet

says that in later times some will abandon the faith and follow deceiving spirits and things taught by demons (I Timothy 4:1). Demons are real and will be very busy during the Tribulation Period.

> **Revelation 16:14** They are spirits of demons performing miraculous signs, and they go out to the kings of the whole world, to gather them for the battle on the great day of God Almighty.

A Death Trap

Jesus was talking about the last days when he said, *false Christs and false prophets will appear and perform great signs and miracles to deceive even the elect—if that were possible. See, I have told you ahead of time* (Matthew 24:24, 25). The Apostle Paul said the Antichrist will come *with the work of Satan displayed in all kinds of counterfeit miracles, signs, and wonders* (II Thessalonians 2:9). When the sixth bowl is poured out, spirits of demons will use miraculous signs to lure the leaders of the world and their God-defying troops into that death trap called the great day of God Almighty or the Battle of Armageddon.

What Others are Saying:

Charles H. Dyer: Satan and his human henchmen send the demons to summon the armies. The armies come as allies, not enemies. Armageddon serves more as a staging ground than a battlefield.[19]

David Hocking: When miraculous signs are performed, many people believe God is behind them. The Bible teaches otherwise. While it is possible that God is performing the signs, it is also possible they are being done through the power of Satan or demons.[20]

RELATED CURRENT EVENTS

On Thursday, September 21 (1995), the news swept around the world of the extraordinary miracles of milk-drinking Hindu statues. Never before in history has a simultaneous miracle occurred on such a global scale. Television, radio, and newspapers eagerly covered this unique phenomenon, and even skeptical journalists held their milk-filled spoons to the gods—and watched, humbled, as the milk disappeared. The media coverage was extensive, and although scientists

and "experts" created theories of "capillary absorp-
tion" and "mass hysteria," the overwhelming evidence
and conclusion was that an unexplainable miracle had
occurred. . . . [21]

> **Revelation 16:15** "Behold, I come like a thief! Blessed
> is he who stays awake and keeps his clothes with him,
> so that he may not go naked and be shamefully ex-
> posed."

KEY POINT

Those who refuse the
Mark will be blessed
when Jesus returns,
but those who take it
will be exposed.

A Thief In The Night

It is Jesus who says, *I come like a thief.* People do not usually
expect thieves or they would prepare. This means the coming of
Jesus will be a surprise, but what is Christ talking about? It cannot be the Rapture because by this time that will have already
occurred. And who will be surprised? It cannot be the Church,
because they went in the Rapture. This is a reference to the coming of Jesus at the end of the Tribulation Period. The unclean
spirits will gather the armies of the world at Armageddon, and
only then will Jesus return and catch them by surprise.

Blessed is he who stays awake and keeps his clothes with him is an
encouragement for people to remain faithful. This garment
(clothes) is the righteousness of Christ. Those who refuse the
Mark of the Beast will be blessed when Jesus returns, but those
who take it will be exposed.

> **Revelation 16:16** Then they gathered the kings to-
> gether to the place that in Hebrew is called Armaged-
> don.

Armageddon

This is the only time the word "Armageddon" can be found in the
Bible. Armageddon is Hebrew and is the name of a place in northern Israel (see Illustration #10, page 240). When translated, the
word means "Mount of Megiddo." The Mount of Megiddo is a
large hill just west of the Jordan River, in the Plain of Esdralon.
The Euphrates River will dry up to allow the 200 million man
army to approach from the East. Demons will go forth from the
Satanic trinity (Satan, the Antichrist, and the False Prophet) and
gather other armies from all over the world.

Illustration #10

Megiddo—Modern day map showing location of the city of Megiddo. It has become a symbol for the final battle of good and evil because Armageddon translated is "Mount of Megiddo."

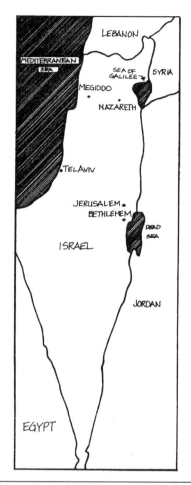

What Others are Saying:

KEY Symbols:

Seventh Bowl Judgment
"It is done!"

Charles H. Dyer: The gathering of the armies at Armageddon is not the climax of world history. One final bowl of judgment must still be poured out on the earth before Jesus returns to claim his throne.[22]

> **Revelation 16:17** The seventh angel poured out his bowl into the air, and out of the temple came a loud voice from the throne, saying, "It is done!"

The Last Judgment

The seventh bowl judgment will be the last. It will be poured out into the air, and then a voice from the throne of God will say, *It is done!* Just before Jesus died on the cross he said, *It is finished* (John 19:30). Just before Jesus returns to earth he will say, *It is done!* The remaining events will bring an end to Satan's reign.

> **Revelation 16:18** Then there came flashes of lightning, rumblings, peals of thunder and a severe earthquake. No earthquake like it has ever occurred since man has been on earth, so tremendous was the quake.

Off The Richter Scale

When the seventh bowl is poured into the air something will happen to the atmosphere. Great flashes of lightning will explode to the ground, and thunder will rattle the earth. Fires will break out, and a tremendous earthquake will shatter the land.

```
Major Earthquakes Of This Century
(40,000 or more deaths)
```

Date	Location	Deaths	
1908, Dec. 28	Messina, Italy	83,000	
1920, Dec. 16	Gansu, China	100,000	
1923, Sept. 1	Yokohama, Japan	200,000	
1927, May 22	Nan-Shan, China	200,000	
1932, Dec. 26	Gansu, China	70,000	
1935, May 31	Quetta, India	50,000	
1970, May 31	Northern Peru	66,794	
1976, July 28	Tangshan, China	242,000	
1988, Dec. 7	Northwest Armenia	55,000	
1990, June 21	Northwest Iran	40,000	[23]

> **Revelation 16:19** The great city split into three parts, and the cities of the nations collapsed. God remembered Babylon the Great and gave her the cup filled with the wine of the fury of his wrath.

☞ **GO TO:**

Isaiah 13:4–6, 19, 20; Jeremiah 51:7, 25, 26 (prophets)

Remembered Again

This great earthquake will split the great city of Babylon into three parts, but it will still stand. This cannot be said for other cities because they will be leveled. Every city on earth, except Babylon, will be in ruins as the end of the Tribulation Period approaches.

With Babylon still standing, it will come into remembrance before God. One of the three angels (Revelation 14:8) predicted Babylon's doom just a short time before this. The Old Testament prophets predicted her doom long before that. It will be time for those prophecies to be fulfilled. She will get *the cup filled with the wine of the fury of his wrath.*

Remember
This . . .

A second angel followed and said, *Fallen! Fallen is Babylon
the Great, which made all the nations drink the maddening wine
of her adulteries* (Revelation 14:8).

☞ **GO TO:**

Isaiah 24:19–23 (drunk-
ard)

> **Revelation 16:20** Every island fled away and the
> mountains could not be found.

Creation Backwards

The surface of the whole earth will be changed. Every island will
sink beneath the water. Every mountain will be leveled. The
prophet Isaiah said the floodgates of heaven will be opened. The
earth will reel to and fro <u>like a drunkard</u>.

What Others
are Saying:

John Hagee: The earth will quake so severely that the islands
of the sea will disappear. Puerto Rico and Hawaii will be covered
with water. Every building, every wall will crumble. Millions will
be trapped beneath the rubble with no one to come to their aid.[24]

Peter and Paul Lalonde: According to sources from Energy,
Mines, and Resources in Canada there were, from 1900 to 1969,
about 48 earthquakes that registered 6.5 or more on the Richter
Scale. This is an average of *6 per decade.* From 1970 to 1989 there
were 33 earthquakes measuring 6.5 or more. This is an average of
17 per decade. From January 1990 to July 1990 there were 10
earthquakes of 6.5 or greater. This is 10 major earthquakes in just
six months. And from July 1990 to October 1992 there were 133
earthquakes which measured at 6.5 or greater. This averages out
to *600 per decade.*[25]

☞ **GO TO:**

Exodus 9:18–25 (sev-
enth plague)

> **Revelation 16:21** From the sky huge hailstones of
> about a hundred pounds each fell upon men. And they
> cursed God on account of the plague of hail, because
> the plague was so terrible.

Hail Bigger Than Bowling Balls

The <u>seventh plague</u> in Egypt during the days of Moses was hail
mixed with fire. It was directed against Isis, the cow-headed goddess of the air. Giant hail killed the cattle in the fields and broke
down all the trees.

coconuts falling on people

This plague will be much worse. These hailstones will weigh more than 100 pounds apiece and will beat the earth with a fury. What effect will this have on mankind? Will people finally repent of their sins and avoid hell? No. They will still blaspheme God.

Study Questions

1. Who tells the angels to pour out the bowls of wrath?
2. Why will people have to drink blood during the Tribulation Period?
3. What will happen to the kingdom of the Antichrist and how will it effect people?
4. Who will the blessed be during the Tribulation Period?
5. What will the evil spirits do to gather men for the battle of Armageddon?

CHAPTER WRAP-UP

- When the seven bowls of God's wrath are poured out his judgments will come to an end.
- After the third bowl is emptied, the angel in charge of the waters and the Tribulation Saints will proclaim these judgments to be just and true. (Revelation 16:5–7)
- The Euphrates River will dry up to make way for the coming of the kings from the East. (Revelation 16:12)
- Three spirits will come out of the mouths of Satan, the Antichrist, and the False Prophet to summon the kings of the earth together for the Battle of Armageddon. (Revelation 16:13–16)
- After the seventh bowl is poured out a great earthquake will rock the planet, destroying all cities except Babylon, which will split in three parts. (Revelation 16:18, 19)

REVELATION 17

CHAPTER HIGHLIGHTS

- Mother of Prostitutes
- From the Abyss
- An Eighth King
- Babylon, the Mother, Destroyed

Let's Get Started

Get ready. Chapter 17 is one of the toughest chapters to understand in the Bible.

At the close of Chapter 16 we read, *God remembered Babylon the Great and gave her the cup filled with the wine of the fury of his wrath*. He will give Babylon this cup during the Tribulation Period, and the next two chapters will provide some idea of why God seeks to destroy this city.

Chapter 17 tells us about a Babylonian woman who has a double identity: she is a mother, and a city. This is one of the keys to understanding Chapters 17 and 18—recognizing that Babylon the Great is *both* a woman and a city at the same time.

As a *mother*, Babylon the Great is a failure. She is a prostitute and the Mother of Prostitutes. The Bible tells us that a prostitute is more than just a woman who *physically* commits sexual sins. A <u>prostitute</u> is also a person who *spiritually* has stopped following the true God and has turned to idol worship. Babylon the Great abandoned the true God and has raised her daughters (false religions) to do the same. She is the mother of false religions who wants all her daughters to grow up in her *one-world prostitute religion*. The names of some of her daughters are New Age, Satan Worship, Mother Earth Worship, Globalism, Hinduism, and Islamism. Her daughters talk about love and peace, but none of them love Jesus, and none of them talk about peace with God through Jesus. Her daughters' followers are a collection of religious people who will be left behind when the true Church is raptured.

As a *city*, Babylon the Great is also a failure. She is the birthplace of the Mother of Prostitutes and many of her daughters.

☞ **GO TO:**

Exodus 34:15, 16; II Chronicles 21:11–13 (prostitutes)

Revelation 19:7 (Bride of Christ)

Jeremiah 31:32 (wife of God)

adulterous: *spiritual prostitutes (people who take up false religions)*

KEY POINT

The key to understanding Chapter 17 and 18 is recognizing that Babylon the Great is both a mother and a city.

KEY Symbols:

Babylon

Mother of Prostitutes
- her daughters are false religions

a city of sin
- center of one-world prostitute religions

center of one-world government
- her daughters will marry adulterous kings

Something to Ponder

☞ GO TO:

Revelation 17:15 (waters)

Revelation 4:6 (sea)

Revelation 15:2 (fire)

Revelation 17:1 (masses)

ecumenism: *the effort to merge all the world's religions into one giant world religion*

During the Tribulation Period, Babylon (the city) will be filled with **adulterous** kings. She will open her doors to one-world government, one-world religion, and global trade. People intoxicated with big government, big money, global commerce, and a lust for pleasure will flock to her. She will even entice these adulterous leaders to marry her daughters which will represent a merger of one-world prostitute religions with one-world government.

Shortly after the Tribulation Period mid-point, the prostitute's sons-in-law (the kings of the earth) will become "wife abusers." They will kill the prostitute (one-world religious system) and her daughters (the individual false religions). Near the end of the Tribulation Period, God will pour out his wrath on Babylon where many of the sons-in-law live. Jesus will return and destroy Babylon the mother and Babylon the city.

Obviously, kings cannot marry a religion. Think of it spiritually. Just as you and I are <u>the Bride of Christ</u>, and Israel is the <u>wife of God</u>, these adulterous kings will marry false religions in the sense that they will espouse the doctrines of the false religions. They will co-operate with the False Prophet and the Antichrist in pushing a false religion on the world. Think about what is going on in Washington. President Clinton wants to pass "Fast Track" so he can sign trade agreements without Congress being able to make changes. Some members of the House will not vote for it because of things in it like teaching abortion to other countries. House members want these things changed, but President Clinton is determined to use trade to force a moral issue on other nations, and to bind this nation to his view. In a sense, those who support him are married to him on this issue.

> **Revelation 17:1** One of the seven angels who had the seven bowls came and said to me, "Come, I will show you the punishment of the great prostitute, who sits on many waters.

She Sits On The Masses

John will be invited to look at the punishment of Babylon the mother, the great religious prostitute who sits on many waters. This is a revelation of what God plans to do with this harlot religious system.

In the Bible, seas and <u>waters represent great masses</u> of people.

They represent people, nations, and tongues. The fact that this wicked woman is pictured as sitting upon these great masses is an indication that she will be supported by them, and she will exercise control over them during the Tribulation Period.

What Others are Saying:

Arno Froese: The political roots of **ecumenism**, the united world church, are in Rome; the spiritual roots go back to Babylon.[1]

Ed Hindson: This will be the final phase of the New World Order. The idea of a new world religion of peace and cooperation is already being proposed. Religious unity has been endorsed by Pope John Paul II, the Dali Lama, and leaders of the World Council of Churches.[2]

KEY Symbols:

Babylon

MOTHER

sits on the masses and has control over them

Hal Lindsey: I expect to see more and more mergers between Christian denominations and more emphasis on ecumenism.[3]

Jack Van Impe: In a further bid to bring the world to one point of view, there is now a movement afoot to establish a permanent "United Religions" (UR) organization. A charter setting up the UN-style group is currently being drafted, and a facility to promote this point of view may well be open in the near future.[4]

> The Declaration (Council for a Parliament of the World's Religions—Declaration on a Global Ethic) states, "We affirm that there is an irrevocable, unconditional norm for all areas of life: for families and communities; for races, nations, and religions; there already exists ancient guidelines for human behavior which are found in the teachings of the religions of the world and which are the condition for a sustainable world order."[5]

RELATED CURRENT EVENTS

> Pope John Paul II has prophesied that there will be unity of faith and all religions will be worshiping together by the year 2000 A.D.[6]

> There is an unspoken alliance today between powers inside the Vatican and leaders of major international humanist organizations who would change the Roman Catholic Church from a sacred institution to one whose

primary function is to act as a stabilizing social force in the world. They see the church as the only global structure able to do this. The one obstacle is John Paul II. He is seen as a defender of **medieval traditions**. They want a pope who shares their more liberal, globalist view. [7]

Something to Ponder

Understand that Pope John Paul II is a proponent of religious unity. However, he fears the *form* of unity that is taking shape around him. He sees unity coming and would like for it to be more Christian than it appears it will be. He opposes the falling away that he sees taking place. Unfortunately, powers inside the Vatican are trying to transform the Roman Catholic Church from a sacred institution to a secular institution—from an institution that promotes Christ and Christian values to an institution that promotes the world approved social values. In other words, they want to transform it into a prostitute system. Instead of taking the Christian view on abortion, gay marriages, women in the priesthood, etc., it will promote the secular view.

Remember This . . .

The Church in heaven looked like a <u>sea of glass</u>.
The Tribulation Saints in heaven looked like a sea of glass <u>mixed with fire</u>.
Babylon the Great (the mother) will sit on the <u>masses of the world</u>.

☞ **GO TO:**

Luke 8:26–36 (possession)

I Timothy 4:1 (deceiving spirits)

harlot: *unfaithful religious people*

deceiving spirits: *demons*

non-monotheistic religions: *religions that believe in many gods*

> **Revelation 17:2** With her the kings of the earth committed adultery and the inhabitants of the earth were intoxicated with the wine of her adulteries."

No More Separation of Church and State

The **harlot** religious system will commit adultery with the kings of the earth. She will conspire with world leaders to produce a merger of religion and government. Here it finally is! A religious system united with a political system to manipulate the people of the earth into a false government-approved religion.

The *wine of her adulteries* is a <u>reference to demon possession</u>. This wicked woman will cause people to be led astray by **<u>deceiving spirits</u>**.

Grant R. Jeffrey: Pope John Paul II (see Something to Ponder) is constantly calling for the nations to abandon their opposition to world government.[8]

Jack Van Impe: Teachings of **non-monotheistic** Eastern religions have infected even the Church itself, driving it increasingly toward **apostasy** and a **laissez-faire** interpretation of God's Word. With widespread religious deception so out of control, it is easy to understand how worldwide ecclesiastical trends are leading to the dawn of a one-world church controlled by the spirits of Satan.[9]

Ed Hindson: A false prophet of international fame will suddenly emerge to gain control of the world religious system and use it to reinforce the worship of Antichrist.[10]

```
Delegates from more than 170 sovereign nations will
attend the United Nations Fourth World Conference on
Women in Beijing, China (held in September 1995). It
will represent the most radical, atheistic, and anti-
family crusade in the history of the world. . . . It
is a mystery, in fact, how such enormous threats to
our spiritual and cultural heritage could have slith-
ered into our midst without due notice or alarm. .
. . Make no mistake about it: Most of what Christianity
stands for will be challenged during this conference.[11]
(Even our President's wife, Hillary Rodham Clinton,
attended this conference.)
```

Pope John Paul II is in favor of a one-world religion, but he wants it to come about under his terms. *He* wants to be the one who decides what this one-world religion will stand for, and what it will reject. For example, he does not want Catholics to become Protestants. He wants Protestants to become Catholics. He is for unity, but under his leadership and his terms. He believes whoever replaces him as the next pope will not be as committed as he is. He believes he will be replaced by someone who will relinquish church beliefs for a secular world view. And he believes he will be the *last* faithful pope. The next pope could be the False Prophet.

What Others are Saying:

apostasy: *to completely forsake one's faith or religion*

laissez-faire: *letting people do as they please*

RELATED CURRENT EVENTS

KEY POINT

The saved, regardless of religion or denomination, will be raptured, and the lost, regardless of their religious beliefs, will be left behind.

Something to Ponder

Something to Ponder

☞ **GO TO:**

Revelation 13:1 (Antichrist)

Revelation 17:18 (great city)

KEY Symbols:

Scarlet Beast
ANTICHRIST

Woman
BABYLON, THE MOTHER
AND THE CITY, OVER
THE ANTICHRIST

☞ **GO TO:**

Jeremiah 51:7, 8 (wine)

Holy Grail: a legendary golden cup that some say was used to catch the blood of Jesus when he was dying on the cross

communion: the ritual of taking bread (his body) and wine (his blood) to commemorate the death of Jesus

Some experts take a very anti-Catholic stance on Revelation. I have tried to avoid that. The one-world religion will have a lot of Catholics in it, but it will also have a lot of Protestants and other religions too. The saved, regardless of religion or denomination, will be Raptured, and the lost, regardless of their religious beliefs, will be left behind.

> **Revelation 17:3** Then the angel carried me away in the Spirit into a desert. There I saw a woman sitting on a scarlet beast that was covered with blasphemous names and had seven heads and ten horns.

The Woman Rides The Beast

John was taken in the Spirit to a desert where he saw something strange—a woman sitting on a scarlet beast. We already know the beast with seven heads and ten horns is the Antichrist. Since the woman will be sitting on the beast, we must assume that her prostitute religion and the Antichrist will exist on earth at the same time.

At first the Antichrist will support her one-world religion and be under her authority, but things will eventually turn sour between the two. Their relationship will be hindered by the woman's double identity. Remember she is both the mother, the false religious system, and the great city, Babylon. We see from this that all three—the false religious system, the city of Babylon, and the Antichrist—will exist during the first half of the Tribulation Period.

> **Revelation 17:4** The woman was dressed in purple and scarlet, and was glittering with gold, precious stones, and pearls. She held a golden cup in her hand, filled with abominable things and the filth of her adulteries.

The Holy Grail?

The purple and scarlet clothing with glittering jewels indicates she will be a prostitute of royal stature. She will be adorned in the trappings of her rich lovers, and appear enticing and appealing to the world.

Look at the golden cup she will be holding. Will it be the **Holy Grail**? Will she take **communion** with it? She may want the world to think that, but she will really be holding a cup *filled with abominable things and the filth of her adulteries*. When the false religions drink from this cup, they will <u>drink the wine</u> of adultery—symbolic of deceiving spirits and demons.

Today, many people think our modern society is too enlightened to believe in the existence of demons. More conservative Christians disagree. Those who accept the authority of the Scriptures accept the existence of demons. They are no less dangerous than Satan, for they are his cohorts doing his will. All who have not accepted Christ are subject to their evil influence. It is unfortunate, but this includes many of the world's religious and political leaders.

Ed Hindson: Materialism and selfism will replace spiritual values. Mankind will be left in the mindless pursuit of material prosperity as the basis for meaning and value in life.[12]

Hal Lindsey: I have found this about religion. The more false a religion is, usually the more wealth it has. And the more true a religion is, usually the less material things it has. And it doesn't seem to care about it. And I've seen the Christian church become poverty stricken spiritually as they have become wealthy materially.[13]

> **Revelation 17:5** This title was written on her forehead: **MYSTERY** BABYLON THE GREAT THE MOTHER OF PROSTITUTES AND OF THE ABOMINATIONS OF THE EARTH.

Birthplace Of Abominations

The prostitute's title reveals where she will come from and what she will do. She will come from Babylon and be associated with Babylon again during the Tribulation Period. She will be known as the Mother of Prostitutes and the Mother of Abominations. Many evil and adulterous practices will flow from her.

David Jeremiah with C.C. Carlson: A false religious system was born on the plains of Shinar in ancient Babylon, where the first world dictator, Nimrod, defying God, <u>built a tower</u> that would

Babylon, The Woman
dressed in purple and scarlet
- prostitute of royal stature

gold, precious stones, and pearls
- trappings of her lovers

a golden cup
- wine of her adultery

What Others are Saying:

☞ **GO TO:**

Genesis 11:1–9 (tower)

mystery: *a hidden truth*

nihilism: *all existence is senseless and there is no possibility of an objective basis for truth*

Nirvana: *the final heaven of Buddhists; a state of perfection*

What Others are Saying:

reach to heaven. This tower was used for studying the stars and established the basis for astrology. From the very beginning, Babylon was associated with sorcery and astrology.[14]

Arno Froese: In order to have fellowship with them, she (the prostitute) drinks the wisdom of many religions. Whether this is Buddhism, Hinduism, or Islam, all are welcomed by the "harlot Babylon." It makes no difference that the Lord Jesus is merely one of a thousand gods for the Hindus, nor does it mean anything that for Buddhists only works and **nihilism** count in **Nirvana**. It is said that they all (many waters) lead to the one God. . . . What difference does it make? We can still have fellowship with one another, can't we?[15]

Remember This . . .

The prostitute, which is the one-world religious system, originated at the <u>Tower of Babel</u>, which is located at Old Testament Babylon(see Illustration #9, page 211). Babylon was destroyed, but it is being rebuilt along with the Tower of Babel in Iraq. The prostitute is going full circle. She was born in Babylon and she will go back there before she dies.

☞ **GO TO:**

Revelation 17:2 (drunk)

> **Revelation 17:6** I saw that the woman was drunk with the blood of the saints, the blood of those who bore testimony to Jesus. When I saw her, I was greatly astonished.

Drunk With The Blood Of Her Victims

The prostitute will not only <u>make others drunk</u>, but she, too, will be drunk on the blood of the Tribulation Saints. This great ecumenical religious system will be actively involved in the persecution and death of God's people. She will be so determined to establish her one-world religion that she will actually be filled with the blood of the saints.

What Others are Saying:

Grant R. Jeffrey: Obviously, Mystery Babylon, the apostate pagan church of the last days, will not develop overnight. Such an ecumenical organization, involving many diverse religious groups, will be created by negotiation and conferences over a number of years leading up to the beginning of the seven-year tribulation period. It is therefore quite probable that we will witness the initial steps toward this one-world church of the last days before the Rapture takes the Christians home to heaven.[16]

> **Revelation 17:7** Then the angel said to me: "Why are you astonished? I will explain to you the mystery of the woman and of the beast she rides, which has the seven heads and ten horns.

Confusion

God's angel perceived that John was astonished and maybe even confused, so he told John he would explain two things: the mystery of the woman, and the mystery of the beast with the seven heads and ten horns. The remaining verses of Chapter 17 are about this—the meaning of the beast and identity of the woman.

> **Revelation 17:8** The beast, which you saw, once was, now is not, and will come up out of the **Abyss** and go to his destruction. The inhabitants of the earth whose names have not been written in the book of life from the creation of the world will be astonished when they see the beast, because he once was, now is not, and yet will come.

Out Of The Abyss

The beast existed prior to John's lifetime —*once was*, did not exist when John received this revelation—*now is not,* but will reappear at some unspecified time in the future—*will come.* The beast will have Satanic ties to the **subterranean abode** of demonic spirits since he will come *out of the Abyss.* He will eventually *go to his destruction* since God will cast him into the Lake of Fire. And he will take his followers, *the inhabitants of the earth whose names have not been written in the book of life from the creation of the world,* with him.

Ed Hindson: A world leader will quickly arise on the international scene promising to bring peace and economic stability. He will receive the support of the European Community and eventually control the whole world.[17]

When the fifth trumpet sounds, Satan will open the Abyss and release the demonic spirits being held there.

☞ **GO TO:**

Revelation 19:20 (Lake of Fire)

Revelation 9:1–11 (Abyss)

Abyss: *the place where God is holding the worst of the demonic spirits*

subterranean abode: *their prison beneath the earth's surface*

KEY POINT

The beast once was, now is not, but will come again.

KEY Symbol:

Beast
ANTICHRIST
scarlet

What Others are Saying:

Remember This . . .

☞ **GO TO:**

Jeremiah 51:24, 25;
Daniel 2:35–45
(mountain)

KEY Symbols:

Seven Heads/Hills
seven kings
- kingdoms or world
  governments

> **Revelation 17:9** This calls for a mind with wisdom. The seven heads are seven hills on which the woman sits.

Put On Your Spiritual Wisdom Cap

Interpreting this verse requires spiritual understanding of the Scriptures (not of world geography). The seven heads on the beast are seven hills on which the woman sits. This seems simple enough, but it is not as it appears. Revelation 17:10 tells us these seven hills are not seven actual hills, but are seven kings (kingdoms or world governments). Herein lies the problem. Is this: 1) a religious system/city that sits on seven hills, 2) seven kings, or 3) both? The Bible tells us that hills or <u>mountains</u> are a symbol of kingdoms. Therefore, the seven hills must be seven kings or kingdoms.

Still, some experts say the *seven hills* is a reference to Rome (the city on seven hills). Even if right, this is only saying the prostitute will control, and be supported by, Rome.

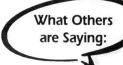

What Others are Saying:

Charles H. Dyer: Identifying the prostitute as Rome because of the seven hills has some serious flaws. The first flaw is the assumed relationship between the woman and the hills. The seven heads are attached to the beast, not the woman. . . . The seven heads do not identify the location of the prostitute because she is not part of the beast. . . . The woman sits on the whole beast, not just on the heads. . . . It is far more consistent to view the harlot's "sitting" as describing her control over the seven mountains instead of pointing to her physical location.[18]

David Hocking: To identify the seven heads as the seven hills (mountains) of the city of Rome is ignoring the clear statement of verse 10 (Revelation 17:10) that the seven mountains are seven kings.[19]

> **Revelation 17:10** They are also seven kings. Five have fallen, one is, the other has not yet come; but when he does come, he must remain for a little while.

☞ **GO TO:**

Daniel 9:27 (length)

KEY Symbols:

Seven Kings
*seven Gentile world
kingdoms*

Seven Kingdoms

The seven heads are seven hills, and they are also seven kings. The word "kings" can also be translated "kingdoms." It makes more sense in this case to say the seven heads are seven kingdoms, because history and Scripture reveal that there have been seven Gentile world kingdoms.

Five have fallen are the five Gentile world kingdoms (Assyrian, Medo-Persian, Greek, Egyptian and Babylonian) that existed *before* John's lifetime. *One is* refers to the sixth kingdom (Roman) that existed during John's lifetime, and *The other has not yet come* refers to a seventh future kingdom (the Revived Roman Empire) which will exist *after* John's lifetime. This seventh kingdom will remain *(He must remain for a little while)* for the duration of the seven-year Tribulation Period.

What Others are Saying:

David Hocking: The seven kings can represent political empires or kingdoms as well as individual rulers.[20]

Hal Lindsey: Here (John) is referring to those great world empires from the time of the original Babylon of Nimrod's day which have been dominated by the false occultic religion of Babylon.[21]

Remember This . . .

> The seven Gentile world kingdoms are the Assyrian, Medo-Persian, Greek, Egyptian, Babylonian, Roman, and Revived Roman Empire (Revelation 12:3).

> The seventh future kingdom, the Revived Roman Empire, will last for seven years (one week of years) from the day the Antichrist signs a seven-year covenant to protect Israel. Seven years will be the <u>length of the Tribulation Period</u>.

> **Revelation 17:11** The beast who once was, and now is not, is an eighth king. He belongs to the seven and is going to his destruction.

☞ GO TO:

Revelation 17:8 (beast)

Globalists: those who want to create a one-world government

KEY Symbols:

Eighth King

ANTICHRIST

out of the seventh kingdom (Revived Roman Empire)

New World Order

An Eighth King

The beast who once was, and now is not is the Antichrist. He is an eighth king (or kingdom). *He belongs to the seven* means he will be one of the seven already mentioned. Since he is yet to come, he must come out of the seventh Gentile world kingdom which will be the Revived Roman Empire.

As *an eighth king* he will take over the seventh Gentile world kingdom and establish his own brand of world government—a New World Order. The Antichrist will rise to power in that government, take it over, and transform it into a Satanic state.

What Others are Saying:

Remember This . . .

Hour of Trial: the Tribulation Period

KEY POINT

God will keep the faithful from the hour of trial.

KEY Symbols:

Ten Kings

ten rulers of the ten divisions of the world government

have not ruled before

will rule for one hour (Tribulation Period) with the Antichrist

Ed Hindson: **Globalists** are now insisting that national governments should surrender their sovereignty to a one-world government. Such a government would operate through a world headquarters, a world court, and even a world military.[22]

The beast who once was, and now is not, is the beast that will come out of the Abyss—the Antichrist.

> **Revelation 17:12** "The ten horns you saw are ten kings who have not yet received a kingdom, but who for one hour will receive authority as kings along with the beast.

An Hour Of Trial

The ten horns are ten kings (see GWDN, page 199) that will rule with the Antichrist. This presents a picture of what the end-time world government will be like. The Antichrist will rule the world which will be divided into ten divisions. In charge of each division will be a separate leader who will answer to the Antichrist.

Another significant point: The ten kings will receive authority for one hour. *One hour* is a Biblical term that means a short time. In this case, it means the ten kings will reign with the Antichrist for the duration of the Tribulation Period. The significance of this is the fact that Jesus promised to keep faithful believers from the **Hour of Trial** that is coming upon the world. Obviously there will be a pre-Tribulation Rapture (Revelation 3:10). The Church will not be on earth during the one hour reign of the ten kings with the Antichrist.

What Others are Saying:

Remember This . . .

Hal Lindsey: In my opinion, this unquestionably refers to the European Economic Community, which I believe is destined to bloom into the last great world empire represented by the seventh head with the ten horns (see page 184).[23]

Since you have kept my command to endure patiently, I will also keep you from the hour of trial that is going to come upon the whole world to test those who live on the earth (Revelation 3:10).

> **Revelation 17:13** They have one purpose and will give their power and authority to the beast.

Puppet Kings

The ten rulers will be under the Antichrist. They will be nothing more than puppet kings who submit to him.

Dictators usually come to power by using one or more of these tactics: violence, force, or political trickery. After coming to power, they usually have to continue to use force to stay in power. Because of that they usually outlaw basic freedoms such as the freedom of assembly, freedom of speech, and freedom of worship. According to the Bible, the Antichrist will do these things too, but he will be worse than any previous dictator.

Something to Ponder

> **Revelation 17:14** They will make war against the Lamb, but the Lamb will overcome them because he is Lord of lords and King of kings—and with him will be his called, chosen, and faithful followers."

Called, Chosen, And Faithful

At the end of the Tribulation Period the Antichrist and his ten puppet kings will make war against the Lamb and his <u>called</u>, <u>chosen</u>, and <u>faithful</u> followers. Unfortunately for them, the outcome was determined long ago. The Lamb will defeat them in the Battle of Armageddon because he is the Lord of lords and King of kings.

> **Revelation 17:15** Then the angel said to me, "The waters you saw, where the prostitute sits, are peoples, multitudes, nations, and languages.

Worldwide Deception

The waters that the prostitute sits on in Revelation 17:1 are peoples, multitudes, nations, and languages. This base of power and support will give the prostitute religious system tremendous control. She will ensnare and deceive people on a worldwide scale.

☞ **GO TO:**

II Timothy 1:9 (called)

Ephesians 1:4 (chosen)

Matthew 25:21–23 (faithful)

KEY POINT

Only those who are *called, chosen,* and *faithful* will be with Jesus.

KEY Symbol:

waters
peoples, multitudes, nations, and languages

☞ **GO TO:**

II Thessalonians 2:4 (he is God)

Revelation 17:16 The beast and the ten horns you saw will hate the prostitute. They will bring her to ruin and leave her naked; they will eat her flesh and burn her with fire.

Babylon, The Mother, No More

During the first half of the Tribulation Period the Antichrist (the beast) will be submissive to Babylon (the mother and her false religious system, and the city and its one-world government). Now John tells us that the Antichrist and his ten puppet kings (the ten horns) will rise up against Babylon at the mid-point of the Tribulation Period.

The Antichrist will enter the Jewish Temple in Jerusalem and declare himself to be God. Obviously there is no more room for Babylon and her one-world religion and one-world government. The Antichrist cannot be God and subject to those who worship him at the same time. So someone must go! The Antichrist and his allies will destroy the prostitute's religious system. They will confiscate her expensive clothing, gold, and precious stones, and they will persecute and kill her poor deceived people. The fact that they will *eat her flesh and burn her with fire* is indicative of the intensity and totality of the prostitute's end. Nothing will remain.

What Others are Saying:

John Hagee: But what the Antichrist does not realize is that God has sovereignly moved to give him the ability to overthrow the Babylonian system—and that soon it will be the Antichrist's turn to experience a judgment that is swift, total, and dreadful. [24]

David Jeremiah with C.C. Carlson: Here is a clear warning against the marriage of politics and religion. Whenever we see that liaison, history has shown that it ends in violent divorce.[25]

David Hocking: It is possible that the destruction of the woman will come at the middle of the Tribulation Period or shortly thereafter. This would explain the terrible persecution by the Antichrist in the last half of the Tribulation.[26]

Something to Ponder

This wicked woman, Babylon, has two identities. In addition to being a prostitute, she is also an actual city. This verse is about the destruction of the prostitute. The destruction of the city will come later.

> **Revelation 17:17** For God has put it into their hearts to accomplish his purpose by agreeing to give the beast their power to rule, until God's words are fulfilled.

☞ **GO TO:**

Daniel 7:25 (give them power)

Antichrist, The Puppet

This is an interesting verse. The Antichrist doesn't know it, but he really is a puppet king just like the ten under him. God will plant the idea of destroying the false religious system into his heart and the hearts of his ten puppet kings. Destruction of the prostitute religious system is the reason <u>God will agree to give them power</u>. They will be instruments in his hand to accomplish his purpose and fulfill his words.

> **Revelation 17:18** The woman you saw is the great city that rules over the kings of the earth."

☞ **GO TO:**

Isaiah 13:19, 20 (rebuilt)

Babylon, The City, Rebuilt

This verse identifies the woman. She is the great city that rules over the earth. Unfortunately, this is not clear enough for some experts because they want to **spiritualize** everything in Revelation. Depending upon who the expert is this city could be Rome, Jerusalem, New York, the United States, part of the European group of nations, or a nation in control of those nations.

I believe this woman is the actual ancient city of Babylon and that her reconstruction is near completion. There are several prophecies about literal Babylon that must be fulfilled. Chapter 18 covers the fulfillment of those prophecies. We must not attempt to spiritualize these verses that clearly teach that <u>Babylon will literally be rebuilt</u>.

spiritualize: not taking anything literally

KEY Symbols:

The Great City
ancient city of Babylon

Charles H. Dyer: Babylon will claw its way to the heights of power and influence one last time. . . . The Bible's prophecies will be fulfilled when someone announces that Babylon will become their capital. . . . Babylon will again become the capital of an empire in the Middle East.[27]

Peter and Paul Lalonde: Are we moving toward a world religion in our day? One example that suggests this may be the case was the convening of the Parliament of World Religions in the summer of 1993. Over 150 religions from Buddhism to Catholi-

What Others are Saying:

cism were represented at this meeting. The outcome of the meeting was "The Declaration of a Global Ethic" which sought to outline the core values and beliefs common to all faiths.[28]

Stanley E. Price: The ecumenical movements under the pope's leadership are leading to *religious* Babylon (Revelation 17); the world trade movement to *commercial* Babylon (Revelation 13:11–18; 18); and the New World Order to *political* Babylon (Revelation 13:1–10). After the Rapture, the whore of religious Babylon will rule the revived empire for three and one-half years, be overthrown, and the Beast of political Babylon will become ruler on planet earth (Revelation 17:16, 17).[29]

Something to Ponder

It seems that the confrontations with Iraqi President Saddam Hussein will never end. The world must wonder why it is so important to make him toe the line. It is simply this: Saddam's defiance is a threat to the New World Order (world government). If he can defy the world government, others can defy the world government. It is important to show the world that the New World Order is not a paper tiger to be trifled with. Rogue nations like Iraq are going to have to submit to a higher authority (world government), in order for the threat of nuclear war and the spread of chemical and biological weapons to end.

* * *

Remember This . . .

Sometime during the 1980's Iraq started rebuilding the ancient city of Babylon with the hope of turning it into a major tourist attraction. About $6 million a year was being spent on archaeological work and construction. At the same time the nation was involved in a war with Iran and Saddam Hussein was looking for a way to stir Iraqi anger against the Iranians. He remembered that Persia (Iran) helped destroy ancient Babylon. He decided to pour hundreds of millions of dollars into rebuilding Babylon and to use it as a reminder that Iran had previously attacked the city. Many of the ancient buildings, including the famous Tower of Babel, have now been rebuilt.[30]

GOD'S WORD FOR THE BIBLICALLY-INEPT

Study Questions

1. Who is Mystery Babylon the Great?
2. What was the condition of John when he saw this vision? What does his condition mean?
3. What is the significance of the prostitute's clothing and the golden cup in her hand?
4. What is a "mind of wisdom" and how can it be obtained?
5. Who will cause the beast and the ten horns (kings) to hate and destroy the prostitute?

CHAPTER WRAP-UP

- An angel will show John the punishment of the prostitute who sits on the scarlet beast. She is the one who the people of the earth will commit adultery with. (Revelation 17:1–5)

- The woman who sits on the beast is Babylon the Great. She, the Mother of Prostitutes, will kill so many of the saints who follow Jesus that she will be drunk on their blood. (Revelation 17:5–6)

- The beast who will come out of the Abyss and go to his destruction will astonish many because he was, wasn't, and yet will come. His seven heads represent seven kingdoms—the beast is the eighth kingdom that will come out of the seventh. (Revelation 17:8–11)

- The ten horns are ten kings who will rule with the Antichrist during the Tribulation. Their only purpose is to give their power to the eighth king (the beast). (Revelation 17:11–14)

- God will accomplish his purpose by planting the idea of destroying Babylon, the mother, into the minds of the beast and his ten puppet kings. (Revelation 17:16, 17)

REVELATION 18

CHAPTER HIGHLIGHTS

- A Resplendent Angel
- A Heavenly Voice
- Fall of Babylon
- Heavens Rejoice
- Millstone-Sized Boulder

Let's Get Started

Chapter 17 described the destruction of Mystery Babylon's first identity as a one-world prostitute religious system. This chapter describes the destruction of Mystery Babylon's second identity as a city that is home to a one-world political and economic system. The destruction of these two entities will rid the world of a lot of its problems.

Tim LaHaye: What all of this means is not too difficult to grasp. The one-world government, the one-world religion, and the one-world banking system that makes possible the commerce of the world is already gathering momentum. It is just a matter of time before it decides to locate in a single spot. That spot will be Babylon.[1]

What Others are Saying:

> **Revelation 18:1** After this I saw another angel coming down from heaven. He had great authority, and the earth was illuminated by his splendor.

☞ **GO TO:**

Ezekiel 43:2 (presence of God)

An Illuminating Angel

After witnessing the coming destruction of the one-world prostitute religious system John received a new revelation. He saw another angel coming down from heaven that will tackle the powerful and wealthy one-world political and economic system. When this angel arrives it will not be the sun, moon, or stars that light the earth but the angel's glory. This suggests that he will <u>come directly from the presence of God</u>.

☞ **GO TO:**

Isaiah 13:19–22;
Jeremiah 50:38–40
(prophets)

> **Revelation 18:2** With a mighty voice he shouted: "Fallen! Fallen is Babylon the Great! She has become a home for demons and a haunt for every evil spirit, a haunt for every unclean and detestable bird.

The Angel's Prophecy

The angel will prophesy about the future of Babylon the Great. It will fall and become the habitat of demons, the dwelling place of all evil spirits, and the home to all unclean birds. The great and beautiful city will become a dark and loathsome place. This fulfills what the Old Testament prophets said.

Fallen! Fallen is Babylon the Great (Revelation 14:8).

Remember
This . . .

WARNING ▶

Certain scholars suggest the great city described in this chapter cannot be the literal Babylon. They seem to think the current city of Babylon is too small, too remote, and more of a tourist attraction. They overlook what the Antichrist could do if several dozen nations flew in work crews and materials from around the world. A hundred nations with unlimited financing, hundreds of engineers, modern equipment, and thousands of workers could turn Babylon into a great city virtually overnight.

> **Revelation 18:3** For all the nations have drunk the maddening wine of her adulteries. The kings of the earth committed adultery with her, and the merchants of the earth grew rich from her excessive luxuries."

KEY Symbol:

Maddening Wine
God's wrath

Drunkard Nations

This is a picture of government and business becoming obsessed with, and controlled by, a concept. Every nation on earth has delved into the idea of world government and world trade. By the time the Tribulation Period arrives they will be intoxicated with it. The idea will receive their full support, and the businessmen involved will become extremely wealthy.

What Others
are Saying:

Ed Hindson: The fall of communism has paved the way for a world economy and a world government. The global web is tightening around us every day.[2]

Peter and Paul Lalonde: In the fall of 1994, over 200 spiritual leaders met in Khartoum, Sudan to discuss the need for a world council of religions which would represent all faiths. Such a council would foster cooperation between the world's major religions. Those who attended not only *called for peace and religious harmony between the world's religions* but for a *new political order* as well.[3]

Something to Ponder

Many people ask what prophecy says about the United States. Some students of prophecy think the United States is mentioned in a general way (not by name), but that is mostly speculation and cannot be proved. Others think the United States will collapse or be destroyed because it is not specifically mentioned, but that is also impossible to prove. The United States would be wise to support Israel during the Tribulation Period, but with the Church gone it seems reasonable to conclude that it will be closely aligned with Europe and its Antichrist.

> **Revelation 18:4** Then I heard another voice from heaven say: "Come out of her, my people, so that you will not share in her sins, so that you will not receive any of her plagues;

Don't Fall Into The Same Fate

A voice from heaven will urge God's people to leave Babylon for two reasons: so they will not become involved in Babylon's sin, and so they will not fall victim to the plagues God will inflict on Babylon. Even during this terrible time of God's wrath being poured out we can see that God still cares about his people.

David Hocking: It is clear . . . that God desires to protect his people, and . . . punish Babylon.[4]

What Others are Saying:

J. Vernon McGee: This verse reveals that God's people are going to be on earth to the end (it is not speaking of the Church which has already been removed before the Great Tribulation began).[5]

Genesis 11:1–9 (Tower of Babel)

Tower of Babel: *a tower built to reach to God*

What Others are Saying:

☞ **GO TO:**

Galatians 6:7 (mercy)

Revelation 17:4 (cup)

KEY POINT

Those who offer no mercy will receive no mercy.

RELATED CURRENT EVENTS

Something to Ponder

> **Revelation 18:5** for her sins are piled up to heaven, and God has remembered her crimes.

No Skipping Town

In the Old Testament, God did not overlook what Babylon was doing when she tried to build a tower to heaven, and he will not overlook this. To stop construction on the **Tower of Babel**, he confused their language and scattered them around the world. In the future, to stop their sins from piling any higher, he will burn her to the ground.

David Jeremiah with C.C. Carlson: The sins of Babylon have piled one on another like bricks in the Tower of Babel. Each stone is an indictment about its sick condition.[6]

J. Vernon McGee: The judgment of God may be delayed, but it is sure. It may seem to us that the unbeliever is getting by with sin, but God's judgment is coming.[7]

> **Revelation 18:6** Give back to her as she has given; pay her back double for what she has done. Mix her a double portion from her own cup.

Double Jeopardy

It will seem for awhile that Babylon will be getting away with killing God's people. Her day, however, will come, and when it does, she will be severely dealt with. Those who <u>offer no mercy will receive no mercy</u>. This is true justice.

> The People's Republic of China (PRC) calls its Holocaust *Laogai* (Reform through Work). . . . Dr. Harry Wu estimates that more than 50 million people have been imprisoned in the *Laogai* since 1949. The PRC, in 1984, officially admitted to 20 million. Of the 50 million, Wu estimates that half have died or will die. . . .[8]

It is predicted that in 30 years there will be no Christians in the Palestinian controlled areas of Israel. Palestinian persecution is driving them out of the land where Christ was born.

Babylon's cup will be filled with abominable things.

Remember This . . .

☞ **GO TO:**

Daniel 5:17–31
(Belshazzar)

> **Revelation 18:7** Give her as much torture and grief as the glory and luxury she gave herself. In her heart she boasts, 'I sit as queen; I am not a widow, and I will never mourn.'

The Taller They Are . . .

This godless city will be filled with the proud and haughty. Her residents will declare her beauty, greatness, glory, and her reign over all the earth. They will think she is a queen, and that she is married to the kings of the earth. As such, she is not a widow but a wealthy queen who has nothing to mourn about. They will be self-deceived and will extol her around the world. Never mind the fact that God brought her down in one day during the reign of Belshazzar.

The voice from heaven will say, "Let her torture and grief be in accordance with the way she glorifies herself." This will be one of God's standards of judgment when he remembers Babylon: the great grief of the godly will be turned into glory, and the glory of the godless will be turned into great grief.

David Hocking: The sovereign control of God in the affairs of human history is a constant theme throughout the Bible. God is not a passive observer to human events. He is working them all out for his glory. He is accomplishing his plan on *his* time schedule.[9]

What Others are Saying:

J.H. Melton: When nations become wealthy, they become independent, and no longer sense the need of God. The history of the great nations in the past reveals wealth and prosperity to be responsible for their fall.[10]

Today, many global corporations and world leaders are making decisions for the sole purpose of producing wealth. They cannot see God's love, mercy, and grace because they are only looking for a big return on their investments. Unfortunately, their willing blindness will be no excuse when God decides that their sins are piled high enough.

Something to Ponder

☞ **GO TO:**

Genesis 41:25–37
(Pharaoh's dream)

Genesis 19:1–28 (Lot)

> **Revelation 18:8** Therefore in one day her plagues will overtake her: death, mourning, and famine. She will be consumed by fire, for mighty is the Lord God who judges her.

Quick And Painful

As the home of one-world government and global trade, Babylon will think she is very powerful. She will control powerful weapons and great armies. But compared to the Lord God who will judge her, this highly-touted strength will be like a dart gun.

What no earthly army can do, God will accomplish in one day. First, the angel of death will pass over Babylon. Second, this city which just finished saying, *I will never mourn* will grieve bitterly. Third, this rich city will suddenly run out of food. Lastly, it will be burned to the ground.

What Others are Saying:

Remember This . . .

Peter and Paul Lalonde: Most experts now agree that one major natural disaster, or weather catastrophe, could mean a major food crisis that would be felt worldwide.[11]

The head of a Gentile world kingdom in Egypt was a man called Pharaoh. He dreamed about seven fat cows with plenty to eat followed by seven skinny cows with very little to eat. He thought this was very significant and called in his advisors, but they could not interpret the dream. Then he called in Joseph who told him God is letting Pharaoh know that Egypt will go through seven years of good harvests with plenty to eat followed by seven years of poor harvests with very little to eat. Pharaoh believed Joseph, built storehouses for food, and located them in areas where the food could be easily distributed. The preparations paid off. Seven years of tremendous harvests came followed by seven years of worldwide famine with Egypt being severely affected, but the nation handled it well.

• • •

After moving to the promised land, Abraham and his nephew Lot decided to separate. Lot eventually moved to the city of Sodom. It was a beautiful city, but it was full of injustice and sordid sins called sodomy (homosexuality). Because of this God decided to destroy Sodom and the equally sinful neighbor city of Gomorrah. He sent angels to tell Lot what was going to happen and to get Lot and his family out of Sodom. Lot barely escaped when fire fell from heaven and burned the cities to the ground.

> **Revelation 18:9** "When the kings of the earth who committed adultery with her and shared her luxury see the smoke of her burning, they will weep and mourn over her.

Weeping Kings

The destruction of Babylon will be worldwide news. Kings, dictators, politicians, and those who supported her will see the smoke billowing up into the air causing them to grieve and cry.

J. Vernon McGee: No one dreamed that this great city would be judged. Yet, by the time the sun goes down, Babylon is nothing but smoldering ruins.[12]

What Others are Saying:

> **Revelation 18:10** Terrified at her torment, they will stand far off and cry: "'Woe! Woe, O great city, O Babylon, city of power! In one hour your doom has come!'

A Quick Fate

The kings, dictators, and politicians will shake in fear. Panic will grip them. Their cry of *woe, woe* reveals deep anguish and terror because her destruction will come in *one hour*. A few experts suggest that *one hour* could mean "a short space of time" or "spread out over a few days," but most think it means suddenly or instantaneously. That will add to the panic and terror.

Ed Hindson: The real tragedy in all this talk of global unity is the absence of any emphasis on the spiritual roots of democracy and freedom. The gospel has been blunted in Western Europe for so long that there is little God-conscientiousness left in the European people. Without Christ, the Prince of Peace, there can be no hope for manmade orders of peace and prosperity. There will be no Millennium without the Messiah![13]

What Others are Saying:

> **Revelation 18:11** "The merchants of the earth will weep and mourn over her because no one buys their cargoes any more—

No More Deliveries

Not only will the heads of state weep but so will the world's big businessmen. However, it will not be over the loss of life, loss of souls to hell, or even their own sins. They will weep and mourn over their loss of customers.

> **Revelation 18:12** cargoes of gold, silver, precious stones, and pearls; fine linen, purple, silk and scarlet cloth; every sort of citron wood, and articles of every kind made of ivory, costly wood, bronze, iron, and marble;

Dead Inventory

Purple and scarlet was worn by royalty in John's day. Silk was so scarce at one time it was outlawed. Citron wood was also scarce and highly sought for ornamental purposes. However, during the Tribulation Period, Babylon will import these cargoes frequently. These are the goods of an affluent society. The global traders will pile them up in Babylon, but the Apostle James warned about such things when he said, *Now listen, you rich people, weep and wail because of the misery that is coming upon you. Your wealth has rotted, and moths have eaten your clothes. Your gold and silver are corroded. Their corrosion will testify against you and eat your flesh like fire. You have hoarded wealth in the last days* (James 5:1–3). It will be boom time in Babylon when the billionaires head there, but it will be bust when the ball of fire falls. God gives wealth, but he meant for it to benefit society, not to enrich a few.

What Others are Saying:

Remember This . . .

J. Vernon McGee: These are the products of an affluent society. . . . You will not find a cotton dress or a pair of overalls anywhere in this list.[14]

The woman was dressed in purple and scarlet, and was glittering with gold, precious stones, and pearls (Revelation 17:4).

> **Revelation 18:13** cargoes of cinnamon and spice, of incense, myrrh and frankincense, of wine and olive oil, of fine flour and wheat; cattle and sheep; horses and carriages; and bodies and souls of men.

Even The Souls Of Man

Some more products large corporations of the world will deal in during the Tribulation Period are: expensive perfumes, spices, food, grain, cattle, and even human beings. This is a picture of large corporations that will sell anything for a profit. It is also a picture of businessmen crying because they have lost sales.

It seems almost unthinkable that we would have slavery in this modern world. Nevertheless, slavery is a tragic reality in Sudan and there is virtually no outcry from global leaders or human rights activists around the world. The jihad (holy war) being waged against Christians and non-Muslims in Sudan has caused the death of about 3 million people. Christian and non-Muslim villages are being burned, the men are being killed, and the women and children are being sold in open slave markets for sometimes as little as $10–15 apiece.

What Others are Saying:

David Hocking: One is astonished to find among the items that will be lost to these merchants, the *bodies and souls of men* (Revelation 18:13). Human life will be cheap, and people will be sold as merchandise. One cannot help but wonder if the prostitution and pornography enterprises of our world are not indicated by these words.[15]

David Jeremiah with C.C. Carlson: This world system championed by the beast will dehumanize mankind, as any system without God will do.[16]

From their treasures the wise men gave the baby Jesus gifts of gold, frankincense, and myrrh (Matthew 2:11).

Remember This . . .

> **Revelation 18:14** "They will say, 'The fruit you longed for is gone from you. All your riches and splendor have vanished, never to be recovered.'

To Be No More

The global traders will acknowledge that the Babylonian dream has been destroyed. All her riches and glory will be gone forever.

Oliver B. Greene: Heaven is here announcing to this woman that her playhouse is wrecked forever, and she is down, never to rise again.[17]

David Hocking: The hunger for achievement and accumulation of wealth remains as the dominant factor of people's lifestyles and desires. The "fools" of this world are found daily in every marketplace and place of business (Luke 12:13–21). But judgment day is coming.[18]

Remember This . . .

Babylon has always been associated with wealth. It is appropriately called the Kingdom of Gold in Daniel 2. The most famous gardens the world has ever known are called "The Hanging Gardens of Babylon." They have been designated one of the *Seven Wonders of the World*. In order to make the mountain princess he married feel at home, King Nebuchadnezzar built terraces for gardens that were 400 feet square and went up to 75 feet high. Flowers, shrubs, and trees were planted on those terraces and slaves worked the gardens day and night.

> **Revelation 18:15** The merchants who sold these things and gained their wealth from her will stand far off, terrified at her torment. They will weep and mourn

Shaking In Their Boots

The businessmen who prospered by brokering deals at Babylon will not go near the burned out ruins. They will cry and grieve at a distance because they are terrified at her judgment. Some may stand in their executive suites halfway around the world watching (on television), weeping, and wailing.

Ed Hindson: What is now more clear than ever is that we have taken a quantum leap toward the fulfillment of the Biblical prophecies of the last days. The stage is now being set for the final climatic act in the long history of human drama.[19]

> **Revelation 18:16** and cry out: "'Woe! Woe, O great city, dressed in fine linen, purple and scarlet, and glittering with gold, precious stones, and pearls!

Beauty Isn't Everything

We have already learned that the businessmen of the world will cry because Babylon's great power will not protect her. Now we learn that they will cry because her beauty and wealth will also fail to protect her. It matters not how powerful an entity is, how beautiful or how rich, if God decides it should fall, it will surely fall.

Hal Lindsey: It's not often that you see grown men weeping and wailing, at least not in public, but at this time there will be no pride left in any man. Everything they have will be lost. The panic will be a hundred times greater than that which followed the U.S. stock market crash of 1929.[20]

What Others are Saying:

Something to Ponder

Jesus said, *Do not store up for yourselves treasures on earth, where moth and rust destroy, and where thieves break in and steal. But store up for yourselves treasures in heaven, where, moth and rust do not destroy, and where thieves do not break in and steal* (Matthew 6:19, 20). Good financial planning includes much more than large bank accounts, sound investments, and a diversified portfolio. Everyone needs to think about these things, but the only permanent investments are spiritual. Giving to the Lord's work is truly sound financial planning because it becomes legal tender in heaven. That is the most careful money management of all.

> **Revelation 18:17** In one hour such great wealth has been brought to ruin!' "Every sea captain, and all who travel by ship, the sailors, and all who earn their living from the sea, will stand far off.

☞ **GO TO:**

Matthew 6:19–21 (treasure)

Don't Get Too Close

The sudden destruction of such great wealth in a short time will be catastrophic for multitudes. First, we read that the kings, dictators, and politicians who supported Babylon will cry. Then we read that the global merchants who do business with her will cry. Now we learn that the seamen who transport her goods will cry. Hauling the merchandise of Babylon will be big business, but in one hour her great wealth will be gone. Every sea pilot, every sea traveler to Babylon, all the sailors, and all who will be earning a living on the sea will stand back and mourn the loss of goods, jobs, and business.

J. Vernon McGee: How do we see the luxury of this world? Do we see it as it really is? Can we use it without getting it into our hearts? How would you feel if the luxuries in your life which you have come to consider necessities suddenly went up in smoke?[21]

Ed Hindson: This aspect (a world economy) of globalism is already upon us. No developed nation of any kind can survive today without networking with the global economy. There is almost no such thing as an "American" product that is not dependent on parts, trade, or investments from foreign countries.[22]

☞ **GO TO:**

Ezekiel 27:32 (Tyre)

> **Revelation 18:18** When they see the smoke of her burning, they will exclaim, 'Was there ever a city like this great city?'

Smoldering Ashes

This cry is similar to the lament people heard when the beautiful city of Tyre was destroyed for a second time. Nebuchadnezzar wiped out the original city on the mainland, so the Phoenicians rebuilt it on an island. They made it their capital and turned it into a great trading center. Alexander the Great came along and pushed the ruins of the old city into the sea, making a causeway out to the island. His troops walked out on dry land and destroyed the rebuilt city. People compared that to the sinking of a great ship. They cried and asked, "What city is like Tyre? Who was ever silenced like Tyre?" When people see the smoke of Babylon rising in the air they will ask, *Was there ever a city like this great city*?

☞ **GO TO:**

Revelation 18:10, 17 (one hour)

1 Timothy 6:10 (money)

> **Revelation 18:19** They will throw dust on their heads, and with weeping and mourning cry out: "'Woe! Woe, O great city, where all who had ships on the sea became rich through her wealth! In one hour she has been brought to ruin!

The Captains Cry

This is the third time we are told Babylon will fall in one hour. The sudden nature of her destruction will leave the political, business, and shipping world bitterly weeping, reeling, and stunned. This is a clear sign of what the love of money will do to people. When money is god, and God is gone, what is left but godless grief?

Some think the destruction of this great city in just one hour could mean an atomic or nuclear explosion. The fact that people will not go near it is another indication of that.

1) A mighty angel asked, *Who is worthy to break the seals and open the scroll* (Revelation 5:2)?

2) An angel with great authority and a mighty voice shouted, *Fallen! Fallen is Babylon the great* (Revelation 18:1, 2).

3) A mighty angel picked up a boulder, hurled it into the sea and said, *With such violence the great city of Babylon will be thrown down, never to be found again* (Revelation 18:21).

> **Revelation 18:20** Rejoice over her, O heaven! Rejoice, saints and apostles and prophets! God has judged her for the way she treated you.'"

The Heavens Rejoice

This is something the <u>Old Testament prophets</u> prophesied, the <u>New Testament apostles</u> predicted, and the Tribulation Period Saints will pray for. We should join the angels in heaven in rejoicing when God's Word is fulfilled and the prayers of God's people are answered.

Here we have a difference between God's people and the godless. One group will rejoice and sing the praises of God. The other will grieve and mourn the loss of their god (money). In the end, Babylon will have brought this judgment on herself for mistreating God's people.

> **Revelation 18:21** Then a mighty angel picked up a boulder the size of a large **millstone** and threw it into the sea, and said: "With such violence the great city of Babylon will be thrown down, never to be found again.

Never To Rise Again

This is the third time we have read about a mighty angel. Whether these will be three different angels or the same angel is not known, but the picture is that of a huge stone being violently hurled down into the sea where it will disappear forever. This symbolizes the sudden, violent, and eternal destruction of future Babylon.

Something to Ponder

Remember This . . .

☞ **GO TO:**

Isaiah 13:19–22; Jeremiah 50:38–40 (prophets)

James 5:1–6 (apostles)

KEY POINT

In the end, Babylon will have brought this judgment on herself for mistreating God's people.

millstone: *a large round, flat, stone (doughnut shaped) used for grinding corn, wheat, or other grain*

David Hocking: It will be wiped off the face of the earth with one fatal blow from the hand of Almighty God.[23]

J. Vernon McGee: Like a stone that makes a big splash and then disappears beneath the waves will Babylon come to an end.[24]

> **Revelation 18:22** The music of harpists and musicians, flute players and trumpeters, will never be heard in you again. No workman of any trade will ever be found in you again. The sound of a millstone will never be heard in you again.

Silenced

Everything from entertainment to manual labor jobs will cease. There will be no more music in Babylon, no people going to work, and no craftsmen on the job. She will be silenced forever.

Peter and Paul Lalonde: A truly global economy was not possible until today. Before the advent of modern communication and transportation systems, the world was little more than a collection of economic islands. However, there is no denying the fact that the same generation that saw Israel come back in her land (1948), is also seeing the world's economic focus set clearly on free trade zones, the reduction of tariffs and the building of "the new global economy." As U.S. President Bill Clinton puts it, "this new global economy is here to stay. We can't build walls around our nation. So we must provide world leadership, we must compete, not retreat."[25]

Something to Ponder

The ancient city of Pompeii, Italy was suddenly destroyed by the eruption of Mt. Vesuvius in 79 A.D. Hot ashes, cinders, poisonous gas and smoke killed about 2,000 people. Archaeologists have found shells or molds of human bodies preserved in the hardened ash. The details are so clear that even the expressions of pain and terror on their faces have been preserved.

> **Revelation 18:23** The light of a lamp will never shine in you again. The voice of bridegroom and bride will never be heard in you again. Your merchants were the world's great men. By your magic spell all the nations were led astray.

Who Turned Out The Lights?

The street lights; the lights in the malls, shops, and homes will all be dark. Joyous occassions such as marriages will never been heard again. Babylon will be an utter waste.

The merchants in Babylon will be great men on earth. They will use black magic, sorcery, and demonic practices to lead people astray. The forces of darkness will reign until God turns their lights off.

What Others are Saying:

Peter and Paul Lalonde: The religion of the ancient Babylonians was very heavily influenced by astrology, magic, fortune-telling, and occultism. In recent years our modern world has seen a re-markable increase in interest in the same types of ideologies that made up the Babylonian culture. Businessmen and politicians are having their astrological charts drawn up. Political leaders in Russia and Saudi Arabia are reported to use black magic, or consult soothsayers for their political ends. Police authorities even use psychics to provide them with clues and tips in criminal cases. In fact, it was reported in late 1995 that the CIA had been using six different psychics over a period of 20 years for intelligence missions.[26]

> **Revelation 18:24** In her was found the blood of prophets and of the saints, and of all who have been killed on the earth."

☞ **GO TO:**

Revelation 13:11 (lamb)

Matthew 24:11 (deceive)

Filled With Blood

Babylon has a long history as the city of Satan. The False Prophet will make his headquarters there during the last half of the Tribulation Period. He will worship the Antichrist and have no tolerance for the people of God. He will kill all those who lack the Mark of the Beast. Babylon's destruction will be well deserved.

The False Prophet came with two horns like a <u>lamb</u>. Lambs do not have horns, so we know he will be a fake in lamb's clothing.

Remember This . . .

Jesus warned that <u>false prophets will deceive many</u> in the last days. The winds of deceit will reach gale force during the Tribulation Period. Beware of any religious leader who speaks ill of Jesus and opposes the scriptures. Any message that contradicts the Bible, no matter how sweet-sounding, is not from God.

Study Questions

1. How many nations have been defiled by Babylon?
2. What will be the extent of Babylon's punishment?
3. What was Babylon's magic spell and does any of it exist today?
4. Whose blood will Babylon be responsible for shedding?
5. What will Babylon use to lead people astray?

CHAPTER WRAP-UP

- An angel will come from the presence of God and declare the destruction of the great city, Babylon. (Revelation 18:1–3)

- A heavenly voice will call God's people out of Babylon so that they will not share in her crimes and judgment. (Revelation 18:4–7)

- Babylon will be destroyed by God in one hour. Her sudden destruction will leave the world wailing and weeping over the loss of money. (Revelation 18:8–19)

- Those in heaven, who suffered at Babylon's hands, will rejoice over God's judgment of her. (Revelation 18:20)

- A mighty angel will throw a boulder the size of a large millstone into the sea. This will represent the totality of Babylon's destruction; she will never rise again. (Revelation 18:21–24)

REVELATION 19

CHAPTER HIGHLIGHTS

- Heavenly Rejoicing
- Marriage Supper of the Lamb
- Second Coming
- Battle of Armageddon
- A Second Supper

Let's Get Started

The terrible judgments of the Tribulation Period will be brought to an end. All rebellion will stop. Man's efforts to bring peace on earth without God will cease, and finally, Jesus will return bringing days of blessing and bounty for all believers.

> **Revelation 19:1** After this I heard what sounded like the roar of a great multitude in heaven shouting: "**Hallelujah**! Salvation and glory and power belong to our God,

Hallelujah: comes from a Hebrew word meaning "praise the Lord"

A Heavenly Roar

After the destruction of Babylon and the worldwide reaction that will follow, the roar of a great multitude will be heard in heaven. This multitude will most likely be the Tribulation Saints, but it may include others such as the Old Testament Saints, the Church, and the angels. Praise will be directed to God because salvation, glory, and power belong to him. Salvation speaks of his deliverance. Glory speaks of his judgment. Power refers to his ability to overcome his enemies.

We Will Give Him Praise For Our/His:

Salvation—his deliverance
Glory—his judgment
Power—his victory

Remember This . . .

☞ **GO TO:**

Romans 12:19 (only
God can avenge)

> **Revelation 19:2** for true and just are his judgments.
> He has condemned the great prostitute who corrupted
> the earth by her adulteries. He has avenged on her the
> blood of his servants."

Blood Repaid

Those praising God in heaven will declare his truth and justice
because he destroyed the one-world prostitute religious system,
and <u>avenged</u> the death of his people. The wicked will not get
away with their sin forever. God will personally repay those who
harm his people. His judgments are true and just because he gives
people what they deserve.

> **Revelation 19:3** And again they shouted: "Hallelujah!
> The smoke from her goes up for ever and ever."

Eternal Fire

This is the second time in this chapter that we hear a shout of
"Hallelujah" in heaven. One Hallelujah is for the destruction of
Babylon, the mother of prostitutes, and the other one is for the
destruction of Babylon the city. However, this verse refers to more
than the destruction on earth. It means they have gone to their
everlasting destruction. The only smoke that will go up for ever
and ever is the smoke of their eternal burning in the Lake of Fire.

**What Others
are Saying:**

*Remember
This . . .*

Tim LaHaye: No wonder there is rejoicing in heaven at the realization that never again will Satan's religious, commercial, or political systems be permitted to lead men astray.[1]

The smoke of their (those who take the Mark) *torment rises
for ever and ever* (Revelation 14:11).

☞ **GO TO:**

Psalm 106:47, 48;
Revelation 5:8, 14,
7:11; 11:16
(worship God)

Revelation 4:4 (elders)

> **Revelation 19:4** The twenty-four elders and the four
> living creatures fell down and worshiped God, who
> was seated on the throne. And they cried: "Amen, Hal-
> lelujah!"

Worshiping The Father

The Church and the four living creatures will fall down and <u>worship the God</u> who sits on the heavenly throne. Here again we see the elders and living creatures falling down as they did before.

David Jeremiah with C.C. Carlson: The angels, the Old Testament Saints, the Church Saints, and the Tribulation Saints will raise their voices in a choir which will reverberate louder than thunder. I've heard great choirs before, but I'm really looking forward to being in this one.[2]

- The <u>twenty-four elders</u> represent the entire Church from Pentecost to the Rapture.
- The elders and living creatures fall down to <u>worship God</u>.

> **Revelation 19:5** Then a voice came from the throne, saying: "Praise our God, all you his servants, you who fear him, both small and great!"

All Join In

It is impossible to say whose voice this will be because both the Father and the Son will be on the throne. The only certainty is that someone on the throne will approve of the heavenly praise and worship. They will invite everyone who serves God to praise the Lord.

J.H. Melton: The element of praise is so often missing in the life and service of the average Christian and the average church. . . . The world would have a different image of Christianity if there were more rejoicing and praise on the part of the people of God.[3]

> **Revelation 19:6** Then I heard what sounded like a great multitude, like the roar of rushing waters and like loud peals of thunder, shouting: "Hallelujah! For our Lord God Almighty reigns.

Thunderous Acclamation

This will be the response to the invitation found in the last verse. All God's servants will shout praises to him because the Lord God Almighty reigns.

What Others are Saying:

Remember This . . .

☞ **GO TO:**

I Chronicles 22:14-16; 23:1-5 (build Temple)

II Samuel 7:16 (covenant)

This brings to mind King David's plans to <u>build the first Temple</u> of God. He bought the Temple site, gathered materials, appointed 24,000 Levites to work on it, 6,000 to oversee the construction, 4,000 to guard the building while it was being built, and 4,000 to play instruments and sing praises to God. Think of it—4,000 people to play music and praise the Lord.

What Others are Saying:

J. Vernon McGee: It takes us all the way back to that <u>covenant which God made with David</u> in which he promised to raise one upon David's throne who would rule the world.[4]

Hal Lindsey: You see, Christ purchased the title deed to the earth at the Cross, but he hasn't yet exercised his *right* to the rulership of this earth. He'll do that when he comes back.[5]

☞ **GO TO:**

Ephesians 5:22-25
(become one)

Matthew 22:1-14
(Jesus)

II Corinthians 11:2
(Church joined)

KEY POINT

The Church is the Bride of Christ.

KEY Symbols:

Wedding Of The Lamb

equipping the saints to reign with him

> **Revelation 19:7** Let us rejoice and be glad and give him glory! For the wedding of the Lamb has come, and his bride has made herself ready.

The Bride Of Christ

This will be a great day in heaven because it will be time for the Lamb's (Christ's) marriage to the Church, the Bride of Christ. God's servants will rejoice and give him glory in anticipation of this event.

A special union will exist between Jesus and the Church similar to the union that exists between a bridegroom and bride upon their marriage. In both instances, the <u>two become one</u>. <u>Jesus is coming back</u> to earth where he and his bride will reign together as one. Before they can reign together, though, they have to be married. The idea is that the Church will be <u>joined together with Jesus</u> in a special relationship that will equip them to reign with him. He will not come back without his people, and they will not reign without him.

What Others are Saying:

Ed Hindson: When the marriage of Christ and the Church is finalized, believers will be in a perfect and fixed moral state for all eternity. In the present era, the Church is engaged to Christ in a relationship that is so binding it is described as a marriage.[6]

Be Ready for the Future Events of the Church!

1) We'll be taken up in the Rapture—I Thessalonians 4:13–18.

2) We'll go before the judgment seat of Christ—I Corinthians 3:12–15; II Corinthians 5:10.

3) We'll attend the marriage and the marriage supper—Revelation 19:7–9.

4) We'll return with Christ for his Millennial reign—Revelation 20:6.

Something to Ponder

> **Revelation 19:8** Fine linen, bright and clean, was given her to wear." (Fine linen stands for the righteous acts of the saints.)

The Bridal Gown

Before its marriage the Church will wear fine linen which is their own righteous acts. A person's deeds will follow one to heaven where they will be worn like a gown or robe. Faith in <u>God makes that possible</u>. When the marriage takes place, the Church will lay their righteousness aside. The holiness and righteousness of Jesus will be imparted to them which will form their clothing for eternity.

☞ **GO TO:**

Philippians 3:9 (God)

KEY POINT

Our deeds on earth will follow us to heaven (Revelation 14:13).

KEY Symbols:

Fine Linen
  our righteous acts on earth

☞ **GO TO:**

Matthew 25:1-13 (ten virgins)

Matthew 22:1-14 (wedding banquet)

Matthew 26:29 (fruit)

> **Revelation 19:9** Then the angel said to me, "Write: 'Blessed are those who are invited to the wedding supper of the Lamb!'" And he added, "These are the true words of God."

Supper Time!

Again John heard an angel tell him to write. This time he was told to write about the Wedding Supper of the Lamb. All those who are invited to attend this supper are blessed or happy.

Robert Frost said a **parable** is a story "that means what it says, and something else besides." Some call them "earthly stories with heavenly meanings." These are pretty good definitions. The English word "parable" comes from the Greek

Something to Ponder

word *parabole* which means "to place beside or alongside of." Thus, a parable is a story that says one thing for the purpose of teaching or illustrating something else. Jesus used them often. He took well known and easily understood truths about earthly things to help people understand difficult truths about spiritual things.

The following two parables help us to better understand the Marriage Supper of the Lamb:

1) The parable of the ten virgins—Just as the ten virgins (people) heard that the bridegroom (Jesus) and his bride (the Church) were coming back for their wedding banquet, so too will Jesus come back to earth with his Church at the end of the Tribulation Period for the marriage supper of the Lamb. Only those who have received the Holy Spirit (those with oil) will be allowed to attend this banquet on earth.

2) The parable of the wedding banquet—This parable tells us about a king (God) who prepared a wedding banquet for his son (Jesus). He sent out invitations, but many of those invited (unbelievers) made excuses for not attending, so he invited others (the Church). One man (an unbeliever) was not wearing the right kind of wedding apparel (fine linen) so he was escorted out. The wedding apparel signifies the kind of righteousness needed to attend the banquet. God provides that apparel to all those who accept Jesus as their Savior. Those who do not have it are not prepared to spend eternity with God. This should not be taken lightly. We cannot go to heaven or attend this feast as we are right now. We must be properly dressed, or we will be cast into outer darkness *where there will be weeping and gnashing of teeth* (Matthew 8:12).

Another verse that provides insight to understanding the marriage supper concerns the Lord's **Last Supper**. Jesus said he will not drink the fruit of the vine again until he drinks it in his Father's Kingdom. His Father's Kingdom is his **Millennial Kingdom** on earth.

What Others are Saying:

J. Vernon McGee: Hear me carefully now: the marriage of the Lamb will take place in heaven, but the marriage *supper* will take place upon the earth.[7]

Hal Lindsey: While Revelation 19:9 pronounces a blessing on the guests at this supper, it doesn't indicate the time or place of it. . . . It's my feeling that the wedding feast of the Lamb and his bride will take place *on earth* at the very beginning of the Millennial Kingdom of God.[8]

I stand at the door and knock. If anyone hears my voice and opens the door, I will come in and eat with him, and he with me (Revelation 3:20).

Remember This . . .

> **Revelation 19:10** At this I fell at his feet to worship him. But he said to me, "Do not do it! I am a fellow servant with you and with your brothers who hold to the testimony of Jesus. Worship God! For the testimony of Jesus is the spirit of prophecy."

☞ **GO TO:**

Exodus 20:3 (no other gods)

I Corinthians 15:3, 4 (death, burial, and resurrection)

Matthew 24:27; John 14:3 (come again)

A Case Of Mistaken Identity

After writing what the angel said, John fell at the angel's feet to worship him. That was the wrong thing to do, and the angel stopped John. He called himself a fellow servant of God and told John to, *Worship God!* During the Tribulation Period multitudes will worship Satan and his Antichrist because the False Prophet will demand it. However, <u>worship of anyone or anything other than God is forbidden</u>.

The testimony of Jesus is an interesting idea. Among other things, Jesus predicted that <u>he would die, be buried, be raised from the dead</u>, and <u>come again</u>. His predictions are his testimony and also prophecy. Everything he predicted is prophecy. Many people do not understand this. They want to throw out or discard prophecy in the Bible not realizing they would be throwing out many things Jesus said. Those who understand this hold to the testimony of Jesus.

Hal Lindsey: Woe to the Christian who minimizes or rejects prophecy in the light of this statement by the angel! It's the same as rejecting Christ.[9]

What Others are Saying:

> **Revelation 19:11** I saw heaven standing open and there before me was a white horse, whose rider is called Faithful and True. With justice he judges and makes war.

☞ **GO TO:**

Daniel 2:34, 35, 44 (prophets)

Matthew 24:30 (Jesus)

Titus 2:13; I Corinthians 1:7 (writers)

The Triumphant Return

This verse is sometimes called the climax of the entire Bible. The <u>Old Testament prophets</u> prophesied this event; <u>Jesus predicted it</u>; and the <u>New Testament writers</u> wrote about it. Everything we

KEY Symbols:

Second Rider on a White Horse

JESUS

Faithful and True
- with justice he judges and makes war

☞ **GO TO:**

KEY Symbols:

Second Rider on a White Horse

JESUS

eyes like blazing fire
- insight, knowledge, and anger

many crowns
- royalty, authority, and majesty

have studied in Revelation has been building up to this. It will be a precious sight to the saints who are still alive on earth when it happens, but a terrifying sight to the Antichrist and his followers.

Heaven will open: It opened the first time when <u>John went up</u> to heaven identifying the Rapture of the Church. It will open a second time when Jesus comes back with his Church.

A rider on a white horse will appear: The <u>first rider on a white horse</u>, the Antichrist, appeared at the beginning of the Tribulation Period. Now, just as in ancient times when mighty warriors and conquerors rode white horses, a second rider on a white horse will come out of heaven to fight and conquer.

The rider (Jesus) will be called Faithful and True: *Faithful* meaning he has done, and will do, everything God asks him to do. When Jesus walked the earth he did everything God asked of him down to the smallest detail. Now when he comes back the second time, he will again do everything God asks him to do. *True* meaning he does everything he says he will do. He <u>said he will come back</u>, and here he fulfills that promise.

With justice he judges and makes war is a reference to the purpose of his coming. He will return as a warrior to judge the inhabitants of the earth. He will deal with their sin, settle their eternal destinies, and establish his reign. What he will do will be just and right, because the earth will have been declared <u>ripe for judgment</u>.

> **Revelation 19:12** His eyes are like blazing fire, and on his head are many crowns. He has a name written on him that no one knows but he himself.

Greater Than Our Understanding

Christ's <u>fiery eyes</u> reveal his insight, knowledge, and anger. He will have full knowledge of each individual and their sins. His many crowns reveal his royalty, authority, and majesty. He will have full authority in heaven and on earth.

He has many names that we know: *Jesus, Lord, Christ, Wonderful, Son of God, Son of Man*, etc. However, when he returns he will wear a special name known only to God. Christians know his name is great, but it is greater than their understanding, since God is the only one who fully understands it.

Concerning his Second Coming, Jesus said, *Watch out that no one deceives you. For many will come in my name, claiming 'I am the Christ,' and will deceive many* (Matthew 24:4, 5). The Apostle Paul said, *The coming of the lawless one will be in accordance with the work of Satan displayed in all kinds of counterfeit miracles, signs and wonders, and in every sort of evil that deceives those who are perishing* (II Thessalonians 2:9, 10). In Revelation 6:1, 2 we saw the Antichrist coming on a white horse. Here we see Jesus coming on a white horse. In Revelation 13:1 we saw the Antichrist rise up with ten crowns on his head. Here we see Jesus coming back with many crowns on his head. It would be wise to remember that Satan is a deceiver who <u>masquerades as an angel</u>.

Something to Ponder

> **Revelation 19:13** He is dressed in a robe dipped in blood, and his name is the Word of God.

A Bloody Robe

The *robe dipped in blood* is a symbol of what is about to take place. The prophet Isaiah tells us it <u>represents the blood</u> of his enemies. He will be coming back to deal with hundreds of millions of unbelievers at the Battle of Armageddon, and it will be a bloodbath.

His name is the *Word of God*. This can be explained by looking at one of John's other books, the Gospel of John. In his gospel, he calls Jesus the <u>Word of God made flesh</u>. It will be Jesus on the white horse, and the judgment at Armageddon will be the work of God.

According to the Bible there is:

1) the *written* Word of God—John 5:39.
2) the *spoken* Word of God—John 3:34; 6:63.
3) the *living* Word of God—John 1:1, 14; Hebrews 4:12.

The Bible is the *written* Word of God. The message of Holy Spirit that filled preachers, evangelists, and others is the *spoken* Word of God. Jesus is the *living* Word of God. He is the one who fulfills the *written* and *spoken* Word of God.

Blood flowed out of the press, rising as high as the horses' bridles for a distance of 1,600 stadia (Revelation 14:20).

☞ **GO TO:**

Isaiah 63:1-6 (blood)

John 1:14 (flesh)

KEY Symbols:

Second Rider On A White Horse

JESUS

white robe dipped in blood
- blood of his enemies

Word of God
- the fleshy expression of God

Remember This . . .

☞ **GO TO:**

Matthew 21:1-11
(donkey)

KEY Symbols:

Army #1
Church

Army #2
his holy angels

Army #3
Tribulation Saints

Army #4
Old Testament Saints

White Horses
victors with Christ

> **Revelation 19:14** The armies of heaven were following him, riding on white horses and dressed in fine linen, white and clean.

What, No Fatigues?

The armies of heaven will follow Jesus. One army will be composed of the entire Church from Pentecost to the Rapture. A second army will consist of the holy angels, while a third army will be all the martyred Tribulation Saints. The Old Testament Saints will comprise the fourth army. These armies will not be dressed in dark colors or camouflage. Not one soldier will have to fight or get bloodied or soiled. The fine linen, white and clean, will prove, when it is over, that his armies will not have to lift a finger. The white horses indicate Christ intends for his followers to share in his glory as a conqueror.

Let's be honest about where the glory really belongs. A famous verse of scripture says, *We are more than conquerors through him who loved us* (Romans 8:37). This victory will not belong to us. It will belong to Jesus. Were it not for his love we would be in the wrong army and would be defeated.

What Others are Saying:

John Hagee: The first time (Jesus) came into Jerusalem he was <u>riding on a donkey</u>. The next time he will come in the final world order. He'll be riding a white horse followed by the armies of Heaven. It will be the greatest mounted posse ever to split the clouds.[10]

☞ **GO TO:**

Ephesians 6:17 (Word of God)

Genesis 1:1-27 (spoke into existence)

John 18:3-6 (fall to ground)

Psalm 2:9; Revelation 2:27 (iron scepter)

> **Revelation 19:15** Out of his mouth comes a sharp sword with which to strike down the nations. "He will rule them with an iron scepter." He treads the winepress of the fury of the wrath of God Almighty.

Sharper Than Any Two-Edged Sword

Jesus will be the only one in this great heavenly army to carry a weapon. The battle will be his to win or lose. His weapon will be a <u>sharp sword, the Word of God</u>.

When this world was created, <u>God spoke it into existence</u>. When soldiers went to the Garden of Gethsemene to arrest Jesus, he spoke and they <u>fell to the ground</u>. At Armageddon he will simply speak to destroy the opposing nations.

Things will change during the Millennium. *Jesus will rule them with an iron scepter.* He will establish a strong set of standards and require everyone to live by them. Crime and unfaithfulness will not be tolerated. There will be no deception, no lies, no murder, no crime, no war. God's brand of righteousness will prevail for a thousand years. Knowledge of the Lord will fill the earth, and Jesus will finally get the worship he so richly deserves.

This will not come about because man has given up his rebellious ways or because man's efforts to establish world peace have succeeded. This will come about because the Son of God has put down the wicked and established his own reign on earth.

KEY POINT

He will speak, and they will fall.

KEY Symbols:

Sharp Sword
Word of God

Iron Scepter
God's standards

Winepress Of His Wrath
judgment of the nations

What Others are Saying:

☞ **GO TO:**

Revelation 17:14 (Lamb)

J. Vernon McGee: Christ is going to be a dictator. A chicken won't peep, a rooster won't crow, and a man will not move without his permission.[11]

> **Revelation 19:16** On his robe and on his thigh he has this name written: KING OF KINGS AND LORD OF LORDS.

Every Knee Shall Bow

Jesus will return as a King to establish his kingdom. Every earthly king will submit to him. Every individual will call him Lord.

The Antichrist and his ten puppet kings will make war against the Lamb, but the Lamb will overcome them because he is Lord of lords and King of kings.

Remember This . . .

> **Revelation 19:17** And I saw an angel standing in the sun, who cried in a loud voice to all the birds flying in midair, "Come, gather together for the great supper of God,

The Second Supper

This is the second of two great suppers mentioned in Chapter 19. An angel will stand in the sun and summon the birds to gather together for a great feast prepared by God.

Remember This . . .

An angel told John to write, *Blessed are those who are invited to the wedding supper of the Lamb* (Revelation 19:9). Those who attend the supper of the Lamb will be *at* the supper, but those who are at Armageddon will *be* the supper.

> **Revelation 19:18** so that you may eat the flesh of kings, generals, and mighty men, of horses and their riders, and the flesh of all people, free and slave, small and great.”

Filled To Overflowing

This predicts the horrible end of the Antichrist's armies. His foolish rulers, mighty men, horses, riders, and troops will become a feast for the birds.

What Others are Saying:

John Hagee: The Second Coming of Jesus Christ to the fields of Armageddon is at once a towering event of human history and the most staggering defeat that any army has ever endured.[12]

> **Revelation 19:19** Then I saw the beast and the kings of the earth and their armies gathered together to make war against the rider on the horse and his army.

☞ **GO TO:**

Revelation 9:16 (200 million)

World War III

The Antichrist is named first because he will lead these armies. His ten puppet kings will join him with their troops from all over the world. The Kings of the East alone will have <u>200 million troops</u>. These armies will have the latest and most powerful weapons known to mankind. Never before have there been so many armies gathered together on one side. Notice why they will gather: *to make war against the rider on the horse and his army.* These armies will gather to fight the Lord Jesus and those who will come out of heaven with him.

Remember This . . .

They are spirits of demons performing miraculous signs, and they go out to the kings of the whole world, to gather them for the battle on the great day of God Almighty (Revelation 16:14).

What Others are Saying:

John Hagee: Yet as the armies of the world converge upon Armageddon on a massive collision course, suddenly their objective will change. Instead of contending with each other, they will unite to fight the armies of the Messiah that descend from heaven to the storied fields of Armageddon.[13]

> **Revelation 19:20** But the beast was captured, and with him the false prophet who had performed the miraculous signs on his behalf. With these signs he had deluded those who had received the mark of the beast and worshiped his image. The two of them were thrown alive into the fiery lake of burning sulfur.

Captured!

Out of the hundreds of millions gathered at Armageddon, only two people will be captured (see GWDN, page 314): the Antichrist and the False Prophet. They will be seized for using <u>miraculous signs</u> to delude people into taking the Mark of the Beast and worshiping his image. They will be judged immediately and cast into the **Lake of Fire**.

☞ GO TO:

Revelation 13:13-15 (signs)

Lake of Fire: *the final abode of Satan and his followers*

David Jeremiah with C.C. Carlson: I believe the Bible. It tells us that heaven and hell are real. It also tells us that Jesus is coming again.[14]

J. Vernon McGee: The two arch-rebels and tyrants, the Antichrist and the False Prophet, have the questionable distinction of being the first two who are cast into hell. Even the devil hasn't been put there yet.[15]

J.R. Church: The Antichrist will be perhaps the greatest intellectual, the greatest politician, the greatest statesman, and the greatest economist who ever lived. But when he usurps the throne of God and gives his allegiance to Satan, he will become the greatest fool.[16]

What Others are Saying:

> **Revelation 19:21** The rest of them were killed with the sword that came out of the mouth of the rider on the horse, and all the birds gorged themselves on their flesh.

Not One Remaining

Not one of the millions of troops will escape. They will all be killed by the powerful Word of God, and the birds will consume their bodies.

☞ GO TO:

I Samuel 15 (Amalekites)

Esther 3:1-15 (Haman)

What Others are Saying:

Something to Ponder

J.R. Church: Christ, the victor, will judge the nations, set up his glorious kingdom and rule over the earth for a thousand years![17]

When Saul was anointed king over Israel, God told him to <u>kill all the Amalekites</u>, including their women and children, and to destroy everything they had including their animals. But Saul only did part of what God commanded. He disobeyed God, let some of the Amalekites live, and took some of their animals for booty. About 500 year later, <u>Haman</u> the Agagite (the royal family of the Amalekites) attempted to have all the Jews killed. By not carrying out God's seemingly extreme command, King Saul opened a door that almost wiped out the entire Jewish nation. Those who do not know the future should be careful about questioning the Word of God.

Study Questions

1. Is shouting a proper form of worship?
2. What is the *spirit of prophecy*?
3. Who are the *armies of heaven*?
4. How will the False Prophet deceive people? Why will he do it?
5. Who will perish at the Battle of Armageddon?

CHAPTER WRAP-UP

- Those in heaven will rejoice and praise God because he has destroyed Babylon and because the wedding of the Lamb has come. (Revelation 19:1–8)

- All those who are invited to the Marriage Supper of the Lamb will be blessed. (Revelation 19:9)

- The Second Coming of Jesus will be marked by his return on a white horse with the armies of heaven behind him. He will destroy the nations of the earth with the Word of God. (Revelation 19:11–16)

- At the Battle of Armageddon Christ will destroy the armies of the earth. He will capture the Antichrist and False Prophet and cast them into the Lake of Fire. (Revelation 19:19–21)

- An angel standing in the sun will invite all the birds of the air to God's supper where they will feast on the dead bodies of those who opposed Christ at Armageddon. (Revelation 19:17, 18, 21)

Part Three

THE MILLENNIUM AND BEYOND

REVEREND FUN

REVELATION 20

Let's Get Started

This chapter reveals something that is mentioned nowhere else in the Bible: The thousand year reign of Jesus on earth or, as we have already called it, the Millennium. Before it can begin, though, two things must happen: Jesus must return, and Satan's rule must come to an end. Chapter 19 covered the Second Coming of Christ, so now it's time to look at the demise of Satan.

Jack Van Impe: To have a thorough understanding of the word "millennium," let's look at the original language derivatives for this word. In Latin, *mille* means "thousand;" *annus* means "years." The Greeks also had a term for this which they called *chilias*—meaning "one thousand." Whenever we use the terms *millennial, millennialism,* or *chiliasm,* the meaning is always "a thousand years."[1]

> **Revelation 20:1** And I saw an angel coming down out of heaven, having the key to the Abyss and holding in his hand a great chain.

The Key To The Abyss

An unnamed, but seemingly ordinary, angel will come from heaven to earth. He will have the key to the Abyss that will be taken from Satan when the devil is cast out of heaven in Revelation 12:7–9. The angel will also have a great chain in his hand.

What Others are Saying:

messianic: *having to do with the Messiah and his Millennial reign*

J. Vernon McGee: It is true that the Millennium is mentioned only in one chapter, but God mentions it six times. How many times does he have to say a thing before it becomes true? He mentions it more than he mentions some other things that people emphasize and think are important. . . .[2]

The Unnamed Angel
key
- open the Abyss

great chain
- to bind Satan

David Jeremiah with C.C. Carlson: How else can we respond to the disciple's prayer, *Thy kingdom come* (Matthew 6:10 KJV), without the literal establishment of that kingdom? The Millennium is needed to redeem creation. We have been told of the terrible devastation of our planet; now it will be made new and beautiful once more.[3]

Hal Lindsey: The heart of the Old Testament prophetic message is the coming of the Messiah to set up an earthly Kingdom over which he would rule from the throne of David. The only important detail which Revelation adds concerning this promised **messianic** Kingdom is its duration—one thousand years.[4]

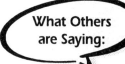
The Dragon
SATAN/DEVIL

the ancient serpent

> **Revelation 20:2** He seized the dragon, that ancient serpent, who is the devil, or Satan, and bound him for a thousand years.

Not Before The Time Is Come

Obviously, since God is omnipotent, he could seize Satan anytime he wants. But the Bible says Satan's arrest will come at the end of the Tribulation Period. God will not jump the gun and violate his own Word. When the Tribulation Period is over, he will send one ordinary angel to seize and bind Satan for a thousand years.

Hal Lindsey: I don't really have any problem believing that God could make such a key and chain, since Satan has never really been free anyway. He's only been able to do what God has permitted. God has had him on a long leash, and now the time has come to pull it in![5]

Jack Van Impe: These are the words (millennial, millennialism, chiliasm) of the early Church fathers, the leaders during the first three hundred years of Christianity. If, in their day, you did not believe in chiliasm—the reign of Christ on earth for a thousand years—you were considered a heretic.[6]

> **Revelation 20:3** He threw him into the Abyss, and locked and sealed it over him, to keep him from deceiving the nations anymore until the thousand years were ended. After that, he must be set free for a short time.

☞ **GO TO:**

Zechariah 14:16 (worship Jesus)

Isaiah 2:4; 11:9 (temptation)

On The Brink

The angel will cast Satan, bound and chained, into the Abyss. This will keep Satan from deceiving the nations during the Millennium. Survivors from the Tribulation (the Tribulation Saints and the living Jews) will repopulate the earth, and people from all nations will go to Jerusalem once a year to <u>worship Jesus</u>.

Multitudes will be born during the Millennium. During that time, the offspring from the Tribulation Saints and Jews will <u>not know what temptation</u> is. There will be no real test of their faith. Satan will be released one more time to try them, and unfortunately, many will fall.

Jack Van Impe: The Targum (Aramaic paraphrase of the Old Testament), Talmud (a vast compendium of Jewish law and lore), and Midrash (an interpretive method to penetrate the deepest meaning of a Hebrew passage) all have concluded there will be a literal thousand-year period when the Messiah will reign on earth.[7]

What Others are Saying:

> **Revelation 20:4** I saw thrones on which were seated those who had been given authority to judge. And I saw the souls of those who had been beheaded because of their testimony for Jesus and because of the word of God. They had not worshiped the beast or his image and had not received his mark on their foreheads or their hands. They came to life and reigned with Christ a thousand years.

☞ **GO TO:**

I Corinthians 6:2, 3 (judge world)

I Corinthians 15:20–23 (resurrection)

Raised At Last

Thrones on which were seated those who had been given authority to judge refers to the Church and martyred Tribulation Saints. They will sit upon thrones and reign with Jesus during the Millennium. They will even be given the authority to <u>judge the world</u>.

KEY Symbols:

Thrones
judgment seats for Christians

The souls of those who had been beheaded refers to the martyred Tribulation Saints. They were beheaded for two reasons: because of their testimony for Jesus, and to fulfill the Word of God. These will be Gentiles and Jews who refused to worship the Antichrist or his image, and refused to take his Mark. After Satan is bound and chained, their souls will appear, and they will be raised from the dead in the fourth and final phase of the <u>resurrection</u> (more on this in next verse).

You have made them to be a kingdom and priests to serve our God, and they will reign on the earth (Revelation 5:10).

Remember This . . .

☞ **GO TO:**

Matthew 27:52–53; Daniel 12:1–3 (Old Testament saints)

KEY Symbols:

First Resurrection

RESURRECTION OF LIFE

believers
four phases

Second Resurrection

RESURRECTION OF DAMNATION

unbelievers
end of the Millennium

> **Revelation 20:5** (The rest of the dead did not come to life until the thousand years were ended.) This is the first resurrection.

Two Resurrections

Jesus said, *Do not be amazed at this, for a time is coming when all who are in their graves will hear his voice and come out—those who have done good will rise to live, and those who have done evil will rise to be condemned* (John 5:28, 29). The first resurrection (see GWDN, page 320) is called the *resurrection of life* or the resurrection of believers. The second resurrection is called the *resurrection of damnation* or the resurrection of unbelievers. This verse reveals that there will be a thousand years between the two.

Perhaps some clarification would help. Some people think that *the first resurrection* means only one resurrection, but that is not the case. The *first* resurrection is a resurrection that began over 1,900 years ago and occurred in four phases (see Time Line #5, Appendix A):

Phase 1—the resurrection of Christ and some <u>Old Testament Saints</u>

Phase 2—the resurrection of the Church at the Rapture

Phase 3—the resurrection of the two witnesses

Phase 4—the resurrection of the Tribulation Saints and the remainder of the Old Testament Saints at the end of the Tribulation Period

Second Resurrection—the unbelievers at the end of the Millennium

The 144,000 and those believers who survive the Tribulation Period will not be resurrected since they will still be alive at the start of the Millennium.

> **Revelation 20:6** Blessed and holy are those who have part in the first resurrection. The second death has no power over them, but they will be priests of God and of Christ and will reign with him for a thousand years.

A Thousand Year Reign

This tells us six things about those who will have a part in the first resurrection:

1) *Blessed*—they will be happy in their eternal state
2) *Holy*—they will be separated or identified as God's special people
3) *Priests*—they will minister to, and serve in the presence of God
4) *Reign*—they will be both a **royal** and a **political priesthood**
5) *A thousand years*—the length of their earthly reign with Jesus
6) *The second death has no power over them*—they will never suffer the consequences of their sin by being cast into the Lake of Fire because they have been redeemed

> **Revelation 20:7** When the thousand years are over, Satan will be released from his prison

Not Him Again

With Satan bound during the Millennium, people will be shielded from temptation and sin. Sickness and disease will not exist and people will live to be hundreds of years old. A population explosion will occur. However, God is no respecter of persons. *Those born during the Millennium* will have to be tested just like everyone else. When the Millennium is over, the Abyss will be opened one more time, and Satan will be released to resume his old ways.

> **Revelation 20:8** and will go out to deceive the nations in the four corners of the earth—Gog and Magog—to gather them for battle. In number they are like the sand on the seashore.

☞ **GO TO:**

Revelation 5:10; I Peter 2:9 (royal priesthood)

Revelation 19:20; 20:10 (Lake of Fire)

royal priesthood: members of Jesus' family who will work as priests during the Millennium

political priesthood: religious people who will hold political positions during the Millennium

☞ **GO TO:**

Isaiah 65:18–24 (hundreds of years)

KEY POINT

Those born during the Millennium will be tested.

☞ **GO TO:**

Jeremiah 17:9; Romans 8:7, 8 (nature of man)

Isaiah 14:12, 13;
Revelation 12:9
(greater then God)

Battle of Gog and Magog:
a great rebellion against
God following the
Millennium

Gog and Magog: the
prince (Gog) and his tribes
(Magog)

What Others
are Saying:

KEY POINT

Rebellion is man's
nature, and unless we
are born again, we
will never change.

☞ **GO TO:**

Psalm 87:2, 3 (City)

Genesis 19:24 (Sodom
and Gomorrah)

Hebrews 12:29 (fire)

KEY Symbols:

Camp of God's People
Jerusalem (City of God)

World War IV—One Last Try

When Satan is released he will pick up where he left off. He will go out once again to deceive the nations.

Tempting those who were born during the Millennium will prove that eliminating sin is not as simple as changing our environment. Something is wrong with the very nature of man's heart. Rebellion is our nature, and unless we are born again, we will never see change.

At the **Battle of Gog and Magog** Satan will repeat what he tried at the Battle of Armageddon. He will try one final time to become greater than God by gathering a great horde of people from all over the world, including those from **Gog and Magog**.

J. Vernon McGee: Because the rebellion is labeled "Gog and Magog," many Bible students identify it with the Gog and Magog of Ezekiel 38–39. This is not possible at all, for the conflicts described are not parallel as to time, place, or participants—only the names are the same.[8]

Hal Lindsey: War is one of his (Satan's) favorite enterprises. He gets together some of the descendants of the enemies of Israel (Gog and Magog) who were born during the Millennium, and surrounds Jerusalem.[9]

> **Revelation 20:9** They marched across the breadth of the earth and surrounded the camp of God's people, the city he loves. But fire came down from heaven and devoured them.

Foiled Once Again

Jesus will reign from Jerusalem, the City of God (*the camp of God's people*), during his Millennial reign. Satan's army will march across the earth and surround the city, but just as God destroyed the cities of Sodom and Gomorrah, he will again consume Satan's army with fire from heaven.

"God is love" is one of the great truths of the Bible, but we should also remember that *God is a consuming fire*. It is interesting that the only thing stopping the attack on Jeruselum is fire from heaven and the destruction of Satan. The message here is to not harm the things God loves.

> **Revelation 20:10** And the devil, who deceived them, was thrown into the lake of burning sulfur, where the beast and the false prophet had been thrown. They will be tormented day and night for ever and ever.

Gone Forever

Satan will not be allowed to lure people into destruction any longer. His deceptive career will be brought to an end when he is captured and thrown into the Lake of Fire where the Antichrist and False Prophet already reside. Unfortunately for them, they will not be destroyed, but will suffer unending torment.

David Hocking: Those who are cast into hell are not annihilated as some religious groups teach. They experience torment forever and ever; it is an everlasting fire into which they are cast. Satan deserves it, and the justice of God demands it (Matthew 25:41).[10]

Hal Lindsey: I'm sure this doesn't bring any joy to God's heart. This creature, Satan, was God's most beautiful creation and here he ends in terrible infamy.[11]

> **Revelation 20:11** Then I saw a great white throne and him who was seated on it. Earth and sky fled from his presence, and there was no place for them.

The Great White Throne

This is the *judgment seat* (see GWDN, page 321) of Almighty God. The one who will be seated on it is not identified, but we have already seen that all <u>judgment has been committed to Jesus</u>. When preachers say people will have to face the judgment of God, this is the judgment most people think about. However, the only ones who will appear before this judgment seat are those who are lost.

 Earth and sky fled from his presence is something that little is known about. The consensus seems to be that earth and heaven will be moved to make room for the **new earth** and **new heaven**. *There was no place for them* appears to indicate the <u>old earth and old heaven will be destroyed</u> after being removed.

KEY Symbols:

Lake of Fire
LAKE OF BURNING SULFUR

hell
Satan, Antichrist, False Prophet, and unbelievers

> **What Others are Saying:**

☞ **GO TO:**

John 5:22 (committed)

Isaiah 66:22 (new earth)

Matthew 24:35 (old)

new earth: *another earth that will replace the one that now exists*

new heaven: *another heaven that will replace the one that now exists*

KEY Symbols:

Great White Throne
God's judgment seat for unbelievers

John Hagee: When Scripture tells us that heaven and earth will pass away, you can be sure that this world will definitely end. There will be a last baby born, a last marriage performed, a last kiss, a last song, a last hurrah.[12]

☞ **GO TO:**

Galatians 3:10 (none will reach heaven)

Exodus 32:33; Revelation 3:4, 5; 22:19 (Book of Life)

Revelation 21:27 (Lamb's Book of Life)

> **Revelation 20:12** And I saw the dead, great and small, standing before the throne, and books were opened. Another book was opened, which is the book of life. The dead were judged according to what they had done as recorded in the books.

They Get What They Have Coming

The dead will stand before Jesus as he sits upon the Great White Throne. They will come from all walks of life: small and great, poor and rich, laborers and managers, peasants and kings. They will all stand before the court's judgment bar to be sentenced. Several books will be opened—each one is a "book of works" or a "book of deeds." These books will contain the thoughts, words, and deeds of each individual, and by these things they will be judged.

KEY POINT

By their thoughts, words, and deeds they will be judged.

Another book will be opened—the *Book of Life.* It will contain the names of every person who ever lived, except those whose names were blotted out for sinning against God, denying Jesus, or adding to or taking away from the Scriptures. When a person is born, their name is recorded in the Book of Life. It remains there until they become accountable for their sins and choose to reject Jesus in their life.

When the judgment begins, the dead will get what they knew they had coming. They will be judged by their divine record—their deeds as recorded in God's own books. A surprise will come their way though, for <u>none of them will reach heaven</u>. Only one thing remains—punishment. No mention will be made of salvation or the names in the *Lamb's Book of Life*, because these people did not accept Jesus as their Savior.

John Hagee: On one day still to come, every man, woman, and child will stand before Jesus Christ the Judge and acknowledge that he is Lord.[13]

Hal Lindsey: Some persons standing there will have so hardened their hearts that they accepted the Mark of the Beast during the Tribulation, and their names were immediately blotted out of the "Book of Life."[14]

The <u>Book of Life</u> is the list of all who were born once (every person who ever lived) minus the names of those who were removed for sinning against God, denying Jesus, or adding to or taking away from the Scriptures.

• • •

The <u>Lamb's Book of Life</u> is the list of all who were born twice (every person who truly accepts Jesus as their Savior).

> **Revelation 20:13** The sea gave up the dead that were in it, and death and Hades gave up the dead that were in them, and each person was judged according to what he had done.

All Will Be There

Everyone will stand before the judgment seat, even those from the bottom of the sea. No one will escape the judgment of God because he will raise them all from the dead. He will even raise them from Hades, the temporary abode of the souls and spirits of the wicked. All will be judged as individuals according to their deeds.

The Bible teaches that man is <u>destined to die once</u>, and then he will face judgment. But believers and unbelievers will be raised separately and judged separately. Believers will go before the <u>Judgment Seat of Christ</u> where their works will be judged. The purpose of this is not salvation or we would not be raised at this time. This is a judgment of works for the purpose of receiving rewards or crowns (see Remember This, Revelation 2:10). Unbelievers will go before the Great White Throne where their works will be judged also. The purpose of this is not salvation, but degrees of punishment.

David Hocking: The word *Hades* is used eleven times in the New Testament and is to be distinguished from the word *Gehenna,* which refers to the final hell, the Lake of Fire. Hades is certainly like hell, a place of terrible torment, but it is the temporary abode of the wicked dead who await the Great White Throne Judgment and their final sentencing.[15]

Remember This . . .

☞ **GO TO:**

Hebrews 9:27 (die once)

Romans 14:10; II Corinthians 5:10 (Judgment Seat)

What Others are Saying:

☞ **GO TO:**

Matthew 25:41, 46
(cast into hell)

I Corinthians 15:26
(end of death)

heavenly city: another name for the New Jerusalem (the future home of the Church)

> **Revelation 20:14** Then death and Hades were thrown into the lake of fire. The lake of fire is the second death.

Death And Hades Destroyed

This will be the end of the first death—*physical death*. This is good news for believers but terrible news for unbelievers. They will want to die physically when they are raised from the dead, and <u>cast into hell</u>, but that will no longer be possible. They will have new bodies that cannot be destroyed in the Lake of Fire, so their suffering will be eternal.

This will also be <u>the end of Hades</u>. An intermediate abode for the lost will no longer be necessary. When the earth is destroyed people will be in one of two places: the **heavenly city**, or hell.

> **Revelation 20:15** If anyone's name was not found written in the book of life, he was thrown into the lake of fire.

Will Your Name Be There?

When the sentence is rendered, one's eternal destiny will not be determined by their deeds, but by what is written in the Book of Life. God will make a careful search of the heavenly list.

The names of those who did not accept Jesus before they died will have been blotted out of the Book of Life. Their names will not be found, and they will join Satan, the Antichrist, and the False Prophet in the Lake of Fire forever.

What Others are Saying:

Hal Lindsey: When God opens this book at the Great White Throne Judgment, the only names left in it will be the names of those who have believed in Christ as Savior and Lord. That's why the name of the book is changed from the "Book of Life" to the "Lamb's Book of Life."[16]

Study Questions

1. What will be the crime of those who will be beheaded during the Tribulation Period?
2. What will be the position of those who are raised in the first resurrection?
3. By what will those who stand before the Great White Throne be judged?
4. Is there such a thing as degrees of punishment for unbelievers?
5. Why will individuals be cast into the Lake of Fire?

CHAPTER WRAP-UP

- An angel, carrying a great chain, will bind Satan and cast him in the Abyss for a thousand years to keep him from deceiving the nations. (Revelation 20:1–3)

- Those believers who died during the Tribulation will be raised in the last phase of the first resurrection and will reign with Christ for the Millennium. Those who take part in the first resurrection will be blessed because they will not face the second death. (Revelation 20:4–6)

- After the thousands years, Satan will be released once again to test the faith of the nations. Unfortunately, many will fall and make war against God, but God will destroy them with fire and cast Satan into the Lake of Fire where he will suffer unending torment. (Revelation 20:7–10)

- Christ will sit on the Great White Throne and judge the dead. Those who's names are not found in the Book of Life will be cast into the Lake of Fire to suffer the second death. (Revelation 20:11–15)

REVELATION 21

CHAPTER HIGHLIGHTS

- New Heaven and Earth
- The Holy City
- Second Death
- Gates and Foundations
- No Temple or Sun

Let's Get Started

We have looked at the Church Age, the Tribulation Period, and the Millennium. Now we turn to what lies beyond. Is heaven a real place? Is there evidence of a better life for the human race? What about eternity? These are the questions we will now see answered.

> **Revelation 21:1** Then I saw a new heaven and a new earth, for the first heaven and the first earth had passed away, and there was no longer any sea.

Everything Made New

Here John glimpsed the <u>new heaven and new earth</u>. He noted that they will replace this present heaven and earth, and one of its features will be the absence of large bodies of water.

Bible experts believe there will no longer be large bodies of water to allow for: 1) more room for people, and 2) to change the climate, reduce storms, and eliminate social barriers.

> *Then I saw a great white throne and him who was seated on it. Earth and sky fled from his presence, and there was no place for them* (Revelation 20:11).

☞ **GO TO:**

Isaiah 65:17; II Peter 3:13 (new earth)

KEY Symbols:

New Heaven and New Earth

will replace the present heaven and earth

Remember This . . .

John Hagee: This world will not continue forever. The Second Law of Thermodynamics, otherwise known as the Law of Entropy, declares that all organized systems tend to disorder after time. Like all things, the earth, along with this physical universe, will wear out.[1]

John 14:2, 3 (home)

Hebrews 11:13–16 (Holy City)

Psalm 87:2, 3 (City)

> **Revelation 21:2** I saw the Holy City, the new Jerusalem, coming down out of heaven from God, prepared as a bride beautifully dressed for her husband.

A New Jerusalem

Here the Church will spend eternity. We have learned about the wedding of the Lamb (the marriage of Jesus and his Church). We have also learned that there will be a great marriage supper here on earth when Jesus comes back. Now we will look at the bride's new home. It will be a Holy City. A city separated unto God for a special purpose. A city without sin. It will be called the New Jerusalem because Jerusalem has always been the City of God. God is the source of this city and it will be fresh, elegant, radiant, and adorned like a *bride beautifully dressed for her husband.*

KEY Symbols:

Holy City

NEW JERUSALEM

a bride for her Church

Remember This . . .

I will write on him the name of my God and the name of the city of my God, the new Jerusalem, which is coming down out of heaven from my God (Revelation 3:12).

What Others are Saying:

Hal Lindsey: The new earth as a whole will not be the principal residence of the believers, though they will have free access to it. The New Jerusalem is where Jesus has been preparing mansions for his own and is the capital from which he will rule.[2]

☞ **GO TO:**

I Corinthians 6:19 (dwells in)

> **Revelation 21:3** And I heard a loud voice from the throne saying, "Now the dwelling of God is with men, and he will live with them. They will be his people, and God himself will be with them and be their God.

With His People

Currently, the <u>Holy Spirit dwells in</u> the hearts of all believers, but when the New Jerusalem comes down from heaven things will change. A loud voice will announce that God will dwell *with* his people instead of *in* his people. God will actually live in the New Jerusalem where he will establish a fixed and permanent relationship with his Church.

Arno Froese: This heavenly Jerusalem, "the Holy City," "the Holy Jerusalem," is the ultimate dwelling place of God with man.[3]

> **Revelation 21:4** He will wipe every tear from their eyes. There will be no more death or mourning or crying or pain, for the old order of things has passed away."

Death And Pain Forgotten

He will wipe every tear from their eyes does not mean crying will occur in the heavenly city. It means things will be so different that there will be no need for tears, because there will be no death, loneliness, depression, pain, or suffering.

The old order of things has passed away is a reminder that God will bring an end to sin and death. Everything associated with human sorrow will pass away.

> **Revelation 21:5** He who was seated on the throne said, "I am making everything new!" Then he said, "Write this down, for these words are trustworthy and true."

A Divine Declaration

Following the Millennium, Jesus will not fix or repair this old creation. He will recreate everything. This is more than a verbal promise because he says, *Write this down.* It is a divine declaration from one who cannot lie.

> **Revelation 21:6** He said to me: "It is done. I am the Alpha and the Omega, the Beginning and the End. To him who is thirsty I will give to drink without cost from the spring of the water of life.

☞ **GO TO:**

Matthew 5:6 (thirst)

John 7:37, 38 (freely)

John 4:13, 14 (satisfied)

Never To Thirst Again

The new creation is inevitable because it is the spoken Word of Jesus. He proved his power to create when he fashioned all things at the beginning of creation. As the Alpha and Omega, he is the first and last word in all things. All authority is his. What he declares will be done.

All who **thirst after God** will be given the privilege of <u>freely drinking</u> from the **water of life**. Their thirst for God will be <u>abundantly satisfied</u>.

"I am the Alpha and the Omega," says the Lord God, "who is, and who was, and who is to come, the Almighty" (Revelation 1:8).

Remember This . . .

> **Revelation 21:7** He who overcomes will inherit all this, and I will be his God and he will be my son.

☞ GO TO:

I John 3:2 (children)

Romans 8:16, 17 (heirs)

Heirs With Jesus

All true Christians are overcomers. God is their God. They are his <u>children</u> and joint <u>heirs</u> with Jesus.

What Others are Saying:

Tim LaHaye: One of the most wonderful concepts in the Bible is the father-son relationship between God and a Christian. This verse indicates that it will go on forever in heaven as on earth.[4]

> **Revelation 21:8** But the cowardly, the unbelieving, the vile, the murderers, the sexually immoral, those who practice magic arts, the idolaters and all liars—their place will be in the fiery lake of burning sulfur. This is the second death."

KEY POINT

All unbelievers will be cast into the fiery lake of burning sulfur which is the second death.

The List Is Long

The list of those who will not enter the heavenly city includes:

1) *the cowardly*—those who are too embarrassed, ashamed or afraid to accept Jesus as Lord

2) *the unbelievers*—those who reject Jesus

3) *the vile*—those who defile themselves with abominable sins such as stealing, taking the Mark of the Beast, taking drugs, and drunkenness

4) *the sexually immoral*—fornicators, adulterers, homosexuals, and rapists

5) *those who practice magic arts*—astrologers, Satan worshipers, witches, and warlocks

6) *idolaters*—those who worship anyone or anything other than God

7) *liars*—those who deceive the lost, falsely accuse Christians, falsely claim to be a Christian, or add to or take away from the Bible

---

J. Vernon McGee: The Lake of Fire is eternal, for it is the second death, and there is no third resurrection.[5]

☞ **GO TO:**

Revelation 19:7 (union)

KEY POINT

God loves and judges; saves and condemns.

> **Revelation 21:9** One of the seven angels who had the seven bowls full of the seven last plagues came and said to me, "Come, I will show you the bride, the wife of the Lamb."

The Bride Of Christ

God's nature has more than one characteristic. He loves and judges; saves and condemns. Both of these characteristics are demonstrated here. Imagine, one of the same angels who poured out a bowl of God's wrath is now inviting John to see God's love for his Church.

We already have established that the bride is the Church, but here the angel refers to the city as the bride of the Lamb. In God's eyes, the Holy City and the Holy People are synonymous. The physical identity of the Holy City will include rivers, trees, streets, and mansions, but the true identity of the city will be the Lamb and his bride.

A <u>special union</u> will exist between Jesus and the Church similar to the union that exists between a bridegroom and bride upon their marriage.

KEY Symbols:

The Holy City
his holy people
physical identity
- rivers, trees, streets, and mansions

true identity
- Lamb and his bride

Remember This . . .

Wim Malgo: It is simply because of all the saints and glorified ones who dwell in it. Without these saints this city would not be the bride of the Lamb.[6]

☞ **GO TO:**

Revelation 1:10; 17:3
(in the Spirit)

Ezekiel 1:3; 24:26
(Ezekiel)

KEY Symbols:

The Holy City
will descend from
heaven

What Others
are Saying:

Remember
This . . .

☞ **GO TO:**

John 9:5 (light of world)

Revelation 4:3 (jasper)

KEY Symbols:

Holy City
shone with the glory of
God
brilliance like a precious
jewel, clear as crystal

> **Revelation 21:10** And he carried me away in the Spirit to a mountain great and high, and showed me the Holy City, Jerusalem, coming down out of heaven from God.

Carried Away

While John was <u>in the Holy Spirit</u>, the angel carried him away to a great mountain where he could have a clear view of this marvelous city. It is being built in heaven, but God will cause it to descend to the new earth. How far it will descend is a matter of debate. Nothing is said about it coming to rest on the new earth. It may do that, but it also may remain suspended above. One thing is for sure: what goes on in the Holy City will be more important than what takes place on the new earth. The Holy City will be the headquarters of the new creation.

Rick Joyner: Trances can range from those that are rather mild, so that you are still conscious of your physical surroundings, and can even still interact with them, to those where you feel like you are literally in the place of your vision. This seems to be what <u>Ezekiel experienced rather frequently</u>, and what John probably experienced when he had the visions recorded in the book of Revelation.[7]

John was in the Spirit (an ecstatic spiritual state) which put him in close touch with God and made him able to see visions.

> **Revelation 21:11** It shone with the glory of God, and its brilliance was like that of a very precious jewel, like a jasper, clear as crystal.

The Glow Of Glory

The presence of God in the Holy City will cause it to shine with his glory. His pure <u>light</u> will burst forth in brilliance like the sparkle of a large and expensive jewel.

What kind of jewel is not said, but it will look like <u>jasper</u> (opal, diamond, or topaz) and be crystal clear. Jasper is the first stone in the breastplate of the High Priest (see Illustration #2, page 21). It is opaque and translucent like a diamond, and is a symbol of purity and holiness.

J. Vernon McGee: The diamond seems to fit the description better than any other stone known to man.[8]

Hal Lindsey: The glory and brilliance of Christ and the Father are all that's needed to illumine the entire universe.[9]

> **Revelation 21:12** It had a great, high wall with twelve gates, and with twelve angels at the gates. On the gates were written the names of the twelve tribes of Israel.

Twelve Gates

The Holy City will be surrounded by a thick, high wall with twelve gates. I'm sorry, but Saint Peter won't be standing at the gates, angels will. The name of each of the twelve tribes of Israel will be written on a gate.

The wall will be for security. The same can be said of the angels guarding the gates. The names of the twelve tribes of Israel will be a reminder that the Messiah, the Scriptures, and salvation came through the Jews. Without them the Holy City would not be needed, and the Gentiles would be without hope.

Why does the Holy City need security? No one knows the answer. Some suggest it is a symbol that not everyone has access to God. Only God knows.

Satan tries to copy everything God does. This explains why the rebuilt city of Babylon will have the <u>names of blasphemy</u> written on it.

> **Revelation 21:13** There were three gates on the east, three on the north, three on the south and three on the west.

Three Gates For Each Compass Point

The wall will have four sides with three gates on each side.

The Holy City
  twelve foundations
  each foundation with
    the name of an
    apostle

> **Revelation 21:14** The wall of the city had twelve foundations, and on them were the names of the twelve apostles of the Lamb.

One Foundation For Each Apostle

The city will have twelve foundations. Some experts say these foundations will be stacked on top of each other and will encompass the base of the city. Others speculate that they will be large columns extending down to the new earth like legs or posts.

Each foundation will have the name of one of the twelve apostles of Jesus on it. This is significant because the Bible tells us that the Church is being *built on the foundation of the apostles and prophets, with Christ Jesus himself as the chief cornerstone* (Ephesians 2:20). It says Jesus gave *instructions through the Holy Spirit to the apostles he had chosen* (Acts 1:1, 2). With the help of the Holy Spirit the apostles preached the gospel, won converts, organized congregations, wrote the Scriptures, selected deacons, and taught their followers. They relinquished everything for Jesus and his Church, and were threatened, beaten, imprisoned, and killed. They earned the right to have their names inscribed on the foundations of the Holy City.

**What Others
are Saying:**

J. Vernon McGee: On the human level, the Church was in the hands of these twelve men.[10]

> **Revelation 21:15** The angel who talked with me had a measuring rod of gold to measure the city, its gates, and its walls.

A Golden Rod

A measuring stick in John's day was approximately ten feet long, and the most common material used in heaven seems to be gold. The same angel who talked with John took a golden measuring stick to measure the city, its gates, and its walls.

☞ **GO TO:**

John 14:2 (many
  rooms)

> **Revelation 21:16** The city was laid out like a square, as long as it was wide. He measured the city with the rod and found it to be 12,000 stadia in length, and as wide and high as it is long.

A Giant Cube?

The Holy City will be laid out like a square. Its length will be the same as its width, and its height will equal its length. Some suggest that this will be a pyramid, but others think it will be a cube. Not enough information exists to prove either view.

However, everyone agrees that the Holy City will be enormous. 12,000 stadia is about 1,500 miles (approximately the distance from New York City to Dallas, Texas). A city 1,500 miles long and 1,500 miles wide will be larger than anything the world has ever seen. A city towering 1,500 miles high is almost incomprehensible, but the Carpenter of Israel is <u>building many mansions</u>.

KEY Symbols:

The Holy City
laid out like a square, as long and high as it is wide
12,000 stadia in length

Tim LaHaye: Thus the city itself would stretch from about the eastern seaboard of the United States to the Mississippi on one side and from the Canadian border to the Gulf of Mexico on the other.[11]

What Others are Saying:

Hal Lindsey: This covers a lot of territory, and it implies that millions upon millions of redeemed saints will be there.[12]

> **Revelation 21:17** He measured its wall and it was 144 cubits thick, by man's measurement, which the angel was using.

A Thick Wall

The wall around the Holy city will be 144 cubits (216 feet) thick. It does not matter whether one uses God's measurements or man's measurements, the result will be the same. This thick wall will provide plenty of protection.

KEY Symbols:

The Holy City
its walls will be 144 cubits thick

> **Revelation 21:18** The wall was made of jasper, and the city of pure gold, as pure as glass.

The Purest Gold

In verse 11, we noted that the jasper could be an opal, diamond, or topaz. Although we don't know which one of these it will be, we do know the wall will be made of a gem that is beautiful, hard, and transparent. People will be able to see through it into the Holy City, and the light of God will beam out of the city. The city itself will be made of gold as pure as glass.

KEY Symbols:

The Holy City
wall of jasper
city of pure gold, as pure as glass

The Holy City
  wall foundations
    decorated with every
    kind of precious
    stone

Remember
This . . .

☞ **GO TO:**

I John 1:5 (light)

> **Revelation 21:19** The foundations of the city walls were decorated with every kind of precious stone. The first foundation was jasper, the second sapphire, the third chalcedony, the fourth emerald,

Walls Of Precious Stone

Each one of the twelve foundations of the city walls will be different. The first four will be:

1) *jasper*—a crystal clear gem that could be a massive diamond
2) *sapphire*—a clear blue gem similar to a diamond in hardness
3) *chalcedony*—a greenish agate with possibly a few stripes of other colors mixed in
4) *emerald*—a bright green stone

And the one who sat there (on the throne) *had the appearance of jasper and carnelian* (Revelation 4:3).

> **Revelation 21:20** the fifth sardonyx, the sixth carnelian, the seventh chrysolite, the eighth beryl, the ninth topaz, the tenth chrysoprase, the eleventh jacinth, and the twelfth amethyst.

How Rich Can We Get?

The next eight foundations will be decorated with:

5) *sardonyx*—a reddish white onyx similar to the color of healthy fingernails
6) *carnelian*—a fiery red or blood-colored stone from Sardis
7) *chrysolite*—a transparent golden-yellow stone
8) *beryl*—a sea green emerald lighter in color than the third foundation
9) *topaz*—a transparent greenish-yellow stone
10) *chrysoprase*—a yellowish pale green stone similar to the modern aquamarine color
11) *jacinth*—a violet hyacinth-colored gem
12) *amethyst*—a purple-colored stone

A brilliant rainbow would be just a pale glimmer compared to what these foundation stones will look like. <u>God is light</u>, and his light passing through these many different colored stones will be breathtaking.

> **Revelation 21:21** The twelve gates were twelve pearls, each gate made of a single pearl. The great street of the city was of pure gold, like transparent glass.

The Pearly Gates

With only twelve gates to this extensive city, and each gate being more than 300 miles apart, we know the gates will need to be huge. And each gate will consist of a single gigantic pearl. This emphasizes the great wealth and generosity of God.

The great street is a mystery. Will this city, with a circumference of 1,500 miles long, 1,500 miles wide, and 1,500 miles high have only one street or will one of the streets be called *the great street*? We don't know, but we do know it will be made of pure gold.

> **Revelation 21:22** I did not see a temple in the city, because the Lord God Almighty and the Lamb are its temple.

No Temple

Because of sin on earth, God withdrew his presence from mankind. He had <u>Moses and others build a tabernacle</u>, and later he had <u>Solomon build a Temple</u> where the people would go to worship. He separated himself from them by <u>residing in the Holy of Holies</u> (see Illustration #5, page 153), and having priests serve as mediators.

After the Millennium, however, things will be different. A temple will not be needed since sin will not be present in the Holy City. God will have no need <u>to separate himself from his people</u>. Mediators will not be necessary. The glorious presence of the Father and the Son will permeate the entire city.

The Bible is filled with truths that are difficult to understand but wonderful to speculate on. One of them is the fact that *when he appears, we* (believers) *shall be like him* (I John 3:2). We will have great insight, great love, and everything else that Jesus has. Also, we will not have a sin nature that could separate us from him.

KEY Symbols:

The Holy City
twelve gates were twelve pearls
street of pure gold, like transparent glass

☞ **GO TO:**

Exodus 25:9 (tabernacle)

II Samuel 7:5,13 (Temple)

Leviticus 16:2 (Holy of Holies)

I Thessalonians 4:17 (with the Lord)

KEY POINT

The glorious presence of the Father and the Son will permeate the entire city.

KEY Symbols:

The Holy City
no temple
no mediator

☞ **GO TO:**

Isaiah 60:19, 20; John
1:3–5; 8:12 (light)

Genesis 1 (created)

KEY Symbols:

The Holy City
glory of God gives it
light
the Lamb is its lamp

splendor: their display of
praise, thanksgiving,
worship, and honor

KEY Symbols:

The Holy City
home to the Church,
the Old Testament
Saints, and the
Tribulation Saints

The New Earth
home to Israel, and
those saved after the
Rapture

Something
to Ponder

> **Revelation 21:23** The city does not need the sun or the moon to shine on it, for the glory of God gives it light, and the Lamb is its lamp.

No Sun

The Father and Son are the source of physical <u>light</u>. They spoke light into existence when they <u>created the sun, moon, and stars</u>. But they will do away with these when they create the new heaven and earth because their presence in the Holy City will eliminate the need for other heavenly lights.

Think about this. It means we can be in the Holy City, several hundred miles from God and not need a light. The light of God will cover an area almost as large as the eastern half of the U.S., and it will even be visible in outer space.

> **Revelation 21:24** The nations will walk by its light, and the kings of the earth will bring their **splendor** into it.

World's Brightest Night-light

The new earth will be populated with the children of Israel, and the descendants of those who did not follow Satan in his final rebellion after the Millennium. Nations and leaders already will be on the new earth when the Holy City comes out of heaven. They will walk in the light coming from that city instead of the light of the sun and moon.

The inhabitants of the new earth will travel to the Holy City—not to live but to worship. The Holy City will be the future home of the Church. The new earth will be the future home of Israel and all others who will be saved after the Rapture.

I believe the Jews lost their right to dwell in the Holy City because they rejected the Messiah. The nation and their priests failed, so God established a new priesthood—the Church. We will be the priests in heaven. It was done to make Israel jealous and to remind her of her sin.

> **Revelation 21:25** On no day will its gates ever be shut, for there will be no night there.

☞ **GO TO:**

Isaiah 60:11 (gates always open)

Always Open

The people of some ancient cities opened their gates during the day and closed them at night. The continuous presence of God in the Holy City will mean the continuous presence of light. Darkness will not be known, thereby eliminating any need to <u>shut the gates</u>.

> **Revelation 21:26** The glory and honor of the nations will be brought into it.

Gifts Of Glory And Honor

Visitors will go to the Holy City to give glory and honor to the Lord.

> **Revelation 21:27** Nothing impure will ever enter it, nor will anyone who does what is shameful or deceitful, but only those whose names are written in the Lamb's Book of Life.

☞ **GO TO:**

Genesis 2:8 (Eden)

Genesis 3:1–6 (Satan)

Only Those In The Lamb's Book Of Life

When God created Adam and Eve he placed them in his perfect creation, the <u>Garden of Eden</u>. Then he allowed <u>Satan to enter and tempt them</u> and they fell. God will never allow this to happen again. He will never allow any impure thing to enter the Holy City. Only those with their names found in the Lamb's Book of Life will be permitted to enter.

Study Questions

1. Why do you think John was told to write this down, *these words are trustworthy and true*?
2. Why do you think Jesus can give the *water of life*?
3. When will the Holy City with the streets of gold come down to earth, and how far down will it come?
4. What is the significance of having the names of the twelve tribes of Israel on the twelve gates of the Holy City?
5. Why will nothing impure, shameful or deceitful be allowed to enter the Holy City?

CHAPTER WRAP-UP

- God will create a new heaven and new earth because the old ones will pass away. (Revelation 21:1)

- God will send the Holy City, New Jerusalem, to the new earth. He will dwell among his people and wipe away every tear from their eyes. (Revelation 21:2–4)

- Everyone who rejected God during their lifetime will be cast into the Lake of Fire which is the second death. (Revelation 21:8)

- New Jerusalem will be built on twelve foundations and have twelve gates. It will be laid out like a square and be made of pure gold and precious stones. (Revelation 21:9–21)

- New Jerusalem will not have a temple because God and Christ will be the temple. Likewise, the city will not need a sun because the Father and Son will be the light. (Revelation 21:22–25)

REVELATION 22

CHAPTER HIGHLIGHTS

- River of Life
- Curse Lifted
- A Final Call
- A Final Warning
- A Final Promise

Let's Get Started

We have reached the last chapter in the Bible's final book, and questions still abound. Unfortunately, answers to many questions will not be found here. Instead, John further explains the believer's glorious eternal home, Christ's final promise, a final invitation, and a final warning. As for the unanswered questions, <u>in *his* time he will reveal the answers</u>.

> **Revelation 22:1** Then the angel showed me the river of the water of life, as clear as crystal, flowing from the throne of God and of the Lamb

River Of Life

Up to this point, the angel has been showing John the city's basic framework: foundations, walls, gates, and a street. The Holy City, however, will also contain other things such as water, trees, and fruit. Here we see that it will have a river called *the river of the water of life*. In other verses of Scripture, this water of life is called <u>*living water,*</u> and it is used as a symbol for the Holy Spirit.

God is using a physical substance (water) to help explain a spiritual truth. Living water flows pure, clear, and fresh. It is not murky, stagnant, or polluted. It possesses <u>life-giving qualities</u> that man cannot live without. The *river of the water of life* is portrayed as a river that will possess life-giving powers; water that will restore and refresh, flow in abundance, and satisfy our thirst.

☞ GO TO:

Daniel 12:8–10 (in his time)

☞ GO TO:

John 4:13, 14 (living water)

John 3:1–8 (life-giving)

John 7:37–39 (Holy Spirit)

KEY POINT

We will drink of the waters from which we will never thirst again.

KEY Symbols:

River of the Water of Life
the Holy Spirit

The source of this river will be the *throne of God and of the Lamb*. They will supply life-giving water and the <u>Holy Spirit</u> in abundance to the Holy City. The Trinity (the Father, Son, and Holy Spirit) will be present to meet all our needs.

What Others are Saying:

Remember This . . .

☞ **GO TO:**

Genesis 3:22–24 (Eden)

Luke 24:30–43 (ate)

Hal Lindsey: I don't think it's far-fetched to regard this crystal-clear river, from the throne of God the Father and God the Son, as the continual outpouring of God the Holy Spirit.[1]

To him who is thirsty I will give to drink without cost from the spring of the water of life (Revelation 21:6).

> **Revelation 22:2** down the middle of the great street of the city. On each side of the river stood the tree of life, bearing twelve crops of fruit, yielding its fruit every month. And the leaves of the tree are for the healing of the nations.

Tree Of Life

Picture a great street of pure gold like transparent glass. It will have mansions of gold on each side and a river of crystal-clear water flowing down the middle with rows of trees on each side. This is the magnificent scene John is trying to describe.

KEY Symbols:

Fruit from Tree of Life
fruit for our heavenly diet

Leaves from Tree of Life
for the healing of the nations

The tree of life (see GWGN, page 26) takes us back to the <u>Garden of Eden</u>. Before they sinned Adam and Eve could have eaten from it and lived forever. In the New Jerusalem, rows of the tree of life will grow. The trees will produce a different kind of fruit every month which will provide a continuous supply of food from God. This says something about the heavenly bodies. Just as <u>Jesus ate and drank</u> after being raised from the dead, believers will eat and drink in the Holy City.

Believers will diet on manna and fruit from the tree of life. They will not eat the leaves of the tree because the leaves will be for the healing of those who dwell on the new earth. These leaves will sustain life and add to well-being.

What Others are Saying:

Tim LaHaye: It would be better to translate the word *healing* as health, not indicating that man will be sickly during the eternal order, but that the Gentiles or nations that have been inhuman to each other throughout their known history will be healed in their relationship toward each other and will thus live equitably and fairly.[2]

The Tree of Knowledge caused Adam and Eve to know right from wrong. It is how they learned what sin was. It caused their spiritual death (separation of their soul and spirit from God) and their physical death (separation of their soul and spirit from the body). It *cost* them immortality. The Tree of Life does the opposite. Eating its fruit *brings* immortality.

I will give the right to eat from the tree of life, which is in the paradise of God (Revelation 2:7).

To him who overcomes, I will give some of the hidden manna (Revelation 2:17).

> **Revelation 22:3** No longer will there be any curse. The throne of God and of the Lamb will be in the city, and his servants will serve him.

The Curse Lifted

When Adam and Eve sinned, God placed a <u>curse upon creation</u>: Because of it, women experience pain in childbirth, both men and women suffer sickness, both must today work for a living, and physical and spiritual death came upon mankind. Sin has caused great harm in this *present* creation, but it will not affect the *new* creation. Once God has cast Satan with all his followers into hell, and raised us with new bodies to dwell in his constant presence, all of the curse will be gone.

The Holy City will be the new location of God's throne. We will not be floating on clouds with harps in our hands, but instead we will be praising and serving our God. What we will do is not said, but we have already been told that we will reign as priests and kings. We know that we will find <u>joy and fulfillment</u> in his service.

In the New Jerusalem There Will Be No More:

1) death, mourning, crying, or pain (Revelation 21:4)
2) temple (Revelation 21:22)
3) sun or moon (Revelation 21:23)
4) night (Revelation 21:25)
5) impure, shameful, or deceitful thoughts (Revelation 21:27)
6) curse (Revelation 22:3)

Something to Ponder

Remember This . . .

GO TO:

Genesis 3:14–19 (curse)

Luke 6:23; Revelation 12:12 (joy and fulfillment)

Something to Ponder

You have made them to be a kingdom and priests to serve our God, and they will reign on the earth (Revelation 5:10).

☞ **GO TO:**

Exodus 33:18–23
(Moses)

John 14:8, 9 (Philip)

I John 3:2 (see God)

KEY Symbols:

**Name of God on
Our Foreheads**
*identifies the people
of God*

Remember
This . . .

> **Revelation 22:4** They will see his face, and his name will be on their foreheads.

See God's Face

In the Old Testament, it was <u>Moses</u> who wanted to see the face of God. In the New Testament, it was <u>Philip</u>. God did not allow them to see his face, because if they did, they would die. However, as residents of the Holy City, we will actually <u>see the face of our Father</u> and his Son. The name of God will be written on believers' foreheads to identify them as God's own.

A name stands for much or little depending upon whose it is. When God puts his name on us it is the greatest name of all. It stands for his character, honor, glory, faithfulness, and much more. it means he is seeking his reputation on us.

I will write on him the name of my God (Revelation 3:12).

> **Revelation 22:5** There will be no more night. They will not need the light of a lamp or the light of the sun, for the Lord God will give them light. And they will reign for ever and ever.

No More Night

This is the second time we have been told there will be no night in the Holy City. Lamps, light bulbs, and flashlights will not be needed. We will not need the sun for heat or to grow our crops. God and Jesus will light the entire creation. They will be all that is needed, and believers will have the honor and privilege of reigning with them forever.

**What Others
are Saying:**

J. Vernon McGee: Who knows but what (God) will give to each saint—a world or a solar system or a galactic system to operate. Remember that Adam was given dominion over the old creation on this earth.[3]

> **Revelation 22:6** The angel said to me, "These words are trustworthy and true. The Lord, the God of the spirits of the prophets, sent his angel to show his servants the things that must soon take place."

☞ **GO TO:**

Colossians 1:9 (spiritual understanding)

The Truth Is Found Here

The angel reminded John of the truthfulness of these words. He is giving his assurance that this prophecy is trustworthy and will be fulfilled.

The angel also reminded John of how this message was given. The Lord Jesus sent his angel to give the prophets <u>spiritual understanding</u>. In other words, Jesus is the source of this revelation, and because he is, it must be fulfilled.

The things that must soon take place have already started. In fact, the first part of this prophecy (Revelation), the Church Age, is almost over. Everything from the Rapture to the Second Coming is near at hand.

J. Vernon McGee: *These words are faithful and true* (Revelation 22:6 NKJV) means that no man is to trifle with them by spiritualizing them or reducing them to meaningless symbols. Our Lord is talking about reality.[4]

What Others are Saying:

These are the words of the Amen, the faithful and true witness (Revelation 3:14).

> **Revelation 22:7** "Behold, I am coming soon! Blessed is he who keeps the words of the prophecy in this book."

Remember This . . .

In The Blink Of An Eye

Behold, I am coming soon can be interpreted in at least two ways: *soon* or *shortly*, or *quickly* or *suddenly*. *Soon* or *shortly* means before long. *Quickly* or *suddenly* means *very fast*. This is significant because people get the wrong impression when we say, "Jesus will come very soon." What we should say is, "When he comes, it will happen very fast, in the blink of an eye."

Many people wonder why prophecy is so important. It's importance does not lie in predicting the future. But rather, in the changing of our lives, by giving us a desire and concern for the lost and **unsaved**. The fact is, God means for prophecy to be obeyed, and those who do obey are promised a blessing.

unsaved: *unbelievers (those who have not accepted Jesus as their Savior)*

Remember
This . . .

awe: *great wonder or
profound respect*

*Blessed is the one who reads the words of this prophecy, and
blessed are those who hear it and take to heart what is written
in it, because the time is near* (Revelation 1:3).

> **Revelation 22:8** I, John, am the one who heard and
> saw these things. And when I had heard and seen them,
> I fell down to worship at the feet of the angel who had
> been showing them to me.

Overcome With Awe

John is repeating his claim that he is the human author of Revelation, and that he both *saw* and *heard* the things he writes about.
He was so impressed with the angel that revealed these things to
him, that he was overcome with **awe**, and fell down to worship at
the angel's feet.

> **Revelation 22:9** But he said to me, "Do not do it! I
> am a fellow servant with you and with your brothers
> the prophets and of all who keep the words of this book.
> Worship God!"

God Alone

This is the second time an angel told John not to worship him.
Angels are servants of God, the same as John and the prophets are
servants of God. It is a mistake to worship angels. Only God is
worthy of worship.

> *At this I fell at his feet to worship him. But he said to me, "Do
> not do it! I am a fellow servant with you and with your brothers
> who hold to the testimony of Jesus. Worship God"* (Revelation
> 19:10).

Remember
This . . .

☞ **GO TO:**

Daniel 12:4 (seal up)

> **Revelation 22:10** Then he told me, "Do not seal up
> the words of the prophecy of this book, because the
> time is near.

Leave It Open

When Daniel wrote his prophecy several hundred years before
the birth of Christ, he did not understand some of the things God

had shown him. He wanted an explanation, but the fulfillment of his prophecies were a long time off, so he was <u>told to seal them up</u> until the end time.

Revelation is different. John's prophecy was already unfolding, and the Church Age was taking hold. For this reason, the message was to be left unsealed. God wants people to hear these things now.

> **Revelation 22:11** Let him who does wrong continue to do wrong; let him who is vile continue to be vile; let him who does right continue to do right; and let him who is holy continue to be holy."

A Great Chasm

The time will come when a person's final destiny will be determined and sealed forever. When the **eternal day** dawns, all unbelievers will be condemned and cast into the Lake of Fire. They will be without hope because their eternal condition will never change. On the other hand, all believers will be accepted and given entrance to the Holy City where they will continue to grow and improve. Hope and holiness will always be theirs.

This is a warning regarding the separation of the lost and the saved. A <u>great **chasm**</u> will separate the Lake of Fire from the Holy City that no one can cross. The decisions people make in this life will determine their destiny and seal it forever.

> **Revelation 22:12** "Behold, I am coming soon! My reward is with me, and I will give to everyone according to what he has done.

Heaven Or Hell

This is Christ's personal promise that he will return, and when he does, he will bring rewards with him. He will separate the lost from the saved, and everyone will receive rewards according to the <u>quality of work</u> they have done.

Not much is said in Church about rewards. For the most part it is a neglected message. No one deserves rewards, but we know they will be given because this verse says so. If we would let the goodness of God sink in most of us would do more to honor him, and follow the advice of the Apostle John: we would watch out so that we will be *rewarded fully* (II John 1:8).

☞ **GO TO:**

Luke 16:26 (chasm)

eternal day: the great day of one's final judgment

chasm: the great impassable region that separates heaven from hell

KEY POINT

The decisions people make in this life will determine their destiny and seal it forever.

☞ **GO TO:**

I Corinthians 3:11–15 (quality of work)

KEY Symbols:

Rewards
heaven or hell

☞ **GO TO:**

Revelation 1:8, 17; 2:8;
21:6 (before)

☞ **GO TO:**

Matthew 5–7 (Sermon)

Matthew 5:3–10
(Beatitudes)

Beatitudes: *a proclamation
of blessing(s)*

**Something
to Ponder**

KEY Symbols:

Washed Robes
those who accept Christ

Unwashed Robes
those who reject Christ

> **Revelation 22:13** I am the Alpha and the Omega, the
> First and the Last, the Beginning and the End.

The All In All

Jesus is using three of his titles to identify himself with the Father. He has used them <u>several times before</u>. No one else can use them because they assert his deity. Explain it? No one can. It must be taken by faith.

> **Revelation 22:14** "Blessed are those who wash their
> robes, that they may have the right to the tree of life
> and may go through the gates into the city.

Heavenly Laundry?

Christ's words here imply a choice between washing our robes or leaving them dirty. Those who choose to wash their robes and therefore accept Christ will be blessed with two rewards: access to the tree of life, and permission to pass through the gates of the Holy City. Those who leave their robes dirty by refusing to accept Christ will be rejecting his rewards.

The <u>Sermon on the Mount</u> is one of the most popular and best known teachings of Jesus. It begins with several principles Christians call the **Beatitudes**. Revelation also contains some Beatitudes, but very few people are aware of it. They are:

1) *Blessed is the one who reads the words of this prophecy, and blessed are those who hear it and take to heart what is written in it* (Revelation 1:3).

2) *Blessed are the dead who die in the Lord from now on* (Revelation 14:13).

3) *Blessed is he who stays awake and keeps his clothes with him, so that he may not go naked and be shamefully exposed* (Revelation 16:15).

4) *Blessed are those who are invited to the wedding supper of the Lamb* (Revelation 19:9).

5) *Blessed and holy are those who have part in the first resurrection. The second death has no power over them, but they will be priests of God and of Christ and will reign with him for a thousand years* (Revelation 20:6).

6) *Blessed is he who keeps the words of the prophecy in this book* (Revelation 22:7).

7) *Blessed are those who wash their robes, that they may have the right to the tree of life and may go through the gates into the city* (Revelation 22:14).

> **Revelation 22:15** Outside are the dogs, those who practice magic arts, the sexually immoral, the murderers, the idolaters, and everyone who loves and practices falsehood.

Access Denied

Jesus is providing his own list of those who will not be blessed with access to the tree of life and the Holy City. Instead of fruit from the tree of life, the dogs (those involved in the occult, sexual immorality, idolatry, and lying) will eat the garbage of hell. Instead of access to the Holy City, these dogs will scavenge in the Lake of Fire.

But the cowardly, the unbelieving, the vile, the murderers, the sexually immoral, those who practice magic arts, the idolaters and all liars—their place will be in the fiery lake of burning sulfur (Revelation 21:8).

> **Revelation 22:16** "I, Jesus, have sent my angel to give you this testimony for the churches. I am the Root and the Offspring of David, and the bright Morning Star."

A Star From David

Here Jesus reiterates the first two verses of Chapter 1 by saying that Revelation is a testimony he gave to an angel for delivery to the churches.

The Root and the Offspring of <u>*David*</u> comes from the Old Testament and is a reference to the Messiah. Jesus is the Messiah.

The bright Morning <u>*Star*</u> comes from both the Old and New Testaments. Jesus is identifying himself as the one who will appear near the end of earth's darkest hour (Tribulation Period). He alone will bring a brighter day to the world (Millennium).

KEY Symbols:

Dogs
 those involved in the occult, sexual immorality, idolatry, and lying

Something to Ponder

☞ **GO TO:**

Jeremiah 33:15 (David)

Numbers 24:17; Revelation 2:28 (Star)

> **Revelation 22:17** The Spirit and the bride say, "Come!" And let him who hears say, "Come!" Whoever is thirsty, let him come; and whoever wishes, let him take the free gift of the water of life.

Come!

This is God's *final* call. It is a call for all believers to *Come!*, and a call for all believers to tell all unbelievers to *Come!* The Holy Spirit works in and through the Bride of Christ (the Church), using them to invite all unbelievers to come to Jesus and drink of his salvation, the water of life.

Whoever is thirsty should *Come!* Those who are tired of living without Jesus should *Come!* God invites all who desire to receive his free gift of salvation through his Son Jesus to *Come!*

☞ **GO TO:**

Acts 5:1–11 (Ananias and Sapphira)

> **Revelation 22:18** I warn everyone who hears the words of the prophecy of this book: If anyone adds anything to them, God will add to him the plagues described in this book.

Nothing New

Revelation was given by God, and it is his Word alone. He alone has authority over it. Anyone who adds anything new to the words of Revelation will feel the wrath of God upon him.

Something to Ponder

There are religious groups today that teach God is love, but refute the message of salvation, the wrath of God, the judgment of God, the Tribulation Period, and hell. Wouldn't you call this adding and taking away from the Word of God?

Here are some examples:

1) Jesus is really the Archangel Michael (Jehovah's Witnesses).

2) Hell is really the grave (Jehovah's Witnesses).

3) God, rather than Jesus, was once a mortal human being (Mormons).

4) Worthy humans are going to become gods and goddesses (Mormons).

5) God is a cosmic force, not a personal being (New Age).

6) Eve's sin was a sexual affair with Satan (Moonies).

If God struck down <u>Ananias and Sapphira</u> for introducing sin into the early Church, what do you think he will do with those who do it today?

> **Revelation 22:19** And if anyone takes words away from this book of prophecy, God will take away from him his share in the tree of life and in the holy city, which are described in this book.

Nothing Less

Taking away from this book brings on a second part to God's warning. Anyone who deletes anything from this book risks having his share in the tree of life and Holy City erased. Those who do delete something prove not only that they do not love God or believe in his Word, but that they are destined for the Lake of Fire as well.

The article (*Theologians Opening Heaven's Gate A Bit Wider*) reads, "Five centuries since the end of the Middle Ages, it's likely that modern-day Christians still subscribe to vestiges of that period's classic depictions of heaven and hell: the former a place of infinite peace and joy; the latter a hideous chamber of eternal punishment.

"Last week, the Church of England made international news by joining other church bodies, including its American relative, the Episcopal Church, in rejecting the medieval image of hell, calling it a distortion of 'the revelation of God's love in Christ.'

"The implication was that God is a 'sadistic monster . . . who consigned millions to eternal torment.' "

The word is then that the liberals are again rejecting the doctrine of eternal punishment. They thereby deny the Word of God, but they do so in the name of the love of God.[5]

RELATED CURRENT EVENTS

Many denominations are rewriting their hymnals and worship materials. They have decided to change such words as "him," "darkness," and "blindness" because they do not want to offend women, African-Americans, Native Americans, Hispanics, etc. Some have even produced Bibles and New Testaments that contain an approved **inclusive** language.

Something to Ponder

Should this be considered adding to or taking away from the Word of God?

> **Revelation 22:20** He who testifies to these things says, "Yes, I am coming soon." Amen. Come, Lord Jesus.

One Last Promise

I am coming soon is his final promise! In answer to this promise of the Lord's return, John responds, *Amen. Come, Lord Jesus.* This is a statement of John's personal belief, and he urges Jesus to come back.

 GO TO:

Ephesians 2:8 (saved by grace)

KEY POINT

Grace makes salvation possible.

Remember This . . .

Something to Ponder

> **Revelation 22:21** The grace of the Lord Jesus be with God's people. Amen.

A Final Note Of Grace

These last words of the Bible serve as a reminder that <u>grace makes salvation</u> possible. Grace will keep us out of the Lake of Fire, and let us pass through the gates of the Holy City.

Grace is **G**od's **R**iches **A**t **C**hrist's **E**xpense. *Grace and peace to you from him who is, and who was, and who is to come, and from the seven spirits before his throne* (Revelation 1:4).

Facts About Salvation:

- Everyone needs it (Romans 3:23).
- Everyone can have it (John 3:16).
- Only Jesus can give it (John 14:6).
- Only believers receive it (John 3:36).

Study Questions

1. What will believers have on their foreheads in heaven?
2. What can a person do to be blessed by God?
3. How do we know the words of Revelation are true?
4. What was John's mistake that we read about in this chapter?
5. Who will have access to the tree of life and the Holy City?

CHAPTER WRAP-UP

- The River of Life will flow from the Throne of God through the Holy City. On each side of the river will be the tree of life. (Revelation 22:1, 2)

- The curse of the original sin caused by the fall of Adam and Eve will be lifted when God makes everything new. God will once again dwell among his people and be the light for their feet. (Revelation 22:3–5)

- The Spirit and bride call anyone who is thirsty to *come* and drink freely from the water of life. (Revelation 22:17)

- A final warning goes to anyone who adds to, or detracts from Revelation. Those who do not heed this warning face the plagues contained therein. (Revelation 22:18, 19)

- Christ has a final promise for all who read Revelation: He is coming soon. (Revelation 22:20)

APPENDIX A — TIME LINES

Time Line #1

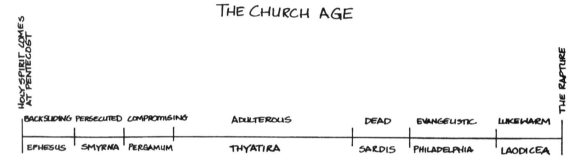

THE CHURCH AGE

BACKSLIDING	PERSECUTED	COMPROMISING	ADULTEROUS	DEAD	EVANGELISTIC	LUKEWARM	
EPHESUS	SMYRNA	PERGAMUM	THYATIRA	SARDIS	PHILADELPHIA	LAODICEA	

HOLY SPIRIT COMES AT PENTECOST — THE RAPTURE

Time Line #2

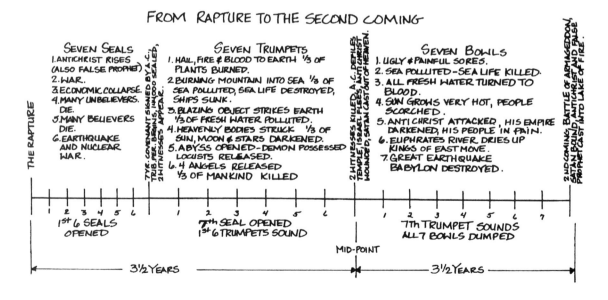

FROM RAPTURE TO THE SECOND COMING

SEVEN SEALS
1. ANTICHRIST RISES (ALSO FALSE PROPHET)
2. WAR.
3. ECONOMIC COLLAPSE.
4. MANY UNBELIEVERS DIE.
5. MANY BELIEVERS DIE.
6. EARTHQUAKE AND NUCLEAR WAR.

7 YR. COVENANT SIGNED BY A.C., TRIB. PER. BEGINS, 144,000 SEALED, 2 WITNESSES APPEAR.

SEVEN TRUMPETS
1. HAIL, FIRE & BLOOD TO EARTH 1/3 OF PLANTS BURNED.
2. BURNING MOUNTAIN INTO SEA 1/3 OF SEA POLLUTED, SEA LIFE DESTROYED, SHIPS SUNK.
3. BLAZING OBJECT STRIKES EARTH 1/3 OF FRESH WATER POLLUTED.
4. HEAVENLY BODIES STRUCK 1/3 OF SUN, MOON & STARS DARKENED.
5. ABYSS OPENED - DEMON POSSESSED LOCUSTS RELEASED.
6. 4 ANGELS RELEASED 1/3 OF MANKIND KILLED

2 WITNESSES KILLED, A.C. DEFILES TEMPLE, ISRAEL FLEES, ANTICHRIST WOUNDED, SATAN CAST OUT OF HEAVEN.

SEVEN BOWLS
1. UGLY & PAINFUL SORES.
2. SEA POLLUTED - SEA LIFE KILLED.
3. ALL FRESH WATER TURNED TO BLOOD.
4. SUN GROWS VERY HOT, PEOPLE SCORCHED.
5. ANTICHRIST ATTACKED, HIS EMPIRE DARKENED, HIS PEOPLE IN PAIN.
6. EUPHRATES RIVER DRIES UP KINGS OF EAST MOVE.
7. GREAT EARTHQUAKE BABYLON DESTROYED.

2ND COMING, BATTLE OF ARMAGEDDON, SATAN BOUND, ANTICHRIST AND FALSE PROPHET CAST INTO LAKE OF FIRE.

THE RAPTURE

1 2 3 4 5 6 | 1 2 3 4 5 6 | 1 2 3 4 5 6 7

1st 6 SEALS OPENED

7th SEAL OPENED
1st 6 TRUMPETS SOUND

7th TRUMPET SOUNDS
ALL 7 BOWLS DUMPED

MID-POINT

← 3½ YEARS → ← 3½ YEARS →

Time Line #3

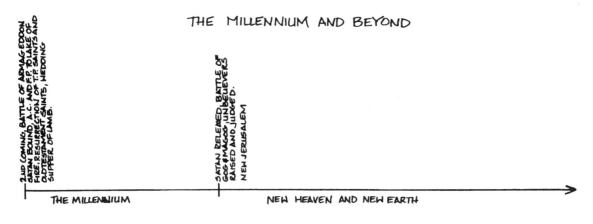

THE MILLENNIUM AND BEYOND

2ND COMING, BATTLE OF ARMAGEDDON, SATAN BOUND, A.C. AND F.P. TO LAKE OF FIRE, RESURRECTION OF T.P. SAINTS AND OLD TESTAMENT SAINTS, WEDDING SUPPER OF LAMB.

SATAN RELEASED, BATTLE OF GOG & MAGOG, UNBELIEVERS RAISED AND JUDGED. NEW JERUSALEM

THE MILLENNIUM   NEW HEAVEN AND NEW EARTH

Time Line #4

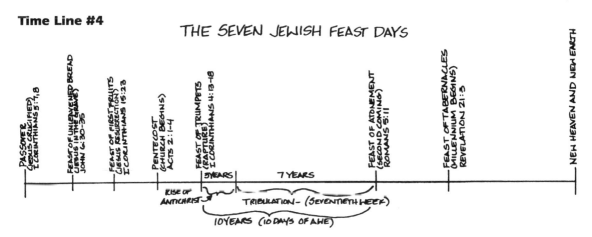

THE SEVEN JEWISH FEAST DAYS

PASSOVER (JESUS CRUCIFIED) I CORINTHIANS 5:7, 8

FEAST OF UNLEAVENED BREAD (JESUS IN THE GRAVE) JOHN 6:30-35

FEAST OF FIRST FRUITS (JESUS RESURRECTION) I CORINTHIANS 15:23

PENTECOST (CHURCH BEGINS) ACTS 2:1-4

FEAST OF TRUMPETS (RAPTURE) I CORINTHIANS 4:13-18

FEAST OF ATONEMENT (SECOND COMING) ROMANS 5:11

FEAST OF TABERNACLES (MILLENNIUM BEGINS) REVELATION 21:3

NEW HEAVEN AND NEW EARTH

RISE OF ANTICHRIST

3 YEARS   7 YEARS

TRIBULATION – (SEVENTIETH WEEK)

10 YEARS (10 DAYS OF AWE)

Time Line #5

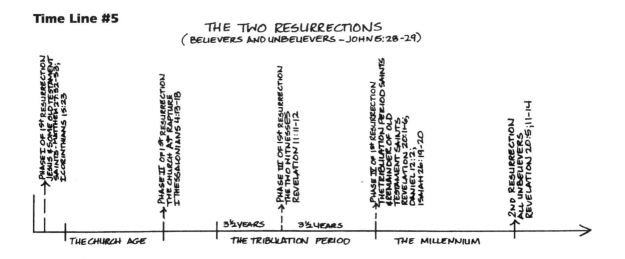

THE TWO RESURRECTIONS
(BELIEVERS AND UNBELIEVERS – JOHN 5:28-29)

PHASE I OF 1ST RESURRECTION JESUS & SOME OLD TESTAMENT SAINTS - MATTHEW 27:51-53; I CORINTHIANS 15:23

PHASE II OF 1ST RESURRECTION THE CHURCH AT RAPTURE I THESSALONIANS 4:13-18

PHASE III OF 1ST RESURRECTION THE TWO WITNESSES REVELATION 11:11-12

PHASE IV OF 1ST RESURRECTION THE TRIBULATION PERIOD SAINTS (REMAINDER OF OLD TESTAMENT SAINTS REVELATION 20:1-6; DANIEL 12:2; ISAIAH 26:19-20

2ND RESURRECTION ALL UNBELIEVERS REVELATION 20:5;11-14

3½ YEARS   3½ YEARS

THE CHURCH AGE   THE TRIBULATION PERIOD   THE MILLENNIUM

APPENDIX B — THE ANSWERS

CHAPTER ONE

1. An angel delivered it to John. (Revelation 1:1)
2. No, because it was given by the one who loves us and died for us. (Revelation 1:5)
3. Everyone alive plus the dead who crucified him. (Revelation 1:7)
4. The good and bad qualities of each church are ideal for instructing all of God's people. (Revelation 1:11)
5. The high priest represents Jesus who intercedes on our behalf. (Revelation 1:13)

CHAPTER TWO

1. They forsook their first love. (Revelation 2:4)
2. They would be persecuted and tested. (Revelation 2:10)
3. They remained true to the gospel even though they were in a city with many pagan temples. (Revelation 2:13)
4. They tolerated Jezebel, a false prophetess, who led many people into sexual immorality. (Revelation 2:20)
5. Let us hear the call to repent and learn these words so that we don't make these same mistakes. (Revelation 2:29)

CHAPTER THREE

1. They had a reputation for being alive but were really dead. (Revelation 3:1)
2. Several of their church members were not true believers. (Revelation 3:9)
3. They were lukewarm—neither totally for Christ or totally against him. (Revelation 3:16)
4. The letter to the church at Laodicea. (Revelation 3:14-22)
5. Be earnest, repent, and open the door to your heart. (Revelation 3:19, 20)

CHAPTER FOUR

1. *Come up here, and I will show you what must take place after this.* (Revelation 4:1)
2. Jasper and carnelian. (Revelation 4:3)
3. Robes of white and crowns of gold. (Revelation 4:4)
4. The seven spirits of God. (Revelation 4:5)
5. We should lay our crowns of pride, selfishness, and control before the throne as a deliberate act of submission to God's power. (Revelation 4:10)

CHAPTER FIVE

1. The destiny of all mankind will be affected by the scroll. (Revelation 5:1,2)
2. The first time he came as a sacrificial Lamb. The second time he will come as the Lion of the Tribe of Judah. (Revelation 5:5, 12)
3. Up until the Rapture, God has been dealing with man as a lamb because he is giving us every opportunity to repent. After the Rapture he will deal with man as a lion. (Revelation 5:7, 8)
4. We have been made a kingdom and priests to serve our God. (Revelation 5:10)
5. There are several reasons: the angels proclaim it along with the living creatures, twenty-four elders, and even the dead. (Revelation 5:11–14)

CHAPTER SIX

1. A bow, but no arrows. (Revelation 6:2)
2. The power to take peace from the earth and to make men slay each other. (Revelation 6:4)
3. The equivalent of a day's wages. (Revelation 6:6)
4. The rider is named Death. He will be followed by Hades. (Revelation 6:8)

CHAPTER SEVEN

1. They will hold back the winds from the four points of the earth. God is still giving people a chance to repent. (Revelation 7:1)
2. They will preach salvation through the blood of the Lamb. The Jews will finally accept Jesus as the Messiah. (Revelation 7:10)
3. Praise, glory, wisdom, thanks, honor, power, and strength. Because God made the sinner's salvation possible. (Revelation 7:12)
4. The twenty-four elders represent Christians of the Church Age. The Tribulation Saints are those saved after the Rapture. (Revelation 7:13, 14)
5. Yes, but once in heaven they will never suffer again. (Revelation 7:16)

CHAPTER EIGHT

1. God is a patient God, and he is giving people time to repent. (Revelation 8:1,4)
2. The death of his Son who died for the sins of the world. (Revelation 8:3)
3. To avenge the death of the Tribulation Saints and to symbolize God's wrath. (Revelation 8:5)
4. God has rained destruction on Egypt and Sodom and Gomorrah, so there is no reason to believe he won't do it again. (Revelation 8:7)

CHAPTER NINE

1. To show mankind that God is in control of our destinies and to turn some hearts back to him. (Revelation 9:4-6)
2. Their faces will resemble human faces. (Revelation 9:7)
3. The Hebrew and Greek names indicate that the locusts will attack Jews and Gentiles. The double name also indicates a double warning of the pain and suffering the locusts will inflict. (Revelation 9:11)
4. Someone speaking for the martyred saints. (Revelation 9:13)
5. Demon worship, idolatry, murder, black magic, sexual immorality, and theft. (Revelation 9: 20, 21)

CHAPTER TEN

1. He has been in the presence of God. (Revelation 10:1)
2. God. (Revelation 10:3)
3. Some of the mysteries include: mystery of lawlessness, the mystery of the Rapture, mystery of Israel's blindness, mystery of God's wisdom, mystery of Christ and the Church, mystery of Christ in us, mystery of the kingdom of heaven, and mystery of godliness. (Revelation 10:7)
4. The two commissions are to assimilate the Word of God into our lives by doing what the Bible says and to spread the Word of God to all peoples, nations, languages, and kings. (Revelation 10:9-11)

CHAPTER ELEVEN

1. Because it has been given to the Gentiles. (Revelation 11:2)
2. An olive tree and a lampstand represent each witness. The olive tree symbolizes that the witnesses are filled with the Holy Spirit, while the lampstand symbolizes that the witnesses will be lights in a dark world. (Revelation 11:4)
3. Because it will be full of wickedness. (Revelation 11:8)
4. The death of the two witnesses. (Revelation 11:10)
5. The death and resurrection of the two witnesses closely parallels the death and resurrection of Jesus. Jesus was crucified but rose from the dead a few days later. The witnesses will be killed but God will breathe life into them several days later. Another similarity is the ascension of Jesus after his resurrection and the rapture of the witnesses after their resurrection. One last parallel is the earthquake that occurred when Jesus died and the earthquake that will occur when the two witnesses are raptured.

CHAPTER TWELVE

1. A woman and an enormous red dragon. The woman is the nation of Israel at its beginning, and the dragon is Satan. The dragon's seven heads represent the seven Gentile world governments, while the ten horns represent ten kings that will reign during the Tribulation. The seven crowns mean the Antichrist will subdue three of those ten kings. (Revelation 12:1-3)
2. 1,260 days equal 3 ½ years and correspond to the last half of the Tribulation Period when the Jews will flee from Satan to the place God has prepared for them. (Revelation 12:6)
3. Michael. (Revelation 12:7)
4. To the earth. Because he has lost his place in heaven. (Revelation 12:9,10)
5. Believers have three ways to overcome Satan: 1) trust in the blood of the Lamb, 2) acknowledge faith in Jesus, and 3) not fear death. (Revelation 12:11)

CHAPTER THIRTEEN

1. Yes. (Revelation 13:7)
2. The False Prophet will perform great deeds. (Revelation 13:12, 13)
3. Patience and faith—many will be captured, killed, experience famine, pestilence, etc. (Revelation 13:10)
4. No. It is the Mark, number, or name of the Antichrist. (Revelation 13:17)

CHAPTER FOURTEEN

1. He heard something like rushing water and loud peals of thunder. This is actually the heavenly multitude singing a new song for the 144,000 who have been redeemed. (Revelation 14:2)
2. Those who die in the Lord will leave their grief and torment behind, enter heaven, and sit in God's presence. (Revelation 14:13)
3. Jesus will reap the first harvest and angels will do the other one. During these harvests the wicked will be taken and thrown into the Lake of Fire. (Revelation 14:14-18)
4. It implies the wicked will be destroyed beyond recognition. There will be nothing left of their former self. (Revelation 14:19, 20)

CHAPTER FIFTEEN

1. We have a concept of angels doing good deeds, but these angels will do deeds of destruction as they pour out the wrath of God. (Revelation 15:1)
2. No! He would be unjust and unrighteous if he did not punish sin, avenge his people, or avenge his name. (Revelation 15:3,4)
3. Jesus is the only one who lived by all of God's standards, the only sinless person to ever live. (Revelation 15:4)
4. The wrath of God. (Revelation 15:7)
5. To keep everyone out. (Revelation 15:8)

CHAPTER SIXTEEN

1. A voice from the Temple—Jesus. (Revelation 16:1)
2. Because they shed the blood of the saints and prophets. (Revelation 16:6)
3. His kingdom will be plunged into darkness, and men will gnaw their tongues in agony. (Revelation 16:10)
4. Those who watch for Jesus and keep their garments. (Revelation 16:15)
5. They will perform miraculous signs. It will be a time of great deception. Not all miracles are good miracles. (Revelation 16:14)

CHAPTER SEVENTEEN

1. She is the mother of prostitutes and of the abominations of the earth—a great ecumenical religious system. (Revelation 17:5)
2. He was *in the Spirit.* Capital "S" means he was under the influence of the Holy Spirit when he had this vision. (Revelation 17:3)
3. Her clothing indicates wealth and an alliance with the world leaders. The golden cup indicates an attempt to appear righteous, take communion, and simulate the true Church. (Revelation 17:4)
4. A "mind of wisdom" is one that can interpret the things of God and understand the prophecies and symbols. It is obtained by studying the Scriptures. (Revelation 17:9)
5. God. (Revelation 17:17)

CHAPTER EIGHTEEN

1. All of them. (Revelation 18:3)
2. She will be paid double from her own cup, given torture and grief to match the glory and luxury she gives herself. She will reap what she sows. (Revelation 18:6,7)
3. Sorcery, astrology, and cultic practices. These are very prominent today. (Revelation 18:23)
4. The prophets, saints, and all who are killed on earth. Babylon's rich and powerful will promote policies that will cause the death of these people. (Revelation 18:24)
5. Magic. (Revelation 18:23)

CHAPTER NINETEEN

1. Yes. (Revelation 19:6)
2. The testimony of Jesus. His predictions about: future events, his death, burial, resurrection, end-times, plagues, deception, and false Christs. (Revelation 19:10)
3. The Church, angels, Tribulation Period Saints, and Old Testament Saints. (Revelation 19:14)
4. He will deceive people with miraculous signs, and he will do it to get them to receive the Mark of the Beast and to worship his image. (Revelation 19:20)
5. All those who take the Mark of the Beast and worship his image. (Revelation 19:21)

CHAPTER TWENTY

1. They will refuse to worship the beast or his image and refuse to take his Mark on their foreheads or their hands. (Revelation 20:4)
2. They will be priests of God and of Christ and will reign with him for a thousand years. (Revelation 20:6)
3. By what they have done as recorded in the books. (Revelation 20:12)
4. Yes. They will be judged according to what they have done. (Revelation 20:12, 13)
5. Because their names cannot be found in the Book of Life. (Revelation 20:15)

CHAPTER TWENTY-ONE

1. Some may doubt the importance or significance of Revelation. Some do not believe in the Rapture, Tribulation Period, Second Coming, or wrath of God. These are the words of one who cannot lie. (Revelation 21:5)
2. All authority is his. He gained the authority and paid the price when he died on the cross. (Revelation 21:6)
3. The Holy City will come down after the new earth is created, but no one knows how far down it will come. (Revelation 21:10)
4. The twelve names will be a reminder to all who enter the city that the Messiah, Scriptures, and salvation came through the Jews. (Revelation 21:12)
5. God allowed Satan to defile the present creation, but he will never let that happen again. (Revelation 21:19-27)

CHAPTER TWENTY-TWO

1. The name of God. (Revelation 22:4)
2. They can keep the words of this book by obeying what it says. (Revelation 22:7)
3. Because John testifies to everything contained in Revelation. (Revelation 22:8)
4. He fell down to worship an angel. (Revelation 22:8)

APPENDIX C — THE EXPERTS

David Breese—President of World Prophetic Ministry, and Bible teacher on *The King Is Coming* television program. (World Prophetic Ministry, P.O. Box 907, Colton, CA 92324)

J.R. Church—Host of the nation-wide television program *Prophecy in the News*. (Prophecy Publications, P.O. Box 7000, Oklahoma City, OK 73153)

Charles H. Dyer—Professor of Bible exposition at Dallas Theological Seminary.

Arno Froese—Editor of *Midnight Call* and *News From Israel*. (Midnight Call, Inc., 4694 Platt Springs Road, West Columbia, South Carolina 29170; News From Israel, P.O. Box 4389, West Columbia, SC 29171-4389)

Billy Graham—World famous evangelist and author. (Billy Graham Evangelistic Association, 1300 Harmon Place, P.O. Box 779, Minneapolis, MN 55440-0779)

Oliver B. Greene—Former Director of The Gospel Hour, Inc., author, and radio show host.

John Hagee—Founder and pastor of Cornerstone Church, and President of Global Evangelism Television.

Charles Halff—Executive Director of The Christian Jew Foundation, radio host for *The Christian Jew Hour,* and featured writer for *Message of The Christian Jew.* (The Christian Jew Foundation, P.O. Box 345, San Antonio, TX 78292)

Gary Hedrick—President of The Christian Jew Foundation, radio host for *The Christian Jew Hour,* and featured writer for *Message of The Christian Jew.* (The Christian Jew Foundation, P.O. Box 345, San Antonio, TX 78292)

Ed Hindson—Minister of Biblical Studies at Rehoboth Baptist Church in Atlanta, Georgia, Vice President of *There's Hope,* adjunct professor at Liberty University in Virginia, and an executive board member of the Pre-Trib Research Center in Washington, D.C.

David Hocking—Pastor, radio host, and Director of Hope For Today Ministries. (P.O. Box 3927, Tustin, CA 92781-3927)

Noah Hutchings—President of The Southwest Radio Church, one of the oldest and best-known prophetic ministries in the world. (P.O. Box 1144, Oklahoma City, OK 73101)

Jack Van Impe—Co-host, along with his wife Rexella, of a worldwide television ministry that analyzes the news in light of Bible prophecy. (Jack Van Impe Ministries International, P.O. Box 7004, Troy, MI 48007)

Grant R. Jeffrey—Best-selling author of six books. (Frontier Research Publications Inc., Box 129, Station "U," Toronto, Ontario M8Z5M4)

David Jeremiah—President of Christian Heritage College, Senior Pastor of Scott Memorial Baptist Church in El Cajon, California, and radio host of *Turning Point.* **Carole C. Carlson**—Author/co-author of nineteen books including the best-selling *The Late Great Planet Earth* with Hal Lindsey.

Tim LaHaye—Best-selling author, President and founder of Family Life Seminars, and husband to Beverly LaHaye, Director of Concerned Women of America.

Peter and Paul Lalonde—Founders and co-hosts of *This Week in Bible Prophecy.* (This Week In Bible Prophecy, P.O. Box 1440, Niagara Falls, NY 14302-1440)

Hal Lindsey—Called by many the father of the modern day prophecy movement, President of Hal Lindsey Ministries, and author of more than a dozen books with combined world-wide sales exceeding 35 million copies. (P.O. Box 4000, Palos Verdes, CA 90274)

Wim Malgo—Former founder of Midnight Call, Inc., and the author of several books. (Midnight Call, Inc., 4694 Platt Springs Road, West Columbia, SC 29170)

J. Vernon McGee—Former host of the popular *Thru the Bible* radio show. (Thru The Bible Radio, Box 100, Pasadena, CA 91109)

Dennis Pollock—Pastor with the *Christ in Prophecy* radio program. (Lamb & Lion Ministries, P.O. Box 919, McKinney, TX 75069)

Stanley Price—associated with the Southwest Radio Church. He has written articles for one of their many publications, *Bible in the News.* (Southwest Radio Church, P.O. Box 1144, Oklahoma City, OK 73101)

David Reagan—Host of *Christ in Prophecy*, and author of the first-ever picture book on prophecy for young children, *Jesus is Coming Again.*

Jerry Tyson—Writer for *Bible in the News*, a publication of The Southwest Radio Church. (P.O. Box 1144, Oklahoma City, OK 73101)

Vera K. White—Christian educator and free-lance writer. (Eco-Justice Working Group, National Council of the Churches of Christ, Room 812, 475 Riverside Drive, New York, NY 10115)

To the best of our knowledge, all of the above information is correct. We were unable to obtain information for those experts that are missing.

—THE STARBURST EDITORS

ENDNOTES

Revelation 1

1. Breese, David, *THE BOOK OF THE REVELATION*, Taped Message #DB111.
2. McGee, J. Vernon, *THRU THE BIBLE WITH J. VERNON McGEE*, Volume V, p. 891.
3. Lindsey, Hal, *REVELATION, HOW JOHN WITNESSED OUR FUTURE*, Taped Message # 003B.
4. Lindsey, Hal, *REVELATION, KEYS TO INTERPRETING REVELATION*, Taped Message # 001A.
5. Breese, David, *THE BOOK OF THE REVELATION*, Taped Message #DB111.

Revelation 2

1. LaHaye, Tim, *REVELATION-ILLUSTRATED AND MADE PLAIN*, pp. 34-94.
2. Lindsey, Hal, *THERE'S A NEW WORLD COMING*, pp. 34-56.
3. McGee, J. Vernon, *THRU THE BIBLE WITH J. VERNON McGEE*, Volume V, pp. 901-915.
4. Breese, David. *THE BOOK OF THE REVELATION*, Taped Message #DB111.
5. Van Impe, Jack, *2001: ON THE EDGE OF ETERNITY*, p. 69.
6. Hindson, Ed, *FINAL SIGNS*, p. 61.
7. Malgo, Wim, *THE RULERSHIP OF HEAVEN*, p.162.
8. Hindson, Ed, *FINAL SIGNS*, p.173.
9. McGee, J. Vernon, *THRU THE BIBLE WITH J. VERNON McGEE*, Volume V, p. 909.
10. Maddoux, Marlin, *POINT OF VIEW RADIO, NEWSLETTER*, September 5, 1997, p. 2.
11. Lindsey, Hal, *THERE'S A NEW WORLD COMING*, p. 43.
12. Ibid., p. 43.

Revelation 3

1. Breese, David, *THE BOOK OF REVELATION*, Taped Message # DB111.
2. Hindson, Ed, *FINAL SIGNS*, p. 147.
3. Moody, Adams, *UPDATE*, 1996.
4. Scott, John, *WHAT CHRIST THINKS OF THE CHURCH*, p. 72.
5. Orr, Edwin J., *THE REBIRTH OF AMERICA*, p.63.
6. *U.S. NEWS AND WORLD REPORT*, April 4, 1994, p. 56.
7. Hagee, John, *BEGINNING OF THE END*, p. 32.

8. Hindson, Ed, *FINAL SIGNS*, p. 177.
9. Hagee, John, *BEGINNING OF THE END*, p. X.
10. *MIDNIGHT CALL*, March 1996, pp. 15, 16.
11. Lindsey, Hal, *REVELATION, LAODICEA: THE APOSTLE CHURCH*, Taped message # 008A.
12. Reagan, David, *THE MASTER PLAN*, p. 219.

Revelation 4

1. *THE PROPHECY BIBLE*, Thomas Nelson Publishers, p. 1319.
2. Lindsey, Hal, *THE RAPTURE*, p. 151.
3. Hocking, David, *THE BIOLA HOUR*, Taped Messages # 3371 and 3374.
4. Reagan, David, *THE MASTER PLAN*, p.90.
5. Jeffrey, Grant R., *FINAL WARNING*, p. 306.
6. Hocking, David, *THE COMING WORLD LEADER*, p. 112.
7. Ibid., p. 112.

Revelation 5

1. Lindsey, Hal, *THERE'S A NEW WORLD COMING*, p. 74.
2. Malgo, Wim, *THE RULERSHIP OF HEAVEN*, p. 30.
3. McGee, J. Vernon, *THRU THE BIBLE WITH J. VERNON McGEE*, p. 936.
4. LaHaye, Tim, *REVELATION-ILLUSTRATED AND MADE PLAIN*, p. 132.
5. Hocking, David, *THE VISION OF HEAVEN*, pp. 25–26.

Revelation 6

1. Hagee, John, *BEGINNING OF THE END*, p. 117.
2. Hutchings, Noah, *BIBLE IN THE NEWS*, p. 5.
3. Hagee, John, *BEGINNING OF THE END*, p. 13.
4. Jeffrey, Grant R., *FINAL WARNING*, p. 59.
5. Hagee, John, *DAY OF DECEPTION*, p. 45.
6. Hagee, John, *BEGINNING OF THE END*, p. 130.
7. *DISPATCH FROM JERUSALEM*, November–December 1996.
8. Lindsey, Hal, *MIDNIGHT CALL*, p. 11.
9. *U.S. NEWS AND WORLD REPORT*, June 13, 1994.
10. Graham, Billy, *STORM WARNING*, p. 273.
11. Van Impe, Jack, *2001: ON THE EDGE OF ETERNITY*, p. 176, 181-182.
12. Jeffrey, Grant R., *FINAL WARNING*, p. 228.

13. Hindson, Ed, *FINAL SIGNS,* p. 181.
14. Hagee, John, *DAY OF DECEPTION,* p. 49.
15. Duck, Daymond R., *ON THE BRINK,* p. 152.
16. Worldwatch Institute, *VITAL SIGNS* 1996.
17. Worldwatch Institute, *VITAL SIGNS* 1996.
18. *THE WORLD ALMANAC,* 1997, p. 131.
19. Graham, Billy, *STORM WARNING,* p. 230.
20. Lindsey, Hal, *THERE'S A NEW WORLD COMING,* p. 88.
21. Van Impe, Jack, *2001:ON THE EDGE OF ETERNITY,* pp. 101–102.
22. Jeffrey, Grant R., *FINAL WARNING,* p. 181.
23. *THE JACKSON SUN,* May 20, 1996.
24. *INTERNATIONAL INTELLIGENCE BRIEFING,* February 1997.
25. Van Impe, Jack, *2001: ON THE EDGE OF ETERNITY,* p. 43.
26. Lindsey, Hal, *THERE'S A NEW WORLD COMING,* p. 93.
27. Graham, Billy, *STORM WARNING,* p. 271.
28. Jeremiah, David, with C.C. Carlson, *ESCAPE THE COMING NIGHT,* p. 112.
29. Lindsey, Hal, *THERE'S A NEW WORLD COMING,* p. 96.
30. *NEWS FROM ISRAEL,* November 1996, p. 23.
31. Graham, Billy, *STORM WARNING,* p. 57.
32. Hindson, Ed, *FINAL SIGNS,* p. 181.
33. Breese, David, *THE BOOK OF REVELATION,* Taped Message # DB112A.
34. Jeremiah, David, with C.C. Carlson, *ESCAPE THE COMING NIGHT,* p. 115.
35. Melton, J.H., *52 LESSONS IN REVELATION,* p. 93.
36. Hocking, David, *THE VISION OF HEAVEN,*p. 46.

Revelation 7

1. McGee, J.Vernon, *THRU THE BIBLE WITH J. VERNON McGEE,* Volume V, p. 949.
2. LaHaye, Tim, *REVELATION-ILLUSTRATED AND MADE PLAIN,* p. 158.
3. Lindsey, Hal, *THERE'S A NEW WORLD COMING,* p. 104.
4. Bennett, Jeff, *THE JACKSON SUN NEWSPAPER,* September 21, 1997, p. 1F.
5. Pollock, Dennis, *Lamb & Lion Ministries, LAMPLIGHTER,* January 1993, p. 5.
6. White, Vera K., *IT'S GOD'S WORLD: CHRISTIANS. THE ENVIRONMENT AND CLIMATE CHANGE, THE ECO-JUSTICE WORKING GROUP NATIONAL COUNCIL OF THE CHURCHES OF CHRIST IN THE U.S.A.,* p. 8.
7. *JERUSALEM DISPATCH,* 1996, p. 1.
8. *AFA JOURNAL,* November/December 1996 p. 15.
9. Lindsey, Hal, *THERE'S A NEW WORLD COMING,* p. 112.
10. LaHaye, Tim, *REVELATION-ILLUSTRATED AND MADE PLAIN,* p. 166.
11. Van Impe, Jack, *2001: ON THE EDGE OF ETERNITY,* pp. 10-11.

12. Jeffrey, Grant R., *FINAL WARNING,* p. 186.
13. *THE WORLDBOOK YEAR BOOK ,* 1993, p. 225.

Revelation 8

1. Van Impe, Jack, *2001: ON THE EDGE OF ETERNITY,* p. 154.
2. *THE WORLD ALMANAC AND BOOK OF FACTS 1997,* p. 304.
3. Lindsey, Hal, *THERE'S A NEW WORLD COMING,* p. 118.
4. Van Impe, Jack, *2001: ON THE EDGE OF ETERNITY,* p. 4.
5. *THE WORLDBOOK YEAR BOOK ,* 1993, p. 226.
6. *TIME MAGAZINE,* December 26, 1994, January 2, 1995.
7. *U.S. NEWS AND WORLD REPORT,* June 26, 1995, p. 20.
8. *INTERNATIONAL INTELLIGENCE BRIEFING,* January 1996, p. 1.
9. *INTERNATIONAL INTELLIGENCE BRIEFING,* February 1997, p. 8.
10. Hocking, David, *THE COMING WORLD LEADER,* p. 156.
11. *COUNTDOWN MAGAZINE FROM THE WASHINGTON TIMES.*
12. *SPOTLIGHT MAGAZINE,* March 6, 1995, p. 15.
13. *THE WORLD BOOK ENCYCLOPEDIA,* 1990, Volume 14, p. 608.
14. Melton, J.H., *52 LESSONS IN REVELATION,* p. 102.

Revelation 9

1. Jeremiah, David, with C.C. Carlson, *ESCAPE THE COMING NIGHT,* p. 128–129.
2. *THE WORLD BOOK ENCYCLOPEDIA,* 1990, Volume 12, pp. 422–423.
3. Hocking, David, *THE COMING WORLD LEADER,* pp. 162–163.
4. McGee, J. Vernon, *THRU THE BIBLE WITH J. VERNON McGEE,* Volume V, p. 968.
5. Greene, Oliver B., *THE REVELATION,* p. 256.
6. McGee, J. Vernon, *THRU THE BIBLE WITH J. VERNON McGEE,* Volume V, pp. 968–969.
7. Melton, J.H., *52 LESSONS IN REVELATION,* p. 106.
8. Jeremiah, David, with C.C. Carlson, *ESCAPE THE COMING NIGHT,* p. 130.
9. Van Impe, Jack, *2001: ON THE EDGE OF ETERNITY,* pp. 37–38.
10. Lindsey, Hal, *THERE'S A NEW WORLD COMING,* p. 127.
11. McGee, J. Vernon, *THRU THE BIBLE WITH J. VERNON McGEE,* Volume V, p. 970.
12. Duck, Daymond R., *ON THE BRINK,* p. 192.
13. Lindsey, Hal, *REVELATION, THE YELLOW PERIL,* Taped Message, DB # 0168.
14. Lindsey, Hal, *THERE'S A NEW WORLD COMING,* pp. 128, 129.

15. McGee, J. Vernon, *THRU THE BIBLE WITH J. VERNON McGEE*, Volume V, p. 971.
16. Hindson, Ed, *FINAL SIGNS*, p. 12.
17. Lindsey, Hal, *THERE'S A NEW WORLD COMING*, p. 130.
18. Hagee, John, *DAY OF DECEPTION*, p. 4.
19. Van Impe, Jack, *2001: ON THE EDGE OF ETERNITY*, p. 69.
20. Hutchings, Noah, *BIBLE IN THE NEWS*, March 1995, p. 14.
21. Tyson, Jerry, *BIBLE IN THE NEWS*, March 1995, p. 12.
22. Hagee, John, *DAY OF DECEPTION*, p. 76.
23. Jeffrey, Grant R., *FINAL WARNING*, p. 180.
24. Van Impe, Jack, *2001: ON THE EDGE OF ETERNITY*, pp. 70–71.
25. Hutchings, Noah, *BIBLE IN THE NEWS*, March 1993, p. 20.
26. *NEWSWEEK MAGAZINE*, August 1, 1994, p. 37.
27. *MIDNIGHT CALL*, April 1996, p. 19.

Revelation 10

1. Hocking, David, *THE COMING WORLD LEADER*, p. 170.
2. McGee, J. Vernon, *THRU THE BIBLE WITH J. VERNON McGEE*, Volume V, p. 974.
3. Hocking, David, *THE COMING WORLD LEADER*, p. 171.
4. Jeremiah, David, with C.C. Carlson, *ESCAPE THE COMING NIGHT*, p. 138.
5. Lindsey, Hal, *THERE'S A NEW WORLD COMING*, p. 143.
6. LaHaye, Tim, *REVELATION ILLUSTRATED AND MADE PLAIN*, p. 196.
7. Greene, Oliver B., *THE REVELATION*, p. 273.
8. Hocking, David, *THE COMING WORLD LEADER*, p. 172.
9. McGee, J. Vernon, *THRU THE BIBLE WITH J. VERNON McGEE*, Volume V, p. 976.
10. Jeremiah, David, with C.C. Carlson, *ESCAPE THE COMING NIGHT*, p. 140.
11. Hocking, David, *THE COMING WORLD LEADER*, p. 174.

Revelation 11

1. Dyer, Charles H., *WORLD NEWS AND BIBLE PROPHECY*, p. 76.
2. Lindsey, Hal, *THERE'S A NEW WORLD COMING*, p. 150.
3. *PROPHETIC OBSERVER*, January 1995, p. 4.
4. *NEWS FROM ISRAEL*, December 1996, p. 19.
5. Lindsey Hal, *PLANET EARTH-2000 A.D.*, p. 156.
6. Hocking, David, *THE COMING WORLD LEADER*, p. 180.
7. Dyer, Charles H., *WORLD NEWS AND BIBLE PROPHECY*, p. 171.
8. *NEWS FROM ISRAEL*, May 1996.

9. Hagee, John, *BEGINNING OF THE END*, p. 94.
10. McGee, J. Vernon, *THRU THE BIBLE WITH J. VERNON McGEE*, Volume V, p. 981.
11. Hagee, John, *BEGINNING OF THE END*, p. 116.
12. Jeremiah, David, with C.C. Carlson, *ESCAPE THE COMING NIGHT*, p. 143.
13. Hindson, Ed, *FINAL SIGNS*, p. 7.
14. Hagee, John, *BEGINNING OF THE END*, p. 95.
15. McGee, J. Vernon, *THRU THE BIBLE WITH J. VERNON McGEE*, Volume V, p. 983.
16. Jeremiah, David, with C.C. Carlson, *ESCAPE THE COMING NIGHT*, p. 144.
17. *MESSAGE OF THE CHRISTIAN JEW*, November/December 1993, p. 6.

Revelation 12

1. *HARPER'S BIBLE DICTIONARY*, 1973, p. 229.
2. Dyer, Charles H., *WORLD NEWS AND BIBLE PROPHECY*, p. 90.
3. Hindson, Ed, *FINAL SIGNS*, p. 21.
4. Lindsey, Hal, *THERE'S A NEW WORLD COMING*, pp. 222–223.
5. Dyer, Charles H., *WORLD NEWS AND BIBLE PROPHECY*, p. 90.
6. Jeremiah, David, with C.C. Carlson, *ESCAPE THE COMING NIGHT*, p. 149.
7. *BIBLE IN THE NEWS*, October 1995, p. 19.
8. Hutchings, Noah, *PROPHETIC OBSERVER*, January 1996, p. 4.
9. Dyer, Charles H., *WORLD NEWS AND BIBLE PROPHECY*, p. 89.
10. Hagee, John, *BEGINNING OF THE END*, p. 171.
11. LaHaye, Tim, *REVELATION-ILLUSTRATED AND MADE PLAIN*, p. 246–247.
12. Hagee, John, *BEGINNING OF THE END*, p. 171.
13. Hutchings, Noah, *PROPHETIC OBSERVER*, January 1996, p. 4.
14. McGee, J. Vernon, *THRU THE BIBLE WITH J. VERNON McGEE*, Volume V, p. 994.
15. Halff, Charles, *MESSAGE OF THE CHRISTIAN JEW*, September–October, 1981, p. 4.
16. Jeremiah, David, with C.C. Carlson, *ESCAPE THE COMING NIGHT*, p. 156.

Revelation 13

1. Van Impe, Jack, *2001: ON THE EDGE OF ETERNITY*, p. 6.
2. Jeffrey, Grant R., *FINAL WARNING*, p. 86.
3. Hindson, Ed, *FINAL SIGNS*, p. 24.
4. Dyer, Charles H., *WORLD NEWS AND BIBLE PROPHECY*, p. 221.
5. McBirnie, William S., *50 PROGRESSIVE MESSAGES ON SECOND COMING OF CHRIST*, p. 158.
6. *MIDNIGHT CALL*, February 1996, p. 13.
7. *THE SPOTLIGHT*, December 18, 1995, p. 1.
8. Hutchings, Noah, *PROPHETIC OBSERVER*, July 1994, p. 2.

9. *DAVE WEBER REPORTS*, November, 1995, p. 5.
10. Lindsey, Hal, *THERE'S A NEW WORLD COMING*, p. 178.
11. McGee, J. Vernon, *THRU THE BIBLE WITH J. VERNON McGEE*, Volume V, pp. 999–1000.
12. Hagee, John, *BEGINNING OF THE END*, pp. 167–168.
13. Van Impe, Jack, *2001: ON THE EDGE OF ETERNITY*, p. 161.
14. Hutchings, Noah, *PROPHETIC OBSERVER*, October 1996, p. 8.
15. Religious News Service, *THE JACKSON SUN*, November 24, 1996, p. 6A.
16. Jeremiah, David, with C.C. Carlson, *ESCAPE THE COMING NIGHT*, p. 112.
17. Lindsey, Hal, *SOURCE OF ANTI-CHRIST'S AUTHORITY*, Taped Message #021A.
18. Hindson, Ed, *FINAL SIGNS*, p. 109.
19. Ibid., p. 107.
20. LaHaye, Tim, *REVELATION-ILLUSTRATED AND MADE PLAIN*, p. 249.
21. Lindsey, Hal, *THERE'S A NEW WORLD COMING*, p. 180.
22. *DAVE WEBER REPORTS*, February, 1997 p. 6.
23. Jeffrey, Grant R., *FINAL WARNING*, p. 158.
24. Van Impe, Jack, *2001: ON THE EDGE OF ETERNITY*, p. 69.
25. LaHaye, Tim, *REVELATION-ILLUSTRATED AND MADE PLAIN*, p. 256.
26. Hagee, John, *BEGINNING OF THE END*, p. 128.
27. Hagee, John, *BEGINNING OF THE END*, p. 119.
28. Van Impe, Jack, *2001: ON THE EDGE OF ETERNITY*, pp. 78, 79.
29. Ibid., p. 131.
30. Lindsey, Hal, *THERE'S A NEW WORLD COMING*, p. 182.
31. LaHaye, Tim, *REVELATION-ILLUSTRATED AND MADE PLAIN*, p. 258.
32. Hindson, Ed, *FINAL SIGNS*, p. 152.
33. Hagee, John, *BEGINNING OF THE END*, p. 135.

Revelation 14

1. Lindsey, Hal, *THERE'S A NEW WORLD COMING*, p. 186.
2. Hocking, David, *THE COMING WORLD LEADER*, p. 215.
3. Ibid., p. 215.
4. LaHaye, Tim, *REVELATION-ILLUSTRATED AND MADE PLAIN*, p. 267.
5. Lindsey, Hal, *THERE'S A NEW WORLD COMING*, p. 187.
6. McGee, J. Vernon, *THRU THE BIBLE WITH J. VERNON McGEE*, Volume V, p. 1008.
7. Duck, Daymond R., *ON THE BRINK*, pp. 118–120.
8. McGee, J. Vernon, *THRU THE BIBLE WITH J. VERNON McGEE*, Volume V, p. 1009.
9. Melton, J.H., *52 LESSONS IN REVELATION*, p. 151.
10. McGee, J. Vernon, *THRU THE BIBLE WITH J. VERNON McGEE*, Volume V, p. 1010.

11. Melton, J.H., *52 LESSONS IN REVELATION*, p. 151.
12. Greene, Oliver B., *REVELATION*, p. 359.
13. Hocking, David, *THE COMING WORLD LEADER*, p. 222.
14. LaHaye, Tim, *REVELATION-ILLUSTRATED AND MADE PLAIN*, p. 267.
15. Hagee, John, *BEGINNING OF THE END*, p. 173.
16. Hocking, David, *THE COMING WORLD LEADER*, p. 226.
17. Malgo, Wim, *THE WRATH OF HEAVEN ON EARTH*, p. 91.
18. McGee, J. Vernon, *THRU THE BIBLE WITH J. VERNON McGEE*, Volume V, p. 1013.
19. Hocking, David, *THE COMING WORLD LEADER*, p. 226.
20. Melton, J.H., *52 LESSONS IN REVELATION*, p. 156.
21. Church, J.R., *GUARDIANS OF THE GRAIL*, p. 316.
22. Lindsey, Hal, *THERE'S A NEW WORLD COMING*, p. 194.
23. Hocking, David, *THE COMING WORLD LEADER*, pp. 226–227.
24. Lalonde, Peter, and Paul, *THE MARK OF THE BEAST*, p. 188.

Revelation 15

1. Malgo, Wim, *THE WRATH OF HEAVEN ON EARTH*, p. 101.
2. LaHaye, Tim, *REVELATION-ILLUSTRATED AND MADE PLAIN*, p. 283.
3. Ibid., p. 285.
4. Lindsey, Hal, *THERE'S A NEW WORLD COMING*, p. 197.
5. Church, J.R., *HIDDEN PROPHECIES IN THE SONG OF MOSES*, p. 14.
6. Lalonde, Peter, and Paul, *THE MARK OF THE BEAST*, p. 189.
7. Ibid., p. 189.
8. McGee, J. Vernon, *THRU THE BIBLE WITH J. VERNON McGEE*, Volume V, p. 1020.

Revelation 16

1. Lalonde, Peter, and Paul, *THE MARK OF THE BEAST*, pp. 187–188.
2. Church, J.R., *HIDDEN PROPHECIES IN THE SONG OF MOSES*, p. 105.
3. Lalonde, Peter, and Paul, *301 STARTLING PROOOFS AND PROPHECIES*, p. 246.
4. McGee, J. Vernon, *THRU THE BIBLE WITH J. VERNON McGEE*, Volume V, p. 1023.
5. Malgo, Wim, *THE WRATH OF HEAVEN ON EARTH*, p. 116.
6. Lalonde, Peter, and Paul, *THE MARK OF THE BEAST*, p. 263.
7. Lindsey, Hal, *PLANET EARTH-2000 A.D.*, p. 95.
8. Hagee, John, *BEGINNING OF THE END*, p. 116.
9. White, Vera K., *IT'S GOD'S WORLD: CHRIS-*

TIANS. THE ENVIRONMENT AND CLIMATE CHANGE, THE ECO-JUSTICE WORKING GROUP NATIONAL COUNCIL OF THE CHURCHES OF CHRIST IN THE U.S.A., p. 5.

10. Hagee, John, THE BEGINNING OF THE END, p. 116.
11. Dyer, Charles H., WORLD NEWS AND BIBLE PROPHECY, p. 230.
12. Church, J.R., THEY PIERCED THE VEIL, pp.141–142.
13. Lalonde, Peter, and Paul, 301 STARTLING PROOOFS AND PROPHECIES, p. 238.
14. THE JACKSON SUN, January 13,1997 p. 5A.
15. U.S. NEWS AND WORLD REPORT, June 21, 1993, p. 43.
16. COUNTDOWN MAGAZINE, March 1996, p. 6.
17. SPOTLIGHT, January 13,1997, p. 3.
18. INTERNATIONAL INTELLIGENCE BRIEFING, January 1996, p. 2.
19. Dyer, Charles H., WORLD NEWS AND BIBLE PROPHECY, p. 231.
20. Hocking, David, THE COMING WORLD LEADER, pp. 239–240.
21. MIDNIGHT CALL, March 1996, p. 28.
22. Dyer, Charles H., WORLD NEWS AND BIBLE PROPHECY, p. 231.
23. THE WORLD ALMANAC , 1997, p. 304.
24. Hagee, John, BEGINNING OF THE END, p. 116.
25. Lalonde, Peter, and Paul, 301 STARTLING PROOOFS AND PROPHECIES, p. 248.

Revelation 17

1. Froese, Arno, NEWS FROM ISRAEL, January 1996, p. 8.
2. Hindson, Ed, FINAL SIGNS, p. 103.
3. Lindsey, Hal, PLANET EARTH-2000 A.D., p. 308.
4. Van Impe, Jack, 2001: ON THE EDGE OF ETERNITY, p. 83–84.
5. CPWR JOURNAL, September, 1994, p. 3.
6. Hutchings, Noah, BIBLE IN THE NEWS, p.9.
7. U.S. NEWS AND WORLD REPORT, Conversation, June 10, 1996.
8. Jeffrey, Grant R., FINAL WARNING, p. 153.
9. Van Impe, Jack, 2001: ON THE EDGE OF ETERNITY, p. 11.
10. Hindson, Ed, FINAL SIGNS, p. 108.
11. SPOTLIGHT, September 11, 1995, p. 5.
12. Hindson, Ed, FINAL SIGNS, p. 108.
13. Lindsey, Hal, REVELATION, THE MYSTERY OF BABLYON, Taped Message #026A.
14. Jeremiah, David, with C.C. Carlson, ESCAPE THE COMING NIGHT, pp. 168–169.
15. Froese, Arno, NEWS FROM ISRAEL, January 1996, pp. 8–9.
16. Jeffrey, Grant R., FINAL WARNING, p. 151.
17. Hindson, Ed, FINAL SIGNS, p. 108.
18. Dyer, Charles H., WORLD NEWS AND BIBLE PROPHECY, pp. 149–150.

19. Hocking, David, THE COMING WORLD LEADER, p. 249.
20. Ibid., p. 249.
21. Lindsey, Hal, THERE'S A NEW WORLD COMING, p. 222.
22. Hindson, Ed, FINAL SIGNS, p. 103.
23. Lindsey, Hal, THERE'S A NEW WORLD COMING, p. 233.
24. Hagee, John, BEGINNING OF THE END, p. 165.
25. Jeremiah, David, with C.C. Carlson, ESCAPE THE COMING NIGHT, p. 177.
26. Hocking, David, THE COMING WORLD LEADER, p. 252.
27. Dyer, Charles H., WORLD NEWS AND BIBLE PROPHECY, pp. 154–155.
28. Lalonde, Peter, and Paul, 301 STARTLING PROOOFS AND PROPHECIES, p. 234.
29. Price, Stanley E., BIBLE IN THE NEWS, July 1996, p. 11.
30. Duck, Daymond R., ON THE BRINK, pp. 118–120.

Revelation 18

1. LaHaye, Tim, REVELATION-ILLUSTRATED AND MADE PLAIN, p. 336.
2. Hindson, Ed, FINAL SIGNS, p. 107.
3. Lalonde, Peter, and Paul, 301 STARTLING PROOOFS AND PROPHECIES, p. 234.
4. Hocking, David, THE COMING WORLD LEADER, p. 259.
5. McGee, J. Vernon, THRU THE BIBLE WITH J. VERNON McGEE, Volume V, p. 1038.
6. Jeremiah, David, with C.C. Carlson, ESCAPE THE COMING NIGHT, p. 178.
7. McGee, J. Vernon, THRU THE BIBLE WITH J. VERNON McGEE, Volume V, p. 1038.
8. Crocker, Gene, Ph.D., SPOTLIGHT, September, 8, 1997, p. 4.
9. Hocking, David, THE COMING WORLD LEADER, p. 261.
10. Melton, J.H., 52 LESSONS IN REVELATION, p. 209.
11. Lalonde, Peter, and Paul, 301 STARTLING PROOOFS AND PROPHECIES, p. 247.
12. McGee, J. Vernon, THRU THE BIBLE WITH J. VERNON McGEE, Volume V, p. 1039.
13. Hindson, Ed, FINAL SIGNS, p. 107.
14. McGee, J. Vernon, THRU THE BIBLE WITH J. VERNON McGEE, Volume V, p. 1040.
15. Hocking, David, THE COMING WORLD LEADER, p. 252.
16. Jeremiah, David, with C.C. Carlson, ESCAPE THE COMING NIGHT, p. 179.
17. Greene, Oliver B., REVELATION, p. 444.
18. Hocking, David, THE COMING WORLD LEADER, p. 252.
19. Hindson, Ed, FINAL SIGNS, p. 107.
20. Lindsey, Hal, THERE'S A NEW WORLD COMING, p. 234.

21. McGee, J. Vernon, *THRU THE BIBLE WITH J. VERNON McGEE,* Volume V, p. 1041.
22. Hindson, Ed, *FINAL SIGNS,* p. 103.
23. Hocking, David, *THE COMING WORLD LEADER,* p. 264.
24. McGee, J. Vernon, *THRU THE BIBLE WITH J. VERNON McGEE,* Volume V, p. 1042.
25. Lalonde, Peter, and Paul, *301 STARTLING PROOFS AND PROPHECIES,* p. 235.
26. Ibid., p. 245.

Revelation 19

1. LaHaye, Tim, *REVELATION-ILLUSTRATED AND MADE PLAIN,* p. 344.
2. Jeremiah, David, with C.C. Carlson, *ESCAPE THE COMING NIGHT,* p. 200.
3. Melton, J.H., *52 LESSONS IN REVELATION,* p. 218.
4. McGee, J. Vernon, *THRU THE BIBLE WITH J. VERNON McGEE,* Volume V, p. 1046.
5. Lindsey, Hal, *THERE'S A NEW WORLD COMING,* p. 238.
6. Hindson, Ed, *FINAL SIGNS,* p. 189.
7. McGee, J. Vernon, *THRU THE BIBLE WITH J. VERNON McGEE,* Volume V, p. 1048.
8. Lindsey, Hal, *THERE'S A NEW WORLD COMING,* pp. 240–241.
9. Ibid., p. 243.
10. Hagee, John, *DAY OF DECEPTION,* p. 63.
11. McGee, J. Vernon, *THRU THE BIBLE WITH J. VERNON McGEE,* Volume V, p. 1049.
12. Hagee, John, *BEGINNING OF THE END,* p. 177.
13. Ibid., p. 176.
14. Jeremiah, David, with C.C. Carlson, *ESCAPE THE COMING NIGHT,* p. 208.
15. McGee, J. Vernon, *THRU THE BIBLE WITH J. VERNON McGEE,* Volume V, p. 1051.
16. Church, J.R., *GUARDIAN OF THE GRAIL,* p. 312.
17. Ibid., p. 312.

Revelation 20

1. Van Impe, Jack, *2001: ON THE EDGE OF ETERNITY,* p. 16.
2. McGee, J. Vernon, *THRU THE BIBLE WITH J. VERNON McGEE,* Volume V, p. 1055.
3. Jeremiah, David, with C.C. Carlson, *ESCAPE THE COMING NIGHT,* p. 213.
4. Lindsey, Hal, *THERE'S A NEW WORLD COMING,* p. 252.
5. Ibid., p. 256.
6. Van Impe, Jack, *2001: ON THE EDGE OF ETERNITY,* p. 17.

7. Ibid., p. 28.
8. McGee, J. Vernon, *THRU THE BIBLE WITH J. VERNON McGEE,* Volume V, p. 1058.
9. Lindsey, Hal, *THERE'S A NEW WORLD COMING,* p. 261.
10. Hocking, David, *THE COMING WORLD LEADER,* p. 288.
11. Lindsey, Hal, *THERE'S A NEW WORLD COMING,* p. 262.
12. Hagee, John, *BEGINNING OF THE END,* p. 85.
13. Ibid., p. 68.
14. Lindsey, Hal, *THERE'S A NEW WORLD COMING,* p. 264.
15. Hocking, David, *THE COMING WORLD LEADER,* p. 290.
16. Lindsey, Hal, *THERE'S A NEW WORLD COMING,* p. 265.

Revelation 21

1. Hagee, John, *BEGINNING OF THE END,* p. 84.
2. Lindsey, Hal, *THERE'S A NEW WORLD COMING,* p. 271.
3. Froese, Arno, *NEWS FROM ISRAEL,* June 1996, p. 15.
4. LaHaye, Tim, *REVELATION-ILLUSTRATED AND MADE PLAIN,* p. 430.
5. McGee, J. Vernon, *THRU THE BIBLE WITH J. VERNON McGEE,* Volume V, p. 1067.
6. Malgo, Wim, *A NEW HEAVEN AND A NEW EARTH ,* p. 156.
7. Joyner, Rick, *THE FINAL QUEST,* p. 11.
8. McGee, J. Vernon, *THRU THE BIBLE WITH J. VERNON McGEE,* Volume V, p. 1069.
9. Lindsey, Hal, *THERE'S A NEW WORLD COMING,* p. 275.
10. McGee, J. Vernon, *THRU THE BIBLE WITH J. VERNON McGEE,* Volume V, p. 1070.
11. LaHaye, Tim, *REVELATION-ILLUSTRATED AND MADE PLAIN,* p. 437.
12. Lindsey, Hal, *THERE'S A NEW WORLD COMING,* p. 274.

Revelation 22

1. Lindsey, Hal, *THERE'S A NEW WORLD COMING,* p. 277.
2. LaHaye, Tim, *REVELATION-ILLUSTRATED AND MADE PLAIN,* p. 443.
3. McGee, J. Vernon, *THRU THE BIBLE WITH J. VERNON McGEE,* Volume V, p. 1077.
4. Ibid., p. 1077.
5. Breese, David, *DESTINY BULLETIN,* March 1996, p. 1.

INDEX

Ruler of all Rulers—16, 25
Russian—186

S

sackcloth—157
saints—110
salvation—15, 110, 279, 332
sanctified—19
Sardis—27, 45, 52
Satan—127, 175
Satanic Bible—137
Satanic trinity—79, 239
Satan's Army—169
scorpion—130
Scott, John—47
scroll—147, 148
sea of glass—70, 248
seal of God—53, 129
sealed—107
second angel—210
second bowl judgment—231
Second Coming—24, 290
second death—34
second glassy sea—222
second plague—237
second rider on a white horse—285, 286, 287
second seal—91
second trumpet—121
seed of Israel—170
seraphim—70
serpent—196
servant—13, 71
seven angels—22, 225, 246
seven archangels—116
seven bowl judgments—86, 230, 240
seven churches—15, 19, 20
seven eyes—78
seven Gentile world governments—171, 255
seven golden lampstands—19, 24, 25, 28
seven heads—170, 184, 188, 254
seven horns—78
seven kingdoms—254
seven lamps—69
seven plagues—227
seven seal judgments—86, 115, 229
seven spirits—14, 45
seven stars—22, 24, 45
seven thunders—143
seven trumpet judgements—229
seven trumpets—116
seven-sealed scroll—75
seven virtues—15
seven world governments—183
sevenfold—110

sevenfold nature—15
seventh plague—120
seventh seal—116
seventh trumpet—151, 164, 177
Seventieth-Week of Daniel—116
sharp sword—289
shekinah glory—22
sign—169
silence—125
sin—16
sixth angel—216
sixth bowl judgment—236
sixth plague—230
sixth seal—98, 105
sixth trumpet—132
slander—190
Smyrna—27, 32
Sodom and Gomorrah—76, 82, 88, 120, 160, 269, 300
Son of Man—20, 71
song of creation—72
song of the Lamb—223
Sovereign Lord—145
Spirit—30, 31
spiritual sword—37
subterranean—127
subterranean abode—253
Sun of Righteousness—22
synagogue—32, 51
synagogue of the Lord—32
synagogue of Satan—32, 51

T

Temple—152, 153, 161, 183, 224, 317
Temple Mount—153
Ten Commandments—225
ten crowns—184
ten days of awe—86
ten horns—170, 183, 256
ten kings—256
ten regions—185
ten rulers—183
ten thousand times ten thousand—81
testimony—14
third angel—212
third bowl judgement—231
third great sign—221, 222
third seal—92
third trumpet—122
thirst after God—310
three evil spirits—237
three great signs—222
throne—297
throne of God—15
Thyatira—27, 38
Tower of Babel—133, 252, 266

transgressions—80
travail—170
treasure—32
Tree of Life—113, 322
Tree of Knowledge—323
Tribulation Period—24, 41, 69, 79, 86, 101, 110, 132, 138, 145, 151, 161, 171, 179, 184, 193, 217, 226, 255, 279, 299, 307,
Tribulation Saints—96, 97, 118, 233
Trojan Horses—41
true God—49
trumpets—86
twelve foundations—314
twelve gates—313
twelve pearls—317
twelve tribes—77, 169
twenty-four elders—69, 72, 110, 165, 280, 281
two witnesses—151, 157, 159, 209

U

unbelievers—163
unnamed angel—296
unwashed robes—328

V

valley of Megiddo—218
Van Impe, Jack—29, 92, 95, 112, 119, 120, 134, 137, 139, 185, 190, 196, 200, 247, 249, 295, 296, 297

W

washed robes—328
water baptism—70
water of life—310
waters—257
Weber, Dave—195
Wedding Supper—283, 284, 292
white horse—88, 94
wife of God—246
wine of God's fury—212
winepress—289
winning crowns—18
witness—18, 162
woman—169, 178, 250, 251
Word of God—25, 148, 287
Word Made Flesh—16
Wormwood—122
worthiness—81, 115
wrath of God—201

Y

yeshivas—153

Z

Zionist—153

JUST FOR TEENS!

• **Learn more at www.learntheword.com** •

The Bible for Teens—Learn the Word™ Series

Who says Bible study has to be boring? Finally, there is a Bible commentary that meets the needs of today's teens by explaining biblical principles and Scripture in a fun, informative, and entertaining format. Adapted from *The Bible—God's Word for the Biblically-Inept™.*

(trade paper)   ISBN 1892016516 $14.99

Bible Bytes for Teens: A Study-Devotional for Logging In to God's Word

Teens can focus on byte-sized Scripture passages and related teaching to get clear spiritual direction for their day. Also included are reflective study questions and a power-packed design that teens will love.

(trade paper)   ISBN 1892016494 $13.99

What's in the Bible for . . .™ Teens

By Mark Littleton and Jeanette Gardner Littleton

Written to teens, this book explores biblical themes that speak to the challenges and pressures of today's adolescents, such as relationships and peer pressure. Helpful and eye-catching "WWJD?" icons, illustrations, and sidebars are included.

(trade paper)   ISBN 1892016052 $16.95

AND FOR WOMEN . . .

Bible Seeds: A Simple Study-Devotional for Growing in God's Word

Especially for women, this book combines Bible study, devotional readings, word studies, practical application, and room to write. Make this book your very own portable garden for growing in God's Word.

(trade paper)   ISBN 1892016443 $13.99

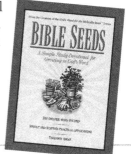

What's in the Bible for . . .™

From the creators of the ***God's Word for the Biblically-Inept™*** series comes the innovative ***What's in the Bible for . . .™*** series. Scripture has certain things to say to certain people, but without a guide, hunting down *all* of what the Bible has to say to you can be overwhelming. Borrowing the user-friendly format of the ***God's Word for the Biblically-Inept™*** series, this new series spotlights those passages and themes of Scripture that are relevant to particular groups of people. Whether you're young or old, married or single, male or female, this series will simplify the very important process of applying the Bible to your life.

What's in the Bible for . . .™ Couples *Kathy Collard Miller and D. Larry Miller*   **WBFC**
(trade paper)   ISBN 1892016028   **$16.95**

What's in the Bible for . . .™ Women *Georgia Curtis Ling*   **WBFW**
(trade paper)   ISBN 1892016109   **$16.95**

What's in the Bible for . . .™ Mothers *Judy Bodmer*   **WBFM**
(trade paper)   ISBN   1892016265   **$17.99**

• **Learn more at www.biblicallyinept.com** •

Purchasing Information
www.starburstpublishers.com

Books are available from your favorite bookstore, either from current stock or special order. To assist bookstores in locating your selection, be sure to give title, author, and ISBN. If unable to purchase from a bookstore, you may order direct from STARBURST PUBLISHERS®. When ordering please enclose full payment plus shipping and handling as follows:

Post Office (4th class)
$4.00 with a purchase of up to $20.00
$5.00 ($20.01–$50.00)
9% of purchase price for purchases of $50.01 and up

United Parcel Service (UPS)
$5.00 (up to $20.00)
$7.00 ($20.01–$50.00)
12% ($50.01 and up)

Canada
$5.00 (up to $35.00)
15% ($35.01 and up)

Overseas
$5.00 (up to $25.00)
20% ($25.01 and up)

Payment in U.S. funds only. Please allow two to four weeks minimum for delivery by USPS (longer for overseas and Canada). Allow two to seven working days for delivery by UPS. Make checks payable to and mail to: **Starburst Publishers®**, P.O. Box 4123, Lancaster, PA 17604. Credit card orders may be placed by calling 1-800-441-1456, Mon–Fri, 8:30 A.M. to 5:30 P.M. Eastern Standard Time. Prices are subject to change without notice. For a catalog send a 9 x 12 self-addressed envelope with four first-class stamps.